SHOULDERING RISKS

SHOULDERING RISKS

THE CULTURE OF CONTROL
IN THE NUCLEAR POWER INDUSTRY

Constance Perin

PRINCETON UNIVERSITY PRESS   PRINCETON AND OXFORD

Library of Congress Cataloging-in-Publication Data

Perin, Constance
Shouldering risks : the culture of control in the nuclear power
industry / Constance Perin.
p.   cm.
Includes bibliographical references and index.
ISBN 0-691-07003-2 (alk. paper)
1. Nuclear power plants—Risk assessment. 2. Nuclear power
plants—Safety measures. 3. Nuclear industry—Risk management.
4. Business anthropology. I. Title.
TK9152.16.P47   2005
621.48'35—dc22   2004013299

British Cataloging-in-Publication Data is available

This book has been composed in Sabon

Printed on acid-free paper.∞

www.pupress.princeton.edu

Printed in the United States of America

10 9 8 7 6 5 4 3 2 1

For all those on whose shoulders rest the unusual risks,
foreseen and unforeseeable, of these times.

Contents

Preface

The Culture of Control

SHOULDERING RISKS their designers have foreseen, bullet trains, jumbo jets, manned space capsules and stations, nuclear power plants, offshore oil rigs, and supertankers deliver services, goods, and knowledge we have come to rely on. Heroic in their ambitions, in the amazing materials making them possible, and in the immense amounts of money and the millions of people mobilized to design and operate them, these technologies maintain uncanny control over gravity, friction, and temperature to defeat known dangers. Their size, reach, beauty, and raw energies awe us. When accidents take or threaten lives and destroy or degrade ecologies, awe turns to anxiety, horror, grief, and mistrust. Wary of that possibility, designers devise worst-case scenarios and try to preclude them. Although that reduces the odds of accidents, the outcomes of any one are likely to be major—hence, "high consequence" or "high hazard" technologies, as they label themselves.

Shouldering risks no one has foreseen is left to those standing watch on the bridge between designers' intentions and how they are being realized. Even with wide safety margins and detailed operating procedures, missteps, missing resources, miscommunications, or mistakes have to be found and put right before they can turn into a tragic flaw. More often than we hear about, and most of the time, those responsible for handling risks—boards of directors, engineers, executives, managers, operators, regulators—defuse worrisome situations, prevent surprises, and keep any that appear from becoming more serious.

Even so, short of an accident, missteps can have "high consequences" for public trust and for productivity. Testifying in October 2003 to their inability to stave off eight "severe incidents" in "just the last few years," presidents and other executives of nuclear utilities in Hungary, Germany, Japan, United Kingdom, and the United States told an audience of about four hundred "how their organizations descended unperceived into a situation where both plant staff and management failed to see disaster lurking." After "the degradation in safety was revealed," repairs and lost revenue cost "hundreds of millions and even billions of dollars." At this biennial meeting of the World Association of Nuclear Operators (WANO), whose theme was "transparency and openness," the audience "sat spellbound as their peers described, with the bitter benefit of hindsight, how this could happen, even to organizations that were once seen as industry stars," *Nucleonics Week* reported. Formed in 1989 as a global response to the 1986 accident at Chernobyl, WANO provides members with peer assessments and technical assistance. "The world nuclear power industry is in danger, threatened by the negligence and complacency" of those companies that "had not heeded earlier signs and, in many cases, are still suffering the financial, social, and political consequences," WANO executives cautioned at this Berlin meeting.[1]

The reasons for these incidents, utility executives and WANO peer reviews said, were "negligence in cultivating a safety culture due to severe pressure to reduce costs following the deregulation of the power market"; not "paying attention to detail"; taking "safety culture for granted"; "overconfidence"; "production bias"; ignoring "significant operating experience"; engineers' "arrogance and complacency"; safety plans without "follow-through." WANO's chairman Hajimu Maeda "warned that even if the public understands that nuclear energy has advantages, 'that is not the same as public acceptance.' "[2]

"Transparency and openness" are certainly remarkable and welcome in an industry not known for plain public speaking. Those reasons nevertheless recite a litany I have been hearing since 1990 when, as a member of a research group at the Massachusetts Institute of Technology and as a total outsider to this industry, I began to study the kinds of knowledge and ways of thinking its experts bring to bear in reducing operating risks.[3] By 1996, I had been invited into eleven nuclear power stations and a few utility headquarters in the United States and abroad, and to national and international industry conferences and technical workshops. I also had joined two teams of experts on invited peer visits at two plants abroad, under the auspices of the International Atomic Energy Commission (IAEA). From men and women who are chemists, control room operators, design and system engineers, electricians and electrical engineers, executives, health physicists, human resource managers, line and middle managers, maintenance supervisors, occupational safety specialists, outage managers, risk analysts, station managers, and others, I heard what "operating safely" means to them and saw how they try to improve the ways they do that.[4] More recently, at three other U.S. nuclear power stations I revisited four events occurring a few months earlier with those involved in them and in analyzing them. Of the many kinds of feedback that control relies on, experts' self-studies crystallize their understandings of how and why control is lost, recovered, and maintained.

Although not classified as "severe incidents," the reasons for these events not only echo that litany, but they also reveal a pattern long a concern of the nuclear power industry, its regulators, and the public. After

analyzing an event designated "significant" for somehow threatening reactor safety margins, experts' best intentions to prevent repetition or further trouble go unrealized too often for comfort, theirs and ours. Standard
practice is for an internal team to drill down to a "root cause," elaborate
on "contributory causes," and, through reverse engineering from the unwanted outcome back through its inputs, develop recommendations to
prevent recurrence. Annually, at plants in the United States and Canada
experts make from two hundred to ten thousand self-reports of problematic conditions, ranging from housekeeping flaws to significant events,
and of those, some thirty to fifty come under an internal review team's
scrutiny.[5] With this high volume of self-reports and self-analysis, the industry expects to ward off surprises and preclude repeats.

But not all event analyses turn out to have been sufficiently thorough,
nor are all recommendations effective or carried out. In thirty-seven events
involving safety-critical systems at U.S. nuclear power plants between
1992 and 1997, not only had previous errors not been identified earlier,
but failures to correct already known problems came to light. These gaps
were four times more numerous than errors involved in the event itself,
according to a study the U.S. Nuclear Regulatory Commission (NRC)
published in 2001.[6] In those same events, previously recommended
changes not carried out contributed to 41 percent of them, and in about
20 percent, utility and plant managers had not responded to industry notices of equipment defects nor to recommended revisions in operating
practices.[7] The longer problematic conditions persist, the less predictable
and controllable system interactions become. Risk estimates that calculate
the probabilities of equipment malfunctions do not also calculate the
probabilities that these self-defeating patterns will be present.

The chance discovery in 2002 of long festering erosion on the head of
the reactor vessel at the Davis-Besse plant in Ohio (one of the incidents
discussed at that WANO meeting) revealed those same patterns. According to after-the-fact scenarios of the damage this could have triggered,
the NRC and the International Atomic Energy Agency calculated that its
severity would match that of the accident at Three Mile Island (1979).
These patterns appear in other risky technologies, as for example, in the
space shuttle program of the National Aeronautics and Space Administration. In its inquiry into the 2003 loss of the *Columbia* shuttle and its crew,
the Columbia Accident Investigation Board found issues in NASA's work
systems and analytic processes similar to those contributing to the 1986
Challenger accident.[8]

At the same time as the nuclear power industry has made fundamental
improvements in reducing operational risks, those self-defeating patterns
persist and the reasons for serious trouble remain the same, across national borders. That is what *Shouldering Risks* tries to explain, by asking

a back-to-basics question: What *kind* of problem is it to reduce the risks of operating a nuclear power plant? Early in my field studies, a station manager in the United States introduced me to about forty managers and supervisors at their "plan of the day" meeting. Unexpectedly, he added, "The reason I've welcomed her is that as a cultural anthropologist, she sees the things we take for granted around here in a different way. She might help us to do the same, so we can get even better at what we do." Despite the strengths of this industry's culture of control, I conclude, "getting better" is possible but not as a matter only of doing the same things better. To lessen the number of events occurring at all and to increase the frequency of sound analyses and effective recommendations—the most fruitful ways to prevent "severe incidents"—it is a more fundamental matter of reconsidering this industry's culture of control.

Like any culture, it is an intricate system of claims about how to understand the world and act in it. In this high hazard world, technologists' explicit claims pivot around the dynamics of control theory, meshed with productivity concepts such as optimization and efficiency, to produce protective bywords such as command and control, defense in depth, feedback, margins of safety, procedures, rules, system reliability, training. These technically correct claims before the fact cannot be the end of it, however. When the switch is turned to On and risks appear in real time, it becomes apparent that technologists do not—cannot—incorporate into their control calculations the contextual dynamics that inevitably accompany operations. That neglect is intentional, inspired by the goal of designing self-consistent, workable systems according to analyses and simulations that assure the lowest possible probability of an accident—workable, that is, under eventualities designers have imagined. A peopled technology operating in the world is, they claim, a source of variability and instability to be minimized by maximizing automation, standardization, and training. Once operating, when control is threatened or lost, however, assumptions underpinning those technical claims come to notice: assumptions about the relationships of humans to machines, models to reality, ambiguity to certainty, rationality to experience, facts to values. Those assumptions and the practices they support, *Shouldering Risks* proposes, are sources of persisting troubles and patterns.

To realize this industry's original promises—to mute the divisive and deadly politics of oil and to squelch the harmful consequences of burning wood and coal—remains a goal of many here and abroad. For others, the risks of operations and of those throughout the fuel cycle outweigh those promised benefits. In any case, promises to shoulder the risks of nuclear power production cannot be confused with the ways they are being kept, here and now and for the lifetimes of current plants and of those being built. That fact is not lost on the thousands of scientists, engineers, and industrialists worldwide searching for technical improvements to make good on them. At one U.S. station, however, an engineer sighed in frustration, "We're technical people, but most of our problems are cultural." To keep cultural promises—to turn "safety culture" into more than a catchphrase—far fewer analytic resources are at hand or called upon. Until up and running, risky technologies are sheltered from the influences of competition and downsizing, missing documentation and trend analyses, legal culpability and regulatory penalties. In designers' thinking there is little room for such worldly matters; they surface as those frustrating "cultural problems" for owners, operators, and regulators.

For real-time operations, the concepts and methods of the physical and engineering sciences lack sufficient scope. When machinery develops flaws, people make mistakes, or unexpected situations arise and going by the book becomes irrelevant, maintaining control depends, at the least, on situational intelligence, foresight, and, above all, on the interpretation of signals of many kinds. But relatively little engineering thought or other intellectual capital has been invested in analyzing the contextual dimensions of risk handling and risk reduction, compared to that invested in estimating risk probabilities. That neglect is one consequence of a hierarchy of credibility at the center of this culture of control, which esteems evidence deemed measurable and discounts that which is not. As pervasive as that hierarchy is across many domains of practice, it can work against realizing the very aims of this and other high hazard technologies. Noting "sharp limitations in the current state of knowledge about how risk is handled in human organizations," a British study group in The Royal Society calls for a more "robust knowledge base" for designing the "social and administrative" changes often recommended "in the aftermath of major accidents." The "research map is a bit like the population map of Australia, with almost everything clustered round the edges and hardly anything in the central conceptual areas."[9] *Shouldering Risks* tries to fill in some of that vast space.

• • • • •

At the book's center are three chapters in which those responsible for daily operations at three plants discuss four events. At Arrow Station, a complicated repair of a critical component in containment displays a panoply of control dynamics. Station managers considered this event to be so serious that they put three review teams to work, each with somewhat different aims. At Bowie Station, each of two unrelated events, brought on by seemingly simple mistakes of experienced people, display some of the industry's demographic dynamics and its ambivalence toward the costs and benefits of outages for repair and refueling. At Charles Station, what turned out to be an ominously dangerous situation, found by chance, reveals the practical consequences of distinguishing "nuclear" and "nonnuclear" "sides" of plant design and operation.

These chapters sustain three perspectives on the events: reports of event review teams that analyzed each for the record; verbatim insights and observations of about ninety experts' excerpted from my transcripts of our taped discussions; and my queries, observations, and reflections on this and other kinds of evidence. Those, and my ordering of that evidence, represent my "different way" of seeing: concern with experts' ideas, concepts, knowledge, language; with their ways of thinking expressed in everyday practices; and with their understandings of their working relationships. Taking off from experts' reports and from their insights are excursions into wellsprings of the issues and themes they bring up, not to second-guess their analyses but to accumulate historical, technical, and conceptual sources of unrecognized elements in this culture of control. My excursions travel into the research of others and draw on my archive of other experts' observations and experiences as reported at workshops, technical meetings, and peer reviews, as well as on my discussions at other nuclear power stations (chiefly Overton Station, whose operations I had previously observed through its different operational phases). Maintaining the integrity of each perspective extends the spirit of my station visits: a collaborative critique toward understanding. As an Arrow Station expert said, heatedly objecting to a team report that compared its event with one more serious, "Events never die, they live on to be misinterpreted in the future!" Or reinterpreted along different lines, as I do in my reflections and as readers will through their own frames of reference.

To set the stage, chapter 1, "Complexities in Control," begins with brief highlights of the industry's last twenty-some years. In the United States, that history culminated in 2000 in the NRC's revised reactor oversight process, which reemphasizes industry self-regulation. Oversight and self-analysis both depend on two pervasive but often unremarked elements of any station's culture of control. One I call the tradeoff quandary, an ever-present negotiation among priorities, resources, and risks, technical and financial. In the customary course of operations, managers and experts face the quandary frequently, but when repairs or an unacceptable condition might force the reactor off line, the stakes become more apparent. A second element is each station's multiplicity of specialists and the continuing influence of the industry's naval origins. Risk handling continuously raises the question of how well or poorly distributed, integrated, and credible specialists' varieties of knowledge and interpretation are. The chapter ends with a description of the industry's approach to event analysis and improvement initiatives and an overview of my research strategy. Chapters 2, 3, and 4 then revisit the events.

The last two chapters respond to that motivating question, "What *kind* of problem is it to reduce the risks of operating a nuclear power plant?" Both offer several concepts for characterizing the ways of thinking and kinds of knowledge that risk handling depends on. In chapter 5, "Logics of Control," I examine the interplay of the calculated logics that estimate risk, the real-time logics of handling risks, and the policy logics that the tradeoff quandary uses and produces. A seemingly inevitable parade of self-contradictions, practical dilemmas, and paradoxes depends on and seeds those policy logics, such as the blame and penalties that can stifle information about trouble; the need for narrow specialties at the same time as systemic awareness is expected; the testing and repair that can introduce new risks; standardization and routinization that diminishes flexibility and adaptation. Not recognizing or not considering how to approach this infrastructure of conundrums itself can precipitate risk escalating conditions. That lived partnership of calculated, real-time, and policy logics comes clear in an unusually detailed study by cognitive scientists of control room operators' actual work practices. I find there a general model of risk reduction, whose animating principle is as much in force as is the principle of command and control: the principle of doubt shadowed by discovery. Calculated logics and policy logics, based almost exclusively on that principle of executive control, carry the most weight, however. The one principle can readily accompany the other, but that hierarchy of measurable and unmeasurable or, as we say, hard and soft knowledge, puts a thumb on that scale. Adding heft are several constructs guiding the NRC's oversight process.

That knowledge hierarchy pervades today's culture of control. Chapter 6, "Intellectual Capital for Regulation and Self-Regulation," proposes that crediting "hard," "objective," and "quantitative" knowledge and discounting "soft," "experiential," and "qualitative" knowledge have two consequences for reducing risk. One is to limit the scope of evidence event reviews consider: that can stymie effective recommendations for technical and nontechnical improvements alike. Another is to impoverish theories of risk estimation and risk handling in complex industrial systems generally. A mode of thinking about parts, components, and assemblies transferred from engineering design and testing methods into operations I call the parts template, together with the project template, another mode transferred from the construction phase into operating, can obscure interdependencies among parts and among specialists' different kinds of knowledge. Those modes of thinking foster understandings of reactor technology as being little more than the sum of its parts, rather than as a peopled technology using and producing invaluable technical and contextual knowledge about its condition. The persistence of those patterns of ineffective or unimplemented changes owes much to that misapprehension.

The crux of reactor control is configuration control: keeping track of expectable interactions within a complicated, often opaque system and responding promptly to those not expected. Close coordination among many specialists' perspectives and knowledge is key. But, the three event chapters show, often vexed relationships among the kinds of knowledge and ways of thinking of specialists in design and in operations, in maintenance and in operations, in support services and everything else can impede exchanges. That compartmentalization has a prominent and negative place in this culture of control, affecting the adequacy of information and analysis. Again, constructs guiding the NRC's oversight process can exacerbate that, as can the generally low status of "maintenance" relative to other specialties. Although that status is a staple of the industrial world, in this as in other high hazard technologies, the analytic and practical contributions of maintenance specialists are as vital as any of those of others, as serious events and accidents keep telling us. To fleets of aging reactors that expertise is increasingly indispensable.

Shouldering Risks ends with a thought experiment for reimagining a culture of control grounded in an expanded system of claims: it does little more than acknowledge the depth and breadth of the culture of control already demanded by the inner work of operating at least risk.[10] The ultimate goal is to create conditions more likely to increase the frequency of effective and implemented CORRECTIVE ACTIONS and decrease the frequency of events. The conditions would maximize specialists' exchange and analysis of information. That depends on maximizing the communicative, observational, and interpretive competencies on which configuration control depends. This is the kind of problem it is to reduce the risks of operating a nuclear power plant, this experiment proposes.

That problem is entirely cultural and entirely pragmatic: the tradeoff quandary centers on evaluating the significance of evidence bearing on "nuclear safety," a term with the specific meaning of maintaining the capacity to shut down the reactor without releasing radiation at levels harmful to employees and to the public. An officially designated "significance determination process" judges daily the extent to which any operating condition or activity affects that capacity. To acknowledge that process as a prime element of the culture of control, this thought experiment entwines an axis of meanings with the axis of functions along which experts' activities are now arrayed. That acknowledges equally the observational and interpretive work that safe shutdown requires and that the principle of doubt and discovery demands.

To imagine cultures of control focused as much on knowledge and meanings as on departments and parts recasts the kinds of work and competencies risk reduction requires. That suggests other criteria for conceptualizing work systems, for the contents of technical and engineering education, and, no less, for the architecture of working arrangements and relationships. Worldwide, questions about competencies are timely: even now nuclear-related industries are short of specialists, including executives and managers.[11] Any next generation of nuclear power technology will confront that problem, as will another option also on the far horizon: new initiatives in the basic science of burning plasma offer the prospect of fusion energy technology, another hazardous source of ozone-friendly energy that some experts say may be possible by mid-century.

Shouldering Risks moves from an immersion in experts' insights to excursions into wellsprings of this industry's culture of control. To enter into this world at this level of specificity, is, I believe, a necessary step for reimagining its culture of control, and perhaps those of other risky technologies. That said, some readers may want to begin with chapter 1, choose one of the event chapters, and after reading chapters 5 and 6, return to the other two. The event in chapter 2 is apparently the most complicated, the two events in chapter 3, apparently the least, and in chapter 4, an event centers on the process of evaluating the significance of trouble.

• • • • •

Although nuclear power production is one among other industries in the high hazard category, its complexities and the public ambivalence surrounding it obviously set this technology apart. Around the world as of March 2004, 439 nuclear power plants were operating and being upgraded, 30 were being built, and 34 were planned or on order. After fifty years of the "atoms for peace" program, which President Dwight D. Eisenhower advocated after the Second World War, nuclear power plants are for the first time new, middle-aged, and old. Some present familiar risks, some that are new; some operate in relatively stable social, financial, and political environments, some in those less so. The world has long passed the point of debating only whether nuclear power plants should be built at all or built where proposed. With 439 operating plants, whether one favors this energy option or not, their safe operation is obviously in the world's best interests, as is safely decommissioning those beyond repair or otherwise shut down, and, not least, securely protecting the fuel cycle and disposing of its waste.

Operating commercial reactors 2004
   United States 103, France 59, Japan 53, Russia 30, United Kingdom 27, South Korea 18, Germany 18, Canada 17, India 14, Ukraine 13, Sweden 11, Spain 9, China 9, Belgium 7; Bulgaria, Czech Republic, Slovakia, Taiwan, each 6. Between 1 and 5: Argentina, Armenia, Brazil, Bulgaria, Finland, Hun-

gary, Lithuania, Mexico, Netherlands, Pakistan, Romania, Slovenia, South
Africa, Switzerland.
Under construction
India 8; Russia 6; Japan 3; China, South Korea, Taiwan, Ukraine, each 2;
Canada, Iran, North Korea, United States, each 1.[12]
Planned or on order
Japan 13; South Korea 8; China 4; Canada 2; Argentina, Brazil, Finland,
India, North Korea, Pakistan, each 1.[13]

Over the nearly twenty years since the 1986 accident at Chernobyl, the
United States's 103 operating plants have come to meet about 20 per cent
of the national demand for energy. Since 1991, the average capacity factor
(actual output compared to potential output) has increased 40 per cent;
as of 2002 it rose to 91 per cent.[14] At the same time, the industry has
been experiencing new kinds of financial risks as many states deregulate
electricity markets. The NRC's revised regulatory regime, still being re-
fined, is taking hold as utilities and stations continue to reduce staffing
and budgets, experience mergers, and rely increasingly on contractors.
All that has been accompanied by a shift to separating ownership of generating operations from that of electricity distribution. These changes come
at a time when developing a "new generation" of commercial reactors
remains high on the industry's agenda.

As "indebted to Descartes and Newton" as we are "for fine examples of
well-formulated theory" on which science and engineering depend, says
Stephen Toulmin, philosopher of science at the University of Southern
California, "humanity also needs people with a sense of how theory
touches practice at points, and in ways, that we feel on our pulses."[15] For
the many concerned with those touching points in this and other high
hazard enterprises as they are today and being planned for tomorrow—
executives and operators, legislators and investors, designers and scholars, shareholders and policy analysts, and for us as citizens—our task is
to reimagine their cultures of control.

· · · · ·

Consider *Shouldering Risks* an attempt at preventive maintenance: replacing an invisible cultural apparatus manufacturing a neglect of the world
in which heroic technologies come to life. Once we dismantle and inspect
that cultural machinery and prepare to reassemble it, we might begin to
imagine how its design and operational arrangements would change
with different claims relying on different assumptions. That would allow
us to evaluate their consequences not only for reducing operational risks,
but also for reconsidering the premises of the many institutions—educa-

tional, financial, governmental, legal—bringing high hazard technologies to fruition.

From inscriptions, relics, ruins, and scrolls we infer much about the claims of societies that built the ambitious artifacts of the past—amphitheaters, canals, churches, pyramids, ships, temples, tunnels. We are in a position today to know these things for ourselves, and to choose. This book is meant to help us think through how things *could* stand, what could be otherwise in a future in which high hazard technologies are vulnerable not only to what has already been foreseen but to what has become much harder to foresee at all.

Heroic technologies not only express the maturity of industrialization after its first 150 years. They also test that maturity. How can scientific, engineering, and financial sophistications bringing us so many marvels also become wiser in the ways of the world?

Acknowledgments

To the many people who spoke with me at nuclear power stations and elsewhere in the nuclear power industry in the United States and abroad, my thanks beyond words for bringing me into their worlds of thought and practice, generously and encouragingly. Although responsive to my interests, they are in no way responsible for my observations and interpretations nor for my representations of technical details.

This work has depended on moral, intellectual, and financial support from several quarters. My observations of the nuclear power industry and plant operations began in 1990 under the aegis of a five-year MIT International Program for Enhanced Nuclear Power Plant Safety, led by Kent Hansen, professor of nuclear engineering at the Massachusetts Institute of Technology and funded through the MIT Office of Sponsored Research by a small international group of utilities and a foundation. Within that program, John S. Carroll, professor of organizational behavior in the Sloan School of Management, led an Organization and Management Study Group, to which I belonged, working about half-time. Our group held several workshops with plant experts and executives; at another, we brought together academic colleagues who were also studying in high consequence industries. Joining us for several months, to our great benefit, was Alfred A. Marcus, professor of strategic management at the University of Minnesota; several graduate students brought back observations, insights, and documents from companies and plants in the United States, France, Germany, Japan, and South Korea (Banaghan 1991; Cho 1995; DiBella 1995, 1993; Hopson 1992; Jaliff 1991; Lal 1992; Marcus 1995; Marcus and Nichols 1999; Roth 1992; Silva 1993; Verma and Marcus 1995; Yakura 1995).

During the study group's life, I twice participated in an international, interdisciplinary workshop of scholars and practitioners in technical and cultural disciplines concerned with operational risks, led by Bernhard Wilpert, professor of psychology at the Berlin University of Technology under the auspices of the Werner Reimers Foundation (Bad Homburg, Germany) and the Maison des Sciences de l'Homme (Paris). I also attended industry conferences, presented talks on panels at the American Nuclear Society, met with members of research and regulatory groups abroad, was a volunteer member of two week-long technical committees at the International Atomic Energy Agency, and under its auspices, spent five weeks as scientific observer with international peer review teams at two nuclear stations outside the United States. In 1997, John Carroll and I put together a workshop with fourteen scholars and eleven engineers, executives, and managers specializing in chemical process safety, funded partly by the National Science Foundation, Program in Decision, Risk, and Management Science (Perin and Carroll 1997). In Europe, research staff in regulatory agencies and utilities in a few European countries shared their findings and concerns. For the collegiality, footing, and fun of that period, I'm ever grateful.

During 1997 and 1998, an individual award from the National Science Foundation made these further field studies possible, through its Division of Social, Behavioral, and Economic Research, Program in Ethics and Values Studies in Science and Technology (#9730605, "'Hard' and 'Soft' Knowledge in High-Hazard Industries"). Between her expert program direction and her philosophic perspectives, Rachelle Hollander and the anonymous proposal reviewers helped me to refine my project and my thinking. By the time I came to write this book, I had visited fourteen stations. At three, I spent a total of about three months; other visits ranged from one to four days; for several days, for a study at MIT's Energy Laboratory funded by the U.S. Department of Energy, I observed and interviewed experts at three U.S. installations formerly manufacturing nuclear weapons.

A grant from the Research and Writing Initiative of the Program on Global Security and Sustainability of the John D. and Catherine T. MacArthur Foundation has helped immensely to make this book possible. Michael M. J. Fischer welcomed me into the milieu most fitting for my interests; as visiting scholar since 1996 in the Program in Science, Technology, and Society in MIT's School of Humanities, Arts, and Social Science, the interests, energies, and stimulation of its students, visitors, faculty, and always helpful staff have sparked my work and persistence. At just the right time, Roger Kasperson invited me to share ideas with a like-minded group at Clark University, as did Lars Ingelstam, then Director of the Program in Technology and Social Change at Linköping University, Sweden.

As indispensable as soft and hard computer technologies have been, MIT's library staff and its collaborative spirit have been more so. Jerry Burke and Edward Mendelson have graciously untangled many a computer glitch, its and mine.

No reader of this book in its various stages can be held to account for what it has come to be, but none can escape my gratitude for their inspiring arguments, corrections, and critiques: John Ahearne, Michael Baram, Vicki Bier, Larry Bucciarelli, John S. Carroll, Elisabeth Drake, Michael M. J. Fischer, Peter Galison, Chris Johnson, William Lanouette, David Lochbaum, Charles Sabel. The two readers for Princeton University Press gave me encouraging handshakes along with nourishing thoughts, and my editor Mary Murrell has displayed an unusual sympathy for the writing enterprise. Kathleen Cioffi and Karen Verde have graced my path through production.

To my delight, Pier Gustafson made the drawings.

Georges Borchardt, as always, has been generous with wisdom and help.

To my lasting benefit, friends, relatives and many other colleagues have been ever generous with critiques, encouragement, patience, and respites.

Reading Notes

AT FIRST USE, technical concepts and terms appear in small caps. To clarify some basics at the outset: REACTOR, UNIT, and PLANT each refer to somewhat different things. "Reactor" refers to the reactor vessel proper; unit, REACTOR UNIT and NUCLEAR STEAM SUPPLY SYSTEM (NSSS) refer to the reactor and its supporting systems (reactor core, pressure vessel, heat transfer equipment, and control and safety systems), also called STRUCTURES, SYSTEMS, AND COMPONENTS (SSCs). PLANT refers technically to that entire system, but in actual usage, "plant" may also refer to an entire generating station no matter the number of units. Yet, as will become clearer, every plant is also understood as having a NUCLEAR and NONNUCLEAR side. Given all that, I use "station" to refer to sites with any number of units, because operational activities in each of its units are, by and large, subject to stationwide policies, procedures, and programs. With "station expert" I honor the fact that, although hierarchies of respect and pay are pervasive, in any job women and men have to become expert at blending their skills with the special demands of this unique system as well as with a station's particular history. Most specialists—MBA, pipefitter, nuclear engineer, occupational health specialist—will need, some say, three to six years on the job before being perceived as seasoned, knowledgeable, and credible in a pinch.

SHOULDERING RISKS

Chapter One

Complexities in Control

NUCLEAR POWER technology is famously complex technically and culturally, from design and construction through operation and into decommissioning, ultimately involving thousands of people, hundreds of techniques
and skills, innumerable components. Once operating, each plant remains
entangled in criss-crossing circuits of suppliers and contractors and en-
meshed in the inevitable politics of financing, budgets, and regulation.
But when first buying reactors, utility executives expected the operational
simplicity of their fossil fuel stations, unaware of the "immense difference." In 1986, the House Committee on Energy and Commerce heard
the chief executive officer of Boston Edison reflect on its first years of
nuclear power operations, from 1972 to 1979.

> Our major management shortcoming then was the failure to recognize fully
> that the operational and managerial demands placed on a nuclear power plant
> are very different from those of a conventional fossil-fired power plant. Boston
> Edison structured its nuclear organization as part of a traditional operating
> arm. . . . The early management problems can be attributed to Boston Edison's
> attempt to manage Pilgrim Station using essentially the same practices as had
> been established for our fossil units without an adequate transition and adjust-
> ment for differences between the two technologies.[1]

Three years later, the former chief executive officer of Detroit Edison
(not affiliated with the then-Boston Edison) echoed that view: "No one
foresaw the complexity of modern-day nuclear power operations. . . . The
feeling was that this new technology would just replace the boiler in a
coal-fired plant. The immense difference between running a nuclear power
plant and a conventional plant was never dreamed of."[2]

Over the last twenty-five years or so, as the industry has come to better
understand the implications of that difference, those complexities—technical, financial, and cultural—have thickened as financial disappointments have mingled with the aftermaths of four shocks.[3] The accidents at
Three Mile Island (1979) and at Chernobyl (1986) delivered the first
major shock. A partial meltdown of Three Mile Island Nuclear Station's
Unit 2 near Harrisburg, Pennsylvania stemmed from equipment failures,
but before operators and managers were able to figure out what was

happening, a loss of cooling water sufficient to uncover the core occurred. No one was injured bodily, nor have studies found that the radiation released has directly affected the physical health of employees or publics. But for some who lived through the company's initial assurances, and soon after were warned of possibly disastrous conditions within the containment, which prompted residents' wholesale evacuation and return, psychological stress has lingered. At Chernobyl, located in Ukraine 80 miles northwest of Kiev, operators were testing the feasibility of supplying the unit's pumps, lighting, and instruments with electricity generated by its turbine, in case of external power failure. When reconnecting disabled safety systems and returning the reactor to its correct condition, they inserted control rods into the reactor core too quickly. That brought on the explosions and fire that killed thirty-one people, exposed millions to radioactivity in Belarus, Russia, Ukraine, and Europe, and contaminated tens of thousands of acres near and far. With its viability under threat from the scale and reach of these accidents—each a "fundamental surprise" that they could occur at all—the U.S. industry and its regulator began to promote major changes.[4]

In earlier days, utility executives not only thought that producing steam from the nuclear reaction was little different from burning coal or gas, they also believed they were buying a ready-to-run technology. Manufacturers promoted the first reactors as "turn-key" plants that promised low construction costs. That started what came to be known as the bandwagon years between 1967 and 1974 when utilities ordered 196 plants.[5] By about 1973, after several had been built and began to operate, utility executives were dismayed to find that although their plants amounted to "loss leaders" for vendors, their production costs zoomed. Getting financing and the license to operate had already taken longer than expected.[6] That broke the spell: between 1974 and 1995, utilities cancelled seventy plants still on order; between 1990 and 1996 the last four ordered plants came on line; between 1967 and 1998, utilities shut down twenty-two plants, of which four had never begun commercial operation.[7]

As the horror of Chernobyl fused with the scare of Three Mile Island, the skepticism of publics and markets had been hardening. Skepticism had been mounting even before the accidents, not only that of avowedly antinuclear publics but also that of financial analysts, nuclear scientists, economists, engineers, and industry insiders no longer bewitched by the optimism and boosterism of the postwar decades. Between 1975 and 1994, Bernard Verna, a nuclear safety expert, wrote 110 columns detailing plant operating experiences for *Nuclear News*, the American Nuclear Society's monthly magazine of news, analysis, and critique.[8] In his last column, Verna concluded, "The industry continues to claim that tremendous progress in operations has been made. . . . I would have to disagree."

In 1990, he says, the NRC found "50 common-mode failure events"; fire barrier regulations have lagged, a "fiasco [that] festered for over 10 years. . . .Years ago, I came to the conclusion that your average designer felt that his designs would hardly ever fail, and tended to neglect provisions for maintenance and repairs." The industry "keeps coming up with too many complicated programs [and] it quite often loses sight of the basics and the practicalities."[9] One of those basics was maintenance, to which the industry applied what it came to call its "fossil mentality" in following the first industrial rule of thumb for keeping costs low: "Run it until it breaks," but then, it found, also pay the costs of forced outages.[10] Nor have many questions about the two accidents been put to rest. Studies continue to analyze, for example, the physics of the Three Mile Island accident and the diminished life chances of thousands affected by Chernobyl's fallout and by decimated land and wildlife.[11]

During a down economy in the 1980s, industry executives and lobbying groups joined to "map out the rebirth of nuclear power. . . . It was a remarkable, perhaps unprecedented situation: a major industry given a forced sabbatical [from expanding] in which to remake itself in light of the lessons it had learned to that point," according to Robert Pool, a science writer, in his 1997 study of the nuclear power industry.[12] In the *U.S. Nuclear Energy Industry's Strategic Plan for Building New Nuclear Power Plants*, first published in 1990 and updated annually, industry leaders and lobbyists laid out in fourteen "building blocks" a detailed plan for developing new generations of reactors. Among other goals were a cost-effective regulatory oversight system; effective low- and high-level radioactive waste programs; and changes in legislation and regulations governing utility ownership and financing. A 1994 update refers to an industry report of 1993, *Strategic Plan for Improving Economic Performance*, which notes that the NRC recognized, in parallel with cost-reductions owners were making, that "to improve nuclear plant competitiveness" meant evaluating "its own contribution to excessive operations and maintenance costs [and it] implemented its own initiative to identify and address regulations and regulatory practices marginal to safety."[13] By 1994 the industry groups writing those plans had consolidated into the Nuclear Energy Institute (NEI), now the industry's central trade association and lobbying consortium.[14] The NEI "coordinates public policy on issues affecting the nuclear energy industry, including federal regulations that help ensure a safe and robust future for our industry."[15]

Survival became the industry's first priority in the mid-1980s as it anticipated a second shock: the deregulation of energy markets. Rate competition would force it to become one electricity producer among all others, putting past guarantees of a "reasonable rate of return" on capital investments in jeopardy.[16] In 1992, the Energy Act allowed states to deregulate electricity rates and consumers to choose suppliers.[17] In the United States as of 2003, the owners of fifty-nine commercial reactors in fifteen states are in retail competition with other electricity suppliers; forty-four reactors are in sixteen states still considering retail choice.[18] One result is that many utilities have sold their nuclear assets to "merchant" companies specializing in operations alone, leaving other companies to distribute what they generate. And at the same time, to reduce costs while increasing output and revenues, the industry took its place on the "re-engineering" bandwagon beginning in the 1980s and continuing today to redesign work and production systems to maximize efficiency.[19] Like others in this movement, this industry's goal has been to eliminate one or two layers of middle managers and supervisors and to reduce the number of employees. Between 1988 and 1991, when Overton Station began to lay off employees and let attrition do its part in its two units, for example, the station reduced the workforce by 7 percent, currently down to about 1,000 from an original workforce of 2,400 (many of whom had arrived during the ten years of plant construction).[20]

The accident in September 1999 at a fuel processing facility in Japan became the industry's third shock. While preparing fuel for an experimental reactor under less than optimum working conditions, three employees at the JCO Company, a subsidiary of the Sumitomo Metal Mining Company Ltd., mishandled enriched uranium and brought about a "criticality" accident (a limited uncontrolled nuclear chain reaction) which continued intermittently for twenty hours. Two of the men died and as of October 2000, 667 people were exposed to radiation (accident response teams, local citizens, temporary visitors, delivery workers, press members); about 56 received doses above annual exposure limits.[21] Japanese officials acknowledge that they first downplayed the accident and delayed public notice and warnings of radiation release. Since then, in Japan's commercial nuclear power sector, other instances of unacknowledged operational failures and falsified repair and inspection records have come to light.[22]

The fourth shock came in March 2002 when station experts at the Davis-Besse Station on Lake Erie near Toledo, Ohio reported that by chance they had found a hole on the head of its reactor vessel "about six inches deep, five inches long, and seven inches wide." This "cavity" was adjacent to a nozzle carrying borated water that penetrates the head of the reactor pressure vessel into the reactor core. After experts had repaired the nozzle and withdrew their equipment, the nozzle's position shifted and made the hole visible for the first time. Borated cooling water carried in the REACTOR COOLANT SYSTEM, which circulates around the reactor core to remove heat, had been leaking from the nozzle since 1990, leaving enough boric acid residue to begin a hole that, once first opened in 1999, subsequent studies found, grew by two inches per year. With a surface area of "approximately 20–30 square inches," it "extended completely through the 6.63 inch thick carbon steel [vessel head] down to a thin internal liner of stainless steel cladding," pulverizing 70 pounds of carbon steel and leaving 3/16-inch stainless steel cladding as the sole boundary of a vessel kept under pressure up to 2,500 pounds per square inch—not the cladding's function. If the hole had gone undetected and the stainless steel liner had failed or the nozzle had been ejected, a loss-of-coolant accident would have been the result.[23]

The NRC gave the plant its lowest rating and shut it down until it could approve the company's plan for repair and restart. On an INTERNATIONAL EVENT SCALE, both the International Atomic Energy Agency (IAEA) and the NRC rated its potential "severity" equal to that of the 1979 Three Mile Island accident.[24] This event was another fundamental surprise: accident scenarios had never considered that nozzle leak deposits could eat into the carbon steel of the reactor vessel, yet leaks had been a generic problem known to the industry since 1990.[25]

The Limits of Regulation and Self-Regulation

As of 2000, owners and the NRC themselves had brought on another kind of "shock," one which both fostered: a revised REACTOR OVERSIGHT PROCESS that revitalizes self-regulation, adopted after being debated and negotiated over several years among various "stakeholders"—the Nuclear Energy Institute (NEI), the Union of Concerned Scientists, nuclear scientists and engineers, station experts, equipment vendors, state departments of public safety, and local citizen groups. The consensus is that besides promising to reduce operating costs, this approach could encourage more conscientious operations and more effective oversight and enforcement. One of the NRC's four goals is nevertheless to "reduce unnecessary regulatory burden" on owners and operators, and, for itself, to "increase regulatory effectiveness and efficiency," "maintain safety," and "maintain public confidence." Cost reduction is central: the industry expects lower costs for meeting license requirements and it and NRC are keeping close watch on the costs of self-regulation. The NRC expects its budget to decrease, partly by reducing its inspection hours from 2,200 hours yearly at "a good performing plant" to about 1,850.[26]

The NRC's understanding of its mission is circumscribed, in part by the demands of the technology itself: to enforce the provisions of the license to operate a nuclear power reactor (and research reactors). That license is predicated on owners' maintaining at all times the capacity to operate without releasing radioactivity above levels defined as not injurious either to the atmosphere or to employees in the course of their work. At all times owners must maintain the capacity to shut down the reactor to prevent UNCONTROLLED RADIATION RELEASE.[27]

With SAFE SHUTDOWN as the central concern of reactor design and the basis for the operating license, the NRC limits its oversight to assessing whether hundreds of pieces of equipment and dozens of operating processes are demonstrably able at all times to eliminate, prevent, limit, or quickly recover from conditions threatening shutdown capabilities as laid out in scenarios of probable ACCIDENT PRECURSOR SEQUENCES. Systems and components designated safety significant along that path must have a backup: the control concept is DEFENSE-IN-DEPTH, or REDUNDANCY, consisting of multiple layers of protective devices and processes as well as emergency response methods. If a safety-critical assembly fails or is out of commission for testing or repair, another must be on the ready. Three such systems do not, however, have backups: the reactor vessel, the cladding around the fuel, and the reactor coolant system are PRIMARY BARRIERS. A fourth primary barrier consists of physical and human SAFE-GUARDS to defend the reactor from internal and external threats or damage. The availability of operable backups and protection of primary barriers, all in the service of shutting down without uncontrolled radio-activity release, together constitute what regulator and industry understand as "nuclear safety," "safe operations," and "plant safety." Those strictures require methods for determining which repairs, components, equipment upgrades, or station practices are more or less necessary for maintaining "nuclear safety." NRC's oversight includes a SIGNIFICANCE DETERMINATION PROCESS that relies in part on PROBABILISTIC RISK ASSESSMENTS, some of which are intended to replace previously "deterministic" methods, where certain "safety-related" components and assemblies had to meet specific thresholds and standards.

The premise of the significance determination process is that there are "safety-related" and "nonsafety-related," "nuclear" and "nonnuclear" sides to every plant. So I learned in 1991 when my regulatory education began in earnest as a member of an IAEA team of seventeen experts making a three-week peer review visit to a station in a Western European country, at its request. Team members came from countries around the world, all as volunteers whose companies or institutions paid their transportation costs. They represented a variety of specialties—health physics, control room operations, station management, regulators, design and system engineers, chemists, maintenance managers. My status was scientific observer, but the IAEA program leaders nevertheless expected my participation in the team's review of one unit at this multi-unit station.

After our first week, a team member learned by chance that about a year earlier one station employee working in the "nonnuclear side" of another unit had been killed, an accident that had been the subject of a special public investigation. There is plant (nuclear) and BALANCE-OF-PLANT (nonnuclear or, in industry parlance, "outside the fence"). The non-nuclear "side" includes the steam generator, turbine, and the switchyard which moves electricity out to a regional grid. Station managers had not discussed the accident in the voluminous preparatory materials supplied to the team, nor did any of those we had already interviewed mention it: that displeased and troubled the members. When asked why, the station director and other managers explained because the death was classified as "mechanical" not "radiological," and thereby outside the team's pur-view of "nuclear safety," they did not see it as relevant. But to team mem-bers, the circumstances under which that death could occur might fore-shadow risk-escalating events elsewhere at the station. The team's final report, delivered in an open forum to utility managers and station employ-ees, laid out these and other concerns, as well as commendations.

Soon after, at Overton Nuclear Station I asked various station experts how they saw the difference between nuclear safety and OCCUPATIONAL, INDUSTRIAL, or PERSONNEL SAFETY, terms used interchangeably. To over-see radiological protection in accordance with NRC limits on employees' levels of radiation exposure, every station has a "health physics" or "radi-ation protection" group. For all other on-the-job injuries, a "health and safety" or "industrial safety" group assures compliance with rules of the Occupational Health and Safety Administration. Overton's managers had recently found ways to reduce head injuries throughout the plant, espe-cially among employees working in the containment; its tight work spaces make those injuries more likely. To me that suggested that the two kinds of safety were then, if not at other times, inseparable. But to everyone, my query itself was puzzling: these were two different matters. All well understood that injuries and accidents can happen in any industry; only the possibility that employees and the public can be overexposed to radio-activity sets this one apart.

For licensed nuclear power plants, the duties of self-regulation come under each station's QUALITY ASSURANCE PROGRAM, which the license has always required. The program is responsible for ongoing oversight of safety-critical decisions and working practices and for the CORRECTIVE ACTIONS PROGRAM which administers internal event reviews. The sta-tions' regular reports to the NRC on the status and condition of desig-nated equipment and programs are another facet of their continuous self-assessment. It has long been standard practice that "plant owners and industry peer groups conduct the majority of the inspections," according to an interdisciplinary working group discussing the proposed oversight process in 1999 (members of Congress, Nuclear Energy Institute, public interest groups, and representatives of the NRC).[28] NRC inspections customarily cover only about 5 percent of all equipment and programs at an "average" plant and about 10 percent at plants with problematic records. The peer group is the Institute of Nuclear Power Operations (INPO), a technical assessment and assistance group, which U.S. utilities formed in 1980 nine months after the accident at Three Mile Island. Its staff of about six hundred makes about the same proportion of inspections as the NRC, but the industry often finds INPO's reviews to be more rigorous than those of the NRC.[29] Insurers set their rates for nuclear power stations with reference to INPO's evaluations, but its assessments are otherwise not publicly available except to the NRC, where they are required reading. A 1993 analysis of INPO reviews made available to Public Citizen, a watchdog group, compared its assessments with those of the NRC: the NRC overlooked two-thirds of the operating issues INPO identified.[30] Nor does WANO (for which INPO was the model and to which INPO belongs) make its peer assessments public.

To help its members meet or exceed their obligations for self-regulation, INPO is a steady source of proprietary systematized programs, techniques, and technical analysis; it does no research. Industry friends and critics alike credit it with spurring plant owners to adopt operational improvements and best practices over the last decades that go beyond regulatory minimums. INPO has also developed metrics for evaluating performance, resulting in improved industry performance overall, such as fewer license violations and reportable events and more time on line producing electricity. Other forces, not least that of industry experts' insight, foresight, professional ethics, self-analysis, and stamina, have also been at work: more experienced senior managers at utilities and stations; a larger database of operating experience, equipment modernization, information technologies; refinements in regulatory requirements; mergers that pool knowledge; and the attention and critiques of state utility commissions, citizens, and groups such as the Natural Resources Defense Council, Nuclear Control Institute, Nuclear Information and Resource Service, Public Citizen, Union of Concerned Scientists.

Withal, the industry knows that "overall" and "on average" can mask not only recalcitrants but "star performers" whose "sentinel events" can harm them all. And, needless to say, owners and managers of this and other high hazard industries often try to keep their doors closed and make chronic complaints about regulation and citizen involvement; some may suppress or punish employees for whistleblowing. By the same token, the NRC has turned a blind eye to repeated infractions at stations other than Davis-Besse.[31]

Self-propelled self-regulation, station by station, nevertheless remains the first line of defense against operating risks. Self-analysis sits well with executives and managers: "When others find a problem," says Gary, Overton Station's manager, "the amount of work and money required to resolve it increases dramatically."

The Tradeoff Quandary

Now, the days of "throwing money" at technical problems are long over, says Marty, an Overton Station engineer, formerly a nuclear submariner. As in the nuclear navy, he said, it had been a matter of looking at problems technically and "deciding what's the right thing to do and worrying about the cost later. So now it becomes much more of a management decision on how to handle the cost and the schedule." Alice, manager of a group of twenty-three in Overton's human resources department dedicated to preventing on-the-job injuries, and Tom, a member of that group, joined in familiarizing me with their approaches to this task. Suddenly, Alice interrupted herself.

> You know, I'm one of the few female managers at the station, and it's really been difficult learning how to hold my own. For a long time in meetings, the men would just look right through me, they wouldn't listen to anything I said, or they'd hear it and then repeat it without so much as a nod to me. But I've stood my ground and I'm getting more attention on these issues.

As our meeting ended, Tom turned to me.

> What she says about the way women are treated here—well, that's the way I see our safety concerns being treated. They'd just as soon we weren't here and they didn't have to listen to us. We're lowest on the totem pole.

> *Why do you think that's so?*

> Everybody's trained to consider production goals first—work should be fast and efficient, and safety only slows it down.

> Just about any piece of equipment, repair, or process required for shutdown capability is costly, partly because of stringent requirements to assure reliability. On the nonnuclear side, maintenance may also include expensive items, but standardized and lower-cost equipment will suffice. In any case, maintenance activities on either side may also require ceasing or lowering electricity output. Then revenues decline while costs rise, as the station buys replacement power to fulfill customer contracts.

> Those constraints and costs combine into a prime element of the culture of control I call the tradeoff quandary. Only in one way does the NRC's

oversight process, old and new, directly address its presence: "[S]uch persons and organizations performing quality assurance functions shall report to a management level such that this required authority and organizational freedom, including sufficient independence from cost and schedule when opposed to safety considerations, are provided."[32] But even as those responsible for quality assurance may have "sufficient independence from cost and schedule," senior managers will nevertheless consider its relation to both cost and schedule, and perhaps, so will the NRC. As straightforward as those words are on paper, little about the tradeoff quandary, decision after decision, is simple. "Safety" is an outcome of how corporate and station managers and experts in many specialties negotiate their way out of the quandary among themselves and with the NRC. More often than not, the negotiations result in maximizing effective risk reduction—those nonevents rarely studied with the same care as events are.[33] The exceptions are, however, impossible to ignore.

What the industry calls its "regulatory burden" refers to what it regards as overly conservative and expensive shutdown requirements. Now it hopes the burden will be lighter under the risk-based significance determination process with fewer specific thresholds and standards. In effect since April 2000 is a "risk-informed" and "performance-based" oversight process with which the NRC rates all plants quarterly. Each plant furnishes numerical indicators of the performance of all safety-significant equipment and processes evaluated against probabilistic risk assessments (PRAs) or INDIVIDUAL PLANT EVALUATIONS. Only when the NRC finds those numbers wanting, in combination with its on-site inspections, will it require owners to make improvements. In chapter 5, I discuss details of this process.

Cost aside, the special requirements of this technology can make the quandary itself a precondition to troubles that may culminate in "severe incidents" and "sentinel events." Hewing to time limits on the downtime of safety-related equipment can create schedule pressures recognized industrywide as sometimes contributing to near-misses and events. Regulatory sanctions exacerbate the pressure: exceeding those limits can be a violation of technical specifications and must be reported to the NRC immediately, possibly resulting in civil penalty.[34] Despite controls built into equipment, procedures, reporting relationships, work planning, and scheduling—all intended to reduce operating and productivity risks—events often demonstrate that station experts are unwillingly enrolled in a perpetual master class in irony: control strategies and techniques may make it more difficult to reduce risk and may increase it.[35]

Protect, perturb, produce, profit: each imperative is on the table in tradeoff negotiations. Activities to *protect* the capacity for safe shutdown can also *perturb* the system, which can introduce new risks. When the same protective activities reduce time on line, they reduce *production* output and revenues; when unforeseen problems require time for repair or money for parts, they can reduce *profits*. Managers and experts enter the quandary whenever deciding schedules, equipment purchases, repair priorities, and budgets and whenever deciding whether to come off line or reduce power to investigate a problem or fix a broken part.

The crux of the matter is CONFIGURATION CONTROL. The redundancy concept requires keeping backups in ready condition; that testing and repair work itself changes the reactor system's configuration. Even though a DESIGN BASIS allows for variations in mode and output level to accommodate maintenance, the premise of most probabilistic risk assessments (PRAs), the source of estimates of accident frequency, is that the reactor is at full power (90–100% power). (Appendix 1 lists typical modes.) PRAs are not likely to consider, or may have only weak methods for considering, the future risks that perturbing activities may introduce. To keep the plant's parameters where they must be according to technical specifications, configuration control in real time—some of it automated, but most dependent on experts' observations and data interpretations—becomes paramount.[36]

Many routine industrial practices also make configuration control a preoccupation. Equipment modifications sometimes have to depart from design blueprints to align them correctly in place, after which AS-BUILT DRAWINGS have to be made. When as-builts are unavailable (backlogs happen), station experts may be in the dark about how a system or piece of equipment is actually configured. Or the design basis may be incompletely documented, a gap that has spawned a consulting specialty. Modifications may require new rules and procedures, which have to be WALKED DOWN (field tested and observed) to verify their steps and clarity: ambiguously or incorrectly written rules and procedures can affect configuration control. Modifications may also change work practices, introducing unfamiliar or infrequent tasks; radiation dose levels for unanticipated tasks have to be calculated; hence PREJOB BRIEFINGS serve as a protective barrier for just about every work order.

Protective activities often come up against the production imperative: "That's why we're here, to produce electricity!" station experts say. Because reducing power or going off line to deal with puzzling conditions may introduce interactions that PRA calculations have not allowed for, there has been the widespread belief that a plant is "safest when running" in light of the trouble that TRANSIENTS—brief shifts in operating modes and configurations—can introduce (just as flight risk escalates during take-offs and landings). Further reinforcing the production imperative are the meanings that regulators and markets ascribe to the amount of time a plant is off line in forced outages (or in scheduled outages exceeding an industry benchmark): signals of low productivity and of TROUBLED plants. To keep up output, managers may stay on line or delay repairs. When they do and an event ensues, reviews are likely to ascribe it to NONCONSERVATIVE DECISION-MAKING, a standard cause category. Until the early 1990s, the industry also relied on an opposite motto: plants are "safest when in outage," and not producing power. An international pattern of incidents during shutdown forced regulators to acknowledge risk-producing conditions stemming from decay heat at low power, which had never before been estimated; outage protocols now include risk analyses and mitigation techniques.[37]

Tradeoff decisions are complex technically and financially, often leaving little room to maneuver. A Finnish nuclear power station, for example, relies on eleven internal departments and external groups for exchanges of "information and influence [on] safety-related decisions, although economic aspects are considered within the same framework," according to Jussi Vaurio, a nuclear engineer and specialist in probabilistic risk assessment. Each department may also rely on consultants and contractors for analyses of the technical and administrative processes in question. Beyond each control room and executive office, then, a wider ecology of influence pervades the tradeoff quandary. But influence is not equal internally: even though they are peers in a senior management group, reactor engineering and operations managers are likely to have more say than maintenance managers.[38] To "manage risks" at any particular time is to strategize through a narrow passage to emerge without harming employees, publics, or shareholders.

To understand more about its tradeoff quandaries in real time, in 1994 Electricité de France (EDF) created "Safety/Availability Monitoring Units" to acknowledge "conflicts" among "a wide-ranging set of requirements": for "nuclear safety," for "personnel safety, health physics and competitiveness," and for "environmental protection." "Safety" here means shutting down or reducing power when worrisome conditions or repairs require; "availability" means staying online, preferably at full power. The monitoring units revisit the choices of EDF control room operators and managers, as well as those of corporate managers about schedules and resources. They study decisions that led to incidents as well as to "well-managed situations," not as oversight or "real-time management" but to create "transparency" for conversations about the conditions that led to operating choices made with "safety consciousness."[39] Those self-studies are unpublished; generally, we have little to go on for understanding how tradeoff negotiations proceed in real time, nor do we learn enough about how those same processes prevent and recover from trouble. Instead of "safety," which implies an absolute condition, I speak, as do many in high hazard industries, of *reducing* and *handling* risk to capture the realities and dynamics of the quandary.

The Davis-Besse finding made it clear that regulators take an active role in tradeoff negotiations. It was by chance, as I have said, that station inspections, responding to the most recent NRC bulletin on issues in pressurized water reactors, found the hole in the vessel head. Neither NRC nor INPO field inspections had seen the hole previously, yet for about fifteen years both had warned, citing operating experiences elsewhere, that regular inspections of the reactor head for corrosion were a must. Several times over the years, knowing about the nozzle leak, the NRC had allowed the company's managers to delay inspections in this inaccessible and high-dose area: they require an outage. The 106-page report of the "Davis-Besse Lessons Learned Task Force" made up of NRC's technical experts couples "NRC" and "the industry" on nearly every point. "The NRC and the industry regarded boric acid deposits on the [reactor pressure vessel] head as an issue that required attention; however, the NRC and industry did not regard the presence of the boric acid deposits on the . . . head as a significant safety concern because they expected that boric acid crystals would form from flashing steam and such crystals would not cause significant corrosion."[40] Nor had the industry accepted analyses that led Electricité de France in 1991 to respond immediately to a fainter signal of nozzle trouble on its pressurized water reactors, the only type in its fleet; EDF has since replaced forty-two of fifty-four susceptible reactor vessel heads.[41] The NRC task force found that ineffective corrective actions contributed to recurrences of "boric acid leakage and corrosion events," and that managers had not kept current with findings about operational issues elsewhere. "Also, the NRC failed to adequately review, assess, and follow up on relevant operating experience to bring about the necessary industry and plant specific actions to prevent this event." The regulator "accepted industry positions" and failed to consider the issues independently.[42]

Several months after the Davis-Besse find, INPO sent to its members a nine-page critique marked " 'Red: Immediate Attention.' " A "nuclear industry expert," violating INPO's secrecy rule, gave the *New York Times* a copy. The reason for the disclosure, the person said, according to the *Times* story, was "to have the industry take it to heart." "The report, not intended for distribution outside the nuclear industry . . . said that the FirstEnergy Nuclear Operating Company had fallen prey to 'excessive focus on meeting short-term production goals' and [showed] 'a lack of sensitivity to nuclear safety. . . . The lessons learned from the Davis-Besse event are universal in nature and should be reviewed by all nuclear stations.' "[43] Local newspaper accounts quoted NRC and company officials who expressed "surprise" about "the nature and extent of the damage," and, this briefing paper by the Union of Concerned Scientists continues, "There [had been] similar statements of surprise . . . about the nature and extent of damage" to nozzles at another plant, "about the nature and extent of the damage to the steam generator tube" at a third plant, "about the nature and extent of the damage to . . . piping"—among others. "Child-like wonderment is endearing on Christmas morning. It is dangerously irresponsible when consistently applied to nuclear safety. . . . The NRC must stop allowing plant owners to conduct fewer inspections and to defer inspections for economic reasons."[44]

On center stage in every tradeoff quandary are basic elements of a station's culture of control: what information is available, how experts interpret its significance, the choices they consider, and the priorities at issue. The industry's rubric, "safety culture," is less specific. That phrase first appeared in a 1986 International Atomic Energy Agency (IAEA) report on the Chernobyl accident, repeated later but without elaboration in 1988. In 1989 the NRC issued a policy statement asserting that plant management "has a duty and obligation to foster the development of a 'safety culture' at each facility and to provide a professional working environment, in the control room and throughout the facility, that assures safe operations."[45] By 1991 an IAEA report titled "safety culture" defined it as "that assembly of characteristics and attitudes in organizations and individuals which establishes that, as an overriding priority, nuclear plant safety issues receive attention warranted by their significance."[46] Determining that significance in particular contexts is, however, the crux of the quandary.

Within the NRC the one group for which "safety culture" has had more specific meanings is the NRC's Advisory Committee on Reactor Safeguards (ACRS), responsible for developing accident scenarios and risk assessment methods, or probabilistic risk assessments (PRAs).[47] To parallel metrics available for equipment reliability and failure rates, which are largely the basis for PRAs, the committee has long tried to initiate research on metrics for "safety culture" from evidence about managerial strategies and operational arrangements. But the NRC itself had previously halted such studies "abruptly" and "rudely," according to George Apostolakis, professor of nuclear engineering at the Massachusetts Institute of Technology and member of the ACRS, and at the time, its chairman.[48] The NRC commissioned one study in the 1980s from several managerial, social, and psychological researchers, and in the late 1990s, the other, in progress at a federal national laboratory, was developing methods for incorporating such data into PRAs.[49] In 2002, while the committee was hearing from the chairman of the NRC Oversight Panel inquiring into the Davis-Besse event, Apostolakis said: "for the last 20–25 years this agency has started research projects on organizational/managerial issues that were very abruptly and rudely stopped right in the middle because, if you do that, the [industry] argument goes, regulation follows. So we don't understand these issues because we never really studied them."[50] Nor do those in other risky technologies, the committee learned from a study it commissioned. "Safety Culture: A Survey of the State-of-the-Art," published in 2002, finds that none have developed "safety culture" risk metrics. There is a "regulatory dilemma," the report said: conditions "important to safety culture are difficult, if not impossible, to separate from the management of the organization. . . . Historically, the NRC has been reluctant to regulate management functions in any direct way. Licensees have been even more reluctant to permit any moves in that direction. The argument is, of course, that licensees are responsible for the safe operation of their facilities, and they must be permitted to achieve safety in their own operating environment in the best ways they know. The closest NRC has come to evaluating management performance is the SALP program [systematic assessment of licensee performance]," which the industry criticized "as lacking objectivity," a central motivation for revising the oversight regime.[51]

Although the NRC maintains the expectation announced in its original "safety culture" policy statement, oversight practices approach it only "through a variety of indirect means," including a "baseline inspection program [that] does touch on programmatic areas—including, in particular, the problem identification and corrective action processes—that provide important insights on safety culture." In this speech to an INPO conference of CEOs in November 2002, NRC's then-chairman Dr. Richard A. Meserve, physicist and lawyer, elaborated on the moral of the Davis-Besse story. "[N]either the [new] reactor oversight process nor the prior inspection program worked as we had hoped at identifying the [vessel head] problem at an early stage." In fact, NRC had awarded the station a "green" rating based on its performance indicators showing no "significant findings" from baseline inspections. "It was only as a result of the deeper inspection in the aftermath of the discovery of the corrosion that we have uncovered the pervasive problems that existed at the plant. Since the underlying cause of the failure was a problem with safety culture, [this] episode presents the fundamental question as to whether the NRC's approach to assuring an adequate safety culture is sufficient." The industry's objections are to "subjectivity" when "objectivity" is wanted.

First, there is the concern that any attempt to regulate and evaluate safety culture is necessarily very subjective. The concept of safety culture has core ingredients on which perhaps all can agree, but the precise limits of this somewhat amorphous concept are hard to discern. Moreover, given that the concept is not crisply defined, it is not surprising that neither the NRC nor other organizations have found an unambiguous way to measure it. As all of you are aware, one of the driving forces for the development of the Reactor Oversight Process was the desire to provide a more objective and transparent method of performance assessment that could be applied equitably and uniformly over the entire industry. The inclusion of safety culture as a direct element of regulation and inspection is inconsistent with this objective to the extent that safety culture does not lend itself to objective measurement.

Invoking the example of other countries with "programs to regulate safety culture in the direct ways that the NRC has heretofore avoided," Meserve cites the British example of a license condition that requires utilities' self-review of the safety consequences of changes such as mergers, acquisitions, and downsizing, which regulators can then assess.[52] The possibility of oversight of "safety culture" is worthy only of discussion, Meserve nevertheless reassured his audience.

That was borne out in July 2003, when the ACRS, after a public hearing on the question with a cross-section of industry experts, reported to NRC's chairman Nils Diaz that although most industry experts could agree on notable attributes of "safety culture," the link to performance was difficult to quantify—attributes such as "instilling employees with a 'questioning attitude,' having a conservative decision-making process at the facility, and adopting personal accountability. . . . 'We conclude that the regulatory framework for monitoring aspects of safety culture is largely in place. . . . This framework is appropriately performance based. . . . Broader evaluations of safety culture, such as management emphasis on safety and personnel attitudes, belong to the industry,' " said ACRS chairman Mario Bonaca.[53]

That the vessel head hole at Davis-Besse was found before it could wreak "high consequences" is, in this scheme of things, however, a strike against its becoming a beacon for sustained change. An industry insider commented to me matter-of-factly that Davis-Besse is a "blip": the deaths and radiation exposures in the Japanese criticality accident will have more effect on the industry as a whole, he said. That has happened before: a near-accident at the Browns Ferry station in Decatur, Alabama in 1975 did not inspire the depth of soul searching that followed the 1979 meltdown at Three Mile Island.[54] That has been a sad cycle among high hazard enterprises: when not an "accident" but an "event" with no evident consequences for public or employee health and safety, the corporate pattern is a spurt of attention and resources for "safety" and for fostering a "safety culture." After improvements take hold and they grapple anew with a tradeoff quandary, managers will misread those improvements as signals that those resources are no longer needed. The cycle begins again, turning seasoned safety specialists cynical: "Are accidents actually required to reset the incentive system in competition with cost?"[55]

What will or should be considered "safety culture" and how to demonstrate and document it, by regulation and self-regulation, remains unambiguously ambiguous to all players, mainly because, as the industry claims, it does not "lend itself to objective measurement."[56] That maintains the assumption, however, that everything else in the culture of control does, or should.

Concerns, Commitments, and Control

Other dimensions of the tradeoff quandary came through to me gradually. After a few orienting visits to nuclear power plants in the United States and abroad in the early 1990s, I observed self-improvement efforts, mostly at Overton Nuclear Station. Re-engineering initiatives had stimulated some, others came from station experts' own analyses or were in response to INPO assessments or NRC findings. Later, I focused on the outage phase when the reactor is off line being refueled or shut down to accommodate scheduled repairs, when contractors double or triple the on-site population and operations staff take on other tasks. The work system reverses for the duration: an outage manager takes charge, replacing the unit's operations manager. All are trying to accomplish thousands of pieces of work that have, most agree, "impossible deadlines" leading to long days: "We divorce our families for the duration."[57] Recently, I've made these inquiries into the event review system.

In each situation, experts were changing their ways of working, critiquing them, or entering into what they call that "second world" of outages. The customary order of things—ways of approaching uncertainties and reducing their risks—was somehow in flux. These four events at Arrow, Bowie, and Charles Stations had also been occurring while, station by station, the industry was redefining itself, churning up a sea of distractions with mergers, acquisitions, re-engineering. Top to bottom, many station experts were unsure of their jobs, their reporting lines, their next assignment, and how the chain of command was working. And under new owners and new policies for compensation, benefits, and promotion, and being reinterviewed for their current jobs, many were unsure of where they and their families stood financially. In American corporations over the last decades, much of all employees' work, on top of what they sign on for, is to cope with such ripple effects to create enough clarity and coherence to get their "real work" done.[58] That too was changing: downsizing often collapsed two jobs into one or rotated people into a different

one. Despite all "the unsettlement" and "concern about" yet another reorganization, as one person put it, station experts continued to speak of
"the organization" and "my organization" to refer to the station as a
whole, to their particular unit, to their department, to their work group,
any of which could change quickly, as though to anchor themselves. "Tur-
bulent times," one expert observed, "but we're not assessing their consequences—we're just picking up the pieces."

Because "organization" implies an orderliness itself in question, I began
to parse what was happening through practices I was observing: who does
what, when, where, and why.[59] That brought me to "enterprise," which
speaks better to the kinds of efforts I saw morning and night: a collective
of people with diverse perspectives, skills, and responsibilities trying to
maintain momentum toward several simultaneous goals. To respect that
effort, the tradeoff quandary replaces the vague semantics of "management," and "strategies" and "tactics" become the practices of interest.
Through these dislocations, I hoped to be open to what I might otherwise
overlook.

What I began to see is that no matter how a utility or station's hierarchy
and functions are arrayed, the premises, values, and principles guiding
this technology's operations are accretions of specialists' different concerns and commitments, expressed in their various ways of understanding
and systematizing risk and its control. Operating nuclear power technology demands that multiplicity. For those reasons, I call specialists' concerns and commitments *orders*: their different approaches to making
order out of the technological and financial ambiguities of risk. Each order
is embedded in institutional networks and grounded in different traditions, values, and practices, only some of which have developed with reference to risk reduction in nuclear power production: a corporate order, a
regulatory order, a market and production order, a naval or military order,
and a material order grounded in the physics of the nuclear reaction and
the engineering of electricity production. Nested within those are professional orders (chemistry, engineering, finance, health physics, human resources, management, occupational safety, among others).

Each order relies on its own concepts, techniques, and sources of authority, and although those of each are interdependent, they are not always compatible. How each of those ranks within each order creates its
own hierarchy of knowledge and a bureaucracy of skills, more or less
explicit. Each order has its internal conflicts over those values and over
strategies and tactics, as each has with other orders. As choices get made
and the orders negotiate their concerns and commitments, each contributes to a political economy. That is also, of course, a moral economy,
expressed through priorities and allocations of influence and resources
across those varied concerns. At the October 2003 WANO meeting, the

president of Tokyo Electric Power Company, Tsunehisa Katsumata, spoke harshly about these matters. The company's "nuclear power division" had become " 'a homogeneous and exclusive circle of engineers who defied checks by other divisions, including the management.' "

> Rules covering fitness for service of equipment were "not clear," he said, and didn't allow for flaws as equipment aged, encouraging personnel to ignore the rules. Media attacks on problems at nuclear facilities, he said, put the engineers "on the defensive" and encouraged them to hide faults as long as those faults didn't immediately threaten safety—leading to 16 cases of falsification of inspection and repair records. . . . Compounding this was the engineers' attitude that a "stable supply of electricity [was] the ultimate objective," leading them to make "personal decisions based on their own idea of safety," Katsumata said.[60]

The president of FirstEnergy Nuclear Operating Company, owner of the Davis-Besse plant, Robert Saunders, agreed: "a good operating record at Davis-Besse and the primacy of engineers over operating staff . . . had spawned 'arrogance and complacency'. . . . Management had programs in place, but there was no follow-through, and quality assurance staff reported directly to site management, 'impacting its independence and objectivity.' "[61]

The market order that has come upon a previously protected industry adds a competitive dimension in each order's concerns and commitments. About 60 percent of all U.S. nuclear generating plants are in retail markets, and as some companies continue to own and build fossil fuel plants, they also compete with themselves. Tradeoff negotiations also affect shareholders, stock prices, and borrowing capacity. Each professional specialty, including craft specialties, brings its particular concerns and commitments to the negotiations: the concepts, standards, methods, techniques, and ethics of chemists, chief financial officers, civil engineers, electricians, nuclear engineers, valve artisans.[62] All are necessarily oriented to the physical science of the nuclear reaction and to the engineering science required for making electricity from the nuclear reaction—the material order.

In negotiating the tradeoff quandary, each order seeks to control and diminish the uncertainties it specializes in. Each has its different time horizons mixed with its perspectives on the technological and financial risks involved. For example, to keep radiation doses within acceptable levels, health physicists ask for shorter periods of work from a larger pool of people; that raises costs, which may adversely affect corporate order's market standing. The profusion of orders turns "management" into a matter of walking into the quandary and, ideally, walking out with a consensus among conflicting, contradictory, or paradoxical concerns and commitments sufficient to realize the best intentions of all.[63]

The orders stand each on its own bedrock like islands in an archipelago. Despite traffic among alliances, ranks, and specialties, a surrounding sea keeps each distinctive and insular or stirs up and destabilizes their exchanges. The orders' profusion adds contextual complexities to technological complexities, for which, however, there are no similarly well-worked worst-case scenarios. Only incipiently, then, is the multiplicity of orders also the system of rationalized relationships that "organization" suggests. Or, put another way, the orders siphon into "organization" its ever-puzzling dynamics and its energy. In this high hazard enterprise, their profusion is basic to its culture of control and its consequences.

The White Spaces between the Boxes

As an Overton Station manager and I looked at the station's organization chart, with its levels and boxes for each function and department, he waved his hand over the page, "Those are just the reporting lines. The work gets done in the white spaces between the boxes, up, down, and sideways." The laws governing corporations and NRC's oversight and enforcement duties pen the design of those boxes and white spaces. Corporate order emerges from a utility or company's legal status and the resulting distribution of fiduciary rights and obligations. That wraps around a division of labor defined by the regulator's understandings of how to approach the physics and engineering of risk reduction. A naval order persists and brings its values to bear on the distribution of authority and influence. This industry's origins in the military order of World War II have remained on active duty as the navy's nuclear submarine and ship programs continued to be a source of industry employees for utilities, NRC, and INPO. By NRC mandate, INPO trains and accredits control room operators and other station experts. Besides its peer evaluations, INPO's staff also provides technical assistance; reanalyzes some important events occurring worldwide; maintains a confidential communication system keeping members here and abroad informed about others' "best practices" and industry activities; and conducts short courses on technical matters, including one for senior managers.[64] INPO and WANO constitute orders with as much influence on self-regulation as regulatory order has on enforceable oversight. I elaborate on naval order soon.

Whether corporate headquarters are in a distant city, at the station in another building, or on a top floor of an on-site administration building, their offices are typically executive in size and decor, in contrast to the industrial architecture of the dozens of buildings populating the station proper. Utilities traditionally assign a "plant superintendent" to their nonnuclear stations, and at nuclear power stations (many now renamed "nuclear generating stations"), that title has become "station manager." But

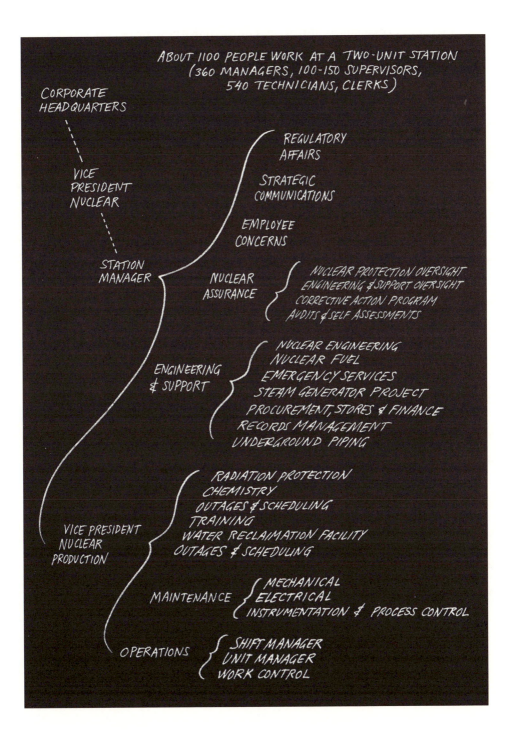

ABOUT 1100 PEOPLE WORK AT A TWO-UNIT STATION
(360 MANAGERS, 100-150 SUPERVISORS,
540 TECHNICIANS, CLERKS)

CORPORATE
HEADQUARTERS

VICE
PRESIDENT
NUCLEAR

STATION
MANAGER

REGULATORY
AFFAIRS

STRATEGIC
COMMUNICATIONS

EMPLOYEE
CONCERNS

NUCLEAR
ASSURANCE
{
NUCLEAR PROTECTION OVERSIGHT
ENGINEERING & SUPPORT OVERSIGHT
CORRECTIVE ACTION PROGRAM
AUDITS & SELF ASSESSMENTS
}

ENGINEERING
& SUPPORT
{
NUCLEAR ENGINEERING
NUCLEAR FUEL
EMERGENCY SERVICES
STEAM GENERATOR PROJECT
PROCUREMENT, STORES & FINANCE
RECORDS MANAGEMENT
UNDERGROUND PIPING
}

VICE PRESIDENT
NUCLEAR
PRODUCTION

RADIATION PROTECTION
CHEMISTRY
OUTAGES & SCHEDULING
TRAINING
WATER RECLAIMATION FACILITY
OUTAGES & SCHEDULING

MAINTENANCE
{
MECHANICAL
ELECTRICAL
INSTRUMENTATION & PROCESS CONTROL
}

OPERATIONS
{
SHIFT MANAGER
UNIT MANAGER
WORK CONTROL
}

that manager is unlikely also to exercise expanded powers over budgeting, hiring, and capital expenditures. Corporate order has exclusive authority over production and outage schedules, customer contracts, fuel purchase and storage, finance, human resources, regulatory relations, and public relations. In response to the Kemeny Commission's finding after the accident at Three Mile Island that utility executives were less informed about and involved in their nuclear station's operations than they needed to be, in most utilities a "vice-president/nuclear" now keeps one foot at the station, the other at corporate. Likely to have been a station manager, senior line manager, or senior officer in the nuclear navy, a vice-president/ nuclear is often the only person with a technical background in nuclear power at the corporate level, except for lawyers specializing in regulatory relations. In corporate councils, the vice-president/nuclear, one among several vice-presidents responsible for diverse assets, is likely to be the station's spokesperson, perhaps also being a one-person "nuclear power subcommittee."

Whatever reporting lines are at any one company or station, they can be only a rough guide to any other's, given variations in patterns of utility and station ownership, the division into generation and distribution companies, the reactor model, and the extent of a utility's diversification into other business interests.[65] The one constant is that by the terms of the license, the operations shift manager is the only person authorized to order a reactor shut down or started up. Up to the time such a decision is needed, the station manager, consulting with line managers (business, chemistry, engineering, health physics, human resources, maintenance, operations, training), is the final arbiter of operational strategies. For operational tactics day by day, month by month, a senior management group meets about twice weekly to review priorities. Their tradeoff quandaries juggle productivity and risk reduction within the budget and schedule handed them. First priorities belong to issues the NRC and/or INPO have fingered; last on any list are what engineers call the "nice to do's" that are plentiful in any technology-driven environment. (Appendix 2 sketches the responsibilities, experience, and education of Overton Station's senior managers at one point in time.)

Stations' social architecture and their orders share the same population pattern, as far as I can tell in the absence of a reliable public demography of this industry. There are relatively few women, people of color, and employees younger than about forty. National and global initiatives aim to increase those numbers: the Nuclear Energy Institute promotes a "women in nuclear" program, and professional engineering groups and university departments are pursuing a "young generation" recruiting campaign. In the United States and varying by region, my guess is that roughly 80–85 percent of all employees are white males, 10–15 percent white females,

5–10 percent black, Asian, Hispanic, Native American females and males. More whites are salaried; more women, people of color, and those in crafts and trades are likely to be hourly employees. For the first time in the United States, in 2002 two women became station managers.

The Nuclear Connection: Naval and Corporate Orders

As the history of industrialization would generally predict and as this industry's specific history determined, naval order has made the most ready conceptual alliance with the command and control principle valued in engineering and corporate orders. The federal Atomic Energy Commission's mandate to promote and privatize nuclear power initiated this military-civilian connection when that Commission migrated from its military origins into the postwar campaign promoting "atoms for peace."[66] Because the nuclear navy has been the stronghold of experience with power reactors, ex-nuclear navy officers and enlisted men and women have populated the industry from its beginning in administrative and technical jobs. INPO's staff is down to about 50 percent ex-nuclear navy from about 85 percent after retirements, attrition, and layoffs, according to industry insiders. So it is for the NRC: "NRC is nuclear navy," one resident NRC inspector remarked off-the-cuff. "They like people who follow orders. People with that background just seem to get ahead faster." As of the mid-1980s, however, the industry began to be less attractive as second careers and for first careers as well. Overton Station's senior managers, many there from construction days, had engineering or technical backgrounds; some came from the navy. According to Gary, its station manager, "We had a history of top people legendary for their wisdom" and for being "overbearing or downright mean"—and who also "turned things around" when they needed to be turned around.

> We don't do a good job of training replacements at this station. We have a history of respected but feared leaders, leaving a legacy of no role models for working with people. All those hired in for the top jobs were same personality types. Talk about changing. I used to make people feel like dirt—just tell them they were wrong. I was too focused on one thing—it was all technical, not thinking of the other consequences.

One of Overton's operations shift managers, Kevin, senior licensed reactor operator, comments that the nuclear navy and commercial nuclear power are "polar opposites."

> We're a highly technical industry, you know, we're not a touchy feely industry. The government on the other hand, the [nuclear] navy, it was

run by a series of megalomaniacs. It was an autocratic society—"You will do it because I'm your boss," and that went down the line. Can't do that here. The navy has millions and millions of reactor hours and miles on ships without an accident. We may also have millions of hours on the bearings of the generator, so to speak—it rotates. But the industry is not the same. They're polar opposites generating power.

Stories of the navy's continuing influences told by those formerly in it, as well as those who had not been, come salted with peppery language; feelings run high. At Overton, Ron, an oversight manager, is talking about a recent event and recalling the past.

I've seen anarchy before. Ten years ago you'd go to meetings and you hoped you weren't called upon to say anything because if you were called upon to talk you were a target.

You were a target?

You were a target.

Who was in charge then?

A former naval admiral. We had a "shoot 'em and kill 'em" attitude. If you weren't bringing good news, if you were the messenger, you did get killed. . . . When we transitioned through the construction of the plant, we had a lot of the construction mentality that followed us, not only down to the worker level but primarily in this manager level and senior manager level, with a lot of ex-navy personnel whose attitude was, "I'll give the order, you follow the order." And so we got to a point where the actual material condition of the plant started degrading—even though we were having some good runs, you could see that the processes, the procedures, the management structure wasn't supporting excellent performance. The NRC got on our case and the management team changed, and things are very different now. But when it was a very autocratic management structure, the workers felt that they had very little voice in addressing problems and helping in the outcome or the resolution of the problems. Now, if I have something I need to relay to the plant manager, I just walk into his office. I mean ten years ago you wouldn't do that. Unless you had a death wish.

Gary lived through that time.

You're in a job for two or three years in the navy, and you can be dictatorial because you want fast results, you're leaving soon for a new job, and any bad feelings have no consequences for you. The military rewards people who get things done, who tromp over people, who see right and wrong with no in-between, and get results. The nuclear industry attracts that.

Licensed reactor operators, keepers of the technical specifications, may take on officer-like status; whether utilities can require them to wear uniforms has been an issue, given that operators themselves, as well as other plant employees, often object to military order in every guise. For some at Overton, ex-navy operators come across as "arrogant," "cocky," "overaggressive," "rude." Even to the NRC: an operations old-timer remarked, "The Nuclear Regulatory Commission finds us arrogant because we stand up for what we believe." Mixed into industry-regulator relationships and into corporate-station-plant relationships is the lingering officer-enlisted man hierarchy, where some managers, especially ex-officers, reenact that superior-subordinate role and brook no dissent. The nuclear navy still has some "old screamers who ruled their ships by intimidation," Douglas C. Waller, congressional correspondent for *Time* magazine, learned a few years ago during his three months underwater observing a mission aboard the Trident nuclear submarine *Nebraska*. One officer knows that the *Nebraska's* captain is "the best skipper he could hope for—very competent. . . . He almost never yelled at people. In fact, it would shock Thorson if he did. [The captain] was a product of the Navy's new leadership, which believed you got just as much out of a sailor by explaining to him and motivating him. A few of the old screamers who ruled their ships by intimidation were still around. [Thorson] had talked to officers on other subs . . . and heard the horror stories."[67] But even this skipper is impatient if his own "do's and don'ts" aren't followed, Waller finds. "Always gird yourself for a grilling. Never—repeat, never—report a problem on the ship to the skipper unless you have a plan in the next breath for solving it. Even if it's a dumb solution, at least offer something."[68] Some industry managers still impose that requirement, and by random report, some still scream and intimidate. Like captains of yore, some, it seems, think of themselves as "kings afloat."[69]

Without necessarily intending to, re-engineering spotlighted the quality of communication generally—among specialists and within the hierarchy—and specifically, all employees' opportunities to speak as well as their capacity for listening. A first task of re-engineering consultants is to develop teams of specialists as sources of their local knowledge. Between a military order and the patriarchal corporate order of an old-line industry, consultants came upon a hard case. Not only had top-down control dominated, but this industry had long been immune to a "human relations" theory of management. Although many station experts readily recognize poor "people skills," as they put it, especially among managers, senior executives, and supervisors, re-engineering and the teamwork it relies on has made them even more apparent. And to the NRC as well: after a few well publicized cases of maltreated or fired employees who became whistleblowers out of frustration at not being heard on safety issues, in 1996 the NRC ratcheted up its criteria for listening to employees' concerns and created sanctions for executives and managers who did not play well with others. Even so, we will hear, "open listening" remains difficult for some. Further inhibiting openness is a blaming system and its "fingerpointing," as station experts call it, induced partly by regulatory and legal orders that require identifiable culprits and partly by customary naval discipline.

As INPO began its search for a president, "We were not looking specifically for a naval officer," recalls an industry executive, "if anything, retired military officers in industry generally had a poor reputation."[70] Out of 107 candidates, however, INPO chose a retired admiral, Eugene Wilkinson, who had been an early protégée of Admiral Hyman G. Rickover, electrical engineer and leader of the team that began in 1946 to develop a submarine power reactor; the navy launched the first in 1953. As his assistant, Wilkinson brought in Zack Pate, who had spent his last three years in the navy as Rickover's special assistant. On July 23, 1979, Rickover himself met with the Kemeny Commission at its invitation. Theodore Rockwell, a chemical engineer and civilian employee in Rickover's Naval Nuclear Propulsion Program and later, an engineer in private practice, was Rickover's friend and biographer. Rockwell reports Rickover's testimony.

> Rickover stated his belief that there was much the commercial atomic power industry could learn from the naval program, but he cautioned against looking for some "magical formula" to be applied blindly and effortlessly. That would not work. The answer lay in all the people involved, from top management to lowest technicians, continuously applying great care to everything they do, and doing so with a competence born of technical training that is both broad and deep. . . . [Rickover] believed that too much attention was being paid to dealing with low-probability accidents and not enough to preventing accidents. The design should assume that even well-trained operators and maintenance personnel will make mistakes, and the design should be able to tolerate such mistakes. He also warned that the design of commercial plants had too many alarms. They sounded under trivial and even [under] normal circumstances, so that operators soon learned to ignore them.[71]

Later, President Jimmy Carter, once a naval officer under Rickover's command, asked him to review the Kemeny Commission's report, and in the "personal views" Carter had asked for, Rickover comments that the industry had placed "too much emphasis" on "research and development" and "not enough on the daily drudgery of seeing that every aspect . . . is in fact properly handled every day by each of the organizations involved."[72] Rickover recommended that "the utilities unite to establish a central technical organization" to supplement their "limited staff"—in 1980 that became the focus of INPO activities. Not knowing that then,

Rickover nevertheless foresaw the clash of orders. To anticipate "the objection that his ideas might not be applicable to private utilities," he pointed out their generality: ". . . Rickover wrote simply, 'Discipline is an essential characteristic of any successful program and of any successful person. The discipline in the naval nuclear program has been successful not because this involves military applications, but because I have insisted upon staffing the program with intelligent, motivated people, whom I hold accountable.' "[73]

Civilian corporate order, despite Rickover's demurral, readily mimics the imperatives of military order, which then conflicts with professional orders whose civilians find it unacceptable outside the encapsulated, total environment of a nuclear submarine or ship. In fact, the question of whether an explicitly military order for plant operations was warranted preoccupied the Kemeny Commission—so recounts Charles Perrow, emeritus professor of sociology and organizational theory at Yale University. Considering if and how this industry differs from all others, a majority of members concluded that "it did not matter" that Three Mile Island was "run like Texas Instruments and General Motors" because industrial "plants are all the same." But members were also saying, "military management" is needed "because they are special," leading one to propose that they consider the model of "the naval reactor program, run with an iron fist, every decision made at the top, nobody budging down below, intense training, intense discipline on the operators." He followed that, however, with a recommendation that the members "ought seriously to consider the question of nationalization." Finally, the Kemeny Commission wrote a report that, Perrow says, "While excoriating everyone, merely said, 'Now let's all do a better job.' "[74]

Rickover's doubts about the compatibility of the two orders also became visible in INPO's approach to reporting its peer assessments to member utilities. In its early years, "utility officials," apparently wary of the naval habit of plain talk, "constrained INPO's enforcement powers" and INPO "carefully restrained" the "wording" in its inspection reports, whose tone was "tactfully diplomatic" so as not to "give ammunition to [industry watchdogs and critics]. . . . The message to INPO was clear: sanitize your inspection reports. . . . And INPO . . . did just that."[75] By about 1986, an INPO self-study found that its strategy of peer pressure for self-regulation had not had its intended effects; there were too many laggards who were placing "too much emphasis" on the reports' "comfort words." That led to a sea change: "greater attention [will be given by the staff] to whether the comfort words can be included justifiably."[76] At the same time, INPO began to send its assessments only to the utility in question rather than to all its industry members.[77] A participant in the earliest risk assessment studies at MIT in the mid-1970s and member of

various INPO committees, who had worked with Rickover and with Wilkinson on plant reviews, recalls that "they were conducted like Rickover
reviews," and although these were always a cooperative effort, the final
versions "were from the perspective of 'I' not 'We.' "[78] Even as naval order
may be dissipating, the image of an "iron fist" remains appealing to some
industry observers: top-down discipline as the prime element of the culture of control.

The Cycle of Self-Improvement: The Event Review System

Of all the feedback streaming from hundreds of sensors, tests, and inspections, it is left mainly to internal event reviews to provide feedback about
technical and contextual dynamics. Event reviews come toward the end
of a cycle designed to catch as many warnings of trouble as possible,
beginning with a report to the corrective actions program of a CONDITION
ADVERSE TO SAFETY AND QUALITY.[79] Every employee, administrative or
technical, and all visitors (contractor, vendor, anthropologist) are expected to identify any material, administrative, or physical condition they
regard as being "adverse." Forms are available at handy locations, and,
increasingly, on computerized kiosks, as the industry aims for a low reporting threshold: nipping problems in the bud can be less costly than
having to shut down production, especially in seasons that may coincide
with favorable rates.

Conditions range widely: by definition, any event is an adverse condition. So are untidy work areas, component malfunctions, missing steps in
a new procedure, faint signals of risk-escalating conditions, employee errors. A downward trend or lack of expected improvement in program,
group, or department also becomes a condition report. Between 1997 and
2002, plants voluntarily responded to occasional questionnaires about
their station's systems for identifying problematic conditions, analyzing
events, and developing recommendations for changes from a "loosely-knit
group of performance improvement professionals" in the United States
and Canada, which began in 1994 to conduct annual workshops "to facilitate sharing of information and best practices" on "human performance,
root cause, and trending" activities. For example, 14 plants reported 30–
40 root cause event analyses in 1997, 40–50 in 1998, 21–30 in 1999. In
2000, responses from 62 plants range from a low of 3 root cause analyses
to a high of 200, and for 2001, a low of 3 and a high of 75.[80]

The reports' authors estimate each condition's level of safety significance, and after the corrective action program staff screens and sorts
them, senior line managers assign priorities: those they designate as im-
peding the path to safe shutdown and threatening allowable dose levels

are at the top. The cycle ends when actions the team's report recommends have been undertaken—an average of 241 days, according to an industry benchmarking study.[81]

A station-specific procedure outlines a local version of a generic review protocol to guide the team's interviews of participants, to be made as soon after the event occurs as possible, and its analyses of station and industry databases, control room logs, and industry data. From those, the team relates only what its members define as the facts drawn from written records and what they declare to be facts sifted from the descriptions and observations of event participants and any others knowledgeable about the circumstances. Resident NRC inspectors are aware of ongoing events and reviews, and although they don't participate in either resolving or studying them, they can speed up team decisions requiring, for example, an interpretation of license requirements.

With a standard ROOT CAUSE ANALYSIS method, the team's inquiries proceed as engineering in reverse, working backward from the unwanted outcome to examine where and why barriers failed to anticipate or prevent it: rules, equipment, drawings, procedures, processes, persons. The team asks a series of "why" questions of each action and outcome to reach consensus about causes they consider most likely, categorizing them by any one of several checklists of "cause codes" promulgated by the NRC, INPO, and consultants. The specific barriers the team deems inadequate, deficient, missing, or not invoked point to "the fundamental cause(s) that, if corrected, will prevent recurrence of an adverse condition," the goal of the analysis. These may be technical failures, managerial shortcomings, types of hand-eye errors, and process deficits and inadequacies. They also cite instances of ERROR-FORCING triggers, as sanctioned by INPO's broad brush: "the aggregate of all management and leadership practices, values, culture, corporate structures, processes, technology, resources and controls that combine to result in the currently existing conditions which affect behavior of individuals at the job site."[82] These appear as cause codes—for example, "overconfidence," "less than conservative attitude," "vagueness in procedures."[83] Senior managers also expect a team to identify to them privately the person or persons responsible for any one "cause." That misstep is likely to become a permanent entry in a person's work history and a possible source of disciplinary actions.[84] Like any blaming system, it creates a dilemma: punishment can bottle up the self-reporting on which self-regulation depends, yet legal, corporate, and professional orders hold employees accountable for their actions.

Customarily, teams circulate drafts to participants and managers for comment before being issued for the record. There may be local, perhaps industrywide, dissension about a report's findings; except as some of

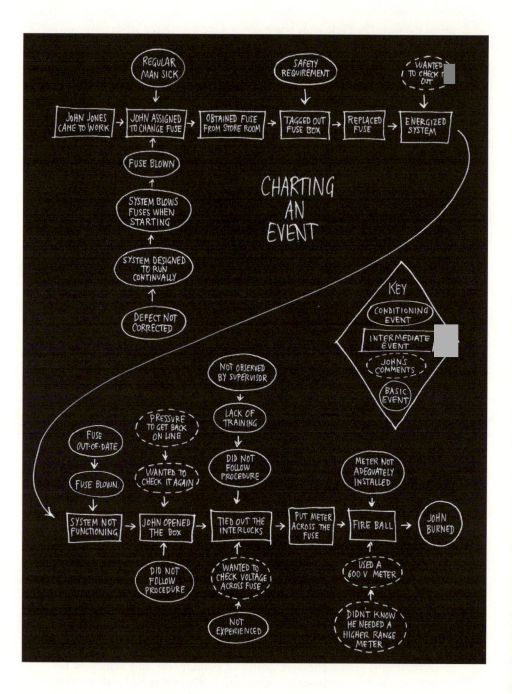

CHARTING AN EVENT

those I interviewed speak of their dissatisfactions and recount that they offered amendments, I have no knowledge of whether and how the teams at these three stations ultimately revised their drafts.

Teams' reports become official renderings of events, likely to be added to an industry database of OPERATING EXPERIENCE; for some safety-significant events, about twice a year INPO makes its own reanalyses and circulates these "significant operating event reports" to members. Reports provide readers with what is likely to be their only knowledge of an event's etiology (aside from an ever-active national and international grapevine). Readers include the station's own employees and managers and those elsewhere, as well as INPO, university researchers and the NRC's staff and consultants.

Event Analyses at Arrow, Bowie, and Charles Stations

To study the event review process, I telephoned corrective actions managers at six stations to ask for their participation, explaining my plans for this phase of my research (1997–2000) and telling them about my earlier participation in a five-year MIT study of "enhancing safety" in the nuclear power industry and other of my related activities.[85] Their concern with that widespread problem of implementing and sustaining self-improvement efforts led managers at Arrow, Bowie, and Charles Stations to agree to revisit an event of their choosing using these criteria: that it happened recently enough for those involved to recall its details; that they regard it as serious; that they would like to take another look at it; that it didn't matter to me whether it was also a violation of their license to operate; and that all I interview are to participate voluntarily and be able to take time for a one-hour individual interview at the station. At Bowie Station, the manager asked that we revisit two events. (See appendix 3 for the study description I sent each manager.)

No manager asked me to sign a confidentiality agreement nor did any impose conditions on my visits; it is my practice in any case not to identify any stations I visit nor identify those who speak with me; one station contributed to my travel costs. Obviously, the stations are self-selected and the people interviewed are only those in the orbit of four events, and then not all of those: some chose not to volunteer or were no longer working at the station, others had no time in their schedules. On the other hand, some interviews came about when one person said, "You ought to see . . ." and that person put me on her or his schedule. When I had follow-up questions about station operations, I caught additional managers, plant staff, and long-term consultants on the fly.

Of 65 nuclear generating stations housing 103 units operated by 42 companies in 31 states of this Union, these are four events from three.

Even if the stations had been selected to represent equally what industry talk labels "star performers," "well-performing plants," and "troubled plants," events raising similar issues and themes are likely to be present at any ostensibly representative station. Besides, "plant" and "station" are too gross to be meaningful: one or two programs within one or two departments may account for a questionable rating as well as for two persistent patterns. Stations designated "star performers" can become has-beens when a single event reveals weaknesses; and "troubled" plants can migrate to exemplary standing after utility or station managers make changes in a few programs.

The pool of people involved in or knowledgeable about the specifics of an event includes those present when it was happening—responsible supervisors, line managers, and senior managers—and members of the review team. The next three chapters draw on the teams' reports, sixty individual interviews, and on notes and tapes from several feedback workshops (more than one at two stations) in which about thirty-five men and four women participated, only a few of whom I had also interviewed; we discussed only their station's event. My account of what happened in each event draws on the teams' reports, translates some of their technical lingo, adds details from interviews, and explains some plant-specific technical and programmatic processes. My version of each team's report consists of both direct quotes and paraphrases of its findings and recommendations. From my transcriptions of the taped conversations, I selected the interview excerpts and edited them lightly for readability; no one refused to allow me to tape our discussion, nor did anyone object to my taping feedback sessions. My questions and excursions draw on my archive of field observations and interviews with other industry experts and managers, as well as professional and academic literatures and industry documents.

The details I offer about each person's biography are sketchy, and except for noting unmistakable nonverbal signs in my interview transcripts {deep sigh}, I do not give my personal impressions of them. Anonymity is my chief priority, and given the industry's demographic skew, I feel obliged to disguise their particulars: if their personal or professional characteristics would readily identify them or the station, I change them. The voices of those in most population categories are nevertheless present in these pages. I also left it to them to bring up anything about their background that they chose to tell me. Although I knew each person's job title from the interview schedule managers prepared for me, to signal my confidence in their credibility, I asked no direct questions about their qualifications or experience. Credibility, it will become clear, is a basic element of the culture of control.

It may seem in the next three chapters that station experts wear only hairshirts and that I'm only looking for trouble. Hardly the case, but asked to revisit events they wish had never happened, experts step up to the plate as the engaged professionals they are. There is no end to the nonevents the people who spoke with me could have discussed with justifiable pride, but no manager ever suggested that, nor to my surprise did station experts themselves bring them up in the course of our unscripted interviews or in feedback discussions. Rather, as you will see, they chide themselves and "the organization."

In these next three chapters I mine station experts' understandings of how their enterprise is and should be ordered as they confront something unexpectedly out of order and try to understand and re-understand the operations of a complicated, potentially dangerous technology. My approach to the taped interviews and internal reports emphasizes the categories and definitions plant experts think with, the meanings they assign to their situations, the practices they believe will be effective and those that disappoint them, the kinds of arguments they make and feel they can make, the ways they negotiate differences of opinion, how they juxtapose technical expertise with common sense. My purpose, then, is not to reconsider or evaluate what happened by the light of models for optimal effectiveness, efficiency, reliability, or rule-following. These events are "failures" in that scheme of things, as the teams' reports often find them to be. Nor do I try to reconcile variations between the accounts given in team reports and the verbal observations of team members and event participants. Some matters seem, from the evidence at hand, irresolvable. Some are evidence of provocative ambiguities lingering in the interstices of the operations of advanced technologies and in our ways of thinking about them. For my concerns, experts' understandings are instead sources of invaluable information about elements of the culture of control. Throughout, that is my task: to identify these as specifically as possible, thereby to make them amenable to analysis.

Whatever wider issues my search for wellsprings may call attention to, event team reports, analyses, and recommendations carry weight in the here and now, coming from those versed in the logics of a particular design basis and technical specifications. The corrective actions these reports recommend will remain on the record and on the table in further deliberations among themselves and with regulators. Those at other stations may take their operating experiences and analyses to heart. The teams' conclusions and recommendations have no choice but to dovetail with the possibilities that each station's ways of working allow—its governance and accountability system, allocation of decision-making authority, departmental responsibilities, and its own possibilities for changing these.

Experts' modes of thinking display aspects of the intellectual capital now seen as relevant for considering the sources of operating risk and for devising ways of reducing it. Discussing the inner work involved in reducing risk, experts allow us into their contained domain. Appreciating that domain in the terms in which they think about it and live in it allows us, as technical and cultural thinkers, citizens, industrialists, and policymakers, to ponder its relation to our own.[86] You will no doubt find, as I do, gaps in my data, observations, interpretations. If they become spurs to your own curiosity and concerns, still another of this book's aims would be realized.

• • • • •

In every scheduled outage a CRITICAL PATH clears the way for high-priority tasks among the thousands of tasks. All those working that path at Overton Station wear a red badge with white lettering to announce that in the maelstrom of activities, they are first in line for resources of all kinds—tools, parts, people, decisions. Clocking their progress along that route is a tight logic controlling system perturbations and assuring the availability of protective devices. Thanks to months of analysis and strategizing, work is expected to proceed transparently from one task to the next—all that can be known ahead of time has been declared.

There is no such critical path through these four events or the event team reports and experts' comments. Like shards and relics lying near the top of a patch of soil, they invite curiosity about the substrates of history, thought, and practices making them. What names can we give to these thoughts and practices? When another culture so reveals itself, or is revealed to those in it or not in it, that naming alone suggests alternatives. Knowing how others make order clarifies our own, even if we dismiss the alternatives for ourselves. Those I name zigzag enough throughout this industry to suggest that, being implicit in its orders' concepts and practices, they rarely get second thoughts about why they exist, nor about how they help or hinder the quest for effective improvements.

Chapter Two

Arrow Station: A Leaking Valve in Containment

STANDING OUT amidst the three dozen structures on Arrow's 50-acre plain is the beehive-shaped reactor containment, its concrete shell lined with 3/4-inch steel, rising inside to about 170 feet. Within its 115-foot diameter are the three primary barriers for confining and controlling radioactivity: the metal cladding around fuel rods in the reactor core; the PRESSURE BOUNDARY of the piping of the REACTOR COOLING SYSTEM; and reactor vessel and containment structure. Accident mitigation systems take over should the reactor cooling system (RCS) or fuel cladding fail. Independent instruments initiate actions to prevent or suppress excess reactivity; standby equipment (including the EMERGENCY CORE COOLING SYSTEM) automatically injects cooling water into the reactor coolant system; various accident scenarios mobilize other control strategies for fires, severe weather, and uncontrolled radiological release and explosions.

The leaking valve sits on the reactor cooling system, an extensive assembly of piping that winds around the reactor vessel to circulate about 100,000 gallons of water per minute heated to about 600°F under very high pressure to prevent boiling—2,000 to 2,250 pounds per square inch. The borated cooling water moderates the speed of the nuclear reaction and absorbs the heat that makes steam; the water also absorbs some radioactivity. Although Arrow's reactor is said to be shut down—not producing power—a low level of fission being produced by the remaining fuel requires a residual heat removal system connected to the RCS to be continuously available. Whether and how this leak affects that availability is the question during and after this event.

Matching the complexity within the containment and the defense-in-depth system of backups and barriers, this event shows, is the station's scaffolding for supporting and carrying out work and for dealing with the consequences of that doubled complexity.

AN ACCOUNT OF A VALVE REPAIR EFFORT

After an extensive maintenance outage, Arrow Station's reactor had been back on line for about a month when a new problem forces managers to shut it down for a week. That restart is difficult: scheduled deadlines are missed twice in a row, and now, after about two weeks back on line, the unit has to come down again.

On a Tuesday, Al and Ben, maintenance mechanics, arrive in containment to repair a leaking valve on the reactor cooling system (RCS). With some protective devices out of service, the reactor mode requires this repair to be done within seventy-two hours or the unit will have to be shut down completely. For the previous ninety minutes, the men have a prejob briefing with their supervisor, Luke, on this "minor maintenance work order," reviewing the task and the tools required; health physics technicians check that they are garbed correctly for doing this job in containment (dress, gloves, and face shields protect them from contamination).

To staunch a leak in the same valve two years earlier, mechanics added packing material (graphoil), and a month ago, inspections revealed a new leak. The valve is unusual in being one of 180 "unisolable" valves out of about 4,000 valves throughout the plant: no other valve on the RCS controls the water coming through it. There are only two alternatives for shutting off flow for a repair. The simplest is to put it on its internal backseat: a stem at the valve's top connects to a disc at its bottom; turning the stem drops the disc into the valve's intake opening as a pressure boundary. Otherwise, repair requires a complicated method that uses liquid nitrogen and special sleeving to freeze the flow in a stretch of piping ahead of the valve. Either way, this valve is in a tight spot with little room for people and tools.

Taking advantage of lower RCS temperature and pressure levels required by other restart work, managers recently moved this job up on the schedule—with pressure down to 350 psia, water temperature at 180°F, a repair becomes possible. About 20 feet above the containment floor, Al and Ben, crouching on a work platform, begin to work. Using a special wrench to avoid hand injuries from leaking steam, Ben puts the valve on its backseat, and as dismantling proceeds, the men see the packing gland (the graphoil container) move up, a sign of a potential leak. At the least, that means that water pressure is too high; at the most, that backseating is unsuccessful. They stop, retighten packing gland bolts to reduce the leak, and report the job's status to their managers. Cooling water on the reactor floor is a violation of the unit's technical specifications and a significant event when the leak rate is at or above 10 gallons per minute.

A series of meetings among managers, supervisors, and technicians begins. Luke reports that the mechanics verify the valve to be fully seated. Managers are convinced that earlier leakage collected in the assembly caused the packing to move up when the bolts were relaxed. They rule out the freeze seal option for two reasons: too little space for the people and equipment needed, and a freeze seal, classified as a temporary modi-

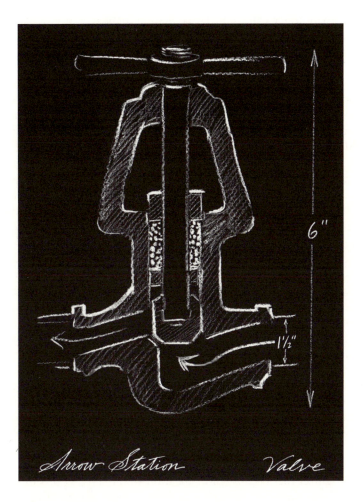

fication when made on a safety-related component, requires at least four days for preparing paperwork and getting approvals. Freeze seal equipment is not on-site—a contractor with expertise and equipment has to be summoned from another state. Maintenance managers continue to consider this a routine valve repacking job; unit managers decide to make another repair attempt after further reductions in RCS pressure and temperature. Radiographing the valve to learn the condition of the backseat is not considered.

On Wednesday, control room operators depressurize the RCS to its minimum (between 30 and 50 psia) and lower water temperature to 140°F, an adjustment that takes somewhat longer than usual because of conflicts with other work underway. Station managers direct engineering to prepare paperwork for the freeze seal option. A worst-case scenario and contingency plans are not discussed.

On Thursday at the morning management meeting (usually attended by 40–50 managers and supervisors) the discussion on this agenda item reviews general problems with backseating and considers a more drastic repair option: to drain the RCS to mid-loop, a major operation usually reserved for refueling outages. Managers dismiss this option because it would take a few days to drain, process, and store radioactive waste water, further delay the restart schedule, and, all around, be costly.

Ray, the system engineer responsible for the RCS, happens to be present to discuss another item on the agenda. He remarks in an aside to Luke that industrywide trend data show the stem/disc connection on this particular brand of valve to be susceptible to breakage. Later, in containment for other reasons, Ray makes a visual inspection of this and similar valve stems. He concludes that because only one thread is visible, compared to 1.5 to 2 threads on three similar valves, there is a possibility that stem and disc are separated. He tells his supervisor, assistant manager, and Luke that he will not issue a condition report (which prompts immediate higher-level managerial reviews), and instead schedules the valve for repair at the unit's next refueling outage. He also requests verification from the nuclear safety analysis group that operating the RCS with stem/disc separation does not constitute a nuclear safety concern.

At Thursday's 3 P.M. management meeting, Rusty, assistant technical support manager, reports on the possibility of stem/disc separation. Steven, the maintenance manager, directs Larry, the mechanical maintenance manager, and Luke to inspect the valve with Ray, to reconcile their opposite conclusions about the stem/disc connection. This does not happen. That day, Mark, a work scheduler newly transferred from another station job, recognizes that because of its location—on the RCS pressure boundary and in containment—together with the potential of a failed backseat, the repair should in any case be designated a HIGHER RISK EVOLUTION, which would subject it to more detailed procedures for job preparation and contingency planning. He so informs Alan, his supervisor (also a newcomer to his particular job). Alan does not communicate this to the management team.

Management meetings continue throughout Thursday night. Some believe that stem and disc are intact. The nuclear oversight group asks that a special procedure for "infrequently performed tests and evolutions" (IPTE) be invoked. That would require contingency plans and senior level approvals. Line management, meanwhile, satisfies oversight's request for what-if scenarios in case the repair fails. Operations claims that a possible leak would not challenge the RCS water inventory—that is, lead to a loss of coolant sufficient to threaten to uncover the core, which would allow the reactor to overheat. Robert, manager in charge of the outage and restart, assures nuclear oversight that stem and disc are intact. Operations does not raise objections to proceeding with the repacking. Again, radiography is not considered, nor are shutdown risk issues discussed.

Managers decide against issuing an IPTE. Some managers come away from discussions of the technical details of a freeze seal believing that its purpose is to isolate any further leakage a new repair attempt might cause, rather than make it possible for valve repair to occur at all, which is its function. They communicate that misunderstanding to upper management. Engineering and maintenance begin to plan an alternative temporary repair to reduce or prevent leakage before and during a freeze seal installation.

On Friday, the "Management Focus Items" agenda at the morning meeting notes the "higher risk" designation, but there is no discussion of its implications for additional planning and risk evaluation, nor does this occur at any of several later meetings.

That afternoon, with RCS pressure under 50 psia and water temperature at 140°F, another repair attempt begins. Because of a delay in arriving at optimum plant conditions, on this shift others substitute for the men originally designated to do the work. Chick and Norm are now up on the work platform, and another mechanic, Mitch, stands on the containment floor to hand up tools and get to a telephone if needed. After checking that the valve is on its backseat, the two mechanics start to loosen the packing assembly. About five seconds later, a leak occurs estimated at between 2 to 6 gallons per minute (about the rate of a bath shower). Mitch scrambles up, angling his way through the tangle of piping, and lying face down over the valve, pushes down on the packing assembly to make it possible for the others to reinstall packing bolts. They manage a temporary clamp that reduces the flow somewhat—the valve lost some of the graphoil packing as well as a key component for holding what remains. They see that the valve's stem threads had "bottomed out," an indication of stem/disc separation. The three mechanics depart containment and make their report.

Kirk, the station manager, calls a management meeting to plan for recovery. He briefs the nuclear oversight/performance evaluation group on plant status and commissions an event review team to assess the reasons why the situation developed. His assistant, Toby, orders maintenance to slow and stop the leak and engineering to arrange for the freeze seal to be installed. The contractor and his equipment will arrive in a day or two.

Others arrive to help in containment and after 10 hours of work throughout Friday night, the leak rate is calculated at 0.25 gallons per minute (a steadily dripping faucet). Maintenance managers and mechanics are working in emergency mode without having invoked appropriate safeguards. Over these few days, in haste several other procedures are not adhered to (for example, performing work on this safety-related equipment does not fit the terms of a "minor maintenance work order").

On Saturday at 5:45 A.M., the engineering manager on duty and maintenance and other line managers revisit the question of issuing the procedure that would designate the repair and recovery effort an infrequently performed test evolution, and recommend against it. At an 8 A.M. management meeting, Jesse, an oversight manager reporting to Richard, the operations manager, recommends the IPTE designation because the unit was not in cold shutdown (defined by the NRC as a "reactor coolant system at atmospheric pressure and at a temperature below 200 degrees Fahrenheit following a reactor cooldown"). The line organization then agrees. By the end of the afternoon, a cylindrical sleeve manufactured on-site is put in place to reduce the leak further. Pumps keep up with removing water on the containment floor; replacement water is readily available; the levels of radioactivity in the water are within safe range for those working in containment. The core is in no danger of becoming uncovered. By this time, radiography confirms the separation of disc and stem. The station operations review committee recommends approval of the freeze seal, a contingency plan, and a safety evaluation.

The source of the stem/disc separation continues to be debated: perhaps a mechanical fracture from overtightening the stem during backseating or from earlier having been backseated "hot" (at high temperature) and then cooled down (a source of metal stress). The valve will be repaired or, more likely, replaced during the next outage when, with fuel out of the core and with the RCS drained to mid-loop, a freeze seal could be installed. A later attempt to remove the backseat assembly failed, Rusty, assistant operations manager, told me. "It's frozen in place. So we're either going to have to cut the valve out or go in and machine the seat out so that we can put a new one in." I said, "As I understand it, it's in a tough spot physically." "Yeah, there's not a lot of room. It requires some pretty significant contortions to get somebody down there."

A nuclear power station's operating environment is "very hostile to human activity." So declares the standard work on maintenance techniques and strategies published by Electricité de France, the French utility that operates the fifty-nine pressurized water reactors producing about 75 percent of that country's electricity.

> It is rare for so many non-repetitive tasks to be concentrated in an industrial environment that is so very hostile to human activity. The forces in this environment are considerable. Temperatures, pressures, the multitude of fluids, mechanical power, omnipresent electricity, even the sheer weight of the equipment

. . . all culminate to make maintenance actions potentially dangerous and to weigh against success. The "nuclear" hazard and the associated radiation protection restraints are simply one more risk, but a risk that is often quite minimal compared to the others.[1]

Moreover, a typical plant has about 100 systems or assemblies of components (each labeled by three-color codes), about 70,000 labeled components, and about 22,000 valves. Many, like this leaking valve, are essential to the defense-in-depth strategy through which backups and other kinds of redundancies and barriers are kept on the ready.

Being Right There

Yes, what *was* the situation of Chick, Norm, and Mitch, the mechanics in containment, when the valve began to leak? Each internal report takes it for granted that readers are able to envision that situation; one report reproduces only a diagram of an intact valve. Otherwise, there are no word pictures or sketches of who was where doing what. Of the three men present when the leak began, only Mitch was available for an interview when I made my station visit.

"Can you draw me a picture of the place where this work was going on?"

Basically you come up a ladder here, about 20 feet above the floor and get on a work platform. Yes, it's a permanent platform. There's a beam that's underneath the platform and it's got another beam that goes up, and you have to crawl between this beam and some of the piping that's here to get down in there. And the same thing with this, this actually goes up in the air like this—I think it's at a 45. So in order to get in here, you have to crawl around this check valve and then get down inside this loop, so there's like an area for two bodies to get scrunched in there. . . . I had to squeeze in order to get in. I had to push myself between the pipe and the beam in order to get in.

And there was a prejob briefing. Was RP [radiation protection] there?

Yes. That was at the [containment] hatch. They briefed us on the rad fields.

And was there some rad in here?

Yes. Depending on where it was, I can't remember all the levels. I would be lying to you if I told you levels.

You had a work order in your hand? Were you carrying tools—did you have to carry any tools up and with you through here?

Arrow Station

At valve in containment

Umhum. We had a work order, we needed some wrenches and some packing and carried it up there.

How did you carry it? In what?

I didn't actually carry the tools. Chick and Norm carried the tools. They were in there a couple of times before me looking at this leak. So they had it already prestaged.

So why were there three of you then, when you came along?

When I came along {deep sigh}? Because they had to crawl down here on both sides of the valve, and I was going in to help them and do anything they needed and coordinate between them and our operations department. . . .

They're scrunched up? Or are they standing? Were they on hands and knees?

They're, uh, {long pause} I'm trying to remember right now. There are some more beams down this side here, and they're actually standing on the beams. There's more structural steel that's down inside there. They were standing on it.

So were they reaching to do the work?

Actually, what they ended up doing was they put a couple of boards across, some planks across some of the boards down there so they could stand on it.

They had to get those up there?

No, actually they came in around back somehow and brought them up underneath there.

It's open underneath?

It's open.

You were with them, but not at the valve. Were you a backup, or what?

I was just out here. Like I said, it was an extra hand, you know, like doing the work in here, there's no place to put the wrench, so they'd hand it to me. I wasn't you know—like I said, while they were in there, if they needed me to run downstairs to make a phone call or something, I was there sort of observing and helping in any capacity I could.

Were you there when they discovered the backseat problem? The stem/disc separation?

When I went in, they [operations] had depressurized and basically reduced the temperature, and said, "Go ahead and repack it." And by our procedure, OK?, it tells us to place it on the backseat and make sure it's on the backseat. In the prejob brief the operations manager said it was already placed on the backseat, nobody had touched it. And when we went in, he gave us permission to go ahead and see if we could turn it in open position to make sure it was on the backseat. And Chick did that, and he felt that it was on the backseat, OK? And by the procedure, it said to verify that the backseat was holding, so we loosen up all our bolts. And we had no water coming on out. We just followed our procedure, and the water appeared after several minutes. I don't know the exact amount of time. We had the bolts unloosened and everything unloosened and we didn't see any water. So we assumed that from following the procedure it was holding.

But then it didn't?

Then it didn't.

And then what did you do?

What did we do? The water pressure was trying to blow what packing rings there were in the valve out of the valve and {sigh} them guys were trying to hold it down, and I came on the top. I crawled in on top and I gave 'em a hand. I pushed down and gave 'em some down force so they could put what packing was in there back in and we could get the bolts back on the valve and try and slow it down. And then we went and notified the shift manager of the problem that we had.

So was that scary?

Not at all. No, I mean it was, yeah, it was a little, I wouldn't say it was scary. I mean it was a little nerve-wracking because something happened that we weren't expecting.

To prepare for that "hostile environment," Mitch and his colleagues had spent the previous hour and a half in a briefing with the radiation protection team, which suited them up for this particular task. They also take in stride the challenge of being "scrunched" and "squeezed." Brian, an oversight specialist whose job is to watch work and provide advice about how to do it at least risk, is "amazed" at the difficulty of access.

You have to climb up a ladder to a platform, and it's stuck out in the midst of a bunch of pipes and other valves and it's very difficult to get at and see. When I finally went up and took a look at it I was amazed at where it was and how they could do the job that they were doing with the equipment, but that's what they're trained to do. It's just not a good place to get to and to work in. I would say it's a probably about 20 feet off the level we're on, you go up a ladder to a little platform, you've got to climb out over pipes and get down in between 'em and it's tucked in—so it's not a good location for what they had to do.

Event Inquiries

Immediately station managers initiate inquiries into the reasons why a "minor maintenance" repair order escalates into a major problem: the leak of cooling water from a valve controlling the pressure boundary of this primary barrier. They first set up an event review team (ERT) to develop an account of what happened and to recommend what needs to be done immediately to regain control over the situation. Then managers order an all-station STAND DOWN or time-out, and all "physical work" in the plant proper stops for about a day and a half while they and first-line supervisors meet with employees for suggestions about, as one person put it, "what they—the managers—could do better." In talks and memos, managers emphasize the utility's priority for "conservative decision-making for work on components that comprise one of the three principal fission product release boundaries." "Conservative" in industry lingo means slowing down the schedule to allow for analysis and reflection, putting in place any possible safeguards for worst-case scenarios, or shutting down the reactor, or any combination of those. A control room shift manager, who is also a licensed reactor operator, formally has independent authority to make the shut down decision.

Besides the root cause analysis team required for a SIGNIFICANT EVENT, managers convene an independent review team (IRT) with a special charter "to assess the decision-making process used by the unit's management team associated with the planning and implementation of [valve] repair activities. . . . The IRT will provide an analysis of: inputs to the decision points, thought processes followed, appropriateness of decisions (conservatism), management standards, organizational level of decisions, barriers to preclude the event, missed opportunities and lessons learned." The root cause analysis team (RCAT) is "to determine why a lack of concern was demonstrated by the involved organizations for a maintenance evolution which violated the barrier of the reactor coolant system without adequate contingencies to re-establish that barrier."

The event review team includes six experts who are otherwise assigned to corrective actions, special projects, operations, maintenance, human performance, and training—these people become the root cause analysis team, with the addition of Clark, a root cause analysis specialist in Arrow's corrective actions program. The independent review team's seven members, regularly assigned to the nuclear oversight group, each concentrates on different "issues" by departments: engineering, maintenance, work planning, operations, nuclear oversight, management oversight. "Management" is the industry's shorthand for "supervisors and above," and when addressing activities within the plant, the term is likely to mean supervisors, or "supervision," and their immediate managers.

Among them, the 14 members of the three teams interview 107 people assigned to about 20 groups.[2] One interviewee is a woman. Their job titles run the gamut: unit director, scheduling and outage manager, operations manager, maintenance mechanic, health physics supervisor, mechanical trainer, work control manager, health physics nurse.

Valve History

All review team members knew that backseating this brand and size of valve had been problematic previously, at this station and in the industry generally: studies found the stem vulnerable to embrittlement and cracking under high temperatures and to excessive force (OVERTORQUEING) when putting it on its backseat. Although managers had added details about its perils to the station's CONDUCT OF OPERATIONS and warnings about backseating the valve when hot, procedures for the backseating task did not incorporate them. The Conduct of Operations, a document required by the Nuclear Regulatory Commission, translates into a "chain of command" the design basis and its defense-in-depth strategy. This document defines the enveloping accountability structure of each function and its assigned responsibilities and authorities and specifies how the operations department is expected to relate to other departments. Each Conduct of Operations is unique to each station—Arrow Station's runs fifty pages.

Ray, the RCS system engineer, provided this overview of the valve's history and of his observations and actions before and after the leak began. I do not know whether the teams had heard this from him, but plant records they consulted during their reviews would provide similar technical information.

> *I notice that in the report you were cited as bringing out the fact that [this brand of valve] could be problematic on the backseat.*

That's correct. If you backseat them too hard, you can get stem/disc separation. On the 3/4-inch valves, we had overtorqued six valves in the past. The reason we were looking at it is it's a [type of] stainless steel stem, which is subject to embrittlement at high temperatures. So we specifically went after those thinking we had an embrittlement problem. . . . And then we sent the broken pieces off [for testing] and found there was no embrittlement—it was strictly overtorqueing. . . . And now this was a 1–1/2-inch valve that failed. It's got the same 2-inch diameter stem, and it was thought it would be difficult to break. You'd really have to put a lot of torque to it. But I was sitting in a meeting with maintenance, and they said they had two mechanics out there who were really trying to get it on the backseat. So I pictured two big burly fellows out there really cracking on that backseat, and I looked at the maintenance supervisor and said, "Stem/disc separation?" and he said, "No, no they didn't push that hard."

But that history includes a repair that left the valve without "enough packing."

[When] this same valve was being repaired [three years earlier], they went in and backseated this valve successfully, and did take out the packing and put in the new packing. We just didn't do the job well. We didn't put in enough packing, and [this time], it turns out there was one too few rings of packing in there. . . . [At that earlier time] it didn't leak—because I asked, I specifically asked, "Did the mechanics wear goggles when they did the job?" Sometimes they'll get a little wet. If they see a little bit of water in there, they don't complain. They just go ahead and do the job, and that's what they're supposed to do. I mean, we have very talented people here. So I asked, "Was there any water at all?" "No." As far as they remember, nobody got wet, and they should have if this thing was leaking, if this [stem/disc] was broken. . . . So that meant that [it was intact when they began working on it this time].

What caught my eye in the report was that you made this comment but it was never picked up.

No, it was picked up. I went back to the maintenance supervisor, who I'd worked with closely as part of a team—one of those many informal teams you develop. And I trusted him when he said, "No, no"—that gives me a little more confidence that it's not a backseat problem. But then, when I was in containment looking at something else, I said, "Well, I really should go and look at that valve." What you do is look at the thread engagement. If this thing's hitting the backseat, then you've got about two threads, two sets of threads, showing. If this thing isn't hitting the backseat, then the stem comes all the way up until it bottoms out, or bottoms up, so to speak. And I saw about maybe a thread showing. Well, I thought, "It's not bottomed out or wholly bottomed out, but it may be as far as it can go. And maybe the threads are hidden."

So I went and looked at the three sister valves and all had approximately two threads showing. I said, "So we're talking the difference of one thread, could be manufacturing tolerances, could be a lot of things, could it be a stem/disc separation?" So I went out and told the maintenance supervisor and I told the work supervisor, the work week manager. . . . And I talked to the shift manager in operations, because those are my customers. . . . And I let them know that they're aware of it, maintenance is aware of it. . . . So I figured maintenance is going to take all the necessary precautions to handle that. And I didn't have a sure thing. I had one thread. Was I going to bet the farm on that one thread? No, I'll let maintenance do their job. {long silence} Oh, and by the way, I also told my supervisor, and he went to the management meeting, and it was discussed there also that we had possible stem/disc separation.

The Teams' Reports

Written in different formats and with different aims, each of the three teams' reports begins with a number of discrete observations and findings of fact, presents conclusions about the event's causes, and ends with the corrective actions it recommends. Asked to provide a quick overview of the event, the event review team writes a six-page report and circulates it within about a week. The root cause analysis team report, about forty pages including attachments, is dated about one month after the event. The independent review team's report is thirty-five pages long; beginning its work four days after the event, about eight days later it makes a "Verbal Debrief of Conclusions," and seven days after that publishes its final report, "Assessment of Management Decision-making Associated with Valve Leakage." Each team circulates its drafts among managers and event participants for comment.

Event Comparison

The Root Cause Analysis Team (RCAT) and the Independent Review Team (IRT) reports feature timelines of the event, references to station documents and records, and a comparison with an event at another station that involved a similar repair. That event, however, brought that station "very close to" a "small break" LOSS OF COOLANT ACCIDENT (LOCA) and risked injury, perhaps death, to employees—a conclusion not disputed in the industry. The comparison hinges on safety significance, both nuclear safety and industrial (or personnel, occupational, or personal) safety. The RCAT report finds the "biggest difference in the work practices applied": Arrow Station arranged a configuration to minimize risk and started the valve work with the RCS at lower pressure and temperature initially, reducing it further after the first attempt failed, while at the other station mechanics drilled on the valve's body while the reactor was on line. That valve cracked and again the unit stayed on line while managers were evaluating that problem. About that event, this IRT report concludes, "Keeping the plant on line and producing power seemed to be the primary focus," which "could have resulted in a Small Break LOCA while performing the task, which would have potentially killed someone" at the station. Not so, in the case of Arrow's valve, where the safety significance "is that it resulted in a Reactor Coolant System Leak."

There are similarities between the two events, however. Each, the teams' reports said, approached the job with "an overconfidence" and each had not planned for a worst-case scenario with contingency plans. The significance for safe shutdown was "much greater" at the other station, the RCAT report declares. The IRT report finds a number of technical differences, but observes several other "similar situations" in their "allocation of roles and responsibilities." Asking whether Arrow Station learned from that station's experience, this team concludes: "Although there are some key physical differences between this and the other event, there are enough similarities" to conclude that Arrow Station had not taken sufficient cues from that event's "lessons learned and corrective actions."

Teams' Observations and Findings

Although each report contributes different kinds of data and points of view, each also speaks to a number of similar themes and issues, many raised by the 107 station experts they interviewed. To convey the contents of more than eighty pages of technical details and observations leading to each team's findings and recommendations, I've put many into direct quotations and abbreviated some into paraphrases, then grouped under my own rough rubrics, presented here in alphabetical order and identified by the team that wrote each one—ERT (event review team), RCAT (root cause analysis team), and IRT (independent review team). The teams' conclusions and recommendations are in the section following.

Category Confusion

"Because this leak did not challenge RCS inventory, control personnel did not interpret a small 'uncontrolled leak' . . . with having an effect on one of the three principal safety barriers, the RCS boundary." (RCAT)

"Operations did not challenge RCS boundary work possibly due to misunderstanding of the situation or possibly because it did not pose a challenge to key safety functions as identified in the [operating procedures]." (RCAT)

Control Lost

"200% accountability for communication and issue resolution not maintained—disk-stem separation issue, freeze seal availability and applicability, high risk evolution designation, leak mitigation strategies and methodology." (IRT)

"Resources for planning the maintenance aspect of the job were not commensurate with the safety significance." (RCAT)

Crisis Mode

"Gate logs show that key managers were spending extra-long days at work . . . fatigue may have contributed to weak implementation of processes." (IRT)

Dis-Organization

"Recent changes in Work Control/Outage Management supervision and management resulted in a lack of knowledge regarding procedural requirements for higher risk evolution communication and reviews." (IRT)

Issues Left Dangling

"Key decisions were delegated without follow-up. . . . A maintenance supervisor was left to sort out disk-stem separation issues with the system engineer. . . . A scheduler noted that the repack work appeared to be a higher-risk evolution—management did not follow through on the additional risk review requirements." (RCAT)

"Lack of Operations ownership and proactivity in staying abreast of issues." (IRT)

"Disc-stem separation issues were brought to the appropriate Engineering and Maintenance Supervision, but the initiator and supervision/management were not proactive in following up on the issue." (IRT)

Let George Do It

"Lack of a questioning attitude: None of the functional areas challenged the maintenance statements that this would be a routine evolution and that adequate contingencies were in place." (IRT)

"Over reliance on Maintenance; Operations did not challenge RCS boundary work." (ERT)

"The management team let maintenance run the repair activities without sufficiently challenging their decisions." (IRT)

Left Hand/Right Hand

"Management, Planning and Operations personnel were aware of the potential risk that a leak during the repacking was a breach of the reactor coolant system barrier. Oversight was not aware of this on the first attempt at repacking the valve." (RCAT)

Information Not Used

"Information was not acted upon appropriately by the organization." (ERT)

"Operating experience for [these] valves' susceptibility to stem/disc separation was not adequately considered when planning the repacking." (RCAT)

"Lack of familiarity with Arrow procedures resulted in requirements for 'higher risk evolutions' not being implemented." (IRT)

Managers' Confusions

"Contingency/alternate method planning was unclear. Some [managers] believed the freeze seal was a [protective] contingency rather than an alternate isolation method." (ERT)

"Miscommunications among managers regarding higher risk planning issues and a lack of rigor in evaluating potential risks." (IRT)

Misinformation

"The actual state of the freeze seal contingency as an alternate method to facilitate the repair was conceptual in that the temporary modification was not prepared, freeze seal personnel were not on site and material was not staged and personnel were not aware that the freeze seal could not be established with a leak at [the valve]." (RCAT)

Missed Steps

"Equipment history not considered in planning the evolution." (ERT)

"System engineer advised the organization of likely stem-disc separation (Unit Director not included). Condition Report should have been issued at this time." (ERT)

"Documentation for safety evaluation issues and freeze seal temporary modification was weak and schedule-driven." (IRT)

"There was a lack of rigor in identifying and facilitating implementation of higher risk evolution processes." (IRT)

"Maintenance was overly optimistic in its ability to deal with what was perceived as a routine activity . . . without planning for the worst case." (IRT)

"Learning from previous events did not result in new, clear instructions being passed on to maintenance or work planning in their procedures." (RCAT)

"The AWO [automated work order] required [the valve] to be placed on the backseat torqued to 70-ft-lbs. prior to repacking. At one point Operations used a crescent wrench and at another point Operations used a cheater bar to verify valve is on the backseat. At no time was a torque wrench used to verify the torque applied to the backseat." (RCAT)

"Temporary devices were installed on [the valve] without the benefit of reviews by Operations, Engineering, or the management team." (RCAT)

Not on Same Page

"The scope of the work was not clear (add packing vs. remove/add packing)." (ERT)

"Miscommunications regarding expectations at several levels—Vice President to Station Manager, Station Manager to Operations Manager and Operations Manager to Supervisor." (IRT)

"Communications were not adequate to ensure all planners, implementers and decision makers were acting on the same information and expectations."

"The organization did not act as a cohesive team in its response to the . . . leak either prior to the valve repair efforts or immediately following [them]." (IRT)

"Miscommunications with senior and executive management regarding contingency plans and freeze seal issues." (IRT)

"Maintenance personnel believed the task was to remove the wiper packing ring, add one or two packing rings, and install a new wiper. Management, Planning, Operations and Health Physics personnel believed the task was to just add packing." (RCAT)

Out of Focus

"Management and Supervision used poor judgment in addressing a number of issues: Failure to radiograph the valve to determine if there was disc/stem separation once it was suspected. . . . Contingency planning for leakage if the backseat did not hold and the leakage got worse. . . . Potential worst case risks associated with repairing this valve. . . . Ownership, roles, and responsibilities associated with the repair effort. . . . Disposition of Nuclear Oversight IPTE concerns. . . . Work performed to mit-igate the leak was not properly documented." (IRT)

"Some Maintenance personnel were not fully aware of the potential consequences of a packing leak as a breach of the RCS barrier." (RCAT)

"The potential for an unisolable RCS leak should have made any of these organizations reach the conclusion that this was 'Higher Risk' work and it required [a stationwide review group] to approve a contingency plan." (RCAT)

"The unit failed to understand the significance of the task being per-formed and the lack of contingency planning to preclude an unisolable RCS leak while performing maintenance." (RCAT)

"Overconfidence: this was a 'routine valve repack job.' " (RCAT)

"The organization did not raise a serious concern about the threat to the RCS barrier . . . did not recognize the importance of this valve as a RCS barrier." (RCAT)

Out of the Loop

"Some Shift Managers lacked knowledge about the [valve] issues and repair activities." (IRT)

"There was less than complete communication about freeze seal contin-gencies, availability, and applications to the rest of the management team." (IRT)

Questionable Training

"The training of the mechanics and operators was deficient. While train-ing may have been adequate for normal repacking evolutions, insufficient attention was paid to possible serious accidents. Experienced operators and mechanics did not know how to check for a stem-disc separation on a valve [being repacked] on the backseat. There appears to be an organiza-tionwide lack of knowledge of the steps needed . . . to verify . . . the back-seat. . . . Training of the work planning, operations, maintenance, techni-cal support and shutdown risk personnel . . . was deficient." (RCAT)

Spread Thin

"Operations management did not sufficiently follow or challenge the issues associated with the [valve] repairs. Operations was not proactive or aggressive. . . ." "Operations delegated some plant ownership to main-tenance." (IRT)

Too Many Cooks

"Various meetings with different players for work control issues results in a lack of a single point of accountability." (ERT)

"There existed a lack of management continuity—different management representatives at different meetings where key issues (higher risk designation, disc-stem separation) were raised." (IRT)

"Some personnel assumed leadership roles while others relinquished leadership roles. . . . [M]anagement was occurring by committee with lack of continuity among the participants and no one individual had the facts needed for an informed decision on how valve repair work should proceed." (IRT)

"The Maintenance department generally assumed the lead, but there was a lack of management in controlling work—decisions were made by committee at meetings and accountability for tasks was not maintained. A single point of control or contact for the issue was not maintained." (IRT)

Warnings Not Heeded

"Verification of valve backseat integrity (the RCS boundary) was delegated down to mechanics performing the work despite precursors." (ERT)

"Oversight had to push quite hard to convince the line that IPTE designation should be considered before and after the leak escalated." (IRT)

"Maintenance showed a less than conservative attitude and lack of sensitivity for a potential unisolable RCS leak." (IRT)

"Maintenance management failed to recognize when a routine repair became more risk significant." (IRT)

Time of the Essence

"Planning a quick turnaround [to repack the valve] and repressurize imposed time constraints on the organization." (RCAT)

"Schedule pressures were a distraction and may have been a factor in decision-making." (IRT)

"Oversight felt work was overly schedule-driven but didn't pursue this with the line." (IRT)

Teams' Conclusions

The Event Review Team did not offer conclusions; its members became the Root Cause Analysis Team.

INDEPENDENT REVIEW TEAM

The team's charge was to focus on decision-making processes.

". . . has concluded that there were multiple causes to this event including:
Overconfidence (routine repacking, done many times before);
Numerous miscommunications (confusions over the word 'contingency,' misunderstanding associated with freeze seal capabilities, possible disc-stem separation;
Lack of questioning attitude and follow-up by the management team;
Misjudgment (not having leak contingency plans in place, failing to radiograph the valve after being told of probable disc-stem separation, IPTE designation);
Lack of Operations ownership and proactivity in staying abreast of issues;
Lack of familiarity with Arrow procedures resulted in requirements for 'higher risk evolutions' not being implemented;
The Arrow organization did not act as a cohesive team in its response . . . either prior to the valve repair or immediately following the various repair efforts;
Schedule pressures were a distraction and may have been a factor in decision-making."

ROOT CAUSE ANALYSIS TEAM

Nuclear/Industrial Safety Significance

"The packing leak had minimal industrial safety significance. . . . Mechanics . . . were wearing appropriate safety equipment including protective contamination clothing and face shields. RCS temperature did not pose a burn threat. . . . The potential consequences to fuel clad damage was nonexistent. . . . The leak did not have the potential to reduce RCS inventory or to affect the decay heat removal system. . . . This event investigation identified a significant work planning and defense in depth deficiency. The work was being performed with only the backseat as the RCS boundary. The potential for backseat failure was not adequately considered. . . . There was no contingency plan for dealing with a leak based on loss of packing. . . . The organization was 'working for success,' overconfidence precluded planning for the worst case. . . . Defense in depth . . . was minimal. The work on the RCS boundary was treated as a routine packing job. Compensatory action planning was limited. There was no immediate plan in place for the workers to stop a leak should the backseat not hold for any reason. Work on any of the three principal boundaries to fission product release commands a special respect above the high standard set for all work within the plant."

Root Cause(s)

"While equipment failure initiated the situation, the fundamental cause of failing to prevent a Reactor Coolant System leak was: Management Control not addressing the Nuclear Safety aspect of working on unisolable Reactor Coolant System boundary valves. This resulted in inadequate work practices that included inadequate verification and validation of an adequate boundary and lack of development of a contingency plan. . . . The backseat is a secondary barrier . . . therefore the structural integrity/ pressure boundary is considered intact. . . . This event is not a violation of tech specs.

"Such deficiencies in training, failure of organizations to learn the proper lessons from others' incidents, and inadequate work practices that applied too much torque to a valve susceptible to stem-disc separation led to this event. . . ."

Preceding its specific recommendations, which follow, the team makes this summary declaration:

"To prevent break-through events as serious as this, fundamental changes will be necessary in the organization, procedures, and practices— and above all—in the attitudes toward Human Performance. As the evidence accumulated it became clear that the fundamental problems are people-related problems and not equipment problems. When we say that the basic problems are people-related, we do not mean to limit this term to shortcomings of individual human beings—although those do exist. We mean more generally that our investigation has revealed problems with the 'system' with regards to the operation, maintenance, planning, and scheduling of work. These are structural problems in various organizations, there are deficiencies in various processes, and there is a lack of precise communication among key individuals and groups.

"A comprehensive system is required in which equipment and human beings are treated with equal importance. The most serious 'mindset' is the preoccupation of everyone with the safety of equipment, resulting in the downplaying of the importance of the human element in nuclear power generation. An enormous effort is always expended to assure that safety-related equipment functions as well as possible, and that there is backup equipment in depth, [but] what the organization fails to recognize sufficiently is that the human beings who manage, operate, perform maintenance, plan and schedule work constitute an important safety system."

Teams' Recommendations

Each report concludes with recommendations its team believes will aid recovery and forestall a similar event. Although recommendations of the independent review team may also become action items, the senior management group is likely to take them under its wing and respond as it sees fit.

EVENT REVIEW TEAM

The report recommends 11 interim corrective actions: fixing the valve, ordering the "work stand down," reconciling "vendor recommendations on valve repair with current operating practices and procedures," evaluating other valves of this brand for stem/disc separation and radiographing the suspects, requiring "radiography verification for repack work on uni-solable RCS boundary valves which could result in loss of inventory," reviewing "the definition of higher risk activities" and defining "a method of elevating those activities for additional focus," and conducting a "detailed root cause" investigation. Given its charge, the team's short-term recommendations center on technical matters concerning equipment and procedures.

ROOT CAUSE ANALYSIS TEAM

The team recommends corrective actions covering a range of technical and administrative issues, some addressed to specific functions and managers:

Work Planning Manager to review the definition of higher risk activities, define a method for assuring additional "focus" on them by Scheduling/ Outage Management, "add RCS integrity to the list of 'Key Safety Functions,' " evaluate the possibility of a "Shutdown Risk team without other commitments" to be mobilized during particular plant configurations and to participate in scheduling and planning meetings.

Tech Support Engineering to evaluate wholesale replacement of this brand of valve.

Unit Director to "administer constructive discipline" to individuals for failing to comply with procedures.

Operations Training to provide training across the station on "higher risk designation" requirements.

Operations to address "the following concern as a caution in the Containment Entry procedure. The freeze seal required bottles of liquid nitrogen to be transferred into the containment. If the bottle builds up enough pressure it vents to atmosphere. A confined-space concern was raised with having personnel in the airlock [a locked-door passage system between outside and inside containment] during this transfer."

The RCAT recommends "Five Compensatory Actions" for managers to take in the short term:

"Management Team [should] reiterate" station's safety standards and principles to Arrow employees, call for a physical work stand down, outline the need for the "application of conservative decision making for work on components that comprise one of the three principal fission product release boundaries, and define and reinforce roles for work management decisions."

"Unit Management should reinforce expectations for clear, concise communications and consider exploring the requirement for three-way communications for transmitting important data and assignments"

"Maintenance/Operations to evaluate additional training" of mechanics on identifying a stem-disc separation, adding operators into training pool.

The team's "Corrective Actions to Prevent Recurrence" (longer term actions) are:

House "the safety expectations (personnel and equipment) needed to work on valves in Automated Work Orders, Maintenance Procedures and Work Control . . . If these conditions cannot be met, adopt [another station's] philosophy that the Station Manager's approval is required."

"Verification of backseat integrity should be standard practice on any system. Mechanics could be seriously injured by being subjected to superheated water or high velocity chunks of packing. . . . Require radiography or other means of verification. . . . Stem thread measurement has proven accurate in identifying stem disc separation."

"Add to maintenance and work control procedures" that an "approved contingency plan" is required under specified conditions.

INDEPENDENT REVIEW TEAM

"Encourage managers and supervisors to solicit input from other parts of the organization as appropriate and establish a **healthy questioning attitude.**"

"Management and supervisory position descriptions should be detailed with respect to knowledge, skills and abilities required to successfully function in the position."

"Newly hired or promoted individuals need to be carefully screened to ensure they meet these requirements. . . . appropriate training should occur before [they] are allowed to function independently."

"Institute a policy where a specific person is assigned the authority and responsibility to address and resolve emerging issues."

Maintenance planning methods should include "methods to contend with the worst scenario, rather than assuming a best case result. Contingencies for potential problems should be planned and available before work proceeds. Maintenance and other departments should actively solicit assistance and expertise from other groups to support development of such contingencies."

Management "needs to strongly reinforce" the utility's "safety standards and expectations." The lessons from the other station's event "must also be learned." The report quotes these in full.

> "Reliance on statements regarding safety ethic is not sufficient. There is a need for management to lead by example; e.g., by encouraging questioning attitudes, by endorsing a conservative operating philosophy, and by continuously demonstrating management commitment to safe, conservative operations;
>
> "Senior Management should hold face-to-face meetings with the employees and appropriate support personnel in order to reinforce management's expectations. . . . in small enough groups to facilitate an open dialog with employees;
>
> "Senior Management should hold face-to-face meetings with all [reactor operator] license holders in order to reinforce the unique responsibility these individuals have in regard to nuclear safety. Management must re-instill in the Senior Reactor Operators that they are ultimately the owners of the plant and that their actions must reflect this fact;
>
> "Management must demonstrate by word and deed that it is committed to conservative operation and that it welcomes input from all quarters that support this end. The staff must realize that when they make a conservative decision, they will be backed up by management."

INSIGHTS AND EXCURSIONS

The issues and themes the teams define as pressure points for change seem to suit the facts of the case, in the ways they approached it. Free from report writing conventions, station experts' insights and experiences suggest some avenues for my excursions into their wellsprings. Whether the industry's "collective way of thinking" needs a "paradigm shift" in light of this "fundamental failure" is a question Richard raises—he is Arrow's operations manager, at the station since its days of construction, after a five-year stint operating reactors in the nuclear navy.

Were there any things the reports didn't address that you think are important?

The final IRT conclusions . . . were very generic in nature. "Here's a series of requirements and general procedures. Everybody should review them and see what they say."

What effect do you think that would have in any case?

We were already doing that at the time, among the soul searching we were doing. It's valuable stuff, but if what you need is a paradigm shift—if there's some fundamental flaw in our collective way of thinking that led to this—going back and reading the procedures does not correct that fundamental flaw. I don't know what went on internal to maintenance, but I think whatever fundamental failure occurred in this case occurred somewhere in the maintenance organization. That's when—when you talk about omissions—that's what surprised me about the report that, again, some fundamental failure occurred and I don't think we addressed what or where it was.

Just in general, not necessarily on this issue alone, what is the status of these event reports? Do they become a point of reference? What importance are they given in the scheme of things?

Events never die, they live on to be misinterpreted in the future. {angrily} Which is why when this event happened, fifteen minutes after the leak there were people shouting, "This is the same as that other station's event!" And in no way was this the same. This was its own unique event which required its own unique treatment, and to attempt to treat it [like] the other event would have been a mistake.

I could see that reading the reports. I think at a very high level of kinds of decisions—not the outcome, not the threat—

Even in the decision-making process, I saw the other event as a high level loss of ethics. They did the wrong thing willingly ordered from the top. [Those managers have left that station.] In this case, I think decisions were made at a much lower level.

What do you base that on?

I base it on reading that station's reports and talking to some people I knew there—that they had discussed it at the management level and that some of those in my kind of level on the management chain were dead set against going with the plan, that they were overruled higher up . . . to keep that unit on line.

In four excursions taking off from the review teams' findings and station experts' discussions, I examine these "collective ways of thinking":

about the relationship between defense-in-depth and primary barriers, about the evaluation of an event's significance, about sources of experts' credibility, and about how categories and their meanings are understood. Together with an examination of the parts template, which ends this chapter, these do not "misinterpret" or even reinterpret this or any other station's event, but try to expand the grounds on which to understand why they occurred at all.

"High Awareness" of "Safety" and "Nonsafety"

The meanings of "primary barriers" appear to be cloudy at Arrow Station. Technically speaking, the RCAT declares, the valve sits on but is not itself a primary barrier. Small as its 1-1/2-inch diameter is, without its being promptly repaired, a leak could end up as tens of gallons of water on the containment floor; that is the reason the work order should have carried a "higher risk" designation. Brian is a performance evaluation specialist in the station's internal oversight or quality group, which regularly observes work as it is being done and offers critique and information for doing it more effectively and with least risk. In the industry for thirty-one years, eighteen of them in the quality group, Brian participated in many of the discussions during the event and afterward worked with maintenance to develop equipment mockups for rehearsing the next repair steps and anticipating their consequences.

> *What would you say was the reason that maintenance did not see this as a barrier problem? Why did they put it in the routine category? How would you explain that?*

I'm not so sure that the barrier situations are well discussed, out to everybody. I think they know, "Yeah, that's important," but it's not put out as one of the three barriers that you have to have a heightened awareness to. The work orders, I believe, didn't show this as high risk or any other problems. There again, when this was discussed, the maintenance supervisor and everybody doing it, "Just go in there and repack the valve, it's a normal job." And that was the mentality almost all the way through it. "What is the big deal, we do this all the time?" And it wasn't til the packing started coming out that they realized that they could lose all of this. Even at that point, my opinion was that they didn't consider this one of the barriers being breached and that this put it in a higher contingency.

And right to this day [about ten months later] I don't believe, even though they talk about it, that there still is a major distinction of the various systems based on that theory. For instance, we just did another valve where it had a leak, and although it wasn't quite the same thing, it was one of the containment valves, kind of like a breach, and here again, at this point there was a heightened awareness—"Is this that type of valve that is breaching a barrier?" and the questions were asked more. But a lot of that was being prompted, I think, more so by oversight and by ops than by the mechanics who were looking at it. They say for the most part, "It's a leak, it's a normal job, get it isolated, we'll go in there and fix it." . . . It's like, "It's a waste of time to put all these contingencies in place for something where we just go in and tighten down on the packing."

An always cramped schedule of "normal" jobs helps to make what-ifs "a waste of time," but on the other hand, concern with "contingencies" may not be in maintenance experts' job descriptions: managers expect these "very talented people" to customize their routinized and standardized skills to the situations any work order puts them into. I commented to Brian:

> *In my research at other plants, ops would sometimes say about mainte-*
> *nance, "Well, maintenance never really has the big picture." Then when*
> *I would try to find out more about that, I would hear maintenance*
> *people say, "Well, we're trained on the pump, or on instrumentation*
> *and control, we know how to do that, we don't know anything about*
> *the larger system. We aren't trained on the larger system." I heard that*
> *enough—not everywhere—to make me wonder what's being said. Is*
> *that the kind of thing that's maybe happening here, that they know*
> *their stuff but their stuff is limited? To think of contingencies you'd*
> *have to be able to think of the larger system.*

I think that our maintenance people here for the most part have a pretty good understanding of the whole system of what they're involved in. It doesn't mean that they don't focus on the job, so to speak. But through their supervision and everything, it's not like they're ignorant of all the plant functions and all they know how to do is turn a wrench and fix a valve. No, I think they're much smarter than that, they're much more educated in the systems and what it does and the problems they could get into.

But to go back to "It's a routine job"—that's what does it. It's that, to me that's the biggest part, that mentality, "We've done this a hundred times," and they don't look at it as "What could happen?"—the what-if. They don't look at that type of thing. . . . And quite often it turns out to be very complicated and they start finding problems that they could have got into. They're starting to accept that more. And the same thing here, their number one concern is, "I've got this little valve out here. What system is it on and what's the worst thing that can happen?"—that's not part of the mentality here. And it doesn't mean they don't know what could happen and they don't know the overall picture of the system.

After bobbing and weaving through that response, Brian continues his analysis, in which cloudy meanings of safe shutdown also appear. It turns out, he claims, that the oversight group itself has lacked "high awareness" of safety issues and of meanings assigned to other "safety" categories.

> I think as far as the safety implications go that there is not a high aware-ness—and there wasn't in our group either, unfortunately. This shows in our own group that we have to be more aware of the various contin-gencies. This became and still is one of the biggest considerations for when we look at jobs. "Is it one of the barriers and are they taking the proper steps?"

How do you account for this? Where would you say this drop off of attention comes from?

> Good question. I think it's many, many years of complacency. We didn't get to where we are because we were doing the right things. And even though people go through training and systems training, and stuff like that, there was not a high awareness of this throughout the plant. It wasn't one of the big things that they stressed. They might stress safety of personnel more than they stressed this barrier system. I think it's that complacency—you know, "We can do no wrong type of thing. We're the best in the world."—when actually we weren't. . . .

"Overconfidence" is a well-exercised cause category, in part, Brian im-plies, because it is based on questionable assumptions underlying the hier-archy of "safety" and "nonsafety" that he says is now gradually being leveled.

> The biggest emphasis we have is on safety systems related to safe shut-down in case of an accident. But there's many systems out there that are equally as important. In fact, we just talked about this this morn-ing. . . . [A fuse blew] and operators couldn't find one to fix it. Well, it isn't considered a category one system [nuclear safety-related]—it's not, I guess, really related to safe shutdown of the plant. So you look at it differently. But {voice rising} it can trip a plant, if you don't have the instrument working, it can cause all kinds of problems. . . . I mean you can trip a plant for no reason. Because you're not taking care of this fuse properly, it can cause other problems. Our emphasis on equipment I think is off base. And this is starting to show up more when we've looked at some of the turbine-driven feed pumps and something like that. "Not related to safe shutdowns," but it's a high cost—it's some-thing that you can't start the plant up without, if they're not working right. . . . There's a lot of implications that you should look at these systems a lot differently than the way we used to.
>
> If you look at it this way, from the history of our operating experi-ence, it's basically everything was geared toward cat one [category

one]—and everything else nobody cared about. Give you an example: I was a QC [quality control] inspector. If you went out and looked at nonQ work, they'd ask, "What are you doing out here? You don't have any reason to look at this." So we didn't. We just went and looked at the important ones, which was a very small part. Well, now we realize that the nonQ is just as important to doing the job correctly too, and the plant is starting to see this. We'll look at anything up there and do the oversight on it. . . . in my group we look at all systems, all manners and types of work. Because we look at all of it as being important. That's a change in philosophy.

Ray is the system engineer responsible for the reactor coolant system. He disagrees with the relevance of "nuclear safety" to this event.

Do you disagree with anything in the reports? Would you add anything?

The IRT report, yes. And I sent e-mails off. I said I think it's counterproductive they brought up the other station's event. That valve was done at 2,000 pounds pressure 600 degrees temperature [while on line], and they worked on a valve that was unisolable from the RCS, and if they broke it, they were going to have a LOCA [loss of coolant accident]. We worked on a valve with 50 pounds pressure 130 degrees temperature, nobody's going to get scalded, there was no personal safety issue, both [IRT and RCA] reports say, "There's no personal safety, no nuclear safety issue." But the team said, "We'll do a comparison," because I believe they were told to do a comparison. They found a lot of things that were similar, so they said, "We'll compare." So the lessons learned from the other station's event weren't picked up here, but the lessons learned emphasized nuclear safety. Even after saying this wasn't a nuclear safety issue, the IRT report emphasized nuclear safety.

I know the maintenance manager asked the question, "How badly can this leak?" My supervisor came back and said, "At worst it's going to leak seven gallons per minute. That's if there's no backseat at all, it will leak seven gallons a minute, because where this stem goes to the valve, the fitting's tight enough that it's going to reduce the leak, really limit the leakage." So they had asked that question, "Is it a nuclear safety issue? Can we keep up with seven gallons a minute?" I've got a [sump] pump that puts out 150 gallons/minute, I've got plenty of water and it's going to be leaking cold water, so if I do have a leak, I can always go back in there because there's no personal safety issues. So they focused on nuclear safety. I focused on nuclear safety and said, "They already know they had the leak. They're dealing with it."

That is, Ray is assured that safe shutdown is not threatened, nor will mechanics be scalded or contaminated: that the leak is under control means there is no "nuclear safety issue." Until he interrupts himself.

{Sudden thought} The [maintenance] organization tried to do this job at 350 psi—I didn't know about that effort till somebody said, "We're shutting down because." That's the first I'd heard about it. So I didn't know we'd tried to backseat that valve and tried to work it hot. But I figured if the organization was willing to take that risk then—

The maintenance supervisor didn't know that either?

The maintenance supervisor knew it because he sent the people out there. I didn't know it. I'm in engineering. I'm the reactor coolant system engineer. And a valve packing wouldn't necessarily come to my attention—just doing a packing job. So if they went out there to try to tighten down on the packing, that's fine. If they're trying to replace packing, now I think we're a little more sensitive to that. We've done this before. We've backseated valves before, we've gone in and changed out the packing. I never know about it. I just know we did that, in containment, and on the reactor coolant system.

What kind of issue is it for you, then, if it's not a nuclear safety or personal safety issue?

What kind of issue?

What kind of issue is a cooling water leak?

I'm still working on that. I believe the director called us out on nuclear safety [the stand down], and again, as I told these people, if you focus on nuclear safety {frustrated tone}—everyone was focused on nuclear safety, and this wasn't about nuclear safety. So everyone was comfortable with some risk. There's a risk that we'll get some RCS water leaking out, but we can recover from that. Everyone was confident that we could recover from a leak, everyone was confident that it wasn't going to threaten anything, and nobody's come through and said that's wrong. All right? So it wasn't nuclear safety and my concern was, that I expressed to the team lead on the IRT, that if you tell people to focus on nuclear safety, what's that doing?

In this particular case it's called a barrier. We have three barriers: the fuel, the reactor coolant system, and the containment. And what we were told was, "Hold the barriers sacred." I'm still working on what that means. I'm not sure what that means. We're supposed to hold those barriers sacred. So when you look at this, we broke the RCS barrier. We got water on the floor. And that's what we really did. And that is called, there's a thing called a "higher risk activity"—I didn't know what it was until after this event. I wasn't even aware of the procedure, which I think is a shortcoming. There's a tool out there that I could have designated this as higher risk. If I knew that, I could have said, "You know, this is a higher risk activity, what's our contingency plan?"

With the one thread—was that enough to put it in that category?

Absolutely. Well, I wouldn't have [not knowing about the procedure]. It turns out a new fellow came into the scheduling group. He looked at this activity and said, "Higher risk." Because he was told that "If you can put one drop of RCS water on the floor during a job, it's a higher risk activity." All right. I don't think we've bought into that. I know we haven't bought into that for higher risk. Once you designated it higher risk, you have to have a PORC [plant oversight review committee] approve a contingency plan. His supervisor didn't know the procedure that well because he's a new supervisor, and the guy who just started in work scheduling knew it and thought it was going to be taken care of. So it got designated higher risk one day, the next day everybody looked at it, there was higher risk on the schedule, but nobody discussed it. . . .

But see, I walked away. As soon as I say "not nuclear safety" and as soon as everyone else says "not nuclear safety," we don't have to do what-ifs. If I thought that was nuclear safety, as soon as I came out of containment, saying "I saw one thread on one valve and two threads on the others," I would have had to be conservative and issue a condition report, and we would have had to address the issue. Because it was nuclear safety I *have* to address the issue and I would *have* to feel conservative.

At that time you didn't think it was nuclear safety.

At that time and today. And both reports specifically state, it's "Not a nuclear safety issue." And both reports specifically state it's "Not a personal safety issue." And the report that went out to the industry clearly stated in a note right under the summary at my request, "This is not a personal safety issue, not a nuclear safety issue and the reason we're taking this so seriously is because we hold the barrier to be sacred." I had to put in some words like that because I didn't want someone else, one of my co-system engineers out there, picking this up and saying, "Are you nuts? It's not personal safety, not nuclear safety. You've got a packing leak. Why don't you just fix it and get on with your life?" instead of all these things that we did.

Clark, the root cause specialist leading the RCAT team, discusses contingency planning. Clark is an engineer who has held various positions in several station departments over the last twelve years.

> Now, we didn't do that, we didn't do that. So we could have done that, we could have utilized all those engineering resources to plan for the worst case. And we still could have done the job and had almost the same scenario [as the event], but it would have been a *known* scenario.

By virtue of his "oversight" role and long tenure in the industry, Brian sees reason to doubt the validity of strict lines around "category one" and "nuclear-safety related" quality control: fuses and reactor coolant systems can interact. While those categories may carry out the letter of the laws that technical specifications lay down, they do not reflect their spirit: the "change in philosophy" of his group—to look beyond category-one activities—fills that gap. For Ray, his systematics seem to be bounded by his responsibilities to "his" reactor coolant system: he did not know that this job could have been marked as "higher risk," nor did he write a condition report about his suspicions of a valve that, in corporate order, "belongs" to maintenance. For Clark, whose root cause analysis specialty keeps him aware of consequences, a "known scenario" would have prevented losing sight of the sacred status of the primary barriers: imagined risks to people and plant would have been planned for. Brian scans, Ray draws boundaries, Clark anticipates: three ways in which professional and regulatory orders approach risks.

"Sacred Barriers and High Risk"

For Richard, operations manager, through less than "stellar" communication, the event sullied "the operations organization," "one of those that got burned badly."

> The job as it was presented to me prior to being done was a "This shouldn't even be on your radar screen. Don't worry about it, nothing can go wrong." That was on the one hand, then on the other hand, when myself and my direct [report] said, "What do you have for contingencies?" we were presented with a contingency plan that turned out not to be a contingency plan. . . . It was contingent on two things. First of all, there was the leak and that the job as it was planned could not result in catastrophic failure. The worst it could result in was a blowing by of packing at a couple of gallons a minute, which would be sufficient [low enough] to allow a freeze seal to be placed on the line. So I was presented with, "The freeze seal was the contingency." The reality of it turned out to be that not only was catastrophic failure possible, I think

there's some communication problem in that the actual work performed may have been different than the work scope that was presented. But in any event, no freeze seal equipment had been ordered. 'Cause at the working level they never considered [the freeze seal] a contingency, whereas at the management level that was presented as a contingency. . . .

Richard soon moderates "catastrophic," but remains concerned that no scenario was in place.

In terms of actual reactor safety, this might not have been the world's worst event. I think that one could have calculated that we had something on the order of four days of reserve water, that even with gravity feed we could have continued to maintain plant safety. But none of that was thought of going in up front because it was, "You can't have this failure, so why do you need to plan for it?" So that valve went wrong at my level for a different reason than on some other levels because to us it was presented as a "This isn't a problem, this is below your radar screen. . . ." This was part of the discussion of, "You can't have catastrophic failure. Since all you're doing is adding packing, you back off on the gland [the repository for packing]. If the gland starts to leak, you retighten the gland." But the job scope as presented to us [and that ops approved] was, "We will only add packing." And it appears that prior to adding packing, packing has got to be taken away. So this is not a stellar example of interdepartmental communication.

So when you say that you got burned, you feel that there's some blame attaching to ops or you don't come out smelling like a rose, or what?

When the unit fails, operations fails. I'm not so concerned about the words in the report that ops should have stopped the job. What I'm concerned about is when push comes to shove and you get to the bottom line, we assure the safety of the plant by how we operate it, and plant safety was not assured in this condition.

It turns out that the haze around primary barriers hadn't dissipated after this event. I asked Richard,

What kinds of arguments seem to make a difference when people in your position are trying to push back on schedule and cost pressures?

Safety. Safety makes a difference. Safety can mean different things to different people, but it doesn't mean you're not going to get overruled or overwritten. Usually we seek to work out a way of making it work [the tradeoff quandary]. The next big challenge we had after this leaking valve event was a feedwater valve that was a direct containment penetration. And in that one, it was about halfway through the management meeting that they realized that they had not invited anybody from operations to discuss the repair plan on this containment penetration. So they called me, and I grabbed one of my supervisors, who was a direct control room supervisor, and brought him in. And we sat there and listened to the plan and said, "No. We're not going to allow you to do this." And that put planning back to square one, to develop a plan that we felt met the safety needs of the plant, not merely the technical needs of going in to repair the unit.

The level of discussion {voice rising} that happened at that meeting, though, was on the same level as that around the leaking valve. The presentation was, "Don't worry about it, nothing could happen." It was a cutaway view of the valve. "We're going to do this, we're going to take off this, we're going to move this." Some of the outfall of that, I was told afterwards, was that I presented a non-teamwork demeanor by going into the meeting and saying I disapproved of the plan. I don't fall easily to peer pressure. That could have been a subtle attempt to [tell me] "Join with the team and get on with it." That's how you lead yourself into events, by the group think, by joining with the team when they'd made up their minds on where they're going. . . .

Why do you think your "demeanor" was an issue, that they felt you were being uncooperative?

I was doing just what I ought to have been doing, which was challenging a decision I didn't buy in on.

Perhaps that was part of the issue—that you weren't brought in at the beginning?

It was part of the issue. It would have been much better had all that been solved outside the room before the meeting ever happened. That goes back to process. There was no process that would have brought me into that at that point.

That's hard for me to understand, in containment. And that if a feedwater valve also affects the RCS in some way, which I assume it does, that an ops involvement wouldn't have been built into the definition of the problem.

Well, there is ops involvement, it's part of the process. It's just that it's a relatively low level involvement for most work. And also that the level of involvement requires a good statement of scope. Every job at some point passes through a [control room] shift manager's hands and that's the ultimate acid test. Most of them pass through twice. They pass through on the front end [work planning] and then just prior to going out [to do the job]. If the statement of the scope of the job is, "I'm putting the valve on the backseat and replacing packing," no warning flags go up. None at all.

Rusty, assistant operations manager, has been at Arrow for sixteen years. He oversees the work of licensed operators in the control room and in the plant; shift managers and their crews report through him to the operations manager. Earlier, Rusty was in reactor engineering; he sits on the plant operations review committee. He too did not know this task should be designated "higher risk."

What did you think of the comparison between this event and the one at the other station, which the IRT's report featured?

The IRT. {long pause} I think the analogy is valid only insofar as both involved work on a reactor coolant boundary and the impact, and that the fact that we were working on one of our three principal fission barriers was not fully appreciated. In the other event, they weren't sensitive to the fact that they were working on an unisolable portion of our reactor coolant system boundary, and again it all comes to those three barriers. That lack of sensitivity. In this event we weren't sensitive to the fact that we were working on one of our three principal fission barriers.

Beyond that I think the analogy is fatuous. I think it is baloney. I think the safety implications and the consequences of the leaking valve event, and our inability to repair it, and the potential consequences of an unsuccessful repair are minuscule in comparison with the safety implications of the other event. If that valve ruptured, there would have been a small break Loss of Coolant Accident. The safety implications would have been extraordinary. Even if we had been unable to put any packing back in, the maximum leak—just because of the construction of the valve and the clearances inside the valve—we would have been well, well within our ability to maintain inventory in the reactor coolant system at that lower pressure. Would it have been a mess? Would it have been a mess to clean up in containment? Yes. But from a safety significant standpoint there is no comparison between the two in my mind.

Jerry, the manager of engineering technical support, considers the comparison.

Clearly the potential for {pause} affecting safety of the public was there at the other station. We were much more deliberate. The other station had taken something and just went way way way too far with it. And [news of that other event] was very much not lost on the industry or

Arrow. Our take on this event was not—I mean we were very conscious of what—we even went over some of the other event's lessons, as I recall, that did come up prior to us getting into it. But at no time, even if we had the packing extrude would we have placed the public at a risk. The safety significance was completely different. And I have a hard time making those two mesh together.

As an outsider, what's interesting to me and perhaps I should be corrected on this—the analogy I got out of it—I saw clearly that these were disparate, but both were RCS boundaries.

Oh yeah, you can make that.

But what you're telling me is that the fact that at the other station there was a boundary breach with a consequence versus a boundary breach without a consequence, that didn't hold in terms of making that analogy convincing.

To me, that was one of the biggest things that I didn't buy in on the IRT report. That was probably the biggest, actually. . . . But we were fairly conscious of the fact that we would remain safe, but we were not—again I can't go back and say it often enough, we did not look at it as a barrier that we should be more cautious with at the time.

Clark, Ray, Rusty, and Jerry, each in his own way, are speaking to a basic principle of risk reduction to assure safe shutdown: timely recovery of control over malfunctions is essential. A near-miss by definition is either the quick avoidance of losing control or the immediate resumption of control. Duration of adverse conditions can be more worrisome than their frequency: longevity can propagate mischief.[3]

If the valve leak had spilled a lot all over the floor, is there a standard scenario for dealing with the consequences that people can just pull up and take a look at? My experience reading Licensee Event Reports [made to the NRC] and talking to people at other plants is that "You never know," they say. "You have that one glitch. Whoops, there's another glitch and the holes start lining up," they say. So that would be one question I would have. That even that scenario deserves to be played out, it would seem. I don't think the water was contaminated in this case.

Very, very mildly. There is no question that that scenario deserves to be played out. And part of an effective, strong work control and work planning process would have considered that. But from the standpoint of nuclear safety, was there a credible failure mode in this repair that could have led to something that challenged nuclear safety? And the answer in my opinion is "No." Would it have caused a mess, and would it have been an inconvenience, could it have led to some people being contaminated, mildly contaminated? Yes. Is that significant? Yes. We should not be dumping water into containment. We should not be getting people contaminated. So I don't want you walking away from this thinking that I don't take it seriously.

What about the issue that came up so often over designating the valve repair simply as a "higher risk evolution"? Does that seem to have been scanted? There was this new scheduler who caught that.

Yes, yes. That scheduler should be commended. He really should be commended. In fact, the idea that this should have been classified as a high risk hadn't even occurred to me. In fact, I didn't even realize that somebody had picked up on that until I read the report. But if you go through the procedures, what does designating an activity a high risk require you to do? It requires you to have contingencies in place, certain people to be notified. If we had done what we were supposed to have done for a high risk evolution, that would have insured that the activity would have been planned adequately, that we would have had compensatory measures and contingency plans in place, procedures in place, and before we went into this we would have known exactly what to do if the repair failed. That is appropriate—totally appropriate. And it would not have kicked us into an IPTE [infrequently performed test evolution procedure].

In a system dependent on defense-in-depth, a primary barrier becomes "weird," Clark says. He was leader of the root cause analysis team.

One thing we learned is that there was another plant that had actually put the station manager right in line with decisions of this nature. I think that that's a good action in that it really says, "Management controls this evolution. This is no longer operators and work planning. For everything that's going on here, managers and supervisors are involved." That is, we have something that's weird and what I mean by weird is single-boundary protection. Typically nuclear plants are defense-in-depth. So here we go away from defense-in-depth, here we go—we're only going to have the single boundary to protect the person, and my concern is more in that area. My concern is more global in that this same situation could occur in a steam plant, you know, to the person working on the valve. So where there's a single boundary evolution it seems we have to elevate this and say, "Management has to step in," since they need to control this tight. From that, the meetings need to be much crisper: "Who has this issue, who has responsibility, who's the lead, and who's assisting the lead." . . . There should be areas that say,

"We're going into single boundary, we need increased management attention, this is an RCS valve, a brand that may have had some other problems, so we may need engineering assistance throughout this whole evolution."

But primary barriers—single-boundary barriers—are as "typical" for nuclear power plants as are defense-in-depth strategies. Clark's concern turns to protecting those working on the valve, not also to preventing the loss of coolant from the RCS. From there, his concern becomes "global" as he likens this leaking valve to those in any steam generating plant.

Acceptance of a nuclear power plant as being its own kind keeps going in and out of focus, as at the meeting on a repair that penetrated the containment wall. Only after the valve repair failed is it acknowledged to affect the RCS pressure boundary on a primary barrier. Only then is Mark's higher-risk designation appreciated. Keep the barriers "sacred," Ray says, because they have no backups. But at the same time, the leak on a pressure boundary is "not nuclear safety" because the threat to the barrier proper did not materialize. The consensus was that recovery was entirely within reach, arrived at in the absence of no "known scenario," however, once accepting the estimated leak rate of seven gallons per minute, which, according to Rusty, would have caused "a mess" but not reduced cooling water inventory to worrisome levels.

"Pieces" and "Silos," Newcomers and Credibility

"Stellar" interdepartmental "communication," as Richard says, appears to have been hard to come by. One afterimage the event leaves is of a connect-the-dots sketch, a staccato of points in a situation where connections of many kinds—among competencies, records, procedures, observations, information—didn't happen. A system engineer's concern is muffled in an informal comment to the responsible supervisor, managers don't register the significance of technical information, a supervisor ignores a manager's directions to inspect the valve, an appropriate procedure is sidestepped, valve precursors aren't considered, radiography for definitive information isn't performed. Dots that had been connected get erased when managers take a minor maintenance work order out of its planned place on a complicated schedule. The rule to "hold the boundaries sacred" is ignored; only a work scheduler new in his job tries to honor its meanings. Managers and mechanics in maintenance are repeatedly said to have been "overconfident" after the fact, but despite doubts raised about the valve's condition, had been left to "do their job."

Steven, maintenance manager, had been in his job for about a year. Previously in instrumentation and control and in operations, at one time he also attended operator license school. Steven characterizes the event as involving "a lot of different pieces."

> This was an attempt to do maintenance that we had performed in the past in an environment that was probably less settled than what we had been exposed to in the past, meaning a lot more things going on. A lot more intensity, I guess, would be a good word for the environment, meaning there was the realization that we needed to finish up so we could get started up. . . . The original maintenance team that was scheduled . . . a titled supervisor, experienced people going in to do the job didn't happen—delays in being able to get plant conditions into the right situation caused that team to change. I see a reluctance on management's part to get actively involved because it was maintenance that had been done before. I see a lot of people trusting the lower levels of the organization based on comments and experience, and all to the point where we probably had an overconfidence for this particular— not probably, we did have an overconfidence based on the people that were originally scheduled to do it, based on the people that were there saying, "Don't worry about it, I got it, we can do this." And then I see it in a worst case scenario once we got to it, meaning the valve was not in the condition we thought it was in, no one took to heart the precursors [earlier problems with this brand of valve] that were identified, meaning "Check the valve condition [backseat] before you try to fix it," and I see us getting into the situation. So if I had to characterize it in just a couple of terms I would say, hectic conditions, overconfidence, and lack of supervisory, management involvement. . . .

He puts himself squarely into that picture.

> I think in this case we minimized the risk, based on the confidence of the people performing the work in my organization. I communicated that upwardly so my part of it is clear in that. . . . Circumstances changed as we went through from who the lead was going to be to who actually got physically out there. So that's an awareness thing on my part. . . . There should have been a better, and we've since adopted it, a better realization of who's in charge, who's the central focal point for information coming in and going out, who is the person who's looking at it overall—meaning there are a lot of different pieces of this, there was an engineering piece, an operations piece, a maintenance piece, and who was watching all of that? And the answer was, "Nobody."

Those "different pieces" are the different departments, functions, or disciplines—orders—often called "silos" standing on the prairies of many if not most stations. Brian, the oversight specialist, was once assigned to reactor engineering.

One question I have is about the kinds of evidence people pay attention to and what kinds they discount. And when you ask that question about this event, and look at the reports again, it becomes sort of a theme. Like the maintenance manager not giving great credence to the system engineer's observations. What does it take for people in different positions—because everybody has their own perspective—to give something credence and credibility?

If I had the answer to that question, I'd bottle it and be a millionaire and retire. I think that ties in with this silo effect that we see in the unit. Yeah, maintenance is a silo, engineering is a silo, ops is a silo, operations doesn't respect the system engineers, so they don't give them the credence that they deserve. You know, engineering doesn't respect ops, so they don't give weight and credence to points that operations tries to make. Maintenance doesn't respect system engineers, so they're not working together. Ops and maintenance don't respect each other so they're not working together. You know, it all leads to the silo. If I had the answer to that question, all our problems would be solved.

Let's take an example that you might be able to call up from way, way back when there was mutual respect. How would you explain the fact that that existed? If we understand that, that could be the seed of understanding why it's missing or what it would take to have it.

I can give a very specific example, and this is something that I can relate to personally. For a lot of years reactor engineering and operations did not have a good relationship. Which hurt. Because reactor engineering and operations has to be right smack in lock step. And it was due probably in most part to the fact that, you know, over in reactor engineering, we did our thing and we did what we felt was best. Specifically, generating the curves that the operators use to actually run the plant—rod worth curves [reactivity values] and everything else. We generated those curves, and we formatted those curves in the manner that was easiest for us to generate and that we felt was good. Well, we're looking at it from an engineer's perspective. So we did what was easiest for us and what we felt was best, and we handed them to the operators. The operators hate 'em. And there was constant tension between us over these curves. And that was a barrier, that was one of the bricks in that wall.

Contrast that now with a reactor engineer that we have who, when it comes time to generate these curves during the shutdown, went over to ops, and said, "Ops, tell me what you need. Here's what we've been giving you, tell us why this isn't good for you, tell us what you want." He even went so far as to come out to training for operating crews, sat there, listened to the operators' comments, got their feedback, took it, went back, and then giving the operators the product that they now can use and meets their needs. Well, there's a big brick that just got pulled out of the wall.

Jerry, Arrow Station's manager of engineering technical support, is remembering a reorganization a few years back.

Re-engineering took a heavily siloed organization, and basically it was like a tornado that came through. {rueful laugh} There's still silos, but most of them are just foundations at this point, and people, attitudewise—I think we changed that dramatically too, in that people are now allowed to want to help out and go help out. You know, some people don't, still—but attitudewise that's what we're striving for, that everyone wants to be positive and contribute. And most people do, it's just their nature.

I asked Richard about "communications between maintenance and ops in general."

In general, they take place based on what the significance of the item is. On this particular job I had talked with both the mechanical manager and the maintenance department manager, and they were the ones that assured me that we couldn't have catastrophic failure and we had contingencies. Engineering also told me we had contingencies ready. They may have believed that at the time they talked to me, which was the day before the job.

When do the silos go away? When is the communication easier?

Communication does take place on an awful lot of levels all the time, or nothing would get done. The silo effect is much less, actually, in the day-to-day work, because at the worker-to-worker level and the first-line level, there is a lot of talk just to keep the stuff moving, going back and forth and having handoffs from department to department. And those are pretty formal and proceduralized also. The silos occur in more philosophical areas. For example, a shift manager deciding he's just not going to allow any [repair or testing] work on that shift because he's too busy, and doing that in isolation from the effect of that on the rest of the unit. Or maintenance deciding, in the case of the leaking valve, "Here's where we're going and we'll defend our position" and "I think I'll keep everybody else out of it so we can do what we want." That's where I come to see the silos. And they exist at my level too, at the level of busyness that most of the managers are at. Talking to another manager becomes a real challenge. . . .

Once managers define and prioritize tasks, Richard adds, getting the work done devolves to those assigned to do it.

If there's a structural problem related to this, it would be that in the course of building the method of getting work through the system the best, that that method does not allow for a lot of external discussion. So a job like this could very easily be planned and executed entirely at the worker level—putting together work packages, scheduling it, making the right plant conditions, going through the reviews that have to happen, or formal reviews that also happen at the worker and first-line supervisor level. And it might not be until this hits the shift manager that he says, "Shit. You're working on our primary boundary. I'm not going to let this happen." So nothing in the process ever says you need management buy-in on a job, no matter what the ramifications of the job are. . . . We probably do on the order of 15,000 work items a year. You can't have management looking at 15,000 work items a year. But at some point certain things should raise the flag, and boundary work on the reactor coolant system is one of those things.

Mark raised that flag and so did Ray. For different reasons, their credibility was at issue: credibility works overtime in this industry, especially that of newcomers. Three newcomers occupy jobs pivotal to the event—Mark, his boss Alan, and Steven, maintenance manager. The independent review team report acknowledges Alan's and Steven's status: "Relatively new supervisor and manager did not recognize the significance of [Mark's] designation." The report does not acknowledge, however, that in a management meeting, it was oldtimers who didn't heed Mark's sensitivity to the job's location. Newcomers may be unfamiliar with many details of plant history, but oldtimers may discount what newcomers know on the grounds of "newness" alone. Out of hand, it seems, oldtimers dismissed Mark's credibility. Nor did Alan, Mark's supervisor, perhaps feeling his way in a new job, look into the reasons for the higher-risk designation on his own, nor did oldtimers familiar with the rationale for that designation pick up on the agenda item.

Not often recognized for their cultural consequences, the auras around the newcomer-oldtimer relationship are nevertheless predictable. And powerful: reactions to anything and anybody "new" move us along a continuum from pleasure to pain and to the fear pain can foster. How oldtimers respond to newcomers depends on many things—how different or unfamiliar they perceive them to be in appearance, speech, education, relative rank, and influence. Newcomers often signal subsequent social or cognitive rearrangements to which oldtimers will be expected to adapt. Steven, maintenance manager, is aware of his situation. "I am a new manager in the organization at that time—I say new from the standpoint of less than a year. My credibility is still being felt out and challenged as we go ahead." Being a newcomer to nearly any group or situation carries its special burdens: how to make one's way into an already established situation by raising just enough interest to be welcomed while dampening old-timers' fears, which they may express through suspicion, perhaps hostility. New, or even different, ideas live through the same initiation and degradation rituals.[4]

The credibility of Ray's observation of the possibility of stem/disc separation was an issue, Steven suggests, because he made it informally.

> And consequently it just wasn't followed up on by the people who were directly into it.

The reports talk about that. What was running through my mind was, "How did Ray present it? Was it critical when they heard it?"

It was not formally presented, meaning, in hindsight, what should have happened was we should have written a condition report which would have gone into the formal corrective action program, which would have gotten formal management reviews. This was a {hesitates}

An aside?

Yes, and that's exactly what it was. You know, "I know you, you know me. Hey, I was just out there looking at this, and I don't see it's correct." That was probably the closest to a formal—and it was in a sense a formal [recognition] because it was brought to a management meeting where it was put on the table as, "Here's what we're seeing, we need to follow up on this," and it was taken by me to my mechanical people. So now you're probably twice removed, in that it travelled from experienced system engineer to manager to second manager—"Here's a condition, I need you to take a look at it, make sure we look at it prior to going in." That was consequently given to a third party, meaning the mechanics that were going in to do the work, and now so far removed with no formal ties, there was no condition report . . . the importance of it diminished as you moved through the handoffs.

When you say in a corrective action, something like "Communication should be improved" or "Take a real hard look at communication"— a technically trained person might say, "Well, that's like motherhood." They can say, "Well, I don't have a procedure for that, I don't have documentation, I don't have a trend analysis, I don't have tools. How am I going to do this?" I'm just making this up. But I don't think that's an unlikely scenario . . . ?

Right. Yeah.

What I'm puzzling over is how would *that person need to hear this to be somehow convinced? What kind of evidence would they need to make them say, "This is a priority"?*

I think it could show up in probably three forms and be acted upon. It could show up in the form of a very credible experience-based person, it could show up in the form of the paperwork, the actual CR [condition report], "Here's what we need to address prior to going there," and probably the third phase, that it is formally put together either in a work package description or in a scheduled activity. So I think it if showed up in any of those—and in this particular case, I'll address each one of them.

From a credibility standpoint, you had a system engineer who was very experienced, very knowledgeable. However, he has some background of not being correct, of being overly conservative, being someone that—and again this was the perception as you got to the end of the handoff line—that, "Yeah, we've dealt with this guy before" {skeptical tone}. From my perspective, I am a new manager in the [maintenance] organization at that time—I say new from the standpoint of less than a year. My credibility is still being felt out and challenged as we go ahead, so when I give direction as someone that came from other than the mechanical side of the organization—maintenance including electricians, I&C techs, mechanics, and planners—I didn't come through mechanical ranks, so my direction to a mechanical person was filtered with, "This guy doesn't have a real great mechanical background. How can he know what we should look at? We know it better than everybody else." Therefore I think there was a filtering mechanism there. So now you've got that option, basically not real solid. We did not put it into a condition report, so from a paperwork standpoint there wasn't anything to flag it there, we did not specifically write it into the repair work order because it was a direction, so it wasn't caught there when it got to the handoff phase, and it wasn't a scheduled activity.

It was a piece of research, basically.

Absolutely. That was really—it was a thought, an idea, and a concept that really just wasn't followed up.

During the root cause analysis team inquiry, Clark had addressed the question of Ray's credibility.

I'm a little unclear about why the reactor coolant system engineer's observations about possible stem/disc separation weren't persuasive.

The [maintenance] supervisor that he talked to was—and I'll describe it from people around the situation—first, [the supervisor] was overconfident and cocky and it was almost to the point of, "That guy [Ray] doesn't know what he's talking about." I talked to the system engineer to try to quantify that, you know, "Did you feel this guy was just blowing you off? Did you feel that he wasn't even going to look?" And the system engineer [Ray] didn't get those same feelings. Ray said, "You know, I've worked with the guy before. I felt he was going to look at the valve before they started anything, but he said he felt that maintenance had the issue." Now the RCS engineer also talked with the shift manager, so I asked him, "You talked with the shift manager about this," and he said, "It was not the primary topic. It was a secondary, tertiary topic."

I said, "OK, what about the shift manager, what did he come back to you and say?" The system engineer at that point said, "I probably was not persuasive enough and didn't identify what I felt could occur if this were a problem. It was more laid out there as, 'There's the smelly fish,' and you know, it wasn't that 'If you touched it that you could get a disease,' you know, and 'Don't go near it, rope it off,' and things of that nature." So the system engineer felt that with the shift manager, he did bring it up, but he felt he was not persuasive enough as to what the concerns and the issues were.

The system engineer wasn't brought in on it at the start, it seems?

Yeah. This was not his primary job to go look at this. It wasn't like, "Stamp this on your head to go look." . . . He was associated with some [power reduction] issues because he was a reactor coolant system systems engineer. . . .

Whose responsibility would it have been then, if this was something he took upon himself? Was he filling a gap, poaching on someone else's—?

What would have happened had this thing been identified as a higher risk issue is that in some of the early planning stages, this job would have got planned as shutdown, cooldown, "We're going to do it in a refuel outage so there's no fuel going to be in the pot." When the planner made the work order that was his intention. . . . And then all of a sudden, [managers move it up on the schedule because plant mode conditions were more favorable]. . . . The planner wasn't asked to go back and look at all the conditions. . . . I think that was a good decision, to look at the valve. Maybe not to go ahead with the work, but to pull it up and inspect it. . . .

Was there an engineer aside from Ray with those responsibilities?

No, there is not normally an engineer for repacking valves. Maintenance considers it skill of the trade, and they repack numerous valves. So, no. But the systems engineer had some concerns, he's familiar with these types of valves. It's his reactor coolant system, you know. It was fortunate that he was going to go in the containment, because if he didn't nobody would have even raised a flag that would have said, "There's a possible stem/disc separation."

So he was in something of an anomalous position giving this advice?

Absolutely. He was not the controlling person on it. He was an irritant—I'll say it that way. I don't necessarily mean an irritant [in a bad sense] but he was off to the side and he took the initiative to go look, and after he took that initiative he communicated that to his supervisor, he communicated that to the maintenance supervisor, he communicated that to the shift manager.

Being "off to the side" so weakened Ray's already dubious credibility that others discounted his knowledge of the valve's history.

Other kinds of "newcomers" also populate this event. Managers took a piece of work out of its place on a schedule, long the frame of reference for all other activities. Why would managers slot this valve repair ahead of its scheduled time? Perhaps because of the backlog of maintenance work, which drives managers to be on the lookout for a system configuration favorable to checking off more of the year's 15,000 work orders. Then, a different repair team replaced the one originally scheduled for the second repair attempt: another "newcomer." On top of that, the work scope was different from what operations had originally expected: only adding packing, not picking out existing packing. Steven characterizes the entire context as a departure from the familiar: "This was an attempt to do maintenance that we had performed in the past in an environment that was probably less settled than what we had been exposed to in the past, meaning a lot more things going on, a lot more intensity." One side effect of routinizing and standardizing for safety's sake is to magnify the significance of disruptions to the expected order of things beyond any they might have intrinsically.

The tradeoff quandary also helped to keep Arrow Station's dots disconnected, according to some. Debates over cost, schedule, and safe shutdown air predictable differences in each order's time horizons. Corporate and senior managers' performance ratings are tied to quarterly financial results, while technical experts' action orientation focuses them on maintaining the technology's integrity. Brian, an oversight manager, comments.

I attended a couple of the meetings where management was involved and where there was a push to do certain things. And there was some push back on it—you know, to make sure that we didn't go crazy on it. . . .

When you say there were things that people were pushing for and back on in that meeting and "going crazy," I don't know what you mean.

Well, not a good term, but we have to be careful sometimes of schedule or cost and that type of thing. And of course we're in a situation of trying to get the plant started. . . . at that particular time it wasn't a good thing to have to drain down [the RCS] and have to go through all that sort of work. And we have to be careful that you don't get caught up in this, "This is no big deal." We have to look past, at times, cost and scheduling to make sure we do all this right. That's the type of push back I'm getting at, where in some cases senior management says, "Look, we're going to do this, right?" We tend to get the feeling that they're pushing, "We have to get this done at all costs," and we, not necessarily oversight, but we, as, you know, an employee have to push back and say, "No, we have to do it correctly and safely"—it's that type of thing.

Brian has company in that observation. Chuck, senior engineer, remembering when he was a shift manager responsible for making shut down decisions, understands managers' "juggling act."

In a situation like this, my feeling as a shift manager is when my boss asks me to do something, my first question, even if it's not outright, but in my mind, "Is it safe? Is what we want to do safe?" That's the first question. The second question is, "Is it legal?" OK. Not that I think my boss would ask me to do something illegal, but he may ask you to do something, and you may turn around and say, "These are the technical specifications and it doesn't fit. We can't do that." If I think it's safe and I think it's legal, then I have to ask if it's the best thing to do or not. Then my responsibility is to give my opinion whether I agree it's the best thing to do or it's not. Unfortunately, what I think you have right now is a high-level management structure that tends to not want to listen to people it doesn't agree with. In other words, they come up with something and if you say, "No, I think it's this . . . ," they say, "Why are you disagreeing with us?" Instead of the open listening. I don't really think that's there right now.

What do you think it takes for it to get there?

{sigh} The right people in management, the people with the right philosophy, the high-level management that will listen to people. At least listen to them and then say, "OK, I understand what you're saying. I disagree with you. This is what I want done." And through the process that I've just described, if my boss did that and it was safe and it was legal and I just didn't think it was the best thing, I'd say, "OK, I'd do it." But I think it's my responsibility to give my opinion. I think we're in a situation now where it's hard to give your personal opinion or even your professional opinion right now on an issue if management is leaning a certain way and you disagree with it. I think you're frowned upon right now.

So if you say that management is "leaning a particular way," would it be possible to say they would be leaning toward schedule issues and cost issues?

Definitely. I definitely think we're—as hard as we say we're not—and we try not to be—I think we are schedule-driven. They tell us not to let the schedule drive you. Unfortunately, schedule is part of life, you have to work to one. The thing is you can't let it become the almighty creature out there that drives everything. . . . And it appears that in this case the better thing to do from operations' standpoint was to take the time, drain to mid-loop, work on the valve, and limit your risk. That was not done.

Competitive pressures that market order displaces onto the "very talented people" responsible for valve maintenance seem to have made it a "waste of time to put all these contingencies in place," time being money. Financial pressures stemming from deregulation and "safety problems" are statistically associated, according to case studies of three previously deregulated industries (aviation, rail, and UK nuclear power). Prepared for the Nuclear Regulatory Commission to evaluate deregulation's implications for the United States nuclear power industry, the study cites a consultant's 1996 recommendation that the NRC should assess "indicators of economic stress and management's response to them" in order to achieve "earlier" identification of problems and their less costly resolution.[5] Not only do "unusual" technical conditions deserve a "higher risk designation," but financial conditions may as well.

"Sitting Back" and "Moving Forward"

As outage manager on shift, Dan, usually a work scheduler, was present during the event, "following the critical path and making sure things were being done in a timely fashion." Dan says that he "didn't think to think" about the meanings of what was going on.

What I see in this is a basically a team breakdown, which is usually the case when you have an event of this nature. Basically, not necessarily any one person or thing, but when multiple barriers break or fail and that results in an event, it's usually the result of lots of people and lots of teams and efforts, and all adding up in one direction to cause the event. So that's my overriding thought when I think about the leaking valve event. It was a team failure. . . .

So this was one of many activities that you were checking off or watching?

It was probably the main activity. I don't remember exactly what else was going on at the time—usually there are multiple activities involved, but I suspect this was the game in town at the time. I can't remember if there was anything else. And so I was checking to see if people were ready to repack the valve, ops had the containment at the right pressure, and engineering was working on the temp mod, and so on and so forth.

While it was going on did you see any of these deficits?

In retrospect I see them. I was certainly one of many. I knew what was going on, I knew pretty much what the plan was, and I never—I, being a team member [of the restart effort as a whole], didn't think to think what else could have happened if the original plan went awry. . . .

Jerry, the manager of engineering technical support in operations, calls this "stepping back" and "sitting back," which is usually the task of "appointed" people.

I don't think information was shared well on what they found when the packing started to extrude. I think there were suppositions made, "Oh yeah, we just put a freeze seal on it, and we can get the freeze seal people in." My organization was tasked with getting that stuff ready, but at no time was there a consideration that this was a time constraint, that we had to hurry up and do it. So I think, as an organization, between communications and how we work together, we really fell down.

The reasons for those fallings down—

Is your interest {laughing}!

Any speculations you want to make around that I'm open to hearing. I don't know what to make of all that.

All right. It was a very busy time for us. I think as a management team, we didn't sit back in our chairs enough. There definitely was somewhat of a sense of urgency at the meetings. I can remember at least one meeting I was at where everyone was sitting back, and we had dialogue for probably up close to an hour, discussing all the different options. It wasn't, you know, "Well, we're going to do this right now." I think the sense of urgency, as I recall, came after we had introduced a leak. Then it was, "Well, we definitely have a problem that we have to address" and "Boy, did we goof up and how are we going to address it and get all our ducks in a row."

But then there was the suspicion of a stem/disc separation—was that in that conversation?

That was a piece of information that got lost for several days. And that was probably the biggest piece of information that got lost next to the high risk [designation]. And no excuses for it. I mean as an organization, we had someone bring something forward [the possibility of stem/disc separation] . . . a key piece of information that somehow we didn't pick up. And why we didn't pick up on it was, I'd have to say {pause} that people doing implementation possibly did not—from a management standpoint they obviously didn't—take that information and step back and go, "What is this going to mean?"

You've mentioned that now a couple of times. When does that happen? What conditions are conducive to this "sitting back," and asking "What does it mean?"

There are two ways to answer that—not right or wrong. It's, "Do we talk about it in a meeting setpoint?" or "Do we just talk about it in a general day?" In a meeting, at least how it's done at most of them, we do have quite a few people who are into details, not just micromanagers, but they're into details and they want to know that we've considered everything. And that's a good thing. . . . But sometimes I believe that that takes the organization into the details, and we're not sitting back. We actually discussed this, part of this stuff, at manager meetings recently. There are usually a cadre of folks who have the ability to sit back. I guess from a behavioral standpoint as an organization, the question is, "Are there people appointed to do that?"

People appointed to do that?

Yeah. That is the question. And the answer at Arrow is the managerial staff is—managers and directors, that's their jobs. Do they have the ability to get caught up in details and not do that job? I think this is evidence that does occur. The conditions that are created to ask those questions—one of the things that helps us tremendously as a management team is our oversight organization, because they do sit back, and they will speak up and say, "We think, based on what I'm witnessing here, that you guys might want to sit back and think about it." Our oversight manager is excellent. That didn't happen this time. And now that you mention it, I don't think I've ever talked to him about why [Ray's] insight [about disc/stem separation] wasn't shared or if it should have been shared.

Planning and implementation are, then, separate domains of thinking and acting, each on a different timetable. Despite cartons of printouts of daily, weekly, and monthly schedules showing "work windows" to meet restrictions imposed by technical specifications and despite frequent "look ahead" meetings, most of what matters to risk reduction and to line managers' assigned goals and expected rewards occurs in the here and now. The daily dynamics of the tradeoff quandary heighten those stakes. The experts who carry out testing, repair, and surveillance activities earn hourly wages, overtime extras, and, for some (like managers), bonuses based on production levels. As employees who cannot claim "careers" often do, nonsalaried employees are likely to think about putting in a good day's work one day at a time. Operational responsibilities devolve to line managers and supervisors, each with a technical specialty, whose goals and the rewards for meeting them are also tied to immediacies: "action plans" chunk their work. Each order works from its own time horizons and its agenda of concerns and commitments.

Mark, the work scheduler who recognized that this work required a "higher risk designation," has a job where his daily goals and rewards depend on looking ahead. So does Dan, usually a work scheduler but a shift outage manager during the time of this event, whose job is "programmed to think a little bit ahead."

Is there something about asking questions when you're trying to always go forward—do people think that asking questions slows things down? Or is this just not a habit that people would have?

I think there's always time pressures. But I don't think there's time pressure of the nature that management would say, "Don't do something because of time pressure" if it was important to do. But of course, there's always time pressure. But "Is it managed?" is really the question. And I believe the management at the unit, if posed a question that would delay things but was important, would explore that. I do believe that. But to answer your question, Yes, there is time pressure, and does that inhibit asking questions? I think at one time it might have at this utility, but I don't believe that's the case anymore.

A habit. I'm not sure of that. I think that would vary a lot from person to person. I would not say that was an organizational habit per se. I think that might be an individual thing. In my specific role in this, I usually tended to ask questions on what could upset the plan for moving forward, or what else has to be done to execute the plan. So in that regard I do ask questions, because my job was to insure that things went off as scheduled. So I would try and think of things that might pose problems to that, so in that regard it's the exact opposite. My job was programmed to think a little bit ahead on what could get in the way and to make sure it doesn't get in the way of moving forward. So that's sort of a built-in asking questions, but not in regard to what else could go wrong. It was more in regard to my job of insuring that things moved forward. So in that regard personally I did ask a lot of questions in that ten-month period I was a shift outage manager.

"Moving forward" can be helped and hindered by "sitting back." Stan, a member of the oversight group, recalls that when he brought up the question of the procedure for an infrequently performed test and evolution, he told line managers, "You guys are out there doing a science project."

I'm the guy in [the IRT report] at the [plant operations review committee] at midnight who said, "has anybody reviewed it as an IPTE to see if it needs a special procedure?" And they hadn't. And I'm the one that said, "Well, I'm going to have to not let you go forward with this until you do this, because you haven't evaluated it, and I think it needs to have a special procedure. You guys are out there doing a science project." Well, it didn't come across quite as strongly or as adversarial, because it was me in the room against the line management.

By the time the IPTE was approved the next day, senior managers seem to have had enough of what Nick (a maintenance mechanic who wrote the original work order that managers moved up on the schedule) calls "bulling our way through it."

In my opinion, it was the typically tunnel approach to getting something done around here, bulling our way through it. It started out as something that should not have been done in the first place, at the time it was done. The plant conditions were never right for it, nor did we realize what the plant conditions should have been. . . . This valve was originally scheduled for a refueling outage when you have a defueled core and the only head of water above it would be the refuel cavity . . . with no fuel in the pot, or even if there's fuel in the pot, it's a lot less head of water and no pressure. And they decided to go in and do this one [with the RCS] under pressure. And it went south on 'em. . . .

Somebody, whoever, or somebody in whatever chain it was, a manager decided to do the valve [move it up on the schedule], they went after the valve, something went wrong. That's when they brought engineering in. There was some words and discussions and misunderstandings, and maintenance then went back out there and removed this packing again, after they had reduced pressure, and it came at 'em again. And at that point it was all rescue attempts. . . . they saw the backseat was not holding and they had to rescue it. That's when the tunnel vision really narrows down. Rescue to stop it from leaking. It's pretty much whatever that costs. . . .

You started out by saying, "That's the way we do things around here"—"tunnel vision, bulling through." Tell me more about that.

Bull-in-a-china-shop stuff. We do it in spite of ourselves. If you persist long enough with something you eventually get it done.

Does that mean that it doesn't have a wider focus, or that the consequences—

Sometimes you have to stop and ask, "What are we doing here?"

The Parts Template

"The biggest failure of the industry is that the views of design and ops are polarized," claims Sam, a systems engineer at Overton Station who long worked in operations. The accidents at Three Mile Island and Chernobyl could have been avoided, Sam said, if "the people with the nuts and bolts knowledge had talked with those on the theoretical side." Operations at Three Mile Island, he claimed, hadn't been prepared for the situation that arose, but some engineers "fully understood what was going on, but weren't talking to them. . . . If I were to judge the quality of a station's operations, it would be how operations and engineering are tied together. There should be less bureaucracy to interfere in their relationship." The disconnects throughout this event inspire this excursion into historical and cultural wellsprings of the "machine bureaucracies"—functionally divided responsibilities—that characterize most high consequence enterprises.

On that three-week peer review of a European plant, we worked in subteams organized by function, meeting daily with our departmental counterparts for discussions and to observe activities, from early morning through lunch into the midafternoon. Then each subteam reported its observations for the full team's analysis. By the end of the second week, one concern we shared was that employees seemed not to be well-informed about other functions' activities. Team members knew that, at the least, most work orders need cross-department discussions. Each morning each subteam met with our counterparts to recount the full team's discussions of the previous afternoon, to give them the opportunity to correct our understandings (English was the official language) or explain themselves further. One morning I mentioned that the team was puzzled by this seeming lack of cross-departmental knowledge. "When we were getting ready for your visit, we felt that we should not speak about matters that others are responsible for, in case we wouldn't provide the team with the right answers." That satisfied our concern. The team leaders were surprised, however: they had not realized that their visit protocol organized strictly by function could lead local experts to distort their actual knowledge and practices.

Similar turf reservations appear in a pilot study of station experts' "mental models." John S. Carroll, professor of organizational behavior at the Sloan School of Management, Massachusetts Institute of Technology, asked four employees—two from maintenance, two from operations—to reanalyze a few examples he had prepared of "problems, surprising incidents, or issues that provoke a need to know more." Occurring at other stations, these had been well publicized within the industry.

> The most dramatic result was the immediate reaction of the maintenance employees when asked to respond to a situation whose presenting symptoms occurred in the control room. They felt very uncomfortable answering "operations" questions; in fact they are trained to refer problems outside their own expertise to appropriate other groups. It was suggested that I would get better results if I asked operations to answer operations questions and maintenance to answer maintenance questions. . . . This reaction demonstrates that . . . this particular plant relies upon a division of labor by expertise. Although this is a necessary feature of reliable operations, i.e., people should not mess with things they don't understand, the unwillingness to address hypothetical issues suggests that the barriers between functional groups may be quite high. . . . [T]he degree of discomfort was much higher for the maintenance than the operations people; there is an understanding that operations is supposed to know about everything and that operations is higher status than maintenance.[6]

"Silos" reflect a walled-off understanding of the division of labor, which, like specialties everywhere, can foster a trained incapacity for taking wider contexts into account. Doing what they're supposed to do, specialists narrow things down—as in the "overconfidence" of the valve mechanics and their supervisors perhaps. To them, one valve out of four thousand is a valve no matter where it is: theirs is a global "skill of the craft" ready to do its part.

In the regulatory and engineering orders of things, stations' silos become like pieces on a chess board. As Steven said, there is "an engineering piece, a maintenance piece, an operations piece," each having a place within a well-understood, institutionalized hierarchy of respect, influence, and authority: design engineering at the top, operations in the middle, maintenance at the bottom, in this industry's version of a machine bureaucracy. And of what is a machine made? Parts: components assembled into subsystems, configured into systems.

Thinking in terms of parts has been a constant from this industry's beginnings. In the early 1960s, General Electric and Westinghouse priced and sold each reactor as a "part" based largely on its design costs, a strat-

egy that ultimately cost them about $1 billion according to some esti-
mates. After selling twelve "turnkey plants" at a fixed price, the companies learned that they had "greatly underestimated how expensive it
would be to build [the total plant]." After vendors stopped selling their
"loss leaders," utilities continued to buy whole plants in "parts," "buying
the reactor from one company, hiring a second to design the plant, a third
to build it, and so on."[7] Today, for example, in four U.S. plants having the
same owners, two nuclear steam supply systems (reactor and associated
systems) are from the same manufacturer, two are each from different
manufacturers; one manufacturer made the turbine for two plants, another for the other two; the design engineering firm for two plants is the
same, the other two each had a different engineer; the construction firm
was the same for three plants, different for one.[8] Those at any station
during its construction lived through the step-by-step process of building
the station part by part, piece by piece for anywhere from six to ten years
before coming on line.

On material grounds, a parts mode of thinking pervades regulatory and
professional orders: every part needed to maintain the capacity for safe
shutdown passes extra reliability tests to meet standards for delivering
the performance engineers have designed it for; every assembly of parts
passes equally rigorous tests for driving out possible malfunctions. Combined into a megastructure, however, built-in reliability, piece by piece,
subsystem by subsystem, may not add up.[9] In a machine bureaucracy experts may also understand their skills and knowledge as themselves parts
susceptible to being more apart from one another than integrated in the
whole: "pieces," "silos," "owners." The division of parts and assemblies
into "category one" (safety) and everything else (nonsafety) heightens the
hierarchy of parts, sometimes inappropriately, we have heard. The NRC's
oversight was previously guided solely by a "punch list" of category-one
equipment (its "deterministic" approach); now it uses a performance- and
risk-based approach, which nevertheless sustains the safety/nonsafety-
related hierarchy. By default, this parts template, as I am calling this system of knowledge and meanings, furnishes what could only generously
be called a theory of this energized technology *in operation.*

The parts template derives from an "epistemology of engineering" identified by Glenn E. Bugos, historian of business and technology at Stanford
University. In his history of another risky technology, the Navy's F-4
Phantom jet fighter, Bugos finds this epistemology in engineers' designing,
prototyping, assembling, and testing practices used in developing the F-4
between 1954 through the 1990s. Those processes accumulate into the
kinds of knowledge designers need and methods for getting that knowledge.[10] In tracing the "typology of testing" through the kinds of feedback

its different phases provide, Bugos identifies the "cognitive foundations of engineering" and the "types of information" engineers find useful "in their dialogue between the hoped-for and the feasible."[11]

The typology of testing for the F-4 jet fighter suggests the structure of the parts template. The McDonnell Aircraft Company, the Navy's contractor, began by "aggregating" new parts as well as re-using the navy's previously accepted, standardized parts.

> McDonnell envisioned success in terms of making the entire weapon system [jet + weapons] perform optimally [and] the material bureaus of the Navy were dedicated to improving its parts. . . . The Navy's [Bureau of Aeronautics] maintained a list of standard parts that had worked in other jets, as well as the [military specifications] that codified the engineering methods successfully used [in the past]. . . . [The Navy] sought certainty . . . by insisting that McDonnell use standardized parts and standard engineering methods for piecing those parts together. . . . The entire aircraft was an aggregation of parts, and the process of aggregation testing continued through increasingly larger assemblies of parts . . . tested . . . [under] conditions of vibration, barometric pressure, heat transfer . . . [which] more closely approached the environment they would encounter in the finished aircraft.

As the parts were assembled, several other kinds of testing followed: "integration" testing of the design of parts subcontracted to other manufacturers, and "federation" testing that combined "in a single black box the various components previously spread around nooks and crannies in the airframe. . . . Federation implied that the sovereignty of the components would be maintained as it was combined into a whole." "Acceptance testing" followed, when the Navy decided whether to "commit the design to production."[12] After that came "real-life" testing: for about twenty-eight months, twelve prototype F-4s went through trials simulating use "in real life situations—most importantly flying it off an aircraft carrier—to expose and correct 'all the little Murphies' that could go wrong. . . . Navy engineers knew that if they could not anticipate all the F-4's failures, they likely would not anticipate all its capabilities." Nor would the Navy otherwise learn what the pilots' contributions would have to be.[13]

> Much of this active testing showed that radical technology, like the new F-4, could be integrated into an established technological system, like an aircraft carrier, only by making short-term demands on the flexibility and ingenuity of the human operators. When the Navy discovered problems that defied McDonnell's effort at a hardware solution, pilots and crews were trained to adapt and compensate for it. Pilot training became increasingly complex as pilots discovered

the Phantom's technical idiosyncrasies. Maintenance crews passed along their knowledge of the Phantom in increasingly detailed handbooks, trouble-shooting trees and rules of thumb.[14]

In the nuclear power industry, two-dimensional simulations and risk assessments have to suffice until a plant is up and running. Then, testing the performance of its "federated" and "aggregated" components requires a complete production cycle extending over many months, under the gradations of power modes, each responsive to load demands and to scheduled component testing, repair, and replacement. Even so, unlike flight experience gained from many takeoffs and landings, shut down and startup are kept to a minimum given the stress on structures and equipment of the enormous energetic and mechanical forces involved.

The nuclear industry's "testing typology" is continuous: utility owners have redesigned and reconfigured parts in every plant operating worldwide ever since any one of them came on line, as a matter of efficiency or the regulatory necessity to integrate technological advances and replace components. The fundamental reactor design remains distinctive, but each plant's history of changes is unique. "Each time the Air Force changed their F-4s, however, or added a part, they made the proven functions of the entire weapon system less certain." That has been no less true in nuclear power plants where control of the system's overall configuration is an incessant preoccupation; configuration error rates can reach unacceptable levels. "Acceptance testing" occurs after every outage during which hundreds of parts are disassembled, realigned, and reassembled: outage success is measured by the number of days the reactor remains on line after startup.

As at Arrow Station, that same "sovereignty of components" prevails, but to mediate among them—to "federate" them—are those stationwide programs for controlling work on every piece of safety-related equipment and process; for example, at Overton Station, the list runs to about eighty programs, (e.g., materials and products, fire prevention, instrumentation performance, maintaining air-operated valves, personal safety, system integrity, technical specification interpretation and clarification, testing piping for erosion and corrosion). Cross-functional or matrixed teams "aggregate" specialists for each program. To "federate" them, their representatives participate in standing committees, technical review groups, and ad hoc task forces. Layered within these are the convoys of peers and colleagues within a station and elsewhere, on whom experts call for information, help, advice, cooperation. Hallway, phone, and lunchtime conversations are also well-used opportunities. "Integrating" as bridging goes on continuously. Although there may be little choice but to exchange among functions and specialties, command-control principles maintain the rungs of the work system's authority ladder: design engineers at the top, licensed reactor operators next, system or field engineers next, maintenance specialists below them, and those in staff and support functions at the bottom. Yet that authority hierarchy and the knowledge hierarchy are not reliably isomorphic, as the freeze seal misunderstandings make clear. Nor is influence: at Overton Station, a corrective actions expert, frustrated at managers' resistance to recommendations, observed, "This job needs more clout than it has here." In any case, writing corrective actions for departmental "interface issues" is so "difficult," the program's staff at Arrow Station says, that few are. When it comes to contextual conditions, corrective actions are likely to do little more than identify a "lack" of "integration" and "federation" among departments and specialists.

Event palliatives are appropriately pegged to parts, but only up to a point, yet the reactor design model also guides event reviews in examining the context of events. In *What Engineers Know and How They Know It*, Walter G. Vincenti, professor emeritus of aeronautical engineering at Stanford University, declares: "Most complex 'devices' are in fact hierarchical systems, design of which can—indeed must—be organized in accordance with that fact. . . . [The hierarchical breakdown] reduces the original problem to smaller, manageable sub-problems. . . . Design as a whole then takes place iteratively and interrelatedly throughout the hierarchy."[15] In reverse, that becomes a "fault tree," as experts move from barrier to root cause, to decompose an event in terms of engineers' intentions and the condition of each part, as artifact and as person. As effective as algorithms are in assembling parts, they cannot assemble social bridges.

The Arrow event review team's main finding is that because maintenance, operations, and senior managers "lost sight" of the reactor coolant system as a primary barrier, they did not consider worst-case scenarios before proceeding. Each left that "part" to others, as did those who were planning a narrowly conceived fix through the containment wall. "And that put planning back to square one, to develop a plan that we felt met the safety needs of the plant, not merely the technical needs of going in to repair the unit," said Richard. He could not allow a part to be mistaken for the whole.

In the aerospace industry, the parts template continues to thrive, and has "serious" consequences for "system safety." In "large projects with significant software components, the software development organization is often totally divorced from the safety organization, and information flow is nonexistent or limited. Software development activities tend to go on in relative isolation from system safety and other engineering activities.

Serious problems can often be traced to such disconnects." So observes Nancy G. Leveson, a specialist in software safety and reliability and professor in MIT's Aeronautics and Aerospace Department.[16]

Even to themselves, each function and its specialists become "parts" and "tools." As Arrow Station's Brian put it about those working the valve repair, "It's that, to me that's the biggest part, that mentality, 'We've done this a hundred times,' and they don't look at it as 'What could happen?'—the what-if. They don't look at that type of thing. . . . And quite often it turns out to be very complicated and they start finding problems that they could have got into." An Overton Station maintenance supervisor was explaining a gap in communication during an outage. "At the backshift turnover, ops pulled out without talking to anyone about what had been going on. We need to get people talking. They're not there just to stroke a valve." "Tool" commonly designates many things: station programs are "tools"; a primary barrier, including a procedure, is a "tool"; a process or method for doing anything is a "tool." "Tools" may put parts together; they can also keep them apart. Ray's "shortcoming," he volunteered, was in not knowing that there was a higher-risk designation available when he first suspected stem/disc separation. At Arrow Station for twelve years, he understands that maintenance "owns" the plant's four thousand valves; he "owns" the RCS. The event review team declares that maintenance was "overconfident," but valves are its specialty: maintenance was playing its part as a part, its "very talented" mechanics acting as "tools" for "a routine repack."

Borrowing from reengineering jargon, a market order of things partitions internal "owners" and "customers." That gives a nod to the dynamics of interdependence and exchange on the one hand and reinforces turf on the other, as in Ray's personalizing: "my" system; "I have pumps." "The maintenance supervisor knew [about the earlier backseating effort] because he sent the people out there. I didn't know it. I'm in engineering. I'm the reactor coolant system engineer." The independent review team declares: "Management must reinstill in the senior reactor operators that they are ultimately the owners of the plant and that their actions must reflect this fact." Respecting others' property rights, groups may keep hands off what they "own" but in the process leave themselves uninformed (operations did not question maintenance activities; Ray and Rusty were ignorant of the existence of the "higher risk" designation). Consulting with others diminishes "ownership" by diluting it, yet leaves intact "ownership" understood as responsibility and accountability. In practice, the responsibilities of any one function nevertheless include nourishing its built-in interdependencies, but the "sovereignty" of parts can starve them. Dan, an outage manager during this event, regrets defining his duties narrowly.

It wasn't necessarily my responsibility, but I have eyes and ears. I certainly could have observed and made a comment, because I did know pretty much most of the activities that were leading up to actually doing the repack.

"Pride of partnership" would better fit the practical circumstances than a mythic "pride of ownership."

Clanship is another kind of partition preventing exchanges, even among and between units at the same station and among those with the same owner in different locations. Station experts everywhere consider their plant to be unique, each having its own operating philosophy embedded in its unique Conduct of Operations and each with a unique history of modifications, notable operating experiences, memorable managers who have come and gone, and paper trails of their relations with regulators, vendors, contractors.[17] Initiation into the clan begins during the years of construction, often a trying—and satisfying—time. "Plank owners" share special bonds, says Richard.

[T]he maintenance manager . . . is one of the people that I would have less tended to go to with a problem. Usually my first hit would be the tech support engineering manager, because he and I are both plank owners. We go back 20–23 years with the unit, developing it. Seventeen years anyway.

A unit's operators are usually licensed only for that unit (sometimes at the same station for two units, if they are identical). At extra cost, Overton's utility deliberately built stations about 100 miles apart with the same reactor technology to maximize exchange of operating experiences and ideas. But over the years, all agree, disappointingly little occurred. There is also the plain resistance clanship fosters: "We're too different to learn anything from them." I have heard peers from the Institute of Nuclear Power Operators at a workshop for about twenty-five operations managers plead with them repeatedly to get and read copies of an international operating experience handbook that INPO prepares on a regular schedule. This became one of the tasks it took on after the accident at Three Mile Island in 1979 when the industry began to acknowledge that utilities needed to document and exchange details about near-misses and equipment issues.[18] Regional differences among workforces and local cultural systems further intensify solidarity. Stations often mark a particular triumph over previous records or an industry benchmark (outage length, days without injury) with posters and parting gifts for visitors such as pens, T-shirts, pins with unit or station slogans and logos. These burnish clan pride—all to the good for morale, of course, especially important in the remote areas where most stations are located: a nuclear generating station is itself a production satellite, a part apart from its corporate headquarters.

One indisputable fact developed only after the Arrow Station event: a radiograph showed separation of the stem and disc. Apparently, work planning did not request radiography, nor did maintenance. Ray, the system engineer, also did not. Nor, said, Leo, the station's freeze seal specialist, had radiography come up while paperwork was being prepared for the freeze seal. Steven talks about Ray's suspicion of stem/disc separation and how his credibility could have been strengthened.

> *Track that for me. If that suspicion had been conceived of in another category, as an engineering study, for example, and it had gone back to engineering and not to maintenance, what would the procedure at the plant be, do you know? Do you write a condition report for the engineering manager?*

> No, no. It probably would have been followed through in a little bit of a different manner. I don't know from a formal procedure standpoint— a condition report would have generated something, there's no doubt about that. That in itself would have generated a formal response, so that could have been a single stopgap, just there.

> *And the response could have been the study?*

> Correct. Which would have in hindsight turned into a radiography shot of the valve to tell us what condition it was in, would have been a formal measurement of stem position, so it's, "Wow, if we can get to this position, something's wrong." So those would have been the follow-ups from an engineering standpoint. First thing they would have done is the radiography shot.

Throughout these discussions, that is the one spontaneous mention of the fact that no radiography was performed before or during the repair attempt. Only engineering is responsible for developing evidence of the valve's material condition; when engineering does not play its part, maintenance is left to its own devices.

Narrowing down to the job at hand, taking a category designation ("minor maintenance") at face value and routinizing a new problem to make it similar to a well-known one—these can cut work off from ties binding it into a larger scheme. Those strategies are expectable responses to overload, ambiguity, complexity. The event as a whole suggests that there may be more to consider. Not only did many players lose sight of where the work was being done, but generally, "there was not a high awareness" of primary barriers throughout the plant. A stubborn "fossil mentality" coupled with the parts template seem likely sources of blind spots and of "overconfidence," reinvigorated by competitive pressures. Nuclear power production becomes a business little different from any other, as when Clark characterizes single boundaries as "weird." Or perhaps he finds it troubling that defense-in-depth isn't the last word in assuring safe shutdown. "Weird," then, that the comforts of the redundancy principle can be illusory. Ultimately, we are all left alone with "primary barriers"—the fuel cladding, the containment, and the reactor coolant system—and with the "safety system" of the "human element," as Arrow's root cause team emphasized.

"Didn't think to think what else could have happened if the original plan went awry," said Brian. Thinking through, contemplating, reflecting, analyzing, and consulting one another: all are said to have been expected after the fact, but job descriptions may not specify them, nor may schedules allow time for them. Yet, these pages show, station experts no matter their job are unmistakably reflective, thoughtful, frank, and insightful, once taking an hour out of an always busy day of moving forward to sit back.

Chapter Three

Bowie Station: A Reactor Trip and a Security Lapse

EACH OF THESE two events puts us face to face with the most familiar and most often invoked "root cause": "human error." One shut down the reactor automatically, the other violated Nuclear Regulatory Commission security regulations, but without similarly serious consequences. Less dramatic and only seemingly less complicated than those at Arrow or Charles Stations, these events illustrate that only by "going behind"—sometimes far behind—the simplicity of a single mistake do relevant technical and contextual dimensions come into view.

Industrial systems all make some room for the inevitability of mistakes even by highly skilled people, in the same way that they take into account historically validated failure rates of components. Finding ways of reducing the risk of making mistakes at all and making fewer of them is nevertheless a constant concern, as is that of reducing the risk of on-the-job injuries. A station's HUMAN PERFORMANCE PROGRAM is involved in improving the reliability of hands-on work in the control room and in tasks of all kinds throughout the plant. Its goal is to prevent errors and bodily injuries through event analysis, training, and work observations. Event analyses increasingly acknowledge the influence of managerial and supervisory "human performance," not as "human error" but as systemic sources of ERROR-FORCING CONDITIONS.

After giving accounts of each event and excursions into some of the issues and themes their review teams and experts' insights raise, I conclude with an excursion discussing characteristics of the culture of control the two events share.

AN ACCOUNT OF AN AUTOMATIC REACTOR/TURBINE TRIP

On the midwatch shift, running from 7 P.M. to 7 A.M., the control room crew consists of the shift supervisor, control room supervisor, three reactor operators, a field supervisor, and six plant operators. Rotating together, the crew is on its second day back from a daytime schedule. Ned, a field or plant operator at the station for fifteen years, is one of six who

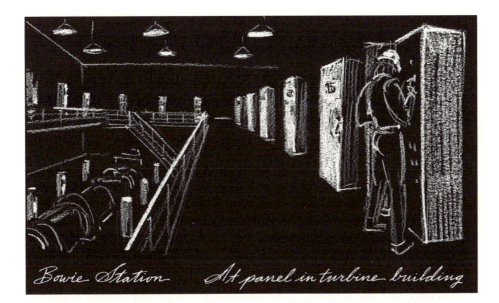

Bowie Station   At panel in turbine building

are trying to pinpoint an electrical ground of some magnitude. An emergency response group in the electrical maintenance department reported the finding in person to the control room, when it became apparent that the ground was not registering on the control room's trouble annunciator.

Alex, a junior reactor operator with several years of experience who had recently become licensed, develops a list of all electrical supplies that could be the ground's source. From that, he and Bob, the shift supervisor, cull only those designated as being nonessential to safe shutdown systems, primarily lighting and heater supply breakers. Because that list is long and the evolution will take a few hours, Bob assigns the work in blocks: operators finish one load list, return to the control room for the next, and each time, Alex, or both Alex and Bob, brief them on its particulars.

The six plant operators work in pairs; one moves around to the designated panels and opens and closes specified breakers. The other stays at the load center elsewhere in the plant where the ground signaled; they are in radio contact with each other and with the control room. The hoped-for result is that after opening a breaker, the alarm at the load center goes off, thereby isolating the ground and making it possible to identify needed repairs. When the midwatch crew begins to implement this troubleshooting plan about 3 A.M., Ned goes to the various panels and his partner stays at the load center. After finishing a few load lists at about 5:30 A.M., and being no closer to finding the ground, Ned comes to the control room for a new list. He goes back out to the turbine building, opens the first panel door on his list, numbered 14S, and as it specifies, cycles all the breakers. The alarm signal remains. The next panel on his list is number 507, also in the turbine building. Opening the panel door, he opens and closes the first breaker, and after opening and closing the second, also without clearing the alarm, he is about to leave when he hears changes in turbine sounds. Immediately, the control room announces a reactor trip over the loudspeaker, and Ned calls to learn what is happening. Not thinking his work is involved, he turns back to close the panel door and sees that its number is 508, not 507, the panel number on his list. He realizes that he must have initiated the trip and further realizes that the first panel where he recycled all the breakers is 14R, not 14S. Panel 507 is at the south end of the second level of the turbine building; 508 is at the north end of the third level and panel 14R is nearby. He radios the control room again to report his mistakes and goes directly there. None of the midwatch crew leaves the station at the end of its shift, waiting for the event review team to begin its interviews. Those end about 11:30 that morning; all are expected back to work by 6:30 P.M. the same day.

Review team members retrace Ned's steps with him in the turbine building and test his self-verification procedures, using a training panel mockup. The final barrier for reducing risk in hands-on work is a procedure called STAR, an acronym for the steps required to confirm to oneself that every action to be taken and then taken matches the action required in the work order in hand. The first step is to *Stop* and get oriented; the second is to *Think*, to understand what the job consists of, to be sure the action is appropriate for current conditions, to consider the expected consequences of actions and decide on actions to take if those consequences do not occur, and to confirm that this is the correct piece of equipment; the third step is to *Act*, to touch the equipment and, keeping a finger on its identifying numbers, match those to the paper work order, and perform the required action; the fourth step is *Review*, to see if the expected response results and then deal with exceptions and to make sure that the action performed is successful. Ned fails the test; he later passes a retest.

Bob, Ned's manager, will have placed a report of his mistakes in his confidential file. The cost of the trip in lost revenues is estimated at $1.5 million; the trip adds a reportable event to the station's regulatory record.

Trip Event Review Team Report

A four-person event review team comes together, including two members assigned from the operations support group to help develop appropriate corrective actions. Art is a member of the corrective actions program group; he often reviews operations' condition reports and participates in event inquiries and root cause evaluations. Greg is with the operations support group as an event investigator. Cal, now in a rotating position, was previously a shift supervisor on the same midwatch crew. Harry, manager of the station's human performance program, joins the team.

In developing information about Ned's actions, the team finds problems with the ground isolation process and observes that breaker labels inside panels are missing. Its report reviews these details.

In wrong panel 14R, all breakers control lighting and Ned's mistakes are inconsequential for plant conditions.

In wrong panel 508, the second breaker Ned opened is unlabeled, but, convinced he was at the correct panel, he correlated it with a "spare" on the breaker list for panel 507. The breaker that Ned opened next, which brought on the trip, had not been "uniquely identified as [having] trip potential."

In panel number 507, "individual breakers" "should not have been included" because this panel "is supplied by a transformer powered off" the load center. That is, panel 507 should not have been in the troubleshooting plan in the first place.

"Load lists . . . did not provide distribution panel locations."

Wrong panel 508 is "physically identical" to 507.

Despite discussing "the potential for a reactor/turbine trip" and reminding operators "to stay away from some specific panels, operator fatigue was not covered in the prejob brief." Load lists omitted panel locations, the prejob brief did not discuss panel locations, and the question of sending out a two-person team for peer checks at each panel did not come up. "The control room staff was overconfident in the plant operator's ability to perform the evolution without error," even though the potential for error was, on the basis of past experience and industry patterns, "more likely" toward the end of the midwatch.

The root cause is "inadequate self-verification and fatigue and overconfidence in performing a perceived low risk evolution," which the team relates to the "prejob briefing which affected the outcome of the event."

The "primary contributing causal factors" are: control room staff's overconfidence in this operator's ability to perform the evolution without adequate backup support; a lack of electrical theory knowledge that electrical grounds are not transmitted through transformers; the lack of a formal process for ground isolation.

Deliberately limited to lighting and heating supplies as a "low risk" evolution, the load list is nevertheless flawed because it is based on an incorrect electrical theory.

The station lacks "an approved formal ground isolation process to ensure operators are provided with the necessary information and guidance to develop and execute an effective plan of action for isolating grounded equipment." In including "subsidiary loads supplied by transformers [powering] off" of the load center, the plan does not recognize that "there is no electrical conduction through the magnetic coupling of transformers [and] grounds can not be sensed across transformers. . . . The ground isolation plan was approved by the unit supervisor and briefed in the control room with all involved personnel in attendance." Licensed operators later disputed this claim on the basis of their experiences with previous trouble-shooting evolutions they had planned and executed.

"Contributing causal factors" are: the trip-making breaker in distribution panel 508 is not uniquely identified inside the panel as having trip potential; the prejob brief could have been enhanced by covering factors that significantly affect human performance (i.e., panel location, operator fatigue, and error-likely situations); load lists used in the ground isolation evolution did not provide distribution panel locations.

An earlier corrective action had called for shift supervisors to conduct one-on-one prejob briefings, but this instruction was not repeated for operators not on shift at the time.

Four months earlier, another operator's failure to self-verify had resulted in a reactor trip; this second trip suggests a possibly systemic issue in that "both events do include [the fact that] backup task verification [a peer check on the spot while one person carries out the task] was not considered because of the overconfidence in these personnel to properly perform the assigned task."

A review of the station's corrective actions database finds that in seventy events over the last three years, employees failed to catch their own error in an increasing trend (18, 24, 28); within the operations department, however, the trend is decreasing (13, 10, 8).

An industry review of similar events over the past three years finds comparable "elements" involved: "night shift" and "late in the shift," which "may have affected the operator's alertness."

The team recommends an immediate "compensatory action": to issue a site-wide briefing sheet to inform all station staff of the "facts of this event" and to suspend all ground evolutions performed by the operations department until a formal process is approved. "Remedial actions" are to compare the event to a previous trip to find "unresolved concerns requiring further action"; to conduct self-verification briefings; to have operations managers discuss the event with other departments for "applicability to their discipline" and to brief their own staff on "the causes and corrective actions of this event."

Nine "corrective actions" are: revise "the *Conduct of Operations* to ensure that error-likely situations, such as fatigue recognition and overconfidence, are discussed in the prejob briefings"; review training curricula to determine "what upgrades are needed for electrical theory training"

and to develop and implement them; develop "a formal process for Operation's ground isolation activities to include as a minimum . . . control of
the evolution from the control room [and] communication of individual
breaker operations"; and to reinforce STAR training for all plant and
reactor operators.

Eight recommendations are for "enhancements": follow up other recommendations with self-assessments; analyze circuit breakers for "single
point failures that could result in a plant trip" and look for other items
with trip potential; add distribution panel locations to load list printouts
that signal their reactor trip potential; install current load list sheets inside
the distribution panels; add the category "prejob brief" to adverse condition report forms; evaluate the increasing trend in self-verification events
and develop corrective actions; and install labels on distribution panels to
warn of trip potential "or significant secondary transient" from specified
breakers.

INSIGHTS AND EXCURSIONS

The issues and themes in the team's findings and experts' insights in our
discussions suggest three problematic conjunctions: between hands-on
mistakes and work schedules, between the original design of the unit and
the demands of operating, and between deregulation and its consequences
for staffing.

"Always Presents Trouble"

For Art, a member of the reactor trip review team who had been a shift
technical adviser and licensed operator, wider conditions and individual
error remain entwined.

> This is one of the one's that's classic. It's like, the operator's out there,
> he's the last one involved. I always ask them, "What did we do to set
> you up?" That's my philosophy on it. And in fact, I think I even asked
> him about going to the wrong panel, "What's the other factors behind
> it? It was late in shift and all that." And he could swear up and down,
> "No, that didn't have anything to do with it. It didn't matter that I was
> going on vacation [the next day]. It's a typical night shift." And I believe
> that, too. I mean what's the cause? Why would you make that kind of
> mistake? It's just the way it goes. I mean you're out there one-on-one
> and such things happen. You reach for the wrong valve or the wrong
> switch. It happens all the time.

It happens all the time?

Sure, it happens all the time. It happens to everybody. It's the reason you have barriers in place to catch them. You see, here he is, five o'clock in the morning and he's out there by himself and he has no buddy with him.

Should there have been a buddy? Is that usual?

I think more and more they're getting to that point, they're checking that.

Bob, supervisor of the control room at the time of the event, recalls:

Part of the review process pointed out that the operator was fatigued, tired. At the time I didn't think so—looking at him, working with him. It may have been true but it didn't show. He didn't say anything. One of the things the report talked about was that the evolution was performed toward the later end of the shift. And sure, there's always—that's one of the things we always consider, especially more so now after this happened. It's late in the shift, if it's a critical evolution, something involved with more hazard to it, more danger to the unit or to the personnel, possibly we should not be doing it. . . .

Did you talk to him yourself after this? Did you get any insights into the reason? It is a puzzle. I mean, psychologists who study human error often come up dry when it comes to what they call lapses or slips.

Yes, I talked to him afterward. All he could say at the time was he was very apologetic. Of course, very. He came up as soon as he heard the plant trip—from where he was at he could hear the equivalent—and he came up as he should and let us know, "Hey, it must, it was me." As a control room staff, we're going through our procedures and at the same time, especially myself as a supervisor, I'm thinking, "What's going on, what's happened?" I need to know what caused the trip so if there's something going wrong we can counteract it. I think he called on the phone and then he came up to the control room, he very humbly said, "I messed up, I was in the wrong, I don't know how it happened, I was in the wrong place." Talking with him later that morning—'cause we ended up staying over for the event review team—before the interviewers started talking with him, he was very—I got the impression from him he realized he was—he was probably half there when he did it. You know, in his mind he was at the right place and he was overconfident. Overconfidence, I think, played the biggest role. "I've been here a long time and I go up there and locate it"—possibly even being in too big of a hurry. I think overconfidence.

Terry, the shift supervisor at the time, points to the closing hours of the midwatch.

From the standpoint of what I would call causal factors, we were on the midwatch—that always presents trouble, you know. And it was late in the shift, it was five o'clock, six o'clock in the morning, and the shift changes at seven, right? Of course, you know, we realize that those are all causal factors, but we try to manage them through different tools and stuff. But it was still a causal factor—it was late in the shift, it was on the midwatch—"Hey, you got fatigue, you know you're not as sharp"—all this stuff kind of plays in.

It plays in, but does it get to be so normal that you don't think about it any more?

Oh, absolutely. You know, the only time it really is thought about is an adverse situation. And you try to sensitize yourself to these causal factors and you automatically try to put compensatory measures in place. In other words, instead of just me sending this guy out by himself, maybe I'll send another guy with him. Peer checking, self-verification, things like that—that's kind of inherent in the business.

None of the four other midwatch operators doing similar evolutions made mistakes, nor do my interviews or the team's report inquire into their prejob briefings or discuss whether peer checks had been considered. Cal, a third member of the event review team, has been serving as an operations specialist on event review teams for two years. Before that he was the shift supervisor on the same crew.

I came from a crew that tended to brief a lot—the crew that did the trip. We tended to brief a lot more than the other crews did. Now as far as whether we actually sat down and thought about "Are you fatigued? Is this six o'clock in the morning and the second midnight?"—I don't think we covered that quite that much before that event happened. What I'm seeing now is a lot more emphasis put on prejob briefs.

The event review team statement was that he knew, he was convinced, he was at the right spot. Have you seen that happen before, with that kind of conviction?

Umm. I think I've even seen it with myself once or twice, where someone pointed out, "This isn't right," and I'd previously looked at it. I'm sure there are other people that have done that.

And he was an experienced person?

Very experienced, yes.

And so you would say that it was the fatigue, toward the end of shift, and all that.

Yes. Umm. I want to say overconfidence on the ability of the person to do that job as far as control room staff was concerned, maybe a little bit of overconfidence in himself, based on his experience, and the number of times he's been in the turbine building, stood the watch.

"Overconfidence" threads the players together: Ned's confidence in taking the assignment in his usual stride and that of the control room crew, which depended on his expertise, no matter the time. The assistant operations manager, Pete, likes people to be "cautious."

I think if you were to take a real close look at errors that occurred in this facility, it's not the guy who's brand new, it's the guy who's had the time to build up his courage. That's the guy that worries me the most. 'Cause he's the guy who thinks he's not going to make a mistake. I want the guy out there who thinks he's going to make a mistake, because he's the one that's going to be most cautious. He's the one that's going to have a peer check, he's the one who's going to double STAR, and then when he's finished doing what's he's doing, he walks off, and comes back and looks again to make sure he did it correctly.

But "caution" has its costs. To Max, the operations manager, I put the question of a design "gotcha."

As far as labeling goes? My understanding on the cabinet was that the external cabinet was labeled and then you opened the door up and got to the breakers, and the breakers are not labeled. So there's not a second wave of checks there.

Just playing devil's advocate—in low light, this punch list of what he's supposed to be checking, you can easily lose your place, it should be double spaced, it should be bigger, etc. So I can imagine myself, fumbling.

Here's one thing I would say. You're probably right. As a matter of fact, I'll take it to the extreme. What we could have done—this is a ground isolation procedure—we're looking for a ground. First of all, the procedure and the process were not very good. We know that. But what we could have done is taken one load at a time and said, "Ned"— good guy, too—"go and go and go to that cabinet and go do it. Not give him a list, but go do it [one by one]. Now, the time to do that— I'm not saying time pressure was an issue—but there are certain balances. That would have been an extreme, to do a ground isolation one item at a time. Let him go out, look at it, spend an hour and come back.
But that starts to push on the parameters of what you're trying to do during the watch, and I would say that there are reasonable expectations that you put upon an individual and although this may not have

been optimum—I don't want to say push back [questioning or doubting him] because it sounds bad—but food for thought—at some point that individual has to be accountable. That's the wrong word—scratch that—he's got to do the right thing. I'm trying to think of an example. I mean, just like you know we all get dressed in the morning. I make sure I've got my tie on, and my belt, you know, I've forgotten my belt before. . . . So I go through that self-check process. In this case, had this individual stopped just for a moment—he was the last barrier—and checked that cabinet, we wouldn't be talking about this today.

If Ned weren't "overconfident," then presumably "being accountable" and doing a "self-check" would include checking himself out: "Am I in a condition to do the work, how pressured do I feel to get it done in a hurry, am I thinking about the end of the shift and my vacation?" To Harry, a manager who oversees the station's human performance program, I put the question:

Could Ned have self-checked and gone to his supervisor and said, "Don't trust me on this one. I either shouldn't do this work or I should be doing it with somebody watching me." Where is that in the system? What response would he have gotten?

We asked him about that, as we were going through the event review. And Ned felt that he wouldn't have a problem approaching his supervisor or approaching the other members of his crew if he felt that he had something challenging his ability to safely and successfully do the job. But there was still something there that in this instance he failed to recognize, or knew that there were some of the indications there [e.g., late in the shift], and felt that he was strong enough to be able to work through those without causing an error.

I asked Max, manager of the operations department, a variation on the same question.

Let's say that of ten error-likely conditions, there were, maybe, three to four present. What if we had asked Ned, as everybody would be asked, "It's up to you to say that these are error-likely conditions in this circumstance that are going to make it harder for you to be good at your job today, or at this moment." What if we said, "You are free to say, 'I cannot really perform this task correctly.' Or 'I shouldn't be here right now, I need to sleep.'" What would happen to such a person?

I honestly believe that that type of feedback would be appreciated. I really do. This is, I think, a unique place to work in that in operations and in many of the areas, we have what's called an open culture. And the culture is fairly facilitative in that if somebody voiced that concern, that concern would be listened to and would be addressed, typically without any type of a penalty. I mean, I honestly believe that. Has it happened in every case? Probably not—it never used to happen years ago. But I believe had Ned said, "Guys, I am tired," if that was the case, or "I think that you're setting me up for failure, here's what I need," there would have been some push back a little bit. But I think as a group we would have come to the right response and it would have been addressed.

Art, a member of the review team who had been a reactor operator, is not so sure.

Well, it's a culture thing. I'm not saying that's never been done, that people have said that, and I think I even have seen that and heard about it or whatever. And the repercussions—if you're saying, "I can't do this tonight, somebody else will have to do it," or whatever, I'm not really sure what the response would be. It would be, "OK, we can get you some help, we'll get someone else," or that maybe all he would have needed to say is, "Send somebody down with me." Those are all valid things to do. But how that would happen here—I don't know if the culture is that far advanced.

The mystery never goes away: Why do skilled people make wrong moves? For some managers, this three-wrong-moves event triggers their spontaneous recall of others, stories they tell in tones drenched in incredulity, stumbling over their words, tripped by black frustration. Pete, the assistant manager of the operations department, is speaking.

I'll tie into a theme there—manipulating the wrong switch, failure to STAR. You have a reactor operator who has a license from the NRC, he's hanging a clearance, getting ready to secure a pump that sends water to one of our chillers that keep our control room cool. He walks back—we got three of those pumps—they're color coded so you can see exactly that red is alpha train, blue is bravo train, yellow is charlie train. We're getting ready to shut down alpha train chiller, chiller's already been secured. Why does he turn off the bravo train pump and end up tripping off the bravo train chillers? I mean red, blue, yellow— he's not color blind. Why did he turn the wrong switch? What were we not doing? Well, there was nobody doing peer check. There was no schedule pressure. Just went back there and turned the wrong switch. It's why, why, why, the why question again. Why did he turn the wrong switch? I don't know. Why didn't he STAR? I don't know, I thought I did. Why didn't he get a peer check? I don't know.

Terry, the shift supervisor, talks about another event "where the error-likely situation became apparent and wasn't recognized." An operator assumed that some fuses "were in the off-position and he needed to turn them on"—the wrong assumption, it turns out.

He would have seen that it was wrong, however, if he had been able to read their current position. But that indicator is a very obscure, benign indication—there's a little notch on the side of the fuse block that reveals the words "on" or "off". . . . The problem is this fuse block is a bakelite material, hard plastic, black, difficult to read, right? It's dark inside the cubicle. All right. So the error-likely situation is, "It's dark. I have inadequate lighting." . . . I'm saying, "Wait a minute guys, you didn't wake up—you should have snapped right there. 'I might screw this up.' " You know, pardon me, but that's what you should feel inside yourself. It's an internal thing, right? And so I said, "Wait a minute, what do we do? You got a flashlight." All my operators carry a flashlight. "All you have to do is turn your flashlight on and look." Now they didn't do that, they didn't take the steps necessary to detect their error. The assumption that they made, that bothered me, but it didn't bother me as much as "Hey, I have something glaring here that should be telling me that I need to take extra precaution."

So what was their response when you said "Use your flashlight"? Did they say "We didn't think of it, we didn't have time," or . . .

Well, one of 'em said, "I just didn't think of it," the other one said, "Well, I didn't have mine." "Oh gosh," I told him, "you're killing me." I'm sitting in my office, right? I said, "Wait a minute. I give you this flashlight, I give you all the batteries, I give you all the bulbs, and in fact if you had come back and said, 'Terry, I left my flashlight,' I'd reach back right here and give you a brand new one. The company would give you a $10 flashlight, just throw it at you, just so that you wouldn't make the mistake." It's not that it wasn't available, and it's not like it's dark in there like it's pitch black—it's just the lighting inside this box is inadequate. I said, "If we have to call electricians to build a light to shine in there, it would be better to do that than assume that we can manage it and not take the steps necessary to remedy the error-likely situation so that we can insure that we get perfect performance." That's really what we're looking for.

And so, they felt, afterward like anybody—it's like anybody, you feel, "Duh." And I don't know, I hate to be presumptuous but I think that we've all been there, oh, oh, oh sure. . . . Any error in the plant, many times the consequence to the plant is usually nil or very small, very rarely do they end up in a situation like this trip. But the supervisory managerial consequences are great. And so, I'll end up with some little human performance issue that I'll have to continue to manage for months and months. So the pain, the real pain is not in these men's arena, it's in my arena. And it's because we're groping to find the solutions.

Art, review team member, revisits Ned's mistakes, shaking his head in bewilderment.

That was what the cause was, he didn't STAR. If he would have starred, he would have looked up there and pointed at that and said that's an 8 not a 7 on that panel. So why doesn't somebody do that when we've told them and beaten them up and trained them and counseled them and talked to them and all that, why do they still make those mistakes? That's the question you're asking.

"We were on the midwatch—that always presents trouble, you know." So it can, according to sleep specialists. And in the nuclear power industry, claims Steven R. Hursh, psychologist at Johns Hopkins University School of Medicine, an aging and depleting workforce, increased demand, increased output, and competition lead to increased time pressure and more fatigue, which increase the risk of error. Sleep deficits accompany "long duty days" and require "recovery sleep," as well as at-work prevention such as peer checks and prejob briefs. Based on studies for the U.S. Air Force, Hursh and colleagues at Science Applications International Corporation developed a "fatigue avoidance scheduling tool" that can also be used retrospectively in event and accident investigations. But the method depends on managers to provide information about schedules and the details of incidents and on employees to keep a sleep history,[1] data that may prove difficult to obtain, given the Nuclear Energy Institute's opposition to the further regulation of working hours (currently the NRC limits work to 12 hours daily during outages, 14 hours when on line).

That industry stance may account for the absence of a corrective action addressing "fatigue," despite the review team's having counted it a "cause." Neither does the team raise the subject in terms of chronic midwatch "trouble," nor is anything made of the fact that the crew was in the second day of its switchover to the midwatch shift. The sole "barrier" or "tool" for "acknowledging fatigue" and preventing the mutual "overconfidence" of operators and supervisors is the prejob briefing. The final "barrier" is the lone person, the "last one involved."

"Elementary Mistake . . . Classic Gotcha"

"Now the operator involved, I don't believe you'll get to talk with him. He's away. But a competent operator, very competent. Been an operator for fifteen years, has quite a bit of experience. Well respected, you know.

And of course this shook him to his foundation, you know, because he has a lot of pride about himself and being a good operator, and how could he be involved in such an elementary mistake that had severe consequences?" So asks Terry, shift supervisor during the event. Bob, control room supervisor, finds the "mistake" a "classic gotcha."

> This evolution I guess it was one of those classic gotcha's, it wasn't a dangerous evolution, it should have been very simple. . . . During the brief, no one asked him if he knew where the cabinet, the panel was located. That's probably because they made the assumption he would know where it's at. I mean, there are a lot of panels, I may not remember where they're at, but I know the general location and I just go up there and find 'em. It might take an extra minute. He knew the general location was mid-deck or 55 foot of the turbine building. If he didn't know, if he had asked in a brief, we have a book of locations in the control room. He didn't ask, he wasn't asked. That was one of the points that came out during the investigation, "Was he asked where the panel was located?" No.

Uncharacteristically, an experienced operator makes an "elementary mistake" expensive in company dollars and in professional reputation. Heads shake in awed disbelief, including Ned's. The mistake is triply *wrong*—a reactor operator includes a wrong panel in the troubleshooting plan, Ned goes to two wrong panels and inevitably opens a wrong breaker—yet, the corrective actions imply, these mistakes are avoidable only by widening the scope of prejob briefings, adding warnings of "trip potential" to breaker labels, improving an existing troubleshooting procedure. Ned is not alone in making the mistake of working on the wrong equipment: such errors of commission, as they are called, are not rare (nor are errors of omission, leaving out a step or not planning a task, such as not designating a work order "higher risk"). Among commission errors, according to a study in one Japanese nuclear power plant, out of a total of 455 near-incidents reported over a 30-year period, the "incorrect selection of equipment or parts" accounts for 46 percent of the total of 219 errors in operations, 32 percent of 177 errors in maintenance, and for 46 percent of 59 errors in radiological control. The second most frequent commission error is working at the "wrong position or location": in operations, 36 percent, in maintenance 49 percent, and in radiological control 27 percent.[2]

At stations built with twin units side by side, experts can make the mistake of working on the wrong *unit*. The Kansai Electric Power Company of Japan studied "unit confusion" in 1995 and 1996 at two of its stations, according to its manager of quality assurance and human factors, Teruo Tokuine. At Ohi Station, an operator opened a valve in unit

1 when he should have opened it in unit 2. The units "have almost the same design, and the operators of auxiliary equipment take care of both units." Their "operating environments" are also similar, yet managers had given "simultaneous" instructions for carrying out different tasks on both units. Before opening the valve with the correct number in unit 1, the operator did not also check the unit number that precedes it; the valve numbers are identical on the two units.[3] The event revealed other kinds of wrongs: each unit's number did not appear in the passageway to it and this locked valve should have been accessible only to a supervisor with a key. About five months later, at the company's Takahama Nuclear Power Station, also with twin units, an operator brought on an automatic shutdown: the relay panels of both units are adjacent; the "unit number is located high on the panel, where it is difficult to see"; the panels are visually identical; the nameplates have an identical appearance and name; the operator "must move from the front to the back of the same panel many times"; the "procedure requires frequent repetition of movements."[4]

"We managers had a feeling of crisis that the awareness of the need to avoid repeating human errors might not have spread sufficiently among all the employees . . . and that the same problems might occur in the future."[5] From a "Human Factors Improvement Promotion Committee" of experts in headquarters and in regional offices came recommendations such as color coding (for doors, walls, columns, and for "work notices and work slips"); additional nameplates; "large unit number signs"; physical partitions between adjacent panels of different units; bar codes on valves for checking by portable terminals. The committee also recommended documenting and publicizing past incidents and inviting "lecturers from other fields, such as railroads and aviation" to speak on human factors and safety.[6]

At Overton Station, two electrical technicians conducting a functional test misread blue-line drawings and inadvertently closed a steam generator valve, which set off a turbine and reactor trip. Afterward, a supervisor broadcast an e-mail to all electrical technicians.

Confusions over drawings are "a potential human factors 'gotcha' that we must be aware of!" In response to a recent event, a great idea was proposed (that some of you have been doing as a good work practice for years to keep you out of deep . . .). THE PRACTICE: While troubleshooting using [drawings] for those devices, links, etc. that do not have the cabinet/box/panel name next to it (the ones with the * next to them with a number that you have to go down to the legend to find what the sucker is), write in red (black, blue, green . . .) ink the cabinet/box/panel name next to the device or sliding link. Uhhhh??? If you understood that, you're ready to come up and write procedures! Simply put . . . mark up your drawings, putting cabinet names, locations, and any other info next to the device, link, or wire that you plan to take some action on. The idea is to use this as a positive self-checking mechanism. A verifier may also use this, placing a check mark or whatever by the markings placed by the doer. . . . Please consider using this work practice as your own. It's simple, won't take much time, and may save your butt one day . . . or someone else's in a very real sense. If you don't understand my ramblings, please see Jack Drew. He's forgotten more than I know about how to keep straight on drawings.

Under good light, I found the blue-line lettering blurred, and commented to the department manager about the low light conditions throughout the plant, compared to those in the control room. He agreed. "We've made the wrong-cabinet mistake hundreds of times but it never tripped the plant before." Maybe "hundreds" is his exaggeration, maybe not. Wrong actions are not rare, yet, according to one root cause analysis consultant, Dr. William R. Corcoran, "most so-called 'root cause trees' and causal factor coding schemes do not include mix-ups. Thus the trending systems of most organizations are incapable of showing how widespread mix-ups are."[7]

"Design-based gotcha's" coming to light in events can also be design-*basis* problems in the original design of systems, structures, and components, from which technical specifications develop. In 1997, spurred by discoveries at Millstone Nuclear Power Station as well as to prepare for the advent of risk- and performance-based regulation and to find ways to reduce "unnecessary regulatory burden," the NRC commissioned an engineering study of design-basis issues (DBI) identified in licensee event reports. Under its deterministic approach, the NRC had made mandatory the repair and/or replacement of all deficient safety-related components and systems; now, each is to be analyzed individually for its significance for safe shutdown.

Between 1985 and 1997, more than 3,100 licensee event reports identified design-basis issues, an average of about 240 annually. Plants licensed before 1975 generally reported more than those licensed after 1984 (older plants, an average of 6.1, newer, 3.6). This engineering study found that increases were a consequence of specific regulatory initiatives (safety system functional inspections and outage modification inspections). The more design-basis inspections, the more design-basis issues that regulators and station staff found, and vice versa. Using 1997 as a checkpoint, the consultants reviewed individually all 1,975 licensee event reports received that year from 110 operating stations to verify their cause determinations; in most cases, NRC staff agreed with station experts' conclusions.[8] Of these, DBIs constituted about 29 percent of the total, and of these 563, the consultants ranked 449 by "potential risk significance." Of those, the majority involved "either minimal risk or no risk significance." Three of twenty-six safety-related systems account for about 58 percent of the potentially risk significant group: emergency core cooling (33 percent), emergency AC power (15 percent) and containment and containment isolation (10 percent). Of all DBIs, fewer than 1 percent were also present in ACCIDENT SEQUENCE PRECURSORS (ASP) according to probabilistic risk assessments—that is, conditions estimated to be implicated in an uncontrolled radiation release. "However, 60 percent (3 of 5) of the ASP events for 1997 involved DBIs. Thus, although the percentage of DBIs that are risk significant is very small, it may be expected that, to the extent that ASP events occur . . . DBIs may continue to be an important contributor."[9]

To overcome design basis issues often requires major modifications and equipment upgrades, which may bring new issues. Under risk-based regulation, these changes will be assessed in terms of ASP scenarios. But, as with any design changes, other issues can arise, especially when "the people with the nuts and bolts knowledge" don't talk "with those on the theoretical side." Testifying to the difficulty of having that conversation is a group of design engineers formerly in the utility's corporate engineering department, who talked about their experiences after working as system engineers for about eighteen months at Overton Station.

> CARL: In design engineering, unless you brought yourself out here on a weekly trip and really buried yourself into it, you'd have few meetings with operators. There was no formal educational process or assigning you out to the plant for three months and let you see how it goes, like writing procedures and seeing how operators deal with signing things on the schedule and what happens in a daily status meeting. We were never offered that opportunity. At one time there was a discussion of rotation, but only a limited amount. The general population of design engineers are not trained as to what's going on out here.
>
> BART: I used to come down about twice a month and on an as-needed basis. It used to be like we were consultants about the long term. I'm now in the plant every day, and it's really been enhanced for me working with the shifts and the craft instead of making two trips a month.
>
> JOE: The change was devastating to me—it took me a year to feel I was making significant contributions.
>
> ANNE: You get thrown from an office environment to a plant environment. It's a lot different. We used to do a minor mod and never knew what kind of problem it was for plant people to actually get it done.
>
> ANDREW: Tasks were so different. I'm dealing with a whole set of different facts. Now you're not concerned so much with the concept of what's going on or what needs to be going on as to the actual operation of the plant. As a designer you're putting it on paper so someone can

go build it. You're incorporating your safety requirements and all this into your design so it's going to be what the plant needs, or what your concept is of what you think they need. And then you come out here and all of a sudden it's a day-to-day business. "Hey I just blew this fuse and I need you to help fix this" . . . so you went from an overall long-term focus to having to deal with something on a day-to-day basis.

BART: Most definitely for the new generation of power plants, there needs to be a trial basis—hands-on work in the field to get appreciation for the maintenance work, the operations work, the performance testing that's done—the limitations that the *physical* plant has versus what it has in a designer's mind. That's been a major realization for me.

Design issues are operational constants, and being "scrunched up" to make a test or do repairs or inspect equipment goes with the territory. Recounting details of their work systems, several Overton experts mentioned "the love pipe." "Oh, it's a pipe you have to hug to get by—so we keep writing 'Love' on it." During the station's construction, vendors installed a major component barely accessible for maintenance, but when station managers complained that it would be "a nightmare" to get at, designers told them, "It will never fail." It did.

" 'Design gotcha's' " originating in the design basis, in modifications, or in black bakelite components can transform into the "benign little transient," which, according to Terry, "major events in the nuclear industry . . . typically start with." But being remote in time and space from the work that the Neds do, design engineers can maintain their "concept of what you think they need" and aren't exposed to "the limitations that the *physical plant* has," which they may exacerbate. The "designer's mind" no less than that of any station expert making "an elementary mistake" needs also to be scrutinized.

"Years in the Trenches"

As the competitive pressures of rate deregulation are reconfiguring nuclear generating stations' demography, newcomers are appearing more frequently in this old-line industry renowned for job security and benefits. The newcomers appear in fewer numbers than the industry says it needs, however, especially since the nuclear navy is no longer a steady source. Newcomers of another kind are like Alex, a recently licensed operator. For several years, he had been a plant or field operator while he worked toward the bachelor's degree that made him eligible for operator license training; nuclear utilities began to introduce a degree requirement after the accident at Three Mile Island. Before rate deregulation and downsizing, oldtimers maintained their majority, partly with the help of an industry tradition, according to one of their number at Overton: "They never fired anyone in this industry. They just put them off into another position."

That confluence of newcomers and oldtimers appears to have watered down Alex's prejob brief, according to Art, member of the trip review team.

What about the management systems here? Do they get a finger pointed at them now and then too, in terms of setting people up?

Oh yeah, we blame management all the time. All our investigations go back to supervisory and management oversight as being less than adequate—organizational problems. I think that's probably—in the majority of them, that is the real cause. You know again, unless the guy maliciously did something wrong, it's always going to fall back on, "How did we set him up?" or "What are we not doing?"

What are your top three of what would be a management systems issue, something you can see over and over again as an issue. Which ones of those do you think haven't gone away?

Umm. {long pause} I think I'd put a lot of it on the immediate supervisors to make sure the guy's not going to screw up, to give him what he needs, his tools. But by the same token, those supervisors are, I'll say, thrown into those positions and they just don't have the time and experience. Management needs to take the responsibility to make sure that they're [supervisors] doing those things and learning those behaviors to help out the guys in the field.

Why do you say they're "thrown into those positions"?

It's just my perspective.

How do you mean?

I look at it from where you had a shift supervisor that's been on the job for ten years, where now you have a shift supervisor that doesn't have that vast experience behind him.

Why has that happened?

One reason it happened is they came and got rid of or replaced all of the old-time shift supervisors that don't have college degrees with the younger men and women that have degrees.

When did that happen?

Probably four or five years ago when the management changed. If you didn't have a degree, they kind of rotated you out, and those were the people that had the ten and fifteen years of experience. Now you have people that I won't say are not competent or not qualified, but they just lack the years of operational time. You know, you just miss that, and you get a whole crew together that's like that, you know they just haven't seen as many things or are in tune with as many things. They respond in different ways and sometimes it works and sometimes it doesn't. That's a culture change that I think sometimes comes behind the scenes here that we rarely put any emphasis on. I mean the guys that I went to [license] class with are now shift supervisors in five years. That may or may not be a long time to some people, but there's a lot to say for having five years as an operator rather than two years or whatever to get promoted to shift supervisor. . . . Ned's been out in the field for the last twelve years, fourteen years, and he had a new control room operator [Alex]. That supervisor-worker relationship, that's a hard one.

Not only is Alex a less experienced reactor operator and Ned's supervisor, Alex also represents a "culture change" that may be difficult for old-timers like Ned to accommodate. Or, Harry, manager of Bowie's human performance program, suggests, it could go the other way—perhaps Alex was shy about giving a briefing to an experienced oldtimer. Harry joined the review team because the event "was thought to be a pure human performance error."

The panels have very clear placards with large lettering on them. Ned said that he physically put his finger on those, looked at his paper work, and in his mind, he read the same numbers on both. And once he did that he felt that he had confirmed the right point, opened up the panel door, and once the panel door was open, then any additional opportunities to validate that you were at the right location really went away. There were organization and programmatic issues dealing with labeling of panels, the labeling of the breakers, the effectiveness of the prejob briefs.

There were in my mind cultural issues in the prejob brief. There's almost an invisible line where, "I understand your strengths, your capabilities, your knowledge, and I don't want to intrude on those by asking some questions that might actually cause you a little discomfort, because you feel I'm asking a question that's intuitively obvious, that's something below you to ask." For that shift, Ned was the most senior turbine building operator. He's been out at the site for, I think, fourteen years or so. And so there was this trust between the crew and Ned to say, "We can give you a very abbreviated brief, we don't need to ask about location, we don't want to insult your intelligence by asking questions that we might ask someone who's not as skilled or as experienced." And that was part of what helped set Ned up, where that prejob brief wasn't as effective as it could have been.

In my conversation with Bob, I raised the question of peer checking. I told him about an event at Overton Station where two craftsmen had been assigned a task, one of whom was designated job captain and assigned to make the peer check, but he didn't.

> We have a case a lot of times in the control room, we have what we call—we have folks from other departments such as engineering that come in and get instant SROs [senior reactor operator licenses], we call them. They have degrees or previous experience like in the navy or at another plant, and to qualify to get a senior reactor operators' license they go through classes. But they don't have the years in the trenches, you might say. And when I started, I started off as a plant operator in the field for the years during construction, then got my RO [reactor operator] license and was an RO for five or six years and then got my senior license, and then became a supervisor. I guess I'm fortunate when I interface with folks in the control room, I've got more seniority, I've been here longer than they have and seen things they haven't, so I feel they listen to me. And that's because I do know, I've seen a lot, I know what I'm doing.
>
> But I see at times, folks that are supervisors, who are the instant SROs, struggle with that, because they're put in a position to supervise even a reactor operator that doesn't have the same level license, but he has more experience. The SRO may come across a situation he hasn't seen before—of course you can't train for everything—so he may not have the knowledge ability to tie everything together just from being here so long—like you know that a little change here causes a change way down the line. So you know the symptoms and what to look for. That hurts them even though they're good supervisors. I've talked to some reactor operators, kind of chastise them [for being down on the SRO], "Don't do that. You know, he [the SRO] may not have the same experiences, but you still need to respect him."

Seniority, qualifications, and experience increasingly do not come together in a single person, as stations recruit to fill positions inside and outside control rooms left by those retiring or laid off.

"Backsliding"

Emphasizing a degree requirement for reactor operator licenses is one of many changes utilities are making to respond to deregulation, or the prospects of it, as well as to the new regulatory regime. By one count, 60 percent of U.S. plants are now affected by a change of ownership or a corporate reorganization: of 103 operating plants in 31 states, 76 are in states moving toward open retail electricity markets.[10] Those changes also mean layoffs and the departure of those with intimate knowledge of, for example, undocumented equipment vagaries and local knowledge that, as Bob said, "a little change here causes a change way down the line. So you know the symptoms and what to look for." The Electric Power Research Institute, a private research firm specializing in electric utilities, heralded a proposed study, "Capturing Undocumented Worker-Job-Knowledge."

> Workforces are aging, expert knowledge and skills are being lost, and qualified replacements are increasingly difficult to find and retain. Furthermore, expert personnel are not always available when needed. The unavailability of valuable knowledge, and, more specifically *tacit* (or undocumented knowledge) . . . can have negative operational, environmental, safety, and economic consequences . . . since such knowledge is unique, known to one or very few individuals or teams, and not available to others in procedures or through normal training. . . . The potential for such problems is expected to grow as deregulation accelerates and companies strive to reduce costs.[11]

In 2000 Exelon Nuclear, a nuclear generating company, announced 2,900 job cuts in the 14 units it operates.[12] Exelon Nuclear had been formed primarily from the merger of PECO Energy, a Philadelphia-based company, Commonwealth Edison of Illinois, and AmGen, which has a British partner. In August 2001, Exelon Nuclear announced the elimination of 138 jobs in the parent company, reducing the total to 300, explaining "that the layoffs were based on eliminating job redundancies and were necessary to deliver electricity at a competitive price."[13]

The latest in a series of layoffs at Bowie Station, which began about five years earlier, came up in a discussion with fourteen people in its corrective actions program, including their manager. Here are a few voices.

> The backlog of maintenance requests is filling up again like it did before. . . . Preventive maintenance is being deferred—the backlog increased by 500 percent since 1995. . . . People think that we're sliding back to the culture that we had before.
>
> Along with the technical side of it, the soft open-ended things we're sliding backwards on also. . . . In the past we had a culture here where you'd shoot the messenger for the problems identified. . . . Now we're kind of backsliding once again to a point where it's a little more difficult to speak up, a little more difficult to bring that up because everyone is working under pressure, people are stressed out or whatever. It starts to show with the simplest request you may make—you may get more negative feedback than you did in the past.
>
> Managers seem to say, "We'll get the workload down to where there are 200 less people who can do it effectively. A few hundred people go

away, and then we figure out what to do, how to manage it, what to cut"—that's the impression I get. . . . We got rid of the bodies, now we're going to figure how to manage it, as opposed to figuring out, "We know we've got a process as lean and mean as possible that we can do with 30 percent less people," so we'll say, "Let four people go—instead of the six who had been asked to leave."

It goes without saying that tradeoff quandaries are the essence of the design of just about anything. In high consequence technologies, negotiating tradeoffs is an expectable, stable, patient process, often formalized with signoffs and conducted with long-term perspectives on the availability of supplies, materials, tools. During operations, tradeoff quandaries also have a permanent place. Especially over the last ten years, as market order has been ascendant, operational tradeoff decisions are likely to be more reactive than prospective, more short-term than long-term (except for those concerning very costly maintenance, such as replacing steam generators). Sudden staffing shifts have been replacing gradual attrition at a time when recruiting and the population of qualified people have lagged. That change of pace puts design tradeoffs to the test: those have assumed a stable operating environment and commensurate margins of safety. In general, whenever there is an unexpected or anomalous situation, whether or not directly threatening safe shutdown—very high winds, for example—the regulatory requirement is that plants monitor and report on this UNUSUAL CONDITION. The instabilities brought on by deregulation and its consequences seem to qualify as worthy of being watched as well.

AN ACCOUNT OF A SECURITY LAPSE

As the start of a refueling and repair outage draws closer, Bowie Station prepares to welcome 1,200 technicians and craftspeople who will more than double its population for the next two months around the clock. As employees of contractors specializing in nuclear power operations and maintenance, they will work with permanent staff members in many departments: mechanical maintenance, instrumentation and control, radiation protection, computer maintenance. Ordinarily, line managers request about eight hundred additional experts every eighteen months for refueling outages of the station's two reactors, each scheduled alternately at times of lowest electricity demand and for the least possible number of days. Now a major component is to be repaired, and even with two months to make it happen, time will be short.

Entrance to any plant requires qualifying for a badge that designates a permitted level of access to plant zones defined by proximity to the reactor core and the expected level of exposure to radiation. Even for repeat contractors, a badge does not carry over outage to outage nor to another contractor; each has a specific expiration date. Every person must qualify for security clearance, administered at Bowie Station by its "access authorization group" of six "coordinators" who review the employment histories and other personal information every pending arrival provides. The group's goals are to prevent entry of those who might damage equipment, harm others or injure themselves, or threaten radiological controls. Those concerns continue after becoming badged, for employees as well; two programs are designed to prevent any untoward behaviors. Under the FITNESS FOR DUTY program, everyone is subject to random drug and alcohol screens (once I waited for mine alongside Overton's station manager), and the CONTINUAL OBSERVATION program, in which supervisors and peers look out for signs of colleagues' stress or fatigue, for example.

In their offices at a gate reserved for contractors on a far side of the site, the coordinators examine each person's file, develop additional information as needed, and interview every person, all to discover the "derogatory information" that would deny "unescorted access" to protected areas, the highest security status. That status confers a picture badge, a coded card for entry into radiological and other protected areas, and a dosimeter for recording radiation exposure. Without that badge, in these areas a contractor has to be constantly within the sight of a station employee with the correct level of access. Not meeting any one of these criteria for unescorted access is cause for its denial: failing to pass a drug or alcohol test within the past three years, being convicted for a criminal offense, failing a standardized personality and attitude test, and providing false information or intentionally omitting requested data. A utility spends about $5,000 per person for these data and for independent background checks to verify their accuracy. Every reviewed file receives a second look from another coordinator as an independent check. When derogatory information is found, the supervisor also reviews the file, and in any case the supervisor has the final say on badge level. Of those experts contractors send, 25–30 percent do not meet the criteria for unescorted access to the zones where most of their work is likely to be performed.

One morning, Meg, a coordinator, reviews the file of a craftsman, Wade, and, on the basis of a preliminary report from the firm making the station's background checks, approves interim unescorted access. Later that day, a follow-up fax arrives with the information that Wade's previous employer reports past "instances" of his failing drug and alcohol tests that were administered as a condition of that employment, but the reports also state that that employer would rehire him if he passes the tests. Seeing the fax the next morning, Meg recognizes that because the failures occurred during Wade's employment within the last three years, it constitutes derogatory and disqualifying information. She does not question Wade about why he had not revealed the information in his work history or in her interviews with him during the initial badging process. Such omissions are themselves cause for denial.

The group's supervisor, Neil, nominally reports to the manager of "plant protection," but that position has been unfilled for several months. Meg telephones him. Because he is filling in for the missing manager, Neil is working elsewhere on the site. She tells him about the information in the fax, and, responding to Neil's question, says that she did not think the information met the criteria for denial, explaining that according to the fax, the contractor would rehire Wade if he passed subsequent tests. Meg assumes that the contractor applies the same three-year rule for re-hire as do nuclear facilities, so, she assumes, the tests must have been mitigated or dismissed if this company had rehired Wade. She does not tell Neil that Wade's failed tests occurred within the past three years, nor did Neil ask. Neil is assuming that the fax relates to information in Wade's file that he failed to pass a drug/alcohol screen in 1985, which Neil had evaluated the day before. Meg adds a memo to Wade's file documenting a review of the derogatory information and approval of Wade's "interim" unescorted access. Upon receipt of additional information, procedures allow that that status may or may not be upgraded to "full" access.

After nearly a month, Wade completes his task for his current contractor, and as is customary, his access to Bowie Station is revoked. Within about a week, Wade applies for reinstatement to work for a second contractor. Another coordinator, Matt, examines his file and sees the fax with the failed-test information. After discussing the matter with Meg, Matt is satisfied that the issue is resolved, but he also sees gaps in Wade's employment record and requests a further background check. In the meantime, Matt interviews Wade about the gaps; feeling satisfied with Wade's replies, he recommends interim access reinstatement. The file then goes to Dale, another coordinator, for the independent check; Dale accepts all previous evaluations of the test-failure and other information and approves the unescorted access.

Two days later, Meg is the first to see a fax coming in on the group's machine, which provides the full background check report Matt requested. But Meg's duties have changed. Andrea is now performing those duties, so Meg documents receipt of the fax in the appropriate database; she does not read it when she puts it into Wade's file. About three weeks later, Meg transfers Wade's file to Dale, who is responsible for upgrading interim access to full unescorted access.

About a week later and before Dale acts on the new information, Andrea reads the full background report. It says that the previous firm had fired Wade for failing the drug screen and when later re-employed, he failed an alcohol screen—both occurred within the last three years, the second one about two months before coming to Bowie Station. Andrea concludes that this meets criteria for denying site access. After Andrea expresses her concern to Meg, Matt, and then to Neil, Neil temporarily deactivates Wade's badge, awaiting additional information.

The next day Andrea requests more information about the failed tests from the background checking firm and calls Wade's then-employer. She also interviews Wade, who says that he had not purposefully withheld the information. He had not remembered the earlier positive drug test and had attributed the more recent positive alcohol test to medications, an explanation, Wade said, that his employer's medical officer had accepted. Because he had continued to work for the firm after the second failed test, he assumed that the issue was "cleared up." The firm now tells Andrea that it decided to keep Wade on because it needed his skills, and besides, the work he was doing for them was nearly finished.

Neil revokes Wade's unescorted access the next day. In the condition report, Neil acknowledges that access should have been revoked two months earlier when the first information about test failures was received. The operations department makes its required report of license violation to the NRC, for which the station could be fined.

Mis-Authorization Event Review Team's Report

In evaluating the event's significance, a three-person team finds that even though this breach did not result in misbehavior by Wade, the access authorization group did not follow procedures and calls the event a violation of NRC requirements. Given the work Wade was doing, the event reveals that there is "a programmatic weakness that could have resulted in more serious consequences to the station and/or its personnel." The team's analysis primarily concerns the ineffectiveness of corrective actions recommended previously after a similar event.

A few months earlier, a temporary worker had twice been granted unescorted access within the last few years despite having had a conviction for drug possession, which, whenever occurring, is cause for denying access. But, the team finds, the corrective actions initiated after that event did not prevent this one. Those corrective actions "primarily . . . [provided] informal training" that focused on that event's "specifics," hence the "scope was limited to communicating expectations and methods" covering only personnel history statements and reports of criminal history. They did not recommend formal changes to processing methods. "Taken in the aggregate," those corrective actions "were narrowly focused and lacked substance." Although another remedial action was a review of past files—which turned up seven other cases of "discrepancies" in granting unescorted access—those findings had not been "recognized" as indicating that the review team's scope "needed to be expanded to address other aspects of the program."

The team's root cause analysis concludes there was "less than adequate management oversight."

"Direct supervision" was meager because the position of manager of plant protection had been vacant for several months; generic concerns for processing records were not followed up; "pervasive verbal communication lapses" resulted in communication failures; "significant discrepancies" between processing activities and "procedure requirements/management expectations" were "unrecognized"; there was a "lack of supervisory involvement during the turnover of long-term responsibilities"; and "management expectations for timely reviews of newly received information which might contain derogatory information were absent."

The reported conversations between Meg and Neil reveal several "human performance issues":

Meg's incorrect assumptions and inadequate understanding of the "approved process for handling" derogatory information; Matt's and Dale's acceptance of Meg's memo and their failure to discuss these matters with Neil, especially Dale's misunderstanding of "independent review," evident in his belief that he could not "revisit previously evaluated derogatory information"; the absence of "management expectations for timeliness of reviews of newly received background information" and the "poor turnover of pertinent information."

Although Dale had concerns about Wade's "extensive criminal history" (which had occurred more than three years earlier), he did not pursue them, "reasoning it best not to 'make waves' with others who had viewed the information differently. His reluctance to challenge his peers deviates from station and group expectations. This issue provides an additional indication that the purpose and method for performing independent reviews is not uniformly understood by Access Authorization personnel."

Human performance "during this event was not in accordance with station and group expectations . . . and is symptomatic of inadequate management oversight. . . . [I]t is the responsibility of supervision and management to be sufficiently integrated into processes that problems of this nature are identified and corrected." In the absence of a manager of plant protection, Neil had also been carrying out some of that position's duties.

The team identifies inadequate management oversight as the root cause; the contributing cause is "the failure of certain Access Authorization personnel to internalize and/or apply long-established station expectations for personnel performance," specifically, making critical decisions with "unverified assumptions," not communicating pertinent information clearly, and not determining whether Wade had wilfully omitted the failed tests.

Compensatory corrective actions are to clarify and document "management expectations" for timely reviews, for the scope of initial and independent reviews, and for immediate notification of receipt of derogatory information, and to "emphasize" the existing requirement that only the supervisor can approve or deny access when derogatory information is involved. Further, program managers should: relieve Neil of duties not related to this program, review all files of those with unescorted access to verify the action taken, conduct a self-assessment, revise its procedures "and/or desktop instructions" to reflect these corrective actions, instigate training on changes, and request an independent assessment of the program "to evaluate the adequacy of actions implemented in response to this event, as well as the overall health of the program."

INSIGHTS AND EXCURSIONS

All those who talked with me conduct the first excursion themselves: they discuss many contributing causes and other themes that do not appear in the team's report, nor does the report recommend corrective actions that their insights and observations imply. The next excursion considers the event's relationship to the meanings attaching to "outage." The last excursion discusses the cultural position of the groups involved in both Bowie Station events.

"Comprehensive and Substantial"

How do this team's analyses and recommendations fare by the same criteria it applies to the earlier team's findings about another misauthorization? That is, are corrective actions now being proposed more comprehensive and more substantial in scope? Are they likely to prevent recurrence of conditions surrounding this and other recent events in this group?

That they fail to meet the criteria is an unavoidable conclusion after hearing the observations readily made by everyone I interviewed several months after the team's report, including the team's own members. Each sketches out conditions affecting managerial inattention and inefficiencies, which go unremarked in the team's report. Despite calling for "expanded scope," the report's palliatives for bringing a neglected program into clearer focus—arousing senior management interest, making self-assessments, assuring a dedicated supervisor—also remain focused only on "the health of the program." That is, this report recommends tightening up the group's operations, procedures, and "guidance," "reiterating existing requirements," and emphasizing retraining. To become more substantial and more comprehensive, the team's observations, analysis, and corrective actions would have had to mention, as the interviews do, what are apparently unmentionables in a review team report.

At the time of my interviews, the access authorization group had been relocated from "security" to "plant protection," one of several responsibilities of Scott, senior manager for "business services." Before that, Bernie, senior manager for "engineering and technical services," had been responsible for security operations when it included the group. Bernie mentions the station's reliance on contractors, workload, and time pressures and provides other details of the event.

> The employment record that contractors fill out has both a place for written comments and for check marks. In that file, the check mark said that he was eligible for rehire, the written remarks said that basically on occasion he'd failed fitness-for-duty tests—"on occasion" {ironically}. The coordinator assumed that because the person was eligible for rehire that somehow those tests had been resolved in the employee's favor, instead of following up. As it turns out, the contractor is not under the same regulations as we are, so they can make those decisions.

> And when we talk to Wade, turned out he had failed one preemployment test, which means he didn't get employed that time. But basically, it's a union hall situation, where the contractors call down to the union hall and say, "I need six of these," and they show up, they give them a fitness-for-duty test, they send them on to wherever they want them, and if they don't, they send them back to the union hall. But then the next time they call, the same cast of characters could show up. When he had a second test he was already employed—I'm not sure why the test was done, random or what, but he didn't pass it. But they made the decision he was OK and that the job was so close to finishing they let him stay.

> Now, you know, although we should have tumbled to this earlier, once you get into it you find the second time he claimed he was on prescription medication and that he thought that test had been resolved in his favor because he had provided their doctor with information about what he was taking, some cold medicine or something. That isn't what the company says—the company says it just wanted him to finish the job. But all that is information that was developed after we made the mistake, unfortunately. Maybe it sort of mitigates the mistake, but it doesn't preclude the fact that we made the mistake.

It is a widespread practice to hire the same contracting companies from outage to outage in order to capitalize on their familiarity with station employees and procedures. NRC security criteria did not extend to the companies' employment criteria at that time (my research at Bowie ended about fourteen months before 9/11/01). Bernie continues.

What makes this a tough issue is that before this event happened, we did an audit and found that a person who had an unresolved arrest had been badged a couple of times. So, he should not have gotten in but he did. In the scale of things this event was a smaller mistake. . . . What we did after that [earlier mistake], we instituted a requirement to basically have people check other people's work—and that wasn't fully implemented the way we wanted because of some of the players and the volume of people coming in. That's been corrected.

The other thing is—and I fault myself for this—when we reviewed the previous event, while it didn't point to this causal factor, there was a gut feeling by the NRC that the supervisor was doing too many things. So Neil wasn't in the building where the work was being done. I think the corrective actions as designed would have been effective. What we failed to do was set the expectations clearly of how we wanted those to be followed. We've now really got a dedicated group, but it's tedious, very detailed work. I think unless the individuals keep their eye on the ball, they're subject to the kind of mental errors that happened in this event. . . . But I do think when you get down to the root cause here that people made wrong assumptions.

And I don't think we took into account the workload pressures on them and the volume being processed. We bring in for an outage about eight hundred contractors. We're getting ready for *this* outage and bring in an additional six hundred, so there's a ramp-up depending on which week it is [before or during the outage]. We can process anywhere from twenty to two hundred people in a week depending on the time each takes. We try to complete the initial badging process ahead of time because you don't want to bring somebody here and basically pay them to sit around waiting. We discovered years ago they were coming here about two weeks before we needed them. And so we did some things to streamline the process [referring to a "total quality management" initiative]. And we're proud of the fact that the process was a plus.

We tried to get our department managers to screen up front—"Don't send us these people hoping they'll get through." Managers see the access authorization group as a necessary evil to get someone in the plant. I really challenged the [line] management team on that. . . . "You do the screening up front, don't make us the last barrier in the chain." We've had better luck since then—I hope it's not just luck, but that the process is better.

That "process was a plus" for the bottom line perhaps, but not for the access authorization group. Before becoming its supervisor about two-and-a-half-years ago, Neil was a member of the group for eight years, and for several years previously, he worked in other parts of the security department but "never carried a gun." Neil mentions the cyclical workload and the pressures speed exerts on quality and on speed's catalyst, cost.

> For every outage we badge at least nine hundred people. So we will see at least 1,200 or more to get that number. And so the files can be as thick as from an inch of paperwork to maybe two or three inches. And all that has to be reviewed. It requires two independent reviews. . . . So now I'm directly supervising the group. I implemented a form recently that, I think, made it easier for the group to know they had to go and look for the type of information that we need to identify. And so in doing that, we just prevented a—I mean we've been using that tool for several months—we prevented a one-hour reportable event from occurring today. By using the tool. I just thought of another barrier to put in place. We had tried training which was, you know, some heard the message or received the message and some didn't. So I felt we needed something physical to see or show. . . .
>
> I've also had two independent consultants in. . . . We look at the big picture, we look at how many people we process and badge to staff up an outage. I'm just taking a wild guess, but maybe when we have two outages in a year's time, we're probably going to touch about five thousand files. So out of the five thousand or more we had two events. I'm not degrading that, but that's not a bad batting average, you know, especially considering the amount of—you know, I'm not condoning the mistakes but considering the information in both events, we self-identified. I think in self-identifying that means that we were doing the job correctly.

Do these outside consultants feel that you had all the resources, the group had the resources it needed to do the work?

They felt that we had what we needed at the time. They say we deal with too much paperwork, we aren't utilizing our computers as much as we can, so there have to be some enhancements of the process, improvements that we have to make. This year will be the first opportunity that we will have where we're not having back-to-back outages, so we'll be able to do some of that. The mentor, he gave me valuable information as far as how to make sure I have my hand on the entire process.

So no one said that there could be more hands at work in this group— the two independent consultants didn't say you needed more help? Do you think you do?

No. I need people that are going to work, pull their share of the load, and I don't see the need for more people. . . .

Have you ever gone to another plant and observed how they run their show?

Yes. In the last year I went to six nuclear power plants and no one I've seen has done any better than this group. They're actually behind the time. We're much more advanced. We're a lot farther ahead than other groups. . . .

Bringing in as many people as we are, it's time pressure placed upon us by the groups [departments] that are bringing the people in. They don't understand that 150 people means we have to look at 150 files and then the next day we bring in 150 people. That means we still have the 150 we had the day before to look at, and each day it's the same thing. . . . But they're yelling and screaming for people, "We need badges." I'm not concerned with how fast we process, I'm concerned about the quality of work that we do. That has been the mode of operations for this group for years—faster, speed it up. I'm saying, "No."

Can you give me an idea of what a dedicated worker can get through in a day?

Each file, depending on the process, it takes about—they probably spend maybe roughly 45 minutes on a file, just doing the whole thing. We work ten hours a day [four days per week]. I work 'em now six days a week, and we come to work at 6:30 in the morning, and we sometimes don't leave until 6 at night. . . . I look at every file. It doesn't mean that I'm infallible and can't make a mistake, same as the peer group. But I think because I haven't handled the file all day, I'll be more in tune to pick out something they didn't see.

Well, so much relies on this team.

Oh, yeah. The station employees never really knew how much we did for 'em until those two events came about. So of course we got negative attention, but I think it's fast approaching positive because we are keeping out some bad elements. We don't want criminals or someone that's an addict of any kind inside of a nuclear power plant. So I take it personally. I like to know someone is going to be as safe as I would be out there. And that's my approach, that's my approach to how I do this job. I know a whole lot of lives could be affected by one mistake. So we need to make sure we're screening and keeping out as many that don't need to be in there.

The catch you made today, maybe there should be a new performance indicator that says this is a positive.

I agree.

It was a near miss that never went anywhere.

Well, and those are not reported. No one ever sees those. Each time we identify someone that doesn't need to be in there, it is a positive thing. I mean we kept them from going inside the plant. We have quite a few that we've prevented. There's very little time to do what we need to do. . . . We have to keep in mind that what we do impacts the budget, so whether we don't hear a word about how fast you badge, we still know that we still affect the outage and the budget costs. So whether it's said or not, it's still there. I try not to put that pressure on the people. My only push would be on me but sometimes you know, it's a big burden. . . .

But I know that in the job that we perform in our area, it can happen again. There's no barrier you can put in place that will prevent it from happening again ever. Not in this job, because of what we're doing. And the NRC understands that and so the task at hand is to communicate that to our own personnel that it can happen again. So I know that it can happen again, and they're [the event review team] like, "Your corrective actions were ineffective." Well, you can say that but then you can also say they were effective because we did identify. No one came in and found these mistakes. *We* found mistakes. Granted, not when they should have been identified, but when you put in all of the circumstances as to why it did not get identified, then it's simple. . . . And I know that this is part of the job—I live every day knowing that it could happen again, just like today we were right on the brink of notifying the NRC again. Where there was a programmatic failure, the system still worked because we found it.

"Self-identifying" is the essence of self-regulation. But at the same time, violating NRC regulations in the first place has to be treated as an event for which culpability and correctives have to be defined. In this case, with the delay in critical peer checks and shifting job responsibilities, the group took a relatively long time to self-identify.

The station's security group supervisor, Hal, is responsible for training, security systems (cameras, intrusion detection devices, carded doors), and operations (at the gate, within the plant). Contractors supply the 140 uniformed and armed women and men staffing physical security; the station employs three technicians to maintain security equipment. After the earlier event, Hal had been assigned to conduct training for the access authorization group in recognizing and dealing with derogatory information. Hal mentions the speed versus cost and quality issue and the troubled history of the group.

I'm in charge of security here. But access authorization is actually a peer group [on his same level in the hierarchy], and it's tied to security obviously very intricately. On this particular event, I really wasn't personally involved in the circumstances surrounding it. I {sigh} was involved in the earlier event due to some of the corrective actions.

What were the corrective actions?

The corrective actions—specifically the one I was involved in—had to do with the evaluation of derogatory information. I presented the training. And then that was determined to be in some fashion inadequate by the individual who investigated the second event. Which, of course, I vehemently object to—{dryly}.

I would think so.

But I was never interviewed for the second event. I was never asked, "What was the content of that training?" So I guess that's where my involvement has been.

Do you have a perspective on both the events from what you know about the access authorization system and what you were assigned to do?

Oh, I have many opinions.

I'm interested in any and all of them.

I don't necessarily agree with the root cause of the second event, which was determined to be management effectiveness.

Where do you think the cause or causes lie? I don't trust one cause.

I don't trust one cause either. I think that there was less than adequate attention upon the actual individuals [in the access authorization group] involved, from a human performance standpoint and a history of their performance over the course of a long period of time. I also believe that, notwithstanding, their behavior is the direct result of the previous management influence that directed the program.

So that was less than satisfactory?

In my opinion, yes.

And has that gone away?

Yes, the management changed, and so the new supervisor, Neil, whom you've met, moved in as the supervisor, but nothing else changed. All of the personnel remained static. And I think that he's had quite a struggle in overcoming some of the culture that has existed in that group from the previous administration.

And what is that culture? How would you characterize that?

Less than adequate attention to detail, and I believe that another contributing cause to these events has been this, our—I have to search for the right word here—our emphasis upon how quickly we could badge personnel versus the quality of our product.

And where does that come from, the large volume?

Oh, I think we're trying to deal with it now. I mean I believe that we're trying to still badge personnel quickly, and that's an economic decision, that's business acumen. But we can't lose sight of the regulatory nature of the work that we're doing and the importance of doing the right thing. I think that currently we're getting that right focus. We're still trying to use business acumen, but we're also trying to understand that we've got to do the right thing. And again I think that's because of our existing management structure.

The problem stems from not only management—the actual individuals—but also from a station mindset that what was important was how quickly we could badge people. We've changed the people part of that and I also believe that we're making the correct change in our station mindset with regard to "Yes, we still need to badge as quickly as we can but not lose sight of the quality product."

And that often means taking longer.

It often means taking longer. That's exactly correct.

Here, the tradeoff quandary pitches regulatory order against market order—"business acumen"—as quality goes toe to toe with the speed expected of short-as-possible outages. But professional orders—the line managers—being judged by the time and cost concerns of market and corporate orders, leave it to regulatory order to take care of itself.

After a few reorganizations following reengineering, the access authorization group has become one of several programs for which Scott, senior manager of business services, is responsible. Unlike the event review team's report, Scott mentions the influences of workload volume, internal group conflicts, the group's isolated location, a general disdain for support functions, a process for augmenting the group, and contractor relations.

It's kind of ironic—we had a situation today which seems to indicate— at least it's one data point—that the fixes we put in place are working. I'll tell you about that in a second. We've got a group of people who basically know the mission. The mission is, "Keep out bad people" {thumping table}. Now, they've been somewhat hamstrung because they didn't have enough real guidance, there was not enough good organization of the files, there was probably some supervisory oversight lacking, there's personality conflicts in the group, and there's apparently some longstanding negative feelings in the group. When you mess that all up together you've got the perfect recipe for trouble. On top of that, when we gear up for an outage, you've got a tremendous volume. So now you've got volume with disorganization beneath it. And a demand for speed. So it's a prescription for failure. . . .

We've done a number of things. We've had an outside person come in to take a look, we've had a former NRC inspector in this area come in and do a self-assessment. We gained a lot of insight from that, and we told the folks in the group, "Look, we're not out to shoot anybody, we're out to fix this so it doesn't happen again. Our job is to control the access on this site." So we tried to take it out of any personal situation, to the extent that we could.

Now, there were some errors that were made, for which one has to counsel those people [a disciplinary action]. So we've changed the procedures, which were also—that's what I was saying—they didn't have enough guidance, proper guidance. So we've done that. We've got the files cleaned up. We've had that audited. We've gone back and gone through every access that we've done for a very long period of time to make sure we didn't have some other problems. We've taken a lot of compensatory actions.

Today, we denied access to an individual—denied access because the system worked. What happened is this individual had been at the plant in a previous outage, had been approved. After he left the site, information came in that said he had a criminal arrest record. The good news is that that came after the fact, so now, the bad news is, why aren't we getting this information faster? That's a problem. But the good news is that when it's in the file, when the negative information is in the file, we denied access. So I'm guardedly optimistic. At least that's one data point that says we're a little bit back on track. So we called the NRC— it's not reportable but we're trying to keep them very informed, and they were very, very pleased. They said, "Your program's now working." So I think we've taken the steps.

Jay works in the corrective action program and conducts event reviews full time. He begins by recapitulating the team's observations, mentions "pure economics" and tells about his own recommendation to senior managers that the access authorization group should stop work to "punt and think."

And what do you see in the environment that might have been a contributing cause? How did you come out on your recommendations?

What I saw was management and oversight of the program in general was really weak, in terms of individuals who did not know their roles and responsibilities. There wasn't the finger on the pulse, the day-to-day looking at the program. Part of it was this supervisor wearing so many hats. And I think the most important thing that that group does is keep people who should be out of plants out of the plant. But it didn't seem like that focus was there. It was more on getting people in the plant in a timely manner. Just the reverse philosophy. That came up a lot. We were talking to Neil and we heard things like, "Well, this is one mistake, but we processed 10,000 people in"—I'm exaggerating the number—and I'm thinking in my mind, "Who cares about the number that are processed in a timely manner? All we care about is that some-body got in that shouldn't have gotten in." Sure, they could get in be-cause our process would allow somebody to get in. But when we know everything about him, that we had information in our hands for two months and that individual was even reinstated when we possessed that information, I thought that was unacceptable. . . . But it was really [a problem of] oversight. It was clear that individuals didn't know their roles and responsibilities, there was no day-to-day oversight.

On the "timely manner" thing, as I understand it at other plants, there is a real problem with that. They want to bring people in at the last minute or as close to the last minute as possible because it costs money to have people hanging around. So, generally speaking, isn't there a lot of time pressure on badging?

Yes, there is.

And where does that pressure really originate? How do people make their requests for contractors—do they make their requests in a timely manner?

I couldn't answer that question.

It's sort of like a funnel, comes right down to the access point. But where is the funnel starting?

I think the funnel starts at the top. The way access works at a nuclear power plant is probably based upon economics more than anything else, a purely economic decision. I'll give you an example. We saw that there were problems in a number of areas of how they do their business [at the top] in general. And so I thought that they should just stop work and reassess everything they were doing. First of all, to determine what are our critical functions and our critical points and reassess those, make sure that we had all the bells and whistles in place to make sure that we were going to make the right decisions. And I thought they really needed to stop work. I think if we had a similar breakdown in the plant in a program related to operating the reactor, we wouldn't restart until we did a stop-work and reassessed everything. So I offered that up to the senior manager. It was a decision of the other senior managers and the site vice-president not to do that. What they did is they got an outside consultant to augment the direct oversight in the interim. He's a very competent man. And I thought the most conservative thing to do was to stop work. We'd had a previous event and had barely averted a level-three violation on it.

It was a little different, but not different enough. And that was what I thought we should do. And just punt and think and stop, and if it costs us money, oh well. The decision was, "We've got a refueling costing money and a major repair, and that's probably too much, going too far." And so they did other things. Whether or not those things were totally apt, I couldn't answer that. But you could see that we're a conservative plant, but the economics of stopping an outage, putting the badging on hold, it was too big. It was their decision to make and they said they couldn't do it.

So I think it's pure economics. You want people in, when you want 'em in, you want 'em in in a timely manner, but you want them processed in correctly and sometimes the two ideals conflict. And that's what happened.

Perhaps the managers assigned each corrective action called for will delve into the substantive and, it seems, systemic issues these several station experts bring up. Although it is not impossible for the "root cause" and "fault tree" format to stretch to include evidence and issues of many kinds, it is striking that team members themselves bring out a noticeably wider range than appear in their report. An overactive parts template seems not only to have censored the wider and more substantive analyses that experts are capable of, but also to have prevented common cause between departments and the access group.

Targeting Outages

A station and its people "live in two worlds," employees say—one while operating, the other a refueling outage every eighteen months when operators shut down each reactor to replace one-third of the fuel assemblies in its core. Although "shut down" or OFF-LINE signals that a reactor is no longer producing electricity, it nevertheless remains at low power, and decay heat remains in the core. Some reactor designs outside the United States permit refueling while on line; here, on-line maintenance (sometimes at reduced power) is increasingly a cost-saving strategy, one governed by NRC requirements for additional planning and safeguards.

Outage targets are under the control of corporate and market orders: be brief, stay within budget, and polish off, say, four thousand work orders without license violations or bodily injuries, all to be accomplished according to that lock-step, critical path. At an industry workshop, operations and outage managers reported that most stations have "outage length and priorities driven by upper management [and] during outage schedule development, [line] managers are usually told the number of days of outage length and are expected to fit the work into that time frame." The Japanese took the opposite approach, on the premise that the benefits of an outage can be measured only by the number of days a unit stays on line after restart: Japanese outages, meticulously planned and lengthy, were followed by record-setting spells of uninterrupted production. They were also a source of correspondingly higher electricity prices, however, and under recent economic conditions, apparently no longer the norm.[14]

When decoupling, testing, repairing, and recoupling hundreds of components and systems preoccupies a doubled workforce around the clock, the station's usual order of things transforms: a separate OUTAGE ORGANIZATION takes charge while, for example, licensed reactor operators, members of the corrective action program, and some administrative specialists switch into assignments for front-line managers and supervisors. Scott, manager of business affairs, explains.

> It's a big shift for everybody. And even folks that aren't in an "outage-direct" role, they're covering for their buddies who are in it. So it's a total system shift. I call it "student body left—hike!" And it's very demanding, very intense, it's long hours. We've really had a goal of short outages from the perspective of the human ability to cope under heavy stress for long periods. In my experience—and I mean I go back to days when the average outage was 120 days—you just survived. And we don't like the short outages from the perspective that we do two twelve-hour shifts, which is very hard because most of us have an hour drive, so that's fourteen hours. All you do in an outage is you eat, sleep, drive to work, work, drive home, go to bed. It's very draining, and it takes a toll on families. You know, we try to attend to that. It's difficult.

> *It's also well rewarded.*

> Yes, it is. Although this upcoming outage will be our third outage in eighteen months—our people are whipped. They're very tired. And I really kind of wonder if a tired element hasn't entered into this particular event a little bit too. People do get to a burnout stage. . . . This outage we've got coming up is a longer, bigger deal. So it's sort of being hit by a wall of water for the third time in a row, you know, and it's

hard. People are very resilient, very energetic, very dedicated. This business is a lifestyle, it's not a job. And, you know, if you can't thrive on that you'd better do something else, because it's going to kill you. It can be a very toxic thing for some folks.

Outages can also be tonics that many may "thrive on." They can inspire innovations in scheduling and performing work that reduce radiation exposure and injuries, for example. Because outage intensity produces results, some stations try to keep that spirit going during operations, perhaps expanding on daily background briefings on plant conditions to keep more people in the loop.

After hearing objections to the tight schedule of a previous outage, managers recently reduced the pressure's "magnitude," according to Jay, a member of the event review team.

> You see more and more a focus on economics, deregulation. We have to be lean, mean. The outage before last, we heard a lot of things that we hadn't heard before in terms of the magnitude of the schedule pressures. The focus was on that: The schedule came first. And there was a lot of feedback—and I'm talking off what I heard, OK?—but for the last outage, that message got through. People talked about the difference—this last one was relaxed. We actually went to four 10-hour days [per week], didn't work people as much, and there's a big difference on that. It looked like they [management] got the message—"Slow down a bit."

Outages seem nevertheless to be regarded as outrages to bottom-line sensibilities. This period of spending while not earning is a target of ambivalence if not diffuse animosity, even though refueling the core is necessary to production, and via preventive maintenance, to reducing the risk of unplanned shutdowns. The specter of outage costs seems nevertheless to darken such longer-term benefits. Senior managers are supposed to think about "urgency in the long run," as an Overton outage manager put it, but, he says, they lack the "patience." The ambivalence extends to any activities whose costs are believed to exceed their apparent or direct monetary benefit or to slow down output. That animosity puts outages into the overhead category, another of Scott's grab bag of duties as senior manager for business services. He ticks off his responsibilities: "finance, human resources, nuclear technology, emergency preparedness, public affairs and external communication, nuclear processing and materials management, contracts and purchasing, and records management and administration." Speaking specifically of the access authorization group, Scott talks about a "negative bias" toward "support groups" as a legacy of naval order.

The group is geographically located way out on the other side of the site so they're somewhat isolated. I think it's a problem, that isolation thing.

They apparently have to be at that gate, but they may also be low on the totem pole, in terms of education, training, and rewards. How do you manage the hierarchy when it's like that?

I think in this business—I don't *think*, I *know* in this business—that because most of the management has come out of the nuclear navy, there's a strong negative bias toward support organizations, and this is a support group. So those groups tend to take an awful lot of flak whether they deserve it or not. They're sort of on the ventilation path.

My comment is to Hal, manager of security.

In my experience with industrial organizations, especially in high technology, anything to do with people is somehow near the bottom of the totem pole.

What do you mean?

Well, the human resources department, for example, in a lot of these industries, is not terribly well resourced and it's not often involved in policy determinations upward. Organizations have hierarchies. That's all I'm saying.

That's true. Security for that matter, in my opinion, has never been high in the hierarchy because we're one of those functions that, like a necessary evil, costs you money. You don't generate a single megawatt of electricity and yet you're required by federal law to be here. "So how can you be as innocuous as possible and cause us to spend as little money as possible and still get the job done?" There are a lot of things going on in our industry as we continue to become competitive. And yet within the security realm, there's a great deal of emphasis coming back on security from the physical protection standpoint. And of course access authorization ties into that, because physical security is to keep the bad guys from attacking the plant, and from an access authorization perspective, continual observation and fitness for duty—that's what we rely on to protect against the insider threat. And so of late and with continuing changes in the industry, the regulator is putting more emphasis upon how well can physical security deter the attack and how good are your access authorization and fitness-for-duty programs.

Between being a "necessary evil" and the target of cost and caste resentments, the access authorization program is, according to Ted, member of the event review team, "a long-running process that's been allowed to basically run itself for years"—an "isolated" program left out in left field, the evidence suggests. So much so that longstanding interpersonal conflicts fester, according to Scott and Hal, but under the "employee concerns program" making changes in assignments is difficult. Scott explains.

We have a problem with changing people out. In the nuclear industry, the NRC has what they call an enforcement rule. [The enforcement rule is the centerpiece of the NRC's employee concerns program for preventing retaliation against employees who speak up.] If you hold a person accountable [for a job infraction, for example], they can file a concern and then they become protected. . . . So moving people around and out and getting them in better slots so everybody's happier is extremely difficult, very time consuming, and fraught with risk. So it makes our job of managing the workforce incredibly difficult. The NRC doesn't understand this phenomenon because the only thing they care about is "Are we addressing safety concerns?" So, you know, they have to have this policy to be able to tell Congress "We're managing this."

You're saying that an employee can say they've raised a safety concern and for that reason they're being shunted around?

Yes, shunted or retaliated against. "They moved me in retaliation for raising a concern." So you're stuck. And I've got a few in this group. So it's going to be a real challenge. I've got to find a way to motivate them in place. I don't have many choices around changing them. Now people know me and they know that I am firm but fair—it's about performance. And I demand performance. And I work twice as hard as anybody in my group, so I think they can work half as hard [laugh]. And yet at the same time I try to be very compassionate and benevolent, but I do really make high demands, have high standards, and don't accept anything but the best.

Hardly unique to this industry, under the "production mentality" work divides into either "direct" or "indirect" contributions to revenues. "Support groups" count only as overhead. Like sailors, they can also find themselves "on the ventilation path."

Administrative or Technical?

"I think the nature of the work is repetitive, I mean it would be boring as the dickens to me, so it tends to get classified low in our hierarchy—you know, 'mindless activity.' And yet it's very important to the site." Scott continues.

What the site doesn't understand or, let me say, what some key managers don't understand, is the importance of this program. That's the next piece of the effort. We've got to educate the site on the importance of the program. These folks [line managers] are smart, once you sit down and talk to them and say, "This is what the mission of this program is, people. I don't want somebody with a bomb inside that plant, or a gun, or anything. And our job as a team is to prevent that." But this particular group has a legal responsibility and it's up to you to help them fulfill that responsibility. You don't help them fulfill that responsibility by bringing people in here who haven't been prescreened. We weren't demanding that our vendors prescreen. We are now. Why should we be the final net? Let's let our vendors, who we're paying to bring these people in—they should have some accountability and responsibility. Now, it's still our ultimate responsibility, but they could help to process a whole lot of it. If you send us some folks that don't get through our process, there has to be a penalty associated with that, contractually. I'm working on that.

I asked Hal,

With so much riding on so many details in so many files, how are people trained to do the work? What kind of training do these people have in fact to do that work? Is there training that can be so specific to access authorization or to the issue of attention to detail and quality?

Yes, all of that. I mean there's no formal training. That's just when you come into this industry what you learn is that there are times when you must cross your t's and dot your i's and nothing less is acceptable. As far as learning the job of doing access authorization, it's on-the-job training. There's no formal training that can prepare you for that. It's a matter of working with someone else who has the experience.

Ted had recently joined the access authorization staff; for the previous two-and-a-half years he prepared condition reports and procedure reviews, among other administrative functions. Ted was one of two people from the group on the event review team, helping to "author the final report." He sees access authorization as being technical, not administrative work, for which "documented" qualifications are needed as much as they are for any other station expert.

There's not a clear understanding of access authorization by a lot of management folks. They think access authorization is an administrative function. It is not, it is a technical function. It is no different in its actual implementation of value to the plant than one of our maintenance mechanics going out and tearing into a particular safety-related pump. . . .

First, there's an exterior threat that will attack the plant using all the good military techniques—all right, there's all that. The second part of the threat is the insider type threat. We spend millions of dollars, guards, guns, that sort of thing protecting against that outside threat. The inside threat we call access authorization, which I believe is a misnomer in itself. The purpose of access authorization is to keep the bad guys out. And it is a technical function . . . there are some specific indicators that are called out in the regulation, called out in our procedure. And I don't believe that that attention to detail, or understanding that this is a technical process, has ever really been fully understood.

What would you call it instead of access authorization? What name has occurred to you?

Oh, access authorization implies we're here to get people in as fast as we can. Just the opposite: my sole job is to keep the bad people out. The bad people, untrustworthy, unreliable, OK. That's the whole purpose. For physical protection we spend millions of dollars a year, which I can completely defeat by signing my name allowing the wrong person in. I don't see any indication that that is understood . . . and I'm referring to management, supervision, peers, people involved in the industry. I can't see their actions clearly indicating that they understand how significant this is. . . .

First of all, to be a mechanic you've got to have certain requirements, certain qualifications, certain skills before you're ever hired for the position. You go through extensive documented training that results in a qualification card, a QCC. The qualification card is signed not only by you, indicating you have completed study—coursework, classroom— that you have completed practical exams, you know how to physically take apart and put back together the component that you're qualified on. Not only do you sign that, your supervisor signs that says, "Yes, I believe this person that's going to be in my charge knows what he's doing," but also in many cases the manager signs that. There is no qualification process, nor has there ever been, for access authorization coordinators. . . . That's why I get the feeling that there's just not an understanding that this is a technical process.

And when you say that they think it is administrative, does that automatically code to you that they think of it as less important?

Oh, it's just paper pushing. "Get 'em in, get 'em in, get 'em in. Can you get 'em in in a day?" And that was *the* criterion—"How fast can you get them in?" That logic indicates that the thought process behind it is fundamentally flawed. You can't get the right answer if you're at that point. Our job in access authorization is to keep the untrustworthy, the unreliable out. Keep the bad people out. Anyone who could say "Can you get him in within a day?" simply cannot understand what they're talking about. . . . I believe they're doing the politically expedient thing in saying "Take your time" to access authorization personnel in getting people in. "Take as much time as you need, do it right, da da da da. Oh, by the way, do you have them in yet? When would you think you would have them in? Is there anything I can do to help you get those people in?" I don't think that supports what we're talking about.

Corrective actions that do not consider the practical implications of distinctions between "indirect" and "direct," "administrative" and "technical," and "support" and "staff," may make it appear that changes have been made, while culturally, the problem stays the same.

The Two Events: Tangential or Essential?

The groups involved in these two events at Bowie Station are, each in its way, oblique to the main action of continuous production. The midwatch is a customary time for background tasks, such as troubleshooting as a "low risk evolution," while work on safety-related distribution panels occurs on day shifts. The midwatch is, for many, a less desirable shift, as well as being one that "always presents trouble," in Terry's experience. In the access authorization group two "necessary evils" blend. Scott's long-term plan is likely, however, to exacerbate the group's off-side status.

If I have my long-term druthers, the access authorization group will be a self-directed work team. It's classical for that. But I got to get the right people in there, I got to have the right oversight, I got to have the program in such shape that we can get to that point. That's probably two years away.

"Self-directed" could be another way of abandoning the group to "run itself," and, of course, a way to reduce mid-management head count. Nor have resources for computer support been a priority for this paperweighted process, according to Ted.

There are some computerized records that we enter, but we've got paper backups on everything. We read things off the screen, write them down on paper, so that someone can read it off the paper and sign their name to it, so we can take that, "OK, approved," and put it back into the computer. . . . I don't know that there's ever been a real champion for the access authorization software. I don't believe there has really been a concerted consistent effort at continuing improvement in the way that the system runs. I have not seen that.

The work of keeping access barriers taut, Ted proposes, is little different from that demanded by "qualified" technical work on safety-related equipment. That suggests another way of thinking about other themes the two events share. A prejob brief is not there to assert authority or to check off a procedure: it is the next to last "barrier" for assuring that a task's intention stands its best chance of being realized. Nor can access authorization be practiced as the "mindless activity" of people seen as being deservedly low in the hierarchy; it is a "tedious, very detailed" *search* for elusive information. Both practices entail literally *thoughtful* work, demanding no less thought than that expected of reactor designers, control room operators, and station managers, for example.

Between the volume of contractors' files whose thousands of details need to be verified and the ever-present possibilities of jack-in-the-box "gotcha's," the goal of "zero errors" in access authorization as in other station groups is, the industry knows well, unattainable, at least, as Ted says, "for any length of time."

And what do you think about zero errors in this group in the future?

Not possible.

Why do you say that?

{sigh, pause} The way that we're conducting our business is much too complex, OK? It is an error-likely situation from the beginning to the end. . . . I believe we're doing better. The idea that we will reach an absolute zero error, I don't believe so, not for any length of time.

The NRC does not expect "zero," but regulators do expect required processes to be effective in anticipating potential glitches and recovering quickly from them. That is the basis for Neil's claim that "self-identifying" their own near-miss is a plus. A rhetoric of "zero" and of "perfection" is meant perhaps for shareholders, Wall Street, regulators, and the public, but when promoted internally cannot help but be met with skepticism born of realism. Errors can be limited but not obliterated: industry realists seek declining trends. Cutting more slack even for presumably "lower-risk" work is one obvious route. For more fundamental help, realists look to event reviews for new understandings. Now that the industry acknowledges that there is little likelihood that most mistakes are "a pure human performance error," or, as Arrow's leaking valve illustrates, a purely technical issue, much rests on whether event reviews also meet Scott's "high standards," for which anything less than "the best" won't do.

Charles Station: Transformer Trouble

A POTENTIALLY DESTRUCTIVE condition comes down upon the shoulders of Charles Station's risk handlers: they have to decide suddenly whether to shut down a reactor, after finding, entirely by chance, an unusual "hot spot" on a transformer located in the switchyard. Whether it merits going off line to track down its source or whether it represents a condition with which they are familiar and can ameliorate without shutting down is the question at the center of their tradeoff quandary. On this nonsafety side of the plant, working without the same guidance as is mandatory on the safety side, they must judge what kind of evidence to believe. The stakes are high: Are they witnessing a situation with possibly life-threatening repercussions, property destruction, environmental degradation, and a long outage at very high cost, or can they treat it with standard practices at lower cost?

AN ACCOUNT OF A "SIGNIFICANT NEAR-MISS" ON A GENERATOR STEP-UP TRANSFORMER

About a year ago, Charles Station bought a $200,000 infrared digitized camera, which, pixel by pixel, registers components' internal temperatures as color-coded images, or thermograms. The station uses the camera for finding problems while equipment is fully energized. In this condition-based maintenance program, maintenance-as-needed replaces scheduled maintenance for certain equipment.

Just after four o'clock on a Wednesday afternoon, Paul, an engineering analyst who does most of the thermography at the station, and Vince, a senior engineer, both in the condition-based maintenance group, are out in the switchyard with Andy and Frank, two industry experts brought in for the week to help evaluate the group's imaging and analysis techniques. All day, they have been moving around the station retaking thermograms of some forty pieces of previously inspected equipment. As Andy takes readings of insulators on the high tension lines in the switchyard, he comments that it's the first time he hasn't observed warm or hot spots in switchyard equipment—a mark of effective thermographic techniques and maintenance. Because the station's infrared camera has a short wave-length better for indoor use, Paul plans its use outdoors on cloudy days; at his request, Andy and Frank brought a long-wavelength camera to check consistency of both results—"and we were within a couple of degrees Fahrenheit across the board."

The group walks inside a chain-link fence to the generator step-up transformer (GSU), an assembly about twenty feet high standing next to the turbine building. Andy aims the camera at one of its six cabinets housing isophase buses (equal phase copper conductors). These receive low-voltage electricity coming from the main turbine through a flexible connection bolted to the top of the transformer. The buses step up electricity from 25 kilovolts to the 345 kilovolts the station sends out over switch-yard lines to a regional grid. Focusing up about fifteen feet, Andy frames the East inspection plate (12″ × 16″) on the housing's panel (5′ × 4′). The calibrated viewfinder registers 256°F, more than double the baseline thermogram Paul made two months earlier. The image today shows a concentrated hot spot, which usually signifies heat radiating from a specific source. The East inspection panels of two other GSU housings register at normal, about 110°F. The four men know immediately that the anomalous condition if verified could pose threats not limited to the operability of the generator step-up transformer.

The energy potentials involved in faulty generator step-up transformers are enormous and instantaneous from two directions—the lower voltage current coming in and the higher voltage going out. The transformer's insulating and cooling medium is 15,000 gallons of mineral oil, flash point 292°F. At the least, an overheated component presents a fire hazard, at the most, the accident record shows, explosions have thrown solid pieces of iron through concrete walls and ripped bushings off a transformer's top—"launching it," as some put it. At another nuclear power plant, the burning transformer tower had landed on top of the turbine building; because available water pressure was too low to reach the roof, the fire burned for about 20 hours before being extinguished. Or there could be a fireball 100 feet high sending burning oil splashing over swaths of ground and onto nearby buildings. Anyone within about 100 feet would not survive. Estimates of the probability of such worst-case scenarios are said to be roughly fifty-fifty.

The threat has to be reported immediately also because the GSU is critical to safe shutdown: it provides power to auxiliary transformers when the main generator is out of service and becomes a source of the on-site power required under an accident scenario in which backup diesel generators also fail. The reactor is running at 100 percent power.

As it happens, the next day is a holiday, and most employees not on shift have left for home. To begin to validate the finding, Paul calls around to find an electrical engineer still on-site. Brad, senior engineer in the technical support group, soon arrives, takes a look through the camera, and agrees that the thermal image signals radiant heat coming from an internal component. The hot spot is confined mainly to the panel cover's inspection plate, radiating outward only at one corner; the bus inside is a few degrees hotter.

That is a pattern not created by the more common problem of circulating current, which spreads hot spots over the housing cover but concentrates them in the corners at bolt holes. On electrical devices with huge magnetic fields, circulating current is likely to appear around discontinuities, such as loosened cover bolts or paint under or around tight bolt heads. Then the device acts like an induction oven and draws current from the bus. The first diagnostic for circulating or induced current is to reduce all possible gaps and recheck temperatures; if no change occurs, the next step is to loosen inspection plate cover bolts and place a cable or grounding strap between two corners of the cabinet cover to change the ground and dissipate the heat more evenly. If the pattern changes, the hot spot is not related to the internal condition of buses and bushings.

Immediately, Paul and Brad call Brad's supervisor Grant at home to report their observations and their conclusion that the hot spot image is unlike that associated with circulating current. About nine months earlier, what was thought to be circulating current appeared on this housing's entire front panel, and about two months ago, grounding straps successfully dissipated it. Paul had taken all the thermograms. Now, Grant decides that with no other indications of there being anything wrong with the GSU, it is highly probable that the hot spot indicates circulating current. He tells them to wait until morning to recheck the readings.

About fifteen minutes later, Brad, Paul, Vince, and Nat, Paul's immediate supervisor, who is at home, make a conference call to Edward, senior engineering analyst in the technical support group, to explore the need for shutting down. Edward, who is also at home, suggests the men talk to consultants specializing in transformer engineering. They next tell Jack, operations shift manager, about their finding; Paul asks him to place caution tape around the transformer as a warning to passers-by and plant staff to stay clear. The generator step-up transformer (a favorite spot for smokers) sits about 25 yards from a parking lot and the access road to the station entrance. About 850 people work at Charles Station.

Paul files an adverse condition report about 45 minutes after taking a number of thermograms. Brad discusses the images by phone with two transformer consultants; both are comfortable with the circulating current theory and a possible troubleshooting plan to check it out. One transformer consultant agrees to come to the station on the holiday. Andy and Frank depart at 5:30 P.M.

Jack asks electricians on duty to inspect the transformer (they observe an already-known problem); then he talks to his boss, Cliff, the operations department manager, and notifies his staff and leaves a message at his home for Mike, manager of the condition-based maintenance group. The adverse condition report and thermograms arrive at the control room around 6:30 P.M., and at 7, Cliff contacts Ralph, the station manager. Meanwhile, a member of Mike's staff who was briefing him by phone on another subject tells him about this situation.

Through the night about a dozen people are looking on or working in the GSU's vicinity; no caution tape is up. On Thursday morning at about 6, a downpour begins. Paul and Brad meet and reaffirm their conclusion that because the radiation and thermal convection data still do not show the whole housing cover to be hot, the pattern differs from thermographic images of circulating current. At 6:30, a thermogram shows no change in temperature. Brad calls Grant, his supervisor, at home and reiterates his and Paul's opinion; Grant discusses the situation with Jack. By 9:30, several supervisors and managers arrive. Seeing no caution tape, Paul puts it up.

Jack questions the accuracy of the thermogram's temperature reading after hearing that, in the rain, the surface of the housing in question is not steaming; Paul tells him that it steamed earlier before the rain cooled it down. Jack requests temperature checks by contact pyrometer; Bruce, an electrical maintenance engineer, climbs to the top of the GSU transformer; the pyrometer registers 170°F, and a few hours later, 230°F. Between 10 A.M. and 11 A.M., still at home, Mike, and Phil, who is manager of the electrical maintenance group, learn that Cliff is calling a 1 P.M. management briefing and decision-making meeting. At 11 A.M., thermograms show no change in temperature. Paul then continues to work with Andy and Frank on the thermography self-assessment elsewhere at the station.

Attending the 1:00 meeting are twenty-one managers and supervisors seated at a conference table and another ten to fifteen people in chairs around the room's perimeter. The meeting lasts two-and-a-half hours. Led by Ralph, station manager, the meeting first hears from Paul's supervisor Nat, who makes a Power Point presentation comparing thermograms from the last scheduled inspection with those taken yesterday. Explaining the bus duct's air cooling system, Grant, engineering supervisor of the technical support group, says that some overheating on the bushing is expectable and the 250°F reading is not unreasonable, but if it is higher than the 300°F seen in the past, the reactor must be shut down in order to check it out. He recalls that the only previous problems with bus links were located at the generator, and they were caused by vibration. Russ, a supervisor in electrical maintenance, observes that attaching a ground to the cover is safe, but it is not safe to take the cover off on an energized panel. Jack, operations shift manager, asks a few questions about possible transformer damage and fire hazard. Ollie, a transformer consultant, thinks the thermograms suggest that the cover bolts are loose, and tightening them may fix the problem, but the increasing temperature and the possibility of oil leaks concern him.

The group discusses three options: to stay on line, attach a ground strap, and tighten the cover's bolts; to go off line for about two days to check out the flexible links between the main generator and transformer; to go off line for at least one week to examine the bushing. There is general agreement that if it were the bushing or the links, heat would radiate around a larger area, but since it is the inspection plate on the cover that is hot, it is probably circulating current. The operations staff presents an action plan: tighten the inspection plate bolting, evaluate for temperature decrease, and if no change, install a ground strap on the inspection cover, monitor it, and if no improvement, revisit the need to shut down to check links and bushing. The consensus is to adopt this plan.

Hank, the station's health and safety administrator, who is responsible for its industrial safety programs, does not learn about the situation until 6 P.M. that day, the holiday, when he picks up a voice mail message at home left about five hours earlier. Although paged once earlier, Hank was too far out of range to receive it, nor did his one staff member get a message. Calling in, he is told that the action plan is in progress and that industrial safety issues are well in hand.

At about 3 P.M., several people are standing around the generator step-up transformer. At Jack's request, Chris, an electrical engineer, climbs up to the panel's cover plate with a pyrometer to validate the temperature. At 4 P.M., Bruce goes up to tighten bolts on the cover. The control room reduces generator output to test its effect on the cover temperature. Paul inspects the hot spot thermographically every fifteen minutes until 5 P.M. No changes occur. The control room increases generator output and fifteen minutes later the temperature increases from 235°F to 245°F.

At 6:15 P.M. the temperature remains at 245°F. Fifteen minutes later, up on the transformer, Chris removes one bolt, preparing to position a strap beneath the cover. Standing at a particular angle, he happens to be able to look into the 3/8-inch bolt hole and immediately reports a visible glow. Jack asks Chris to move over to the West phase plate, where he removes the corresponding bolt. The thermogram Paul takes registers 115.4°F; other images of comparable plates show them between 110°F to 116°F. At 6:45, Paul climbs up to the East bolt hole, positions the infrared camera, and announces an off-scale temperature—greater than 540°F. Jack orders the plant shut down. A soft, or gradual, shutdown begins at 7 P.M., and at 8, now standing on the ground below the GSU, Paul begins hourly infrared inspections of the area until midnight. By 5:45 A.M. Friday, the plant is off line.

That morning at 8:30 Ralph establishes an eight-person event evaluation team "to analyze the overheating condition" and "to correct equipment damage," address the "most probable cause," and "review plant startup readiness." This technical review team is also charged to "review the organizational response for lessons learned" and "to determine if the organization handled the condition correctly from discovery to the decision to shut down," especially with respect to the reasons why the two senior managers of maintenance and electrical were uninformed for eighteen hours. That review is assigned to two additional men designated a subteam to evaluate the "organizational response." They report to the manager of the station's corrective actions program.

At 2:15 P.M. on Friday, plant experts open and inspect the buses and find "significant overheating damage." The technical evaluation team concludes that one of four 3/4-inch aluminum bars (flags) at the transition between turbine generator and transformer had developed a higher resistance and forced the other three to carry more than their rated current, resulting in "severe overheating": aluminum had melted (requiring at least 1220°F) as had copper (at least 1983°F). "With high confidence" the technical evaluation concludes that "a poor or degrading electrical connection" at that one flag initiated the event. The connection "most probably became weakened due to thermal cycling and vibration"; it "had not been torqued [tightened] since the original installation" about twenty years ago, in accordance with vendor instructions. The failed connection, the report concludes, resulted in high resistance to current flow on the other three flexible link connections, which showed significant heat damage ("charred, brittle, torn, cracked"). Because the current continued to register at normal, an automatic relay on the GSU did not set off a plant trip. The team's review of infrared inspections for the previous 16 months, during which circulating current had been observed and reduced with grounding straps, led it to conclude that the "significant internal heating" had not begun until about eight weeks earlier.

At 3:30 P.M., the technical event evaluation review team briefs the station management team on the scenario of the failure and the repairs needed. After a twelve-day outage to replace the 25kV transformer bushing attached to the one flag, the unit comes back on line.

Charles Station
Generator step-up transformer

Circulating current

Hot spot

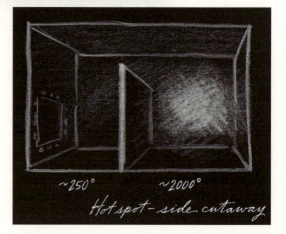

~250°   ~2000°

Hot spot – side cutaway

Witnessing "A New Find"

Paul talks about finding the hot spot, and a few station experts compare the damage they expected to see with what they saw.

Paul, engineering analyst in the condition-based maintenance group, tells his story.

> To be entirely honest, one of the thermography consultants actually had the camera, and he actually identified the hot spot before I got to it. He kinda glanced up to the GSU, "I'll check this," "Yah, Yah," and then he says, "Whoa." I'm "Wow!" and "This is a problem." And it was one of the things that jumps right out at you, it's a no-brainer—it's not always that way—but this was a no-brainer. Anybody that was holding the camera would have compared this housing, "Well, this one was 250 degrees, the one right beside it is 110, there's something different here." . . . . I even have the baseline image from seven months earlier. I could show that it was 90°F, when the weather was colder—all of them were 90°F, 91°F, 92°F. This one was pretty rare. . . . It was the day before the holiday, a half-hour after everyone had left. I called four or five numbers and I finally got one of the electrical system engineers. I say, "You got to come out and look at this, we got a problem." I showed him the camera, I said, "Look at this." And he said, "Oh yeah, I can see this."
>
> So he called Grant, the technical support group's electrical engineering supervisor, and says, "Hey, we have a problem with this." And at the time, Grant felt . . . that it was just a continuation or side effect of the induced current problems that we were having. And we were having a lot of those out there. But I did say to him, "Grant, this isn't the same, the thermal image isn't the same. I feel quite sure that this is radiant heat behind a panel." I had never seen that in the past, something like that. The thermography consultant concurred—he did not feel it was induced current. We both agreed on that. . . . It's not the same thermal pattern because the access panel was hot, but the housing behind it was a few degrees hotter. You can actually see this. You take a big area like this out around the outside, you're getting 200°F, you move in a little bit and it's 210°F, 220°F, all the way to 252°F, the hottest point. That is generally indicative of something behind it that's hot, radiating the heat.
>
> On the phone I told Jack that the thermal pattern was different. On circulating currents, the corners of the panel will be hot. And if the whole panel might be hot, in the corners it will be hotter. . . . Jack felt that we were getting the induced current from the inspection plate. And I said, "I don't think so. . . . The only thing that I said to him, 'cause

he couldn't see the picture—he was going to wait until the morning—was that the thermal pattern was not indicative of induced current. . . . And then he says, "Well, it could be induced current into the whole housing." And I say, "Well, I don't know if I can agree or disagree with that. I don't know. . . . "

After that, I discussed it with my supervisor Nat, and I said to him, "I think we have a real problem here, we're going to be shutting down." But that is a big deal, you're talking a million dollars a day. I was even apprehensive because what if I'm wrong? That's one of the big things. But I did say, "Hey, Nat, you know I really feel that we are going to shut down. This is different. It's a radiated heat pattern." We had a discussion, and then after that, we had a conference call with the system engineer that owns the system and had this similar type of discussion. Shortly thereafter we had another conference call with the unit shift supervisor Jack. Nat pretty much ran the telephone conference, which was probably normal. It was decided that I wouldn't push the issue—"Hey, we need to shut the plant down right now." I did tell him at the end of the conversation, "Hey, Jack, I'm really concerned about this. Somebody in the industry put out a caution paper saying we have had incidents where these things come off the pedestal and launch themselves. I mean catastrophic damage, there are a lot of them that have lost transformers and sometimes take out part of their turbine building. About 50 percent of the time, it launches itself."

I know Jack quite well, we started here at the same time. I did not say, "Hey, Jack, I feel very strongly that this is radiant heat behind it and this is a huge problem, and we should shut the plant right down," because Jack would have really pushed that and he would have done that. He would have wanted more information—he wouldn't have let anyone go home and not address that. I did say, "OK, I don't think that it's circulating current, but I agree that we should check to see what it does in the morning for several more hours." Because generally you have a hot spot, it gets hotter and hotter. And it usually goes up exponentially. "OK, you know in 8 hours or 10 hours I'll be back here. OK, I'll be in here in the morning and see how much it's changed."

And before I got off the telephone, though, I did say, "Hey Jack, I am concerned about this for safety. Please have somebody put caution tape around the GSU, we don't want people in there close to it . . . the potential of killing somebody is real." I came in the next morning, went out to do the survey, the caution tape was not up. . . . The temperatures were almost exactly what they were the night before.

In hindsight, knowing what we know now, that wasn't the prudent decision. OK, it's 140°F warmer [than another cover]—I'm not sure how much of a problem that is. I really didn't have a feel for how high do we need to go [before we shut down]. I did have a feel that with thermographic guidelines . . . we were up into the category where you fix very, very quickly, and usually without even any interpolation or calculation based on what the temperature behind this actually was, if you're taking a direct reading off of something. You would still have fixed that within a week. But if you're talking about a component behind it, and that's based on 140°F on the surface, if you're talking about something behind it—it took a while to find out how far behind. The next day, an engineer . . . calculated that we were talking at the order of 500°F. In actuality it was significantly more than that. . . . To be entirely honest, this was a new find, this was a new type of thermal image that we didn't have any experience on. . . . I wouldn't stand at a bolt hole again.

Paul promoted one corrective action with the technical evaluation team: to install "sapphire infrared inspection windows" on bolted connection boxes.

The Aftermath

Grant, electrical supervisor in the technical support group, compares what he saw after the GSU was opened up with what he had expected to see. It made him feel "very mortal."

> The pieces [conductors] inside are very large links that are made of laminated strips of copper. The copper's only sixty-thousandth of an inch thick, but there are sixty of them laminated together. What I had assumed had happened was that one of those laminated strips had come loose and was touching the side of the cabinet and that's what was glowing and causing the problem. An energized conductor is at about 25,000 volts. . . . As I told the event evaluation team, I felt very mortal because I had my nose about six inches from that the night before, and it was very clear that what was going on inside was much more severe than I had ever envisioned. So in hindsight, I have a lot of safety concerns.
>
> I don't think—well, quite frankly, from the amount of damage I saw—I don't understand how the plant stayed on line. A lot of melting. We actually melted copper, melted aluminum. It was a pretty severe event. . . . We only saw 200°F on the surface. As it turns out we had to have had about 1800°F inside in order to melt aluminum. . . . Once we took that bolt out and realized we had something glowing inside, then . . . the spring of hot metal really became a concern.
>
> At the time I don't think we ever thought that we had that kind of temperature, that kind of fault in there. What we didn't realize was that the housing is aluminum and how well it conducted the heat away

from the event. I mean, theoretically, that could have let go and it could have been a lethal ball of ionized gas, molten metal, in hindsight. . . . We didn't expect that at the one o'clock meeting. Based on previous experience, if they had told me it was at 1800°F, I would have expected to see 500°F to 600°F on the surface of the bus. Our bus is particularly thick at that point, and in hindsight looking at how thick it was, I understand how it dissipated that temperature that well. I'm not sure if the thing had faulted, if the bus might not very well have contained it. But that's not something I would have liked to have tested. Because it very well could have gone and there could have been a fatality involved.

Fortunately, we recognized we had a problem, we shut the plant down in a safe manner and got in and were able to effect repairs before we had a trip, a catastrophic type fault. But there was a huge amount of energy available at that site and if it had let go it could have very easily melted, ionized a large amount of metal.

To Brad, those were "incredible circumstances." Edward, the GSU system engineer, was "amazed."

So you got to remember that the output of the generator phase to phase is 28,000 amps, and going through [the flexible links] was about 22,000 amps—so that's a lot of current goes through each one of these. And this was burned so bad that it was basically the current that was all that was keeping it together flowing through there. I couldn't believe that with that much damage it could still conduct current at that high a rate without showing anything. There was a lot of heat generated by it, but I mean it was continuing to [conduct], which was amazing to me. 'Cause if you look at it, when you got done you could just take the copper and crumble it up. It was completely gone basically. I did not think it was possible to put this much heat on this bushing without causing it to go to ground, which immediately [would have set off a relay signal responding to current imbalance that shuts down the plant automatically]. And so I was quite amazed that we could do as much damage—melt copper on the top of that bushing and that bushing would still continue to function.

Team Reports

About a week after the event, the eight station experts on the "technical event evaluation team" issue a twenty-one-page report, "Generator Step-Up Transformer Low Voltage Bushing Overheating Event: Adverse Condition Report." After recapping the event chronology, the team presents

detailed technical analyses and makes twenty-four corrective action recommendations. The first nineteen address procedures and actions around
retorqueing practices and schedules, flexible link materials and testing,
training and procedures on flexible links, frequency of thermographic inspections, washer issues, and the need to review all electrical distribution
systems before plant restart. One recommendation is to disseminate the
event analysis to all Charles Station electrical specialists and to the industry. Its last four recommendations restate those of its two-man subteam
on "organizational effectiveness."

This team's root cause analysis follows a more or less standard fault
tree analysis, and concentrating on the many technical issues involved,
stays close to the technical competencies of its members, whose recommendations provided the basis for the recovery plan. However, the early
evidence that the two-man organizational response subteam gathered sent
them into unexpected and nonstandard review territory.

"Organizational Effectiveness" Subteam

On the day the plant shut down, Joel, corrective actions program manager, assigned two of his staff, Miles and Doug, to review the "organizational response from initial problem discovery through the plant shutdown decision," a period of 26.5 hours. But the team soon found that
"organizational effectiveness" was the issue.

The "nuclear safety significance" is "small," this team concludes, because "we had both the diesel generators and the reserve auxiliary transformer to supply off-site power after a plant trip or shut down." Citing
the diagnostic work being done on and around the transformer and the
large population walking by the GSU transformer at least twice a day, the
report concludes, "The industrial safety significance was potentially high."

The "primary cause" of the delay in shutting down and continuing to
work at and on the transformer is "Tunnel Vision" in that "actions were
taken and decisions were made without adequately assessing the significance and potential consequences of the overall situation and some available information." ["Tunnel Vision" is one of many standard root cause
categories.] "There had been extensive questioning and exploration of the
hot spot anomaly, by all pertinent levels of Management, during the first
24 hours. To most, it appeared that there were no other reasonable avenues to be pursued. However, with the disassembly of the GSU ductwork,
it became apparent from the actual component damage that the Organization, *as a whole* [bold in original] had failed to achieve as safe and as
conservative an outcome as it could have, for 26.5 hours. The delay in
reaching the shutdown decision had occurred in the presence of considerable industrial safety and business risk. . . . Therefore, the task for this

Root Cause team became one of determining why the organization had not taken more conservative actions, more quickly than it actually did."

In discussions on Wednesday and Thursday, managers asked these and similar questions: "What is the maximum temperature at which the equipment can safely operate? Can the transformer explode? Will relaying protect the transformer? What is the flash point of the transformer oil? With 'definitive, factual answers' only to the last question—292°F—we should have taken precautions to danger tape the area . . . limited the number of personnel in the area . . . [and] not placed personnel on top of the transformer, for extensive periods of time, to take contact pyrometer readings that only confirmed what was already known from thermography. . . . If we were unable to determine that the transformer was *not* going to fail, the conservative thing to have done, from a safety point of view and from a business point of view, would have been to shut down the unit. The station needs to recognize from this event that our culture needs to shift from too strong a production-based behavior toward a more conservative protection (safety) based behavior." The team specifies evidence for its conclusions:

"Briefings and decision-making discussions were oriented to the circulating currents theory alone and did not develop information about the possibility of problems with internal bus work and connections. Obviating circulating current would allow the plant to remain on line, while dealing with internal problems would require shutting down.

"The troubleshooting plan required station experts to work on top of the GSU transformer, at full power, without additional safety measures in effect.

"Thermographic information and industry advice were not adequately used or interpreted throughout the decision-making period.

"Shift managers lack sufficient guidance about who should be notified at the time of such an event."

The team's recommendations for corrective actions:

"Adopt a 'Significance and Consequences' decision-making method or algorithm;

"Develop protocols for calling out people in specific jobs for event support;

"Develop a 'Danger Zone Command and Control' procedure."

Also twenty-one pages, this subteam's report presents background information, station activity logs, data from its two members' interviews with twenty-one people directly involved, and documentation (meeting minutes, the record of thermographic images). In six pages, the subteam presents "Facts, Evidence and Analysis" in terms of three problems:

"Problem 1: Did the organization act in a safe and conservative manner, following the discovery of a hot spot on the Generator Step-up Transformer, through that point in time when the order was given to take the unit off line?

"Problem 2: Did the organization promote and achieve open and honest communication in its activities during this time frame?

"Problem 3: Were notifications of the proper personnel made in a timely manner?"

As background, the report supplies a review of "Industry Operating Experience," followed by "Root Causes and Causal Factors" in two pages. A section on "Generic Implications" discusses the root causes— "Tunnel Vision or 'Group Think' "—together with its recommendations for interim corrective actions, corrective actions to prevent recurrence, and enhancement actions.

The team's recommendations are:

To "develop and implement an Operations and Management tool/ checklist that provides Senior Management guidance on significance and consequence considerations in decision-making";

To "develop and implement a Danger Zone Command and Control expectation similar to a Fire Scene 'Incident Commander' expectation";

To "develop and implement Group Manager level expectations on call out [notification] protocols within their areas of responsibility."

In an appendix, the subteam provides the names and positions of the plant experts and consultants the team interviewed (no names appear on the list made available to me). Its "interview sheet" asks these questions:

Describe the timeline of this event.

Were the appropriate people notified of the thermography finding in a timely manner?

Describe the Industrial Safety conduct, behaviors, attitudes and performance:

Was the troubleshooting decision, to remove the cover bolt, a safe decision?

Was there an effort to limit personnel risk? For example, by restricting the area as much as possible.

Was there caution or danger tagging of the area?

Was there proper use of personnel protective equipment?

Were ladders tied off?

What was the content of prejob briefings?

Were transformer failure scenarios discussed and contingency plans developed?

Was any supervisor or authority clearly in charge of the safety risk zone?

What was done to keep gawkers and sightseers at bay and out of danger?

Was the decision to shut the plant down arrived at in a timely manner?

Between anomaly discovery and now, has anything been done in less than *excellent* fashion? (emphasis in original).

In subsequent discussions, I quote other passages from the team's analysis.

Why the Subteam's Focus Changed

Miles had been at the one o'clock meeting; Doug, previously a manager of quality assurance, had not attended. Doug is speaking.

> Actually the emphasis was not initially on organizational effectiveness because Miles had gone to the meeting and he thought there was a lot of begging for openness on the safety aspects of the issue. In fact, he was very comfortable that it was a very open meeting, one of the better meetings. The concern was because the maintenance manager and the electrical department manager had not been called in when the thermal hot spot was discovered. They didn't know about it until 10:00 the next morning. So that's eighteen hours—they didn't know about it for eighteen hours. And that was the [reason for the] focus on organizational performance, to go and find out why these two senior people hadn't been notified that there was a problem at the station. . . . And within hours of getting into it, we discovered that there was hard and fast evidence that we had a serious problem within minutes of its discovery, which had never gotten to senior management in their decision-making. . . . We started out thinking we would distribute bouquets until we began to document the event chronology and get more deeply into details in the interviews.
>
> Given a worst-case scenario . . . there might have been death, there would have been major equipment damage, there was a high probability of fire and there was a high potential for destruction of parts of the switchyard as well as ground contamination. In addition, if major equipment damage and/or death had occurred, it is highly likely that there would be aggressive prudence and/or wrongful death litigation regarding the management actions taken based on the information available for decision-making.

Having found the hot spot in the first place gave the station a leg up: the station did not, in the subteam's view, capitalize on its "luck." "Delay" is the team's central concern, given "considerable industrial safety and business risk." Limiting faults' longevity, as I have mentioned, may do more to reduce risk than efforts to limit their frequency.

The Reception of the "Organizational Effectiveness" Team Report

After reading the teams' reports, I first interviewed Joel, manager of the corrective actions program, who had selected this event for re-study. Joel, previously an engineering manager at utility headquarters, signed off on the report Doug and Miles wrote—a report that, Joel says, met "with a lot of anger and frustration."

Now it's interesting because when I first heard about the GSU the next day, my first thought was, "Good catch, we really did this well." Because, what I'm thinking is, on first blush, "Here's a serious condition, overheating on the transformer, and we found it using a testing technique of infrared thermography before it became a failure." So I thought, "That's pretty good." And we shut down to fix it. So on the surface, you know, it looked pretty good. And as a matter of fact, Doug and Miles—I think they will also tell you that—when they first heard it, I know Miles in particular, thought, "Hey, good job!" But then we got digging a little more and thinking about it a little more, and that's where we kind of came around to, "You know, we didn't use the thermography because it's a normal thing to do thermography out there, we *happened* to be getting some baseline data, so we found it by luck. We found it late Wednesday afternoon and we didn't shut down until twenty-seven hours later. How come?"

That's when we really started thinking, "Well, what *would* we use for criteria." We realized, "Geez, [in the switchyard] there isn't good hard and fast criteria if you're outside of the technical specs." Technical specs make it very clear that you've got very strict time limits [on work on safety-related systems]. And that's where we just kept thinking, "Here we had a transformer, and we do know there's a hot spot, we didn't entirely know the extent of the condition, and yet we had people crawling around on the transformer. Geez, that doesn't sound like a good idea, you know." So it was more this, once we got going. We started really poking at some of these things, and that's what finally led us to those conclusions.

Now, when we first released this report, there was a lot of anger and frustration at it, because a lot of other people were still back where we were at our first blush, which was, "Hey, good catch! Here we got something before it got us." It took us a lot of effort and time and argument—not arguments but discussion—in trying to convince people that "Hey, if we hadn't been lucky, it would have got us." "Luck is not a robust barrier," as Doug likes to say. You don't want to depend on luck. And that's where we finally started convincing people.

This has been a very interesting root cause [analysis] because of the defensiveness I saw, where people who aren't normally too defensive were quite defensive, and I can't even tell you exactly why, other than we all have some amount of defensiveness whether it be fear, whether it be pride in our own area of responsibility, and we resent people poking holes in it. But there was a lot of pushback on this one, more than I've seen on any other one that we've ever done here. That's why I gave it to you.

Doug recounts how his and Miles's emphasis changed.

Our boss said, "Go find out why these two senior people hadn't been notified that there was a problem at the station." . . . Miles was very concerned about the fact that the organization did not see that we had a significant near-miss. And, as a matter of fact, we had senior and executive management tell us several times that they thought they had done an absolutely stellar job, and they couldn't accept the falsity, the half truths, the errors, how off base [our] GSU report was. . . . The problem was Miles and I couldn't get anyone excited other than our own boss [Joel] . . . about the generic implications of all of that. 'Cause the management team thought it had done an absolutely stellar job of treating the information that it was presented with. Managers are saying, "Some of it didn't come forward, so what? Nothing happened." So [to them] nothing happened.

Vince, the condition-based engineering analyst and one of the original foursome at the GSU, is skeptical about thermography's reliability and cynical toward "Monday morning quarterbacks."

Among the four of you as you looked at what you'd seen, was there any doubt in your minds what this was?

There was doubt in my mind. As to how serious this was. I definitely knew that something was going on, but how serious it was and at what rate it may change, there was doubt in my mind. In fact, the following day I went out to lunch with the two [thermography] consultants while the meetings were going on. I said, "Which way do you think this is heading? What's going to happen here?" And one of them said, "They may be shutting down." Really? I felt kinda—that kinda surprised me. I had thought, "Well, we'll monitor it," that type of thing. 'Cause in my mind it was just probability-wise. It seems unusual that you'd actually go out there and actually find something that's going to fail *now*! You know, you go out there and certain things you're used to. If I went up to a pump and I know what that pump feels like and that thing's shaking off its pedestal, "OK, we have a serious problem here, this isn't going to last much longer." But maybe 'cause I don't have much experience with thermography, the intellectual side, it just seemed that you go out there, generally speaking, you find something and it doesn't look quite right and you monitor it, keep an eye on it, repair, or whatever. But when he said, "I think you'll be coming off line like today or soon," I thought that was, I guess the first time that it really occurred to me that's how serious it was.

So right after they found it and took the picture, the two consultants didn't give you that sense?

I didn't get that sense, no.

Did you discuss with them the circulating current theory at lunch?

At lunch, I don't recall discussing that, no.

'Cause that was the alternative. That it was something they'd seen before. Well, I guess it surprised everybody.

Well, it depends who you want to talk to and how much they want to lie—well, not lie but revise history. The way things go is you've got a certain amount of people that just want to be a Monday morning quarterback, they won't commit to anything, not until they know the facts. Well, then, if they opened it up and said, "We have a high resistance spot here and this was what was causing it or we have"—oh yeah, sure, "Everybody should have known that, I knew that." The thing's melting apart, and then it's, "Well why didn't you take it off line sooner? If it wasn't about to melt apart why did you take it off at all?" I think there's a certain segment of the population that's like that— you're damned if you do and damned if you don't. . . . But you know I thought the timeliness of the whole thing as it was going on, I thought we did a pretty good job. As I recall, it was about quarter of four in the afternoon the day before a holiday and everybody's leaving as we first lay eyes on this, and to have the plant down-powering within twenty-four hours, I thought it was pretty responsive. We had to get people called in. Nobody was supposed to be there that Thursday. We were scheduled to work because we had those guys on contract to come up and do this [Andy and Frank], but nobody else was supposed to be on-site, and who knows where they're going to be at four o'clock. They're going to leave work and go visiting people whatever. To have everybody back in, on the phone, back in on Thursday and have a few meetings, down-powering, looking in, coming off line—I thought it was pretty responsive.

And then a few days or weeks later, people publish a thing saying "You guys aren't too sharp, why did it take you so long?" You know, typical, you know. That's typical. But I was put off a little by that.

The picture, the thermogram didn't seem to be persuasive right off the bat?

Right. Not to everybody. Paul, I think, I don't want to put words in his mouth, but the night before, the night we found it, I think he was relatively certain, pretty certain that it was not a circulating current issue. Now that's not to say that he was certain that there was something in there melting, but he was relatively certain it was not a circulating current thing. And I think he persuaded me to that effect too. I mean, but like I said, we didn't think, "Hey, this thing's"—we didn't just go home that night saying "Oh that thing might melt tonight, so what?" That wasn't our train of thought. But he didn't think it was circulating current.

As lucky as this "new find" was, it could also be "bad news." That seems to have made it hard for many to believe their luck in the first place and to decide what to do with it.

INSIGHTS AND EXCURSIONS

These four excursions treat several issues and themes that station experts illuminate: the semantics of safety, the credibility of evidence and of its interpreters, and the constraints of the tradeoff quandary. Although the one o'clock meeting lasted for over two hours, the one-and-a half page single-spaced report of the discussion made available to me sets out the few details in my opening account of the event. Comments of several who had been in the room, however, appear throughout.

"Shiny and Rusty" . . . "Plant and Balance of Plant"

Two questions preoccupy the organizational effectiveness team. Why, despite evidence of a problem of potentially high magnitude, did 26.5 hours elapse before deciding to shut down the plant? Why were "no additional safety measures" taken to protect those working on and around the GSU? Missing from the decision process, the team concludes, was a worst-case analysis. The station needs a "better tool to assess the significance and consequence of an off-normal condition. The higher the significance and the more undesirable the consequences, the more aggressive the organization needs to be in acting on it and questioning whether we have a solid understanding and basis for action." The station lacks this capability, however, only when equipment not categorized as "safety-related" is involved—that is, equipment not governed by the "logics built into the Technical Specifications" and not unequivocally subject to regulatory oversight. The subteam's report maps these differences between the technical logics of the design basis and the cultural logics of the tradeoff quandary.

For example, if a Diesel Generator is inoperable, we have seventy-two hours to repair it or shut down the unit. When the difficult business versus safety decisions must be made on nonsafety systems, they do not have similar, logically laid out significance and consequence analysis portfolios that help to balance the safety considerations with the long-term, reliable production of electricity. Much of the equipment that could cripple us, as a successful utility, is not prioritized anywhere. The organization needs to be acutely aware of the equipment that we need to make electricity and to safely and reliably conduct business (i.e., the generator, exciter, GSUs, switchyard and the associated support systems).

What counts as safety related and nonsafety related? Edward, senior engineer in the technical support group, refines the distinction with a qualifier: "There's a dividing line" between "safety related, roughly" and "not safety related."

The safety-related equipment is the stuff that is required for safe shutdown, not for the safe operation of the plant. That's the difference. So there's a dividing line of what's safety related roughly and what's not safety related. . . . There is a division [between safety in running the plant and safely shutting down]. I mean we maintain everything, we've got to do that. But there's definitely different requirements depending on whether you're on the safety or the nonsafety side. Especially like from seismic—that's a big one, when there's an earthquake you're required to have shutdown stuff as opposed to [no requirements for] the other stuff.

The logics for the "other stuff" are unlikely to be elaborated to the same extent as they are for the "safety side," says Grant, engineering supervisor in the technical support group.

In [its oversight on] maintenance, the NRC definitely has pulled the entire switchyard almost into what I'd call a safety-related area. It's not really safety related, but you treat it much more like it was.

That was a point that the report also made. That the logic for thinking through this decision is not as well articulated for balance-of-plant as it is for operating.

That's absolutely true. On the nuclear side of the plant you have procedures for almost every contingency and they're written down. If you have this or that event, you go right to this procedure and the control room can almost act without even having to think—just follow the procedures and you'll get to a safe conclusion. On the electrical side of the plant, basically you're developing your plan on the fly.

We have electrical experts here, but on the nuclear side of the plant huge amounts of resources were expended because they had to be, because the NRC required them to develop all these procedures, the emergency operating procedures. . . . It would take an equal if not more expenditure in time, money, and resources to produce EOPs [Emergency Operating Procedures] for this side of the plant without the NRC regulation requirement. I don't think economically we could do that. . . .

I'll give you an example. Another station that was built about twenty years ago, their original electrical tech spec was two pages. That's all the NRC required—it had very limited interest. Our electrical tech spec is about sixty pages because the NRC has gotten more so they realize that a lot of the trips that challenge the mechanical side of the plant came from the electrical side. In many plants originally, you basically spun the turbines, and if there was any problem with the generator or transformers or whatever, you called the host utility who had the electrical people to come take care of the problem. As the NRC became more and more interested in that, that became less and less an option, and you have to have much more control even if you let that group do your work.

In daily parlance, an assortment of categories governed by both regulatory and engineering orders distinguishes equipment and its consequences: "nonsafety related" and "safety related": "nuclear" and "nonnuclear," "plant" and "balance of plant," "the nuclear side" and the "nonnuclear side," the "primary side" and the "secondary side," "the safety side" and "the nonsafety side," "the shiny side" and "the rusty side." And by professional orders: nuclear and civil engineering on "the mechanical side" (the reactor and supporting systems) and electrical engineering and maintenance disciplines on "the electrical side" (generator, turbine, switchyard). Market order also has a word for it, as Paul tells it.

And while [the thermography consultants] were here I wanted them to check the large components, the moneymakers, which happens to be the GSU, the generator step-up transformers. Without them we don't make money. . . . Anyway, we go over to the GSU because it's a moneymaker and start doing a quick scan.

Grant, electrical maintenance supervisor, tries to put the two sides together.

Do you see anything in your work over these years where you would say that you can see—you and your colleagues can see—more of a relation between nonnuclear and nuclear when it comes to electricity issues? Are there any connections that you think are not understood adequately as affecting the nuclear side?

It's all nuclear. Do you mean safety versus nonsafety?

Oh. You say, "It's all nuclear." Well, that's not how it goes—as you said, there's "plant" and "balance of plant."

There's NSSS [nuclear steam supply system, or plant] and balance of plant. Or as we say, the shiny side and the rusty side. You got to remember that there's always been safety-related electrical, like rod control or inverters that support directly the nuclear side of the plant. I think what the NRC pushed is that even though the turbine and the generator are nonsafety, they're important to safety in the plant, in two ways. One is that the best source of power, if you have a problem in the plant, is always the grid. It's an unlimited source and you have multiple sources on it. If the plant loses off-site power you're depending on two diesels to start. They have limited power availability and if one fails you've lost half your power. So the grid is always most reliable. So keeping the off-site power availability, in NRC's terms, is very important to safety.

Second is that many of the accidents that have occurred, or damage or accidents to the mechanical side—the nuclear side of the plant—the initiating event was the loss of the electrical side of the plant. We have a huge amount of energy that is all flowing and passing out of the plant. If the electric side fails and you suddenly have what you call a "loss of load" event, you challenge the mechanical side of the plant tremendously to safely absorb all that energy. You're sending 1150 megawatts out and three cycles later you're not. All that rotating energy, the turbine, all that steam flowing, valves have to stroke, a lot of things have to happen perfectly in order to safely shut the plant down. And in many nuclear events, the precursor has been a trip started on the balance-of-plant side of the plant. So you don't want to challenge the nuclear side of the plant by tripping it off that way.

"Rusty" sides, Grant says, the NRC deems "important to safety" but, as the organizational effectiveness team observes, not important enough to merit a troubleshooting and decision-making logics also oriented to unexpected situations. Nor, Admiral Hyman Rickover observed in his comments on the Kemeny Commission report, had station experts at Three Mile Island been trained on the "direct interaction" of rusty and shiny: "there was no formally approved training program for steam plant operators although there is a direct interaction between the steam plant and the reactor plant. It was the steam plant operators, in fact, whose actions initiated the events which ultimately led to the accident."[1] The basic distinction rests on their public consequences, in Grant's view.

And generally, even if this had gone wrong, and we had lost the transformer for example, there's a very high probability the nuclear side of the plant would have shut down and the nuclear safety of the public would not be compromised. The worst would be an economic impact to the plant and power generation for the region. So there's a different set of consequences too. From my standpoint, not running the plant is a disaster for us as a plant, as a staff, but John Q. Public is not affected other than his price of wholesale electricity may go up. Whereas on the nuclear side, we can potentially affect people off-site. Very low probability, but part of keeping that probability low is putting all these resources into the emergency operating procedures. With the level of consequences for this event I'm not going to hurt anybody off-site. You can't justify the level of resources for that kind of procedure for every possible contingency.

The "primary" side has many "bells and whistles" but when the steam arrives to make electricity, "you hook up any old turbine and any old secondary system" no different from fossil, hydro, or gas-fired plants. Ken, maintenance department manager, talks about these two "sides of the house."

Historically the nuclear industry has taken a very structured approach to the nuclear side or the N triple S [nuclear steam supply system] side of the house in terms of construction—it's more standardized in most cases. There's a lot more seismic issues there, there's a lot more built-in safety features, and with that comes tech specs and the NRC's Final Safety Analysis Review, which also is another layer of protection. Those are requirements to assure you're working within the design concept. On the balance-of-plant side, historically it's just a standard old fossil design, fossil mentality, you know, it's a different approach. The steam comes out of the primary side with all its bells and whistles and protection and envelopes. And here comes the steam and you hook up any old turbine and any old secondary system, no matter what power plant you're at. The boilers may have a little bit more [safety relevance] because they go directly from the reactor to the turbine so they have some other built-in tech specs there. . . .

You don't think about the probabilistic risk assessments that we do on the primary side as much on the secondary side. . . . You know, there's a lot of factories out there that have the same potential, the same energy sources. But a power plant is something different, and especially a nuclear power plant. You know, you don't have the factory mentality, you have to protect the health and safety of the public, and the technology here is pretty powerful. And, yeah, you can just disconnect the containment and all the big cement buildings you see out there and bring in some oil burners and gas burners to make the steam and hook it up and there you go, ready to rock and roll with electricity. You don't have the same controls, regulations, and procedures that you have on the primary [nuclear] side.

Evaluating the reliability of equipment on the "primary side" is not always a stable or "standardized" process, however. Equipment condition can be judged "administratively." Vince, senior engineer in the condition-based maintenance group, explains.

I want to be accurate in what I say. Even on the primary side there's certain situations where you don't have that logic. It's not for every case. I mean if I were to go and take a vibration set of readings, you see we have IST [in-service testing] criteria and IST criteria says, "OK, at this point if the overall vibration level goes above such and such, it's inoperable." That's fine. You see you do vibration analysis, you say "OK, for IST I'm not inop [inoperable]," I'm OK, but I look at it and I'm not where I want to be. It's gone up, it's doubled. Not only has it doubled, but I have these frequencies out here causing it to go up— those are typical for a bearing failure. So now I'm back to my opinion. And you could say, "Hey, this thing, this is not right." Now per your code and everything, I'm OK. But I'm saying, "I don't like this at all," and we're right back into "What should I do, is it operable"?

And when you have that kind of uncomfortable call to make, what do you do?

Try to get buy-in, try to explain it to your supervisor and other people that know about these things and other vibration people around, in the company or down at another plant, or outside the company. Try to get people in on it.

And so what happened last week?

Oh, we stayed on line. We had some—now this is an overall reading— right now we're between 6.3 and 6.5 mils of displacement on this bearing and they had set it [the limit] at, I think 7. Right now where if it reaches 7 we start downpowering. There's [an automatic] trip at 10. The trip point hasn't changed. But that 7 is an administrative limit—it used to be 6. Well, we're over 6, what do we do? Do we downpower now? We get a procedure change. We tell General Electric [the vendor], "Hey." General Electric says, "Why do you have it at 6? Trip's at 10." Well, we used to always run about 3 or 4, so that's why we had it, you know—so is 6 a real good number? So you start getting into that ball game. There's a lot of administrative limits like that that may or may not have the best technical justification for them—"If they're more conservative, so let's go with this."

Divorced legalistically, "nuclear" and "nonnuclear" equipment and processes can remain intimate operationally. Switchyard, generator, and turbine seen as "nonsafety equipment" are nevertheless said to be "important to safety" and "safety related, roughly." Those ambiguities can keep caution uppermost, but they can also reinforce each "side" as being its own "part," as "nuclear" and "industrial" safety are with respect to working conditions and practices: "industrial safety," "personnel safety," "personal safety," "occupational safety" refer to protection from bodily harm, except for radiation protection; the NRC regulates dose control, which is strictly "nuclear" and the province of a station's "health physics" experts. On "personal safety" at Charles Station, Grant remarked:

> We have a philosophy that everyone is responsible for their personal safety, and the supervisors have a responsibility for the safety of the crew. I think that's probably where it focuses, you know, on eyeglass safety, hairnets, safety breathing devices, safety belts, and that type of industrial type safety.

"Our safety group really focuses on the industrial safety part," says Joel, manager of the corrective actions program. "Nuclear safety probably resides most heavily with the operators—everybody's involved with nuclear safety—but the licensed operators are the champions." Hank, the new administrator of what Charles Station calls the "health and safety group," explains his job.

> They hired me on last year to make a change in the behavior of employees here. And I spent a lot of time with their safety program and making sure people were following rules and regulations. Managers were asking, "Was there any support to bring the morale up and for this to be more of a service oriented department—was there enough horsepower?" There wasn't, and employees wanted a change: they wanted more people in the safety department, they wanted some of us out in the field working with them talking to them, less policing and more assistance. So that's where I started.

> *The fact that this event was balance of plant or not on the nuclear side, in the switchyard—is that more industrial safety than nuclear? Is that how the geography is mapped out here?*

> When I say industrial safety I mean employees working on an industrial site, how can they get injured. You've got nuclear safety, you've got chemistry, you have all the different departments. But all these people working on this entire industrial site whether they're working on radiation or components or out in the switchyard, it's industrial. How can someone here get injured? And how am I going to prevent that? That's

what I mean by industrial safety. Coming down the access road, this is industrial safety—you can get hurt anywhere. So I'm really working with all the departments.

The "safety group" can be frustrated in getting heard on the nuclear side, however. Dom, who is Hank's one staff person, comments.

I can't say that there have been any incidents that have made me nervous or made me feel that we need more people or less people [in our group]. Other than maybe getting some help from the technical people that can fix {rising tone} what the plant people see as a need. Sometimes we have a breakdown because people who are [assigned] somewhere else, it's not their priority.

And your group is in a position of intermediary, really.

Exactly.

You're just transferring the request. So, you have no lines into these other organizations directly?

We're trying to develop them. We're trying to get more weight with the engineers. But no, the things we can fix ourselves, we try to. Someone needs a better pair of safety glasses or a better kind of hard hat, we work on those, but the harder issues are kind of, let's say, outside my control. I feel like a little bit of a victim when I say that, you know. I mean I can control a lot but I can't move pipes or design things. We kind of put it to the next group and hope that they move with it as well.

Do you ever ask them to walk it down with you at least, so it gets into their heads?

Some, we have.

If these were matters of nuclear safety, they would be likely to have higher "priority" and be "easier issues" for engineers to pay attention to.

Distinctions born of regulatory and engineering orders shape the approved hierarchy of operational concerns and the geography of work. But those two-sided understandings may not capture operational dynamics nor anticipate the practical ambiguities of those distinctions, as in the turbine vibration Vince was watching. Then, ambiguities can contribute to clarity and to risk reduction in contexts where gradations and variations raise doubts and questions about categorical certainties defined without respect to context. To wrestle with the ambiguities of the GSU's hot spot and to fill that gap between nuclear and nonnuclear logics, the organizational effectiveness team recommends what it calls an "algorithm" used by "a number of utilities to achieve balance in the Prevention (Safety) versus Production decision making and priority setting." This assessment includes the question, "Is this a campaign item—within the station, for the NRC, for INPO, for stakeholders?" "Campaign item" refers to several kinds of issues: those that important outsiders (local community groups, media, shareholders) already have their eye on, those that concern insiders because they represent repeat events or directly affect safe shutdown, and those that concern equipment or procedures already pinpointed for special review by the regulator or by INPO's peer reviews.

The algorithm suggests how discussions within the tradeoff quandary are likely to proceed generally. It asks five questions about consequences, known as "The Five D's," the teams says: "Serious Injury or Death? Uncontrolled, unintended Dose? Significant loss of Dollars? Damage to major plant equipment? Disgrace with Internal and/or External stakeholders (Employees, Owners, Regulators, Public, etc.)? And probably there is a sixth—uncontrolled/unintended Discharge [of radioactivity]." The team's report concludes: "If a significance and consequence assessment tool, such as this, had been run through on Wednesday evening, the significance would have been high on all but one line item ([the GSU] was not a 'Campaign' item). Also, the potential consequences should have triggered concern due to the number of . . . unanswerable unknowns on all but the Dose consequence. [A]n 'unanswerable unknown' must temporarily default to the more conservative, worst case, assumption until it can be answered more favorably." But the semantics of nuclear/nonnuclear, nuclear/industrial, plant/balance-of-plant seem to have made the wait-and-see strategy a viable option: a costly shutdown of "moneymaker" equipment on the "rusty side" versus the least-cost solution (for circulating current) that previously had kept the plant on line.

Those semantics have sustained a rhetoric of public reassurance necessary to this industry from day one: "nuclear side" encapsulates dangers in a concrete containment; "nonnuclear side" claims that otherwise risk levels are no different from those of any other industrial enterprise. As managers and regulators work through the significance determination process situation by situation to decide what counts operationally as "safety related" and "safety significant," they confront the ambiguities those reassurances leave behind.

Crediting Evidence

The thermograms provided the only evidence of an anomaly in the GSU, according to the technical evaluation team's findings, Doug reports. But obstacles to believing that evidence, or believing in the credibility of those citing it, were persistent. Doug observes:

There were no other indications on the transformer, no other differential current, no other temperatures, no other oil filter sample medians, or anything else that would indicate that anything was wrong. No air temperatures on the bus work—nothing that indicated anything else was wrong. It was simply pointed out by the thermography. And the guys that did the thermography recognized immediately that this was different than anything we had seen before. And it was more serious. And the more they looked at it, the more convinced they became, and the stronger and more emphatic they became with their own management trying to get somebody to pay attention to it.

Paul stakes his reputation for betting only on sure things.

In hindsight, should we [the station] have identified what turned out to be happening ahead of time? Well, I think we actually did. Thursday morning infrared wise, we were pretty confident that "Hey, this is caused by something in behind." Another engineer had actually done the statistical analysis [overnight], and he calculated that over 500 degrees was behind there. . . . Given all the variables, that was probably a reasonable guess. And that was enough so that we've got to do something with this. And along about 7 A.M. Thursday, the TSU [technical support group] manager, Mike, came in, and Nat [Paul's supervisor] was there. I'd already been into Nat's office. "Hey, Nat, this is a real problem. We're shutting down—this is a big one. I really feel that this is a major problem." And Mike came along and kinda sat on the edge of the desk, and I said, "Mike, this is a real problem. It's not induced current, it's caused by radiant heat." And I said, "I don't know how hot it is behind there, but it's got to be pretty hot. We're going to be shutting down." He kinda looks at me, kinda raises his eyebrow, and I say, "Mike, you know me," and I said to put it in perspective, "I'll give you 100 to 1 odds." I say, "You know I don't bet unless I'm going win."

During that holiday morning Paul collated the thermograms, presented them to the electrical system engineers and to a transformer expert and vendor representative who were working with them, and then gave "all the information to Nat." Paul recounts:

I laid the pictures out, the before and the after, and I even had some industry data on induced currents, so I could actually show this is what induced currents should look like—"Here's our induced current that we do have on this panel." I was very, very specific: "This picture, this is not induced current." I presented that to the electrical system engineers first thing in the morning, gave all that information to Nat, he put it together in a Power Point presentation [for the one o'clock meeting]. I looked at it, I said, "OK, it's fine." He knew the situation. . . . Should we have actually done that the night before? In hindsight, yes. I don't feel entirely bad waiting until the next morning. I wouldn't again. But under the circumstances I didn't think that was the wrong decision.

At the one o'clock meeting, Grant says, "We didn't believe the accuracy of what Nat was saying about the images. Let me give you an example of how fast it's changed. Two years ago our thermographic camera was a huge boxy affair. In only a year-and-a-half the technology just astound-ingly changed." Charles Station's state-of-the-art digital camera uses a camcorder battery, a major upgrade from the previous one whose infrared sensors required "lugging around a big container of liquid nitrogen." Now the camera "can not only differentiate the temperatures very accurately, but differentiate the temperature gradients, and that's the part you didn't used to be able to do very well. And that's what you need." Paul was the one "guy who was getting all that information, but it takes some time [for others to become familiar with the data]. You know, he can put out a memo and say, 'Yeah it's gotten better,' and we say, 'Yeah, it sure has.' But you need to get out and interact with it—a 'Show Me' kind of thing. So in this particular case—this is a rough way to do it—but it certainly showed me and I'm definitely a believer. And next time I'll know much better how to interpret the results and make a better decision on it."

For about ten years, managers staffed an on-again-off-again thermo-graphic inspection program with several electricians. In one reorganiza-tion, the engineering department took it over, according to Phil, manager of the electrical maintenance department.

So reading that kind of data is not entirely unfamiliar to people here? Well, it could be I suppose.

Well, yeah, even when electricians had the cameras we were data takers, not data analyzers. . . . I think that the ability to interpret the thermo-graphic pictures resides in maybe one person here on-site.

It's kind of interesting—one of the shots that was put up on the over-head at the one o'clock meeting—knowing what we all know now—should have just had us all running out of the room screaming, maybe. There was a picture there that showed this large connection box from the outside—there's really two boxes that you see as one from the out-side—and inside there's an internal wall. And you could see that the heat was being radiated in that one box and not getting through the wall. Now we looked at that and said, "Isn't that interesting?" It didn't click for any of us that that should have told us that this wasn't circulat-ing current, there was something hot in there radiating heat.

I think we could have had somebody in that meeting that was more proficient at interpreting what the pictures were telling us. That probably could have helped us out. And that's probably one of the frustrations for Paul. If anyone else on-site is our expert, it's Paul. I think he spends an inordinate amount of his time gathering data and probably very little, or a limited amount of time, analyzing it.

Cliff, operations department manager, who "facilitated" the one o'clock meeting, acknowledges he "probably had made up" his mind.

This was an unscheduled surveillance. So that was one of the complicating factors. I think that we as a station, as a group, were unfamiliar with the technology. And I don't want to say we didn't believe it, but we maybe misread it. I think the people that did the thermography, the actual technicians that did it, they understood it, but their voice—they were not at the meeting, their next level of supervision represented them. If they were there, it's been so long now, if they were there, the other aspect of it—

They weren't there.

They weren't there?

No.

To be honest, probably I fell hook, line, and sinker [for the circulating current theory] because we had a similar problem with a hot spot and we solved it by tightening a bolt. I probably had made up my mind, now that I think back on it {rueful laugh}.

Others were also hard to convince. Phil, electrical maintenance manager, remembers:

I think that two-thirds of us that were [at the GSU on Thursday morning after the bolts had been tightened and power reduced, then increased] were convinced that we had an overheating connection inside the box and that we had a real serious concern. There were a couple of people there that were not convinced. You know, that wasn't enough for them. They weren't convinced there was a problem, so we just moved the ladder over a little bit to the next box and took a bolt out of there—you would expect to see the same thing inside there. And of course we didn't see anything inside there, so that was enough to convince everybody there that "Yes, we needed to bring the plant down."

"Validation" and "verification" are the watchwords when encountering any off-normal signal. Caution multiplies in this intricate technology, especially when facing the dilemma of over-reading and under-reading hundreds of daily signals. But images are not yet as credible for validation as is evidence from the "outside" of equipment. For Brad, electrical engineer in the technical support group, that evidence is "more measurable and touchable."

> It was stuff that was outside and accessible, as opposed to this, which was inside. The possibility that the currents were running through the housing was what we were looking into, which would cause the heating. Most of the circulating current measurements were done with ammeters and the stuff we could get to, so it wasn't done with the thermographic camera. It was a different way of approaching it. It's really hard to tell what we were seeing on the thermography—we could actually look at the conductors for the other one. On this one, everything was inside something. So it was a matter of how do you reflect the temperature on a conductor out to the outer housing? That was the question nobody really knew how to answer.

Vince, a senior maintenance engineer who was with Paul when the first thermogram was made, sees the images as a "gray area."

> Thermography is best when you can see the object that you're concerned about. If you look at a wire connection you can see it, you're all set. Let's say that connection is behind a panel that you can't open up. You see a warm spot, but what do you really know about it? You're really into a gray area now because then I know that that wire shouldn't be hotter than more than 150 degrees or something. If I have to look through something, [that raises the question of] heat transfer and blah blah blah. You know, if you want to take a heat transfer course and try to do calculations—but in the real world there are certain things you can't calculate, I don't think, unless you know all the details. Well, you don't know all the details, so this is a type of thing we're in with the GSU. Say, OK, I look at the outside of this transformer, I can see this temperature that's not right. Now what does that mean a foot and a half behind it? I don't know. Do I have a point source this big that's throwing out all that heat? So I don't know, until you open it up.

The infrared camera makes it possible to avoid whatever risks attach to opening up this kind of equipment, of course. But that assumption—that "outside and accessible" evidence is more credible—led managers to send electricians up onto ladders with pyrometers (hand-held temperature sensors) to validate the thermographic evidence. Sense data—vibrations and "seeing the object that you're concerned about"—is, for Vince, more believable than images of the invisible, which, he finds, are more "art" than "science."

I think, again, this is kind of my read on it, first off, thermography is still somewhat in the art versus science field as far as interpreting data goes—to some extent, much less so than it used to be, but again, I think we've seen thermography interpretations be dead wrong. I can give you examples where we replaced pipe that's perfectly good because the thermography said it was not good and yet it was good.

Thermographic images can put Jack, the shift manager, on the spot more often than he is accustomed to. When I asked him what he thought about the emphasis on production pressures in the organizational effectiveness team's report, he veered back to the validation question.

I'll tell you the way I feel I need to be challenged if I say, "Shut the plant down." And I should be. And I want to able to come back [to my manager with] with, "You must shut it down because a, b, c, this is this." I couldn't do that. OK. I couldn't validate that. The plan that came out was what I felt was needed to validate whether it was circulating currents. Or what I'm saying is, "Hey, if you can't prove it is, then prove it isn't." And the other things they were going to do was put grounds on different locations and that would move this thing around, this circulating current around, if it was in fact a circulating current. So I feel that we were prudent, because you've got to validate information. You've got information, you've got to validate it.

Now Paul is as good a person as he is, and if you interview Paul, he's just an honest person. But, and I don't mean to say he cries "Wolf!" but he does bring lots of problems up. This isn't like this was the only problem he brought up. As a matter of fact, when we brought the transformers back up after the fix, he was convinced that we got a problem on another transformer because the temperatures were different on that one than they were on the other two, when we were coming up. And it's reasonable that he's bringing these issues to me, but he's bringing 'em to me as, "This is a problem," and I say, "Good, let's look at it and see what we're going to do." . . . And you know, there's nothing wrong with Paul. Any process people have to feel free to bring their issues [to the control room] and you have to validate them. . . .

So you're not claiming that the thermography was definitive, over and above these other things. By the same token, it was an unmistakable hot spot.

It was an unmistakable hot spot. Whether it was definitive, it wasn't definitive to me, but it was leading to, it could not be dismissed as a circulating current picture. Remember, here's a plate, ok? If this whole plate is elevated in temperature, that's more indicative of its being a circulating current, again because it's electrically separated and there's a potential there and there's current passing through it and there's heat. What we had was a plate, mounted on the outside frame, where the bushing was, and the hot spot was substantially on this plate, three quarters of it, but it also went off here. OK. So that was not a traditional circulating current.

There was an anomaly there.

For a plate-induced circulating current. However, the people from the transformer vendor say those things can move anywhere, they can be on a flat piece. . . . So to answer your question, the infrared picture was not definitive, but it was definitive to me that—well, that doesn't sound right. There were enough questions to me that we did need to follow this forward, we just couldn't close the books on it, dismiss it, and agree in that room without doing anything else, saying, "Yeah, this is circulating currents." There was no expert there that would say it was circulating current. They would say, "It certainly looks like it to me. I've never seen a hot spot. I've never seen anything from inside fail like that."

For Jack and others at the meeting, given its more frequent appearance, circulating current is an *expectable* anomaly, or, by now, a condition of an energized GSU for which there is a proven palliative. An unexpected anomaly was beyond practice. I asked Jack:

Was everybody talking who should have been talking?

Yeah, I guess, there were I don't know how many people, somewhere between 20 and 30 people there. Not everybody spoke. There were some people that appeared to have a predisposition that it was a circulating current and they were strong in transformers, and they said, "This is a circulating current," because that's their business. They could say that, and I couldn't really argue with them. But it seemed to be people that were more hoping it was circulating currents because the answer was so much better if it were. And for example, this plate, the screws, these screws on top showed cooler than the plate itself did, and if you saw the thermographic images you could see the color differences. And the person was saying, "That's indicative of the screws being loose and that's why you have this problem."

That normalizing argument did not sit right with Jack, however.

That's really not true, I mean those things are just sticking out further. Now, that [other explanation] was stated, but whether it was accepted or not, it was a theory—a theory that the screws are loose. But it was

like, "Screws are loose, tighten them up, problem will go away." That
was some of the attitude. That would have been great. I would have
loved that if that was it.

*And, so there were the thermograms. Did they keep referring to the
pictures or were they shown once?*

No, we kept going back to them.

I asked Paul if he thought that verifying the infrared data was necessary
or complementary.

In my opinion, maybe just because it's nuclear power and they always
like to have a second check, it's ok to do it once, to verify it. But you
don't need to keep doing it. Was it necessary? No. Because I had my
short-wavelength camera, Andy had his long-wavelength camera, and
we were within two degrees of each other. It was legit. And I felt very
comfortable with that. . . . Now a pyrometer is accurate, but it's very
subjective. You can actually get several degrees difference—me and
you, we would take it a little bit different. And with the camera, once
it's set up, and I tell you it's OK for the distance, the efficiency, and all
that type of stuff, you snap a picture and I snap a picture, it's going to
be within a tenth of a degree. It's going to be very, very close.

Another kind of "tunnel thinking" narrowed the conversation: thinking about the GSU housing per se, not about its connections. At the one
o'clock meeting, Grant mentioned that "the only [electrical] links problems we have had have been right at the generator and that was caused
by vibration" and that during another repair they had replaced "bolts
and washers." Apparently, those comments ended discussion of the conditions of bus, bushing, and connections to the turbine early in the one
o'clock meeting: it was an option that would take the reactor off line for
two days. But as Grant told me, before seeing the damage, he expected
that "one of those laminated strips had come loose and was touching the
side of the cabinet and that's what was glowing and causing the problem."
Only after the fact does the technical team's evaluation note that its "review of the INPO Operating Experience database did show a number of
occurrences of flexible link failures that caused plants to shut down. No
events . . . matched the condition that occurred [at Charles] where the
aluminum connection to the copper plates failed. However, there are a
number of events from failures of flexible connections." The parts template seems to have been laid over the problem, keeping the housing alone
the focus of discussion. It also defined the problem for Edward, the GSU
system engineer, who, despite his title, keeps firm boundaries between
parts. He attended the one o'clock meeting.

This GSU fault is more a distribution issue than it is a transformer issue. I don't have the isophase bus—another system engineer has that. You see the bus itself is not part of mine—I only come to the transformer. The top of that bushing is mine from there down and the backside of that goes to the system engineer for the transformer—I mean for the generator, which includes the isophase bus. And so even though we work together on stuff like that, it's actually his system. But I was a big part of it. But the actual major calling on the bus work and stuff like that, I wasn't really involved in that as much because I was doing most of the work on the transformer and stuff.

At that meeting, Ken, maintenance manager, recalls that doubting was difficult.

I think the question was asked, "What else could it be?" Obviously, [after the fact] there was a loose connection. But then you have this qualified, certified guy who comes in and has twenty years experience. "I don't think it's that, I've never seen that, we haven't experienced that problem."

When giving evidence its due, there is a pervasive industry pattern of taking the word of "credentialed" outsiders over that of insiders, a practice that frustrates and demoralizes the home team when managers, after hearing their recommendations, take action only if outsiders agree.

For Paul, who is well acquainted with the ways that circulating current exhibits thermographically, the first thermogram on Wednesday afternoon was beyond caution: "A no-brainer," he calls the image. "It's not always that way, but this was a no-brainer. Anybody that was holding the camera would have compared this one, 'Well, this one was 250 degrees, the one right beside it is 110, there's something different here,' " which put "us up into the category where you fix very, very quickly." Just as quickly, Paul is "apprehensive because what if I'm wrong?" Like everyone else at a nuclear power plant, he calibrates the freight a shutdown decision carries—"a big deal, you're talking a million dollars a day." And, as they also understand, calling for what turns out to be an unnecessary shutdown can be a "career-closer."

But neither Paul nor Brad are at the one o'clock meeting. Ken, maintenance manager, elaborates.

We made a decision at the time based on the current expertise that we had in the meeting room. We had experts in there telling us what they thought the issues were. We liked that answer. It appeared to us it was technically correct, it kept the unit on line which is our mission, and it didn't seem to be a risky evolution, the people involved were eager, and everything seemed to be jelling pretty well. But the key issue, though, was that there were also people in the organization that had just as strong feelings about what the technical reason for it was—and that was contrary to what we knew at that particular time in the meeting. It had to do with our thermography technical expertise and, for people who really knew about that, this was not a circulating current issue. There was something happening on this particular device. But for some reason, their thoughts and ideas—they didn't sell it or they didn't come forward freely. It wasn't something that was compressed or was something that was intentionally, "I'm not going to listen to you." I think it was one of these things, "Yeah, it's possibly an idea, but we'll look in this area."

That's how I see where our mistake was made as far as looking exactly at what the root cause was, or the maintenance item [the connector flag], to cause the overheating. And the organization from the top down was endorsing it—questioning it, but endorsing it. But they didn't ask some other questions about what risks were there and what really could be the worst thing that could happen. That question wasn't really asked. So my perception is that we made the decision at the time with the knowledge that we had. It was something in our conscious mind that this was the way to go.

The transformer consultants were the "current expertise . . . in the room" who kept everything "jelling pretty well" without considering evidence calling the circulating current theory into serious question. That argument, in turn, wasn't "sold" or "freely" promoted. At the time of the one o'clock meeting, Paul, who might have "promoted" and explained his interpretation, was elsewhere with the consultants, Andy and Frank, to finish their assessment of thermographic techniques. Paul explains.

That was one of the things—we had the thermography experts in here, we were paying them, I don't know, $8,000 for the week or something like that. It was quite a bit to have them in there. So we were trying to continue on and still do other work. I worked fourteen hours a day for two weeks.

I asked Doug what the organizational effectiveness team knew about why Paul and Brad weren't at the meeting.

They weren't even invited. They weren't needed [some thought]. They told their managers what was going on, one was Nat, the other was Mike. Mike and Nat presented the slides that Paul and Brad had put together to the management team, but they didn't understand the information. . . . And we never got a good explanation of why they didn't have them there—they just didn't feel they were necessary. And we also had, visiting here on-site, some of the industry's best thermography

experts that understood the implications of it. But . . . they were looking at other equipment. They discovered this problem and went right
on working with the other equipment. . . . Instead we brought in a
switchyard guy that didn't know anything about thermography. He
said, "That's not a problem."

Doug wasn't at that meeting but had been at many others where a
tradeoff quandary was the agenda.

When you have a meeting and you have very senior people called in on
a holiday and you hold it in a big conference room, and everybody's
focused on, "What can we do to prevent having to shut the plant
down?" and that's the aura of the room, that's the environment. It sort
of chills anybody bringing up something that says, "We've got a bad
problem and we've got to shut down and explore it." It's the production bias as opposed to safety bias, whether it's nuclear safety or industrial safety. Even though the ops manager—a very senior manager in
our pecking order and in our credibility and how we respect that individual in the organization—promoted over and over again in that meeting, "Can anyone else tell me anything that we're not doing right, anything we should be doing industrial safety-wise?" Still, people won't
speak up because there's that chill or whatever in the room so you're
not going to raise the issue.

I've been in that room many times and it's a very uncomfortable,
tense atmosphere. It's not welcome and warm and exploring, and that's
part of why Miles and I proposed the significance and consequence
exercise. That gives you a framework where it's OK to talk about,
"What's the worst possible that can happen? What does this mean in
the worst-case scenario? What is the [safety] significance? Is this a campaign issue with the regulator or with INPO or ourselves because this
has happened a dozen times before? What are the consequences if the
worst thing happened?" But that same ops manager that professed to
do a stellar job in promoting openness and industrial safety said [com-
menting on the report], "This is ludicrous to think that we have to
have something like that to promote discussion. I asked the question,
everybody was free to talk."

*So would the alternative be for him to be the devil's advocate himself?
To show that he was able himself to dream up this other scenario and
have people tell him it wasn't going to happen that way?*

Right. You never hear our senior management doing that. As soon as
it starts to go in that direction—I've been in the room when the chief
nuclear officer said {shouting} "I don't want to hear about that. I want
someone to call the vendor right now and get an expert to tell us that

that's not true." It's just not an open dialogue, what the worst possible case could be.

For the organizational effectiveness team, the costs of shutting down to explore the problem are perhaps the least of it: its report points out that in a worst-case scenario the threat to the GSU is not only the possibility of injury and property loss "in the hundreds of millions," but also the threat of litigation on the grounds of "prudence and/or wrongful death," meaning the "prudency" of management decisions made on the basis of the information available. In the absence of a prefigured decision logic for evaluating anomalies, as mandated on the shiny side, Joel, manager of the corrective actions program, offers an alternative that puts priority on disproving a "worst case" and the "potential" for an explosion.

> If it's critical, like deaths, damage, and so on and you have indications of a problem, then you have to prove you don't have a problem as opposed to something less significant. Now [the way things are] you've got to prove you got a problem before you can take action. OK, "Hey, we're a power plant, we make electricity. If you want me to stop making electricity, prove to me I got a problem." I'm introducing something that's a little different here. I'm saying there are some finite amount of things that are so important that if I have reasonable indications that there's a problem—not, "Hey I think maybe your turbine is not working right." Why? "Well, I just don't think it sounds right." I mean, well I'm going to need a little bit more than that.
>
> But if I have something like a thermographic image that says I got a potential problem, the first question you ask is, "What's the worst it could be?" It's part of determining what space you're in. "Well, the worst it could be is a hot spot inside." Why is that the worst? Well, now we get into a potential transformer explosion, you know, so that's when you start saying, "OK, the worst-case thing is I got a hot spot inside that could result in transformer explosion." Serious stuff. Death, significant plant damage, you know, disgrace, all that stuff. At that point you say, "OK, now let's prove we're OK." How would we prove we're OK? That's the next set of questions. Well, in this case the only thing you could do is what we did eventually—remove the bolt—and even that was luck, by the way. They removed the bolt to put a grounding strap on and the guy happened to say, "Wait a minute, it's glowing in there." We wouldn't even have caught it then. That's another thing we pointed out in the report, that was luck. You've got a hole through the metal and unless you're lined up right, you don't see the glow. So if he had been up higher so that he was just kind of looking into the flange, he wouldn't have noticed. . . .
>
> Picture yourself being the shift manager Wednesday night and someone comes to you and says, "Listen I got a thermographic image and it

shows I got a lot of heat here." So what we kind of did was said, "We're really not sure what it is yet. We've seen circulating current, we kind of think that's probably what it is." So we let ourselves be comfortable with that. But what we're saying *should* have happened is the shift manager should have said, "OK, what could it be? What are the options? What are the potential causes of getting these things? What information do I have to say it's not this worst case? In other words, which of those options can't I live with? I can't live with these four, how do I know it's not that? Well, geez, I don't know. You got one hour to do something to prove to me that it's not that or I start taking the plant down." You tell him to call the station manager and say, "Ralph, here's the situation, I've got a potential here for a transformer explosion, I gave them one hour to show me why it's not that and if I don't get it, I'm shutting down."

That is the other side. Now why wouldn't we do it? Well, that's our livelihood, we make electricity. So you want to be—again, you can get to this whole other line—do you want to be the guy who shuts the plant down and we find out it was really just circulating current? And if that does bother you, why does it bother you? Are you afraid of getting fired? I can't believe that—nobody's going to fire you. But I think now, it's that, "Hey, I look foolish, I look incompetent." Now you get into places [psychology] again where I'm not comfortable.

Even the best-case scenario carries the risks involved in a HARD or sudden shutdown: If the fault had activated the GSU's protective sensors that automatically shut down the plant, that itself puts high stress on important plant equipment and may provoke unforeseen consequences. Brad outlines the consequences of the GSU's "failing," explaining that the switchyard is "nonsafety."

But just like this GSU, the switchyard feeds back into the plant, it all comes from somewhere.

Right.

And if, God forbid, the GSU had, what's the word, "launched"?

That's quite a term. Failed. How about failed?

They've had instances at other plants where it bounces back.

Right. What would have happened in this case was we would have lost one of our power sources. We also have an auxiliary path that comes through some separate transformers. Which would have been the first line of defense. If those had failed we have two diesels after that, so we have a ways to go even after that.

For shutdown?

Right. It probably wouldn't have been a nice trip—probably would have been messy. But we would have, from an off-site power standpoint, we wouldn't have been in that bad a shape. We would have lost maybe one out of four power sources.

"Messy" implies, as everyone in a nuclear power plant knows, that, as Paul put it, "Whenever the plant trips, lots of times other things break and, it's just inherent, that just happens, and it's not uncommon to be down a week fixing these things." But had there been a fault to ground or transformer explosion, the shutdown would have lasted months. The financial risk is considerable, according to calculations Paul made afterward in collaboration with the thermography consultants, partly to demonstrate the wisdom of shutting down, partly to justify the camera's financial value. Using industry data on GSU failures, that analysis showed that under a catastrophic failure scenario in which the transformer would have to be replaced and the plant shut down for seventy-two days, the estimated costs are $74 million; a scenario with no transformer replacement and a fifteen-day outage would run $15 million. The probability of each scenario's occurring was 50 percent, by their reckoning. Charles Station's twelve-day shutdown turned out to cost $12 million. Nevertheless, Paul feels obliged to justify the camera's cost. Out in the switchyard another time, while trying out a new $12,000 zoom lens, he had made another lucky find. "Wow, I got to go out and see what I can find. I got to justify this lens. And in 10 minutes, that's when I found a fault on the 345 KV line in the insulator on the path over to the telephone pole." His camera had also spotted faults on two control rod drives: "You lose those, it's going to trip the plant. . . . I'm a big proponent of thermography. I really feel that it can save the plant on the order of millions of dollars every year."

"This time we were fortunate," the organizational effectiveness team concludes, "but we do not want to depend on luck as a primary barrier to high safety or business risk." As Joel said, that report brought out "defensiveness in . . . people who aren't normally too defensive were quite defensive. . . . and a lot of pushback . . . more than I've seen on any other one that we've ever done here." He revisits the decision process to speculate about the reasons why.

> I think that people took it personally. . . . We had a select few people that really believed it wasn't circulating current, and they didn't effectively bring it forward for management. . . . So that's one thing we have to make sure the organization understands is that if you have a different viewpoint or you feel very, very strongly, that the team's going in the wrong direction, that has to come forward. Or otherwise it will just sit there and set up a culture of "Well, geez, I should have told them but . . ." We don't want that. We want a very free-flowing

communicative, nonpunitive culture. Bring it up even if you've got to shut down the unit or say, "This decision was wrong because of this or that." We need to be able to have that type of communication, a dialogue vertically and horizontally.

Well, there are lots of subtle ways in which that can be turned off. It's not always, "Oh, do tell me everything." It can be said in many ways or preceded by, "You've got to convince me"—it matters, the flavor of how this is encouraged.

We encouraged the wrong decision, no question that we did that. Those individuals that had that information weren't even at the meeting. . . . The expert we had wasn't in the room—he could have provided a response in a dialogue, to key questioning, "What do you mean that this indicates there's an actual hot spot on the other side that's really generating heat?" We need to make it a priority that decision makers have all the players that have all the information, so that when the decision's made that's significantly bad for risk or for production, that the guys that have the mind, the training, the technology, the understanding are there.

Phil, electrical maintenance manager, reflects on Paul's conviction that it was a hot spot.

I get the sense throughout this that . . . in his mind he believed that there was more of a problem or an issue than everyone else. He recognized the urgency of the issue earlier. . . . I had several conversations with him before and after the meeting—he wasn't at the meeting—but I guess I didn't ask as many probing questions as I could have. I really honestly didn't get a sense from him that he was not in alignment with the rest of the organization, that we all thought, if I could place a value on it, that we were all 80 percent sure that it was circulating current. I thought that he was right there with us. After identifying the real problem, the feedback I got was that he had thought all along that it wasn't that, that it was something else, it was a real problem.

I asked Brad, the senior engineer who agreed with Paul from the start, but who had not been at the one o'clock meeting:

When you saw what they had decided in your absence, how did you feel about the steps they took?

Ummm. {sigh} I guess from the data we had, we made an educated decision. As I said, there were two things to do. One was stay up and one was come down. Coming down is always an issue, but when you come down with a large plant like this there's a lot of issues with coming down and getting back up. So it's not just like saying, "Hey, there's no cost either financial or to equipment." So that's what we were trying to do was get the best data we can. I think we arrived at the best decision, with a little bit of luck, I think. . . . We couldn't really pound our fist on the table and say, "Hey, it has to come down," because we didn't have enough data. We had a feeling something wasn't right, but how right and how wrong was a tough proposition. . . . I was comfortable with following up on it. I think it was something that could not be let go. Did I think the unit should come down immediately? No, I don't think I did. But it was not going to be dropped. . . . I wouldn't have left here unless I felt that it was being followed up on. So I think we came up with a good course of action. Looking back in hindsight, I guess you could say one minute it was the right decision, one minute you could say it was a chancy decision, but, you know. . . .

As Edward, systems engineer for the GSU, looks back on the decision process, he provides a clear outline of its tradeoff quandary.

Same as always, when you look back on something, never make assumptions. And every time you do, you say, "I will never make that assumption that this can't happen." But I mean you get narrowed down and when you can get three or four people—and especially when you call some outside people and they all focus in on the same thing—everybody assumes that you're right. And it's very tough to get out of that mold of saying, "OK, let's look at one other step. What would this be if it was . . . ?" even though we weren't thoroughly convinced. And I told them, I said, "I believe it's a 70 percent chance this is circulating current," I said, "but there's a 30 percent chance we got damage and there's something happening in there, and I won't make a commitment to this. And so it was either open up the little thing [bolt] and look in or shut the plant down and go do a full inspection the next morning." . . . It's everything you do in life, you look back, "Could you have done better?" Yeah, probably.

But we made the best call we had at the time trying to continue—we're in the business to make money, produce electricity, so we don't like to shut the plant down. But in the same regard, you're also in it to—if we'd have damaged that transformer, we would have been done for . . . we'd have been down for a month and a half. And that's a tremendous amount of lost revenue. So you have to look at it, "OK, we're not going to damage any equipment, we're not going to go into the safety"—safety is the prime concern—you don't want to hurt anybody or damage equipment, but the thing is you want to make money too. Because if we don't make money, then we're all gone tomorrow {chuckle}.

Grant, electrical supervisor in the technical support group, also revisits the decision process, from which he gained respect for thermography's value.

Based on the information I had at the time and the decision that I made at the time, I would probably make those same decisions again. Now two things are different. One is thermography has progressed rapidly in the last couple of years as far as its ability to detect things. We weren't on the leading edge of knowing how accurate it had become. So thermography in the past had given us a lot of false alarms. It has definitely gotten much better, so I didn't trust it as much as I would now in hindsight.

Second of all, like I said I didn't realize how well that bus was dissipating the energy. Now I know that if I see 150 degrees, 200 degrees outside a bus there is something really cooking on the inside. And with that information I wouldn't make the same decision I made, if the same event occurred. But based on the knowledge and information I had at the time, I think we did the prudent and proper thing.

We found out that because of things we didn't know, the decision process was probably {pause} would probably be changed in the future. And definitely I would not allow anyone up within six inches of the bus in a situation like that again, with the knowledge I have now. . . . Because I don't want to go home some day and tell my wife that I've killed somebody. And that could very easily happen. It's a dangerous place. I think back that I had people up on that ladder, and had myself up on that ladder, and there very easily could have been a fatality.

The event also chastened Phil.

From the practical standpoint, the head of electrical tech support and I had a conversation about the opportunity [to protect those doing the work and onlookers] that was missed and that we could probably improve our communications. . . . The other thing I learned from it was, we had an unknown condition on the transformer but we had some confidence that we could have a real serious problem . . . and we should have had a little—a lot better control over the access to the work area. When the guy was going up and pulling the bolt out, there were people that didn't really need to be there. When I first came on-site [Thursday morning] I don't believe the access to the work area was really under control. It's an area where people tend to hang out for smoke breaks and I don't think anyone was saying, "stay away from here." Stay away from this side of the plant because something might happen. So I think a little bit, a better command and control of the area and access and appreciating the hazard a little better.

When Nat and Mike took on the task of making the presentation at the one o'clock meeting, they were acting as technocrats are supposed to, using their place in their professional orders' hierarchy to deliver messages upward, to buffer those at the top from underlings. Not hearing creditable interpretations of the thermograms and a worst-case scenario, the room as a whole did not determine, as Joel put it, what "space"—the kind of trouble—the plant was in. And so the discussion stayed in the hierarchical space of a corporate, executive conference room whose "aura," in Doug's experience, "sort of chills anybody bringing up something that says, 'We've got a bad problem and we've got to shut down and explore it.'" The status hierarchy outclassed the knowledge hierarchy with no objections from senior managers, line managers, or consultants. But electrical knowledge has no choice but to trump hierarchy, according to Grant.

> Most of my management are not knowledgeable electrically. If you're talking a steam pipe, you know, a thin spot with steam coming out, they would have a very good gut feel of what the dangers were. On the electrical side they don't. And they're totally dependent on those of us who are electrical engineers who tell them that.

Why is such an important component so far outside of plant managers' experience?—a question Grant raises.

> You'd think with an electrical generating plant that most of the management would be very knowledgeable electrically. It's not. Mechanical engineers, the steam guys, run the plant. Ten, fifteen years ago the NRC almost had no interest in the electrical side of the plant because it's considered mostly nonsafety. That has very much changed. . . . The problem is we have a very limited pool of electrical engineers on-site. When we have an event like this we are intimately involved in trying to assess it and repair it. There's no one up here standing back and looking at the big picture—the knowledgeable person to sit back and look at that big picture. When you have a mechanical event, again, because most of the managers [in plant maintenance and system engineering] came up with steam leaks and everything like that, there generally is a manager who's not involved in the day-to-day repairs, who is kind of sitting back and looking at that event.

Again, the part takes precedence over the whole, no matter its size or function. That was true of the "high yard," according to Grant. Until about four years ago when the utility owning Charles Station changed hands, it had been the utility's responsibility to send in "the people who maintain the high lines and do the high voltage work for a living." Now that falls to the station. "At that time I had no high voltage, no high yard experience. I came out of the navy where the highest voltage I had dealt with was 480 volts. It just became a learn-as-you-earn program. And we quickly learned. But I don't have the experience on big transformers like someone who's on these big transformers every day."

Recall that when Vince was explaining the turbine vibration situation and the dilemma of arriving at a threshold number and I asked him, "What do you do?" the phrasing of his response is notable: "Try to get buy-in, try to explain it to your supervisor and other people that know about these things. . . ." "Try" can mean two things: one is that for him, making an analytic case based on his observations doesn't come easily—not unusual among those in technical jobs—and another is that he can make a case, but experience is telling him it will be difficult to get "buy-in" even from his supervisor.[2] That possibility resonates with Paul's difficulties, first, in getting through to Jack, the shift manager (he did not follow through on Paul's request for caution tape around the GSU area) and, second, in not having Nat and Mike, his supervisors, take his readings seriously enough to raise questions of their own at the meeting.

Cliff, the operations department manager, had asked that the outside transformer experts attend the one o'clock meeting as independent observers. He wonders if Paul, and the thermography experts, had been present whether Paul would have said anything in any case.

> I'm kind of speculating—I know the people involved. You see, [thermography's] a new technology—we had industry experts there—I wonder if they [Paul and the consultants] would have spoken up anyways, even if they were at the meeting. Because you get a bunch of high-powered people in a room—I guess is the best way to put it—and Paul's got a personality where he's quiet-spoken anyways and he may not speak up. So with that, all this was in the back of my mind. Even if he was there, would that information have come out?

> *It's not an unusual problem, by any means, for people not to speak up, but is this something that you've seen before?*

> I've had it happen to me. I've had a lot of experience with it. I deal with the executives and the board of directors quite a bit now, so I don't have that problem anymore. But I know I used to {small laugh}. You know, your confidence is—you know, when opinions all are going one way and you're the small fish in the room, so to speak. If you're not 100 percent sure, you usually hold back a little bit. . . . Looking back on this meeting, we had a lot of supervisors there and very few workers. If I had to do the meeting over again, I would have had only people who were knowledgeable about the issue all the way down to the worker level, and had a vertical slice, if you will, of the organization.

So it would have been less intimidating, and you would have had the people that had the right data.

Joel remarks on the luck of the find.

Even if there's no chance of it hurting somebody, the fact that we'd be down for six months could be economically fatal. . . . But shame on us if we don't learn from this reprieve. That's the whole point we try to make in the report—"Hey, nothing bad happened this time, but next time could be completely the opposite."

It will take more than finger wagging to replace primitive status ladders with sophisticated lattices of expertise, especially when it is homegrown—as sophisticated, that is, as the technology they are there to control.

"Biased toward Production"

For the organizational effectiveness team, the station's "production bias" is already coded within the root cause categories of "Tunnel Vision" and "Group Think." Under its heading "Generic Implications," the report elaborates on the station's approach to the tradeoff quandary.

> When we are faced with a problem, we strive to take the least expensive, least intrusive way out of the situation. We tend to avoid the more labor intensive and more difficult, "what if" analysis. In this instance, if it were circulating currents, it would allow us to remain generating electricity and to correct the problem at a reduced cost. We have seen this before; for example, [naming three previous events], the organization focused on production at the expense of prevention. The Management Team needs to be deliberate and conscientious in asking the tough questions. Management also needs to create the environment that welcomes the questions and comments of those who are bringing them bad news or difficult issues. There are other events out there waiting to happen and the organization, overall, needs to be accomplished at asking the questions in the right way when they get here. . . .
>
> We need to balance our production focus with the right amount of safety focus. It is a hard job to balance both and do it well. If we develop a decision tree, and ask the right questions, we will end up doing the right thing. A decision tree is a good tool for Charles, at this time, since we do not have the right culture yet to do this naturally or instinctively (as an everyday way of doing business). A decision tree, however, is only a tool. It is one more barrier that can aid . . . in preventing events but may, like other barriers, fail or not be used properly when it is most needed. Therefore, the management team must expedite the change in culture at Charles from one that is biased toward production to one that is more effectively focused on (and in balance) with prevention (Safety).

I commented to Grant on the team report's emphasis on the influence of the production mentality.

Oh, that's definitely a factor. We all know what it costs, what a day of generation here costs. You're talking, depending on the time of the year, between half a million and a million dollars a day. More than that, even more than the money, there's a great amount of pride in keeping the station on line. And we are very reluctant to shut the station down unless we have to. In fact we're very innovative at finding ways to do repairs and keep the plant running. And we also take great pride in being able to do that. There definitely is a production mentality.

I asked Phil, electrical maintenance manager,

What about the production pressures? Well, I mean coming off line is the last thing anyone wants to do, usually. Was that articulated as. . .

Um. {pause} I don't feel like—you know, there's a very short window where I felt like the decision process was interrupted by or influenced inappropriately. I think it was unfortunate that we waited to have the meeting until one o'clock the following day, but the meeting needed to take place because we didn't have enough information to make any formal decision about whether to bring the plant down. So I wish that meeting had happened earlier. So the normal—what would I say—the normal, proper amount—you know, we don't bring the plant down without having a reason to bring it down. We weren't sure we had a reason yet. That normal healthy decision process was OK, it was elongated, it was longer than it should have been. But I think it was, once those questions were being asked, it was appropriate. . . . I think when we took the bolt out of the first hole and we saw the glowing red that that was enough information, at least for me, to decide to bring the plant down. I think that going over to the second bolt on the second cover and taking it off, where I don't think there was any hazard in doing that, I just don't think it should have been necessary. At that point we had enough information to say, "Bring the plant down."

Who needed to be so convinced? Who was not yet convinced?

The shift manager, the person making the decision to bring the plant down. That decision ultimately lies with—well, it could lie with the station manager but, as we operate a nuclear power plant, if the station manager is not there making decisions, the shift manager is making those kinds of decisions. And he's got a license and he's making 'em.

For Vince, the "production bias" dominates.

The thing I was interested in when I heard you were doing this study— you know people will tell you, the company will tell you, that we don't have this pressure to stay on line and all—well, that's baloney, in my opinion. People feel that pressure, and I'm a bit of an observer of people and I know how other people feel. People do not want to make the call unless they're certain. If they have criteria—you're a control room operator or whatever and you say, "Hey, I've got this checklist in front of me and it says if I get to this point I'm down powering. If I get to this point on whatever, I'm taking this thing off line." . . .

But if they're in an area where it's judgments—"Geez, I haven't seen this before, does this seem right to you? I don't know, well . . ." then they're saying, "Well, you got to tell me if this is OK, 'cause, you know, should I be taking this plant off line?" Well now, people get the pressure and they want to make the right call but they also want to have the support of other people and say, "Hey, this is what I'm thinking, this is my recommendation," and they want to be a little bit more methodical about it. There is a pressure to stay on line.

Do these people also have an incentive to stay on line, with bonuses?

Right. Sure.

Is that as much driving it as . . .

I don't think so. I personally don't think so. I'm also not motivated by money. As much as other people are. I don't think it's the bonus, I think it's more the notoriety or that you can not only hurt your own career, you have the peer pressure, you know a thousand people know, "Hey, you took the plant off line for no good reason." You've got the [local] newspaper, you got not only a thousand people, you got everybody in the company, and it doesn't stop at this station. If you take a 1200 megawatt plant off line you've really made a name for yourself and you don't want to make the wrong call. And also going forward from there to the next time you've got to make a call—you want people to listen to you.

The financial pressure is there whether there's a bonus incentive or not, isn't there? It's the replacement power, it's the . . .

Yes, it's that whole. It's not my personal income that's more, yeah, money to the station. Yeah, that's really the underlying pressure. You're not thinking about your own paycheck, you're thinking about what the company's reaction to it is going to be and that whole reaction is driven by money. Sure. But last week or so when we had that terrible hot weather out here, we had this vibration issue going on with the turbine. And at that time the regional power grid is calling up and saying, "Hey, can you change load on your generator, we want you to carry more bars, we want you do this, we want you to do that." And we're in an area where we're not 100 percent comfortable with the vibrations we have, and you change the loads, you change the vibrations. And there's a lot of pressure in that. {anxiously} We want to go into this box, we want to go into the alterex and start taking more data. Well, every time you go in there you have a, I mean you're into a trip-critical type function where you could bump into the wrong thing and the sucker's coming down.

So what happened?

Well, we stayed on line. But we were still dealing with it. Yeah, we went in and one day we told the dispatcher, "No, we can't change the load, it seems to be increasing the vibrations. We just can't do it," and so he's got to juggle the rest of the whole regional grid. If we had come off line that day, we were told, there weren't going to be brownouts, there were going to be blackouts. So that's the type of—I mean if they came to you and said, "Hey, give me a decision, I want your opinion, and tell me if we should take this plant off line. If we do come off line there are going to be blackouts." {laughter} So there's a pressure there.

Given the limiting conditions of operations that define windows of time in which certain kinds of maintenance can occur while running, the schedule controls just about everything that goes on. The expense of refueling and maintenance outages ratchets up the pressures, which can amplify risk of injury and of equipment malfunctions; at the same time, although everyone is cautioned to be careful and take their time, outages can also be a time when esprit is high and the macho impulse on the ready. Vince sees a paradox.

No matter how many times these jerks tell you "Don't be rushed," they also announce a thirty-five-day outage. Everyday when they print how many hours we lost on the critical path, they just flat out lie to you that you don't have time pressure. They say, "If you 'Do It Right' and you follow the schedule, you don't have time pressure"—shit, of course we have time pressure. But you have to be able to deflect that. Or you have to stop putting that pressure on people. It's ludicrous that they say we don't have time pressure. Already they're hyping this next outage that's going to take twenty-nine days . . . But they work on you for a year and a half about this twenty-nine-day outage. Then you're a couple of days or a week or so into it and you're already behind by twenty-four hours—well, pick a number—there's time pressure. . . . Either you lied to me before, because we can't make up this time, we can't change the past. So if we've lost that day, and the schedule from here on has already been planned, it's going to take another *x* amount of days. We can't recover that time unless we hurry up. Or don't do something. To say there's no time pressure is a farce.

"I've seen people here with burnout on their faces," said Hank, talking about the last outage of about forty-five days.

Knowing that outage schedules usually allow some hours for "emergent work," I said to Vince,

But outages are supposed to be for discovering new problems as well.

No, no, no, no. Don't think that. 'Cause they'll run you right out of here. Outages, well there's no time built into it for that. It always happens. You're talking about theory and reality here, that's the other thing. You're always going to find something unanticipated.

I thought that was the point.

No. The point is to change the fuel, fix what you know that needs to be fixed, and start it back up. That's the point. And there are certain things you're doing—disassemble, inspect, repair—but you're not supposed to find anything new, which you doubtless do.

What may have been "jelling" in that conference room seems to have been the refusal to acknowledge the worst, warding off "honest discussion" and its "bad news" and avoiding a complicated and expensive outage—but not by having compared that to the alternative.

Falling Down

Why was the story the thermographic images were telling spurned in favor of verification procedures that put people directly in harm's way? Managers of a sophisticated high consequence technology introduce a sophisticated technology that can help to avoid trouble before it can start, yet give short shrift to the evidence it produces. A cognitive explanation would have it that loitering behind "group think" and "tunnel vision" was the "availability" or "recency" heuristic: if circulating current happened before, it was happening now. Maybe so. But there were other influences: the semantics of safety (nuclear and nonnuclear, shiny and rusty), the parts template, also motivated by the "two sides of the house" (mechanical and electrical), and, certainly, the tradeoff quandary—all together, these may account for stunted curiosity about a worst-case scenario. Recall Joel's argument.

But what we're saying *should* have happened is the shift manager should have said, "OK, what could it be? What are the options? What are the potential causes of getting these things? What information do I have to say it's not this worst case? In other words, what of those options can't I live with? I can't live with these four, how do I know it's not that? Well, geez, I don't know. You got one hour to do something to prove to me that it's not that or I start taking the plant down." You tell him to call the station manager and say, "Ralph, here's the situation, I've got a potential here for transformer explosion, I gave them one hour to show me why it's not that and if I don't get it, I'm shutting down."

The GSU hot spot was Charles Station's "fundamental surprise," it seems. Ken, maintenance manager, retraces some of its sources.

We've got a number of examples where thermography has helped us out. It's easy to see the temperature heating, to see the aberration of the temperature—"It should be this green but now it's yellow or red"— and what's causing it is usually a loose connection or something like that—a capacitor going bad. In this case, we saw the color, we knew we had a problem, we didn't doubt it. Thermography had found something, credible or incredible—really great visuals—and the explanation of what it could be was where we fell down. What's causing that color? We didn't list all the potential causes and then ask, "What's the probability of those causes and what's the risk if it's this and what's the risk if it's that?" We had the guy who built the switchyard come in and he told us there's no way these connections would be loosened like that and he's been in the business, blah blah blah 19 or 20 years, he's never seen anything like that. What he said didn't happen, *happened*. . . . It was an actual loose connection. . . . I don't know a darn thing about circulating currents, I've spent most of my career in operations and managing people and I don't have that technical background. But I mean the whole team was in that mindset.

Why are managers of a "leading edge" technology not also "on the leading edge of knowing how accurate" the leading edge camera it invested in "had become," quoting Grant. He goes on to say, "thermography in the past had given us a lot of false alarms. It has definitely gotten much better, so I didn't trust it as much as I would now in hindsight." There is, of course, unfamiliarity with interpreting the images the camera produces. As Phil said, hindsight clarified the images: "It didn't click for any of us that that should have told us that there was, that this wasn't circulating current, there was something hot in there radiating heat."

Why did others' analytic capability remain underdeveloped? According to the sketchy report of the meeting during its two-and-a-half hours, among some thirty people present no one advocated shutting down quickly, perhaps because of a "chill" in the room. But perhaps also because those in the room seem to have seen the camera as one "part" (a material object) and its images another part (a representation of temperatures): the camera is just there, but the images demand to be interpreted— "the intellectual side," Vince calls it. The competence to interpret becomes another "part" encapsulated in Paul, not diffused among others, perhaps because, as Grant says, "you need to get out and interact with it—a 'Show Me' kind of thing," an effort that apparently hadn't made it onto managers' "action lists." Yet despite this "new find" of a more anomalous thermal pattern than previously recorded, managers did not open up their circle of familiars to include the three on-site experts able to explain why the images said "hot spot," not "circulating current."

Arriving at the meanings of evidence is, then, partly a technical challenge, partly a contextual challenge of holding an "honest" discussion about puzzling evidence, structured to accommodate appropriate people and questions and to consider a decision's wider implications—a challenge Cliff did not meet in the moment but could define months later.[3] These elements of the culture of control—the interpretive capacities of station experts and of their consultants—in that snapshot of time, together with the material elements of the GSU, pyrometers, infrared camera, reactor at full power . . . fill out our understandings of what this technology in operation consists of.

Chapter Five

Logics of Control

In the mid-1990s, Keith, maintenance manager at Overton Station, was telling me about a memo from his boss. "He says to us, 'Don't write down "personnel error" as a root cause because I won't accept it.' That's going to be tough. This is going to be one of the toughest efforts I've ever been involved in." The event reports and interviews at Arrow, Bowie, and Charles Stations seem to show that since then station experts are finding it easier to speak of systemic issues and of conditions that "set people up" to make mistakes. But they do not also ask, as Richard, operations manager at Arrow Station, does, whether there is a "fundamental flaw in our collective way of thinking." Moving the same pieces around the same board, they play the same game, hoping to do so more skillfully (more training) while paying more attention to the rules (rewrite procedures), to equipment (more inspections), to team signals (more and better cross-department communication), to the referees (listening to oversight), to who does what (reallocating responsibilities), to new techniques (decision-making tools), and to motivation ("reinforce management expectations"). The pattern of issue-by-issue corrective actions this game sets up frustrates Roy, an Overton Station senior manager and engineer. "It's like playing my kids' game, 'Bop the Alligator'—you hit one and another pops right up. What if the list of issues of the month just keeps getting longer? After every incident we go through the exercise of thinking about how we can create an environment where this error won't repeat itself. We can do this ideally, but how can we do it under real-time constraints?"

The four events put us as close as most of us will ever come to knowing what it's like for station experts to identify those issues, to locate their sources, and to think beyond corrective actions limited to technical fixes and "personnel error." This far behind the scenes, we see some of the stagecraft involved in reducing risk and recovering from the consequences of glitches, flukes, mistakes, and surprises. At Charles Station, we see a preview of the legacy of "shiny and rusty" categories, among others, with which the industry and NRC will continue to wrestle in the significance determination process. At Bowie Station we glimpse the cultural machinery of hierarchy, of newcomers, and of the midwatch pulling the strings to put "talented people" into situations where, like Ned, they may act out of character. We learn that a reactor trip costing $1.5 million brought on by his raw mistake has to be taken in stride, compared to the hesitations at Charles Station over a "new find" in a generator step-up transformer, which, in an after-the-fact scenario, could have threatened lives and cost many more millions than shutting down sooner. We see how competitive pressures, layoffs, or attrition, coupled with the sheer passage of time, bring people with fewer "years in the trenches" into a trust and credibility system whose chief criterion has been those years. We witness the slow integration of new diagnostic technologies at Charles Station, and, at Arrow Station, an unexplained reluctance to radiograph a suspect valve.

Each station's "processes for finding, evaluating, and correcting problems is an important fundamental block upon which the new oversight process is built," the Nuclear Regulatory Commission declares.[1] Every year the country over, as station teams produce at least a few thousand event reviews, they are more likely to be singling out alligators by the hundreds than recommending changes in industry paradigms. How might that "collective way of thinking" make room for a second game whose aim is to make event reviews less vulnerable to issue-by-issue corrective actions and more likely to result in effective and implemented improvements? To be a game as good as command-and-control is for safe shutdown, its animating concept has to penetrate the irony the first game sets up: its defense-in-depth principle with its layers of protective redundancies creates the opacities that can prevent systemic conditions from being noticed. To find and expand on another concept, these last two chapters take to heart Nick's rueful response to the confusions at Arrow Station: "Sometimes you have to stop and ask, 'What are we doing here?' " And so I ask, *What kind of problem is reducing the risks of operating a nuclear power plant?*

What I call calculated and real-time logics constitute the first game, based on the principle of command and control and on the risk estimates and scenarios following from it. During daily operations, experts also take orders from a third logics of control culture, policy logics: recurring issues and repeat events are likely to signal the presence of policy matters that executives and managers may not have recognized or did not try to resolve. Policy questions are at the center of the tradeoff quandary: the dilemmas, contradictions, and paradoxes inherent in those fundamental imperatives to protect, perturb, produce, and profit. The presence of those conundrums is not the problem; problems stem from ignoring them or not resolving them appropriately, situation by situation.[2] That goes far to account for issue-bopping, I propose.

I find a model of a second game in a study of the everyday work of Canadian control room operators: its animating concept is *doubt and discovery.* Already incipient in the doubt that the industry encourages with a low threshold for reporting adverse conditions and in the obligatory discovery processes of tests, inspections, and event reviews, that concept is not on a par in intellectual force and stature with that of command and control, I propose.

That is, there are obstacles to developing a second game at all. One way or another, it calls for moderating the strict hierarchy of value the industry now assigns to kinds of knowledge: qualitative and quantitative, unmeasurable and measurable, soft and hard, subjective and objective, substantive and formal. Even though some industry experts recognize that incorporating indicators of, for example, "error-forcing conditions" would allow for more realistic probabilistic risk assessments (PRAs), that persistent hierarchy makes headway difficult. In any case, PRAs can contribute little to operational paradigms that could obviate those patterns of ineffective or unmade corrective actions and neglect of industrywide cautions and advice.[3]

Three Logics of Control Culture

Calculated and real-time logics take their cues from the command-and-control strategy for maintaining the capacity for safe shutdown and dose control. To calculate risk levels for reactor designs, engineers move through a series of deductions to shape high-level control concepts into risk estimates, then into the algorithms, thresholds, and standards that become the design basis, the technical specifications, and the procedures and rules for maintaining control. Once reactors are operating, real-time logics reduce and handle risks that design calculations have not anticipated. The real-time logics of station experts accompany them as they try to hew to procedures and rules. They draw on judgment and inference when interpreting conditions in the moment. They make networks of inductions from their observations, experience, trend data, and circumstantial evidence. For reducing and handling risks, real-time logics keep abreast of the ways in which configuration control was or could be lost or threatened, and when it is, to arrive at steps to regain it. Trees of deductive reasoning structure calculated logics; trellises of inductive reasoning structure real-time logics.

As used in control rooms, on plant floors, and in executive suites, calculated and real-time logics both refer to design basis requirements, but each approaches them differently. The one is metric, the other experiential, the one prospective, the other actual. Until this system is operating, the calculated logics designing it are vicarious and virtual: only later can records of operating experience provide the real-time data with which to reevaluate risk estimates. Others notice these differences. Risk estimation is an "illusion" that "confuses a map with a landscape, a theory of safety with safety itself." So conclude sociologists Wolfgang Krohn and Peter Weingart of the University of Bielefeld after examining how risks had been estimated and then handled in the Chernobyl accident.[4] How do rules derived from risk estimation and practical operating rules relate to each other in the "messier reality which routinely confronts practitioners on the 'inside' of the technological system?" asks Brian Wynne, professor of science studies at Lancaster University. How do the actualities of an "unruly technology" relate to public perceptions of a "neat and tidy" mechanistic image?[5] The 1991 "friendly fire" shootdown of U.S. Black Hawk helicopters, says Scott Snook, member of the Harvard Business School faculty, represents operational situations that require "unique logics":

> Gone is the tightly logical and synchronized rationale that governed system design and rule production at birth. In its place are multiple incrementally emergent sets of procedures, each born out of unique . . . logics grounded in . . . day-to-day pragmatics. . . . Gone is the single rationally designed "engineered world" governed by intricate sets of global rules. In its place is an "applied" world where locally pragmatic responses to the intimate demands of the task dictate action.[6]

In nuclear power technology, routines and scripts are plentiful for predicted situations and for imagined emergencies. For what has not been—cannot be—anticipated inside and outside the control room, experts have no choice but to mobilize their own and others' experience and knowledge for the circumstances—"on the fly," as Grant puts it. Calculated logics are, then, "experience-distant," while real-time logics are necessarily "experience-near," the one context-free, the other context-bound.[7] Real-time logics judge whether conditions need a quick response or deserve to be pondered and analyzed further. Real-time logics depend on synthesizing observations among colleagues and consulting the record of other stations' operating experiences.

The two logics are documented differently. Explicit rationales accompany calculated logics on the nuclear side, based on reliability metrics of the structures, systems, and components of the reactor unit. The design basis and technical specifications embed historical failure rates and set limits on operating modes. On the nonnuclear side, principles of efficiency and optimization reappear in the calculated logics for electricity production and for financial risks, and together with regulatory requirements, these discipline work schedules and prioritize resources.

The rationales for real-time logics appear mainly in conversations and in texts, in training regimens and in a station's Conduct of Operations and "nuts and bolts" handbooks with their rules of thumb.[8] Collated from the experiences of station and industry experts in many specialties, these guides provide "a sense of how theory touches practice at points, and in ways, that we feel on our pulses," in Toulmin's phrase. They use natural language to talk about what is happening, unlike calculated logics, which speak to material and physical conditions in the formal languages of mathematics, statistics, and technoscience. Real-time logics dominate discussion and negotiation but are less likely to be documented.

Calculated logics reach well beyond estimating material and physical conditions for safe shutdown, however; they also model expectations of working relationships. At Overton Station, an outage manager recalled that after the end of construction when the plant began to operate, "Naive engineers just expected people to talk to each other, so no 'integrated scheduling system' had been put in place." An oversight supervisor states: "It's so frustrating, because engineers don't know who they need to talk to. They don't understand how much people in the plant know." Algorithms, it appears, are expected also to automate or obviate conversations and to control exchanges among functions as parts writ large. At Overton Station, the design engineering group organizes its station telephone directory from the top down, by reporting lines, department, and person's name. The directory of the outage management group, responsible for ongoing activities, identifies people by their specialties and responsibilities: its title, "Whoo You Gonna Call?" sits above a sketch of a wise owl.

Being there, having direct experience of an operating plant, makes all the difference, as we have heard from several design engineers now at Overton Station.

> The general population of design engineers are not trained as to what's going on out here. . . . We used to do a minor mod and never knew what kind of problem it was for plant people to actually get it done. . . . Now you're not concerned so much with the concept of what's going on or what needs to be going on as to the actual operation of the plant. As a designer you're putting it on paper so someone can go build it. You're incorporating your safety requirements and all this into your design so it's going to be what the plant needs, or what your concept is of what you think they need.

Scripted and improvisational, static and dynamic, linear and systemic, hierarchical and lateral: two modes of thinking living side by side, each doing its appropriate work, and each drawn upon by the other as the occasion—or turn of mind—warrants.[9] But as things stand, industry experts and station managers understand these logics less as a partnership than as a hierarchy: real-time logics should only execute and implement control methods handed down by reactor, production, and business risk calculations. But when shutdown risk and financial risk are at stake, real-time logics show their muscle, as much in executive offices as on plant floors. We know far less, however, about what accounts for their strengths and limitations than about those of calculated logics. We know after the fact of major accidents, events, and nonevents, however, that technically and contextually real-time logics have been influential if not decisive, as much for good as for ill.

Sustaining this knowledge hierarchy is an ideology, a series of inter-locking assumptions, values, and beliefs.[10] The higher value assigned to calculated logics assumes that quantitative knowledge is more useful for reducing uncertainty. That assumption is often enough correct for some kinds of problems—especially those concerning physical forces and material conditions—that their success, it is believed, outweighs the costs of leaving the qualitative out of account. The relative infrequency of high consequence accidents maintains the general esteem of axiomatic knowledge, codified algorithms, geometric images, and in their wake, expectations of predictability, precision, and stability.[11] Making them and thousands of other technologies possible, which millions of us regard as necessary to the conduct of life as we have come to know it, calculated logics prevail as a cultural benefit.

In situations that are or become ambiguous and less predictable, calculated logics may stall: alone, they are at a disadvantage not only in confronting worldly conditions that disappoint those expectations, but also in deciding what to do next. In calculated logics' semantics, those are "system upsets," "disturbances," and "anomalies" to lock-step chains of deductions. Real-time logics instead have little choice when coming upon the unexpected or murky to view it as a scrambled alphabet out of which meanings must be made to recompose control.[12] Then, real-time logics get into gear, as local experts draw on memories, observations, experience, judgment; on industry studies and on the SKILL OF THE CRAFT; on others' best practices and LESSONS LEARNED from archives of event reports; on high-level design and production strategies and on bottom-line goals and on professional experience; on handy heuristics and rules of thumb.

Even when aware that real-time logics matter to safe shutdown, technologists tend to remain within the orbit of light thrown by the lamp of calculated logics. "If it can't be reduced to a calculation around here, it's not worth thinking about," bemoans Jim, a manager at Overton Station. "Everything is in flow charts with boxes and arrows. I've told engineers, 'You're engineering this problem to death—it's not that kind of problem.' They can't think outside the box. It drives me and a few others here crazy." After learning a trade in the navy, Jim went to college, thinking he'd be an engineer. "I hated it, I hated it. Just making calculations was not satisfying. I changed to an education major and got my soft skills, and got a job in nuclear." Starting as an electrical apprentice fifteen years ago, he leads a group of thirty-seven responsible for testing and maintenance. Recently invited to join an event review team, Jim refused: "I knew that my perspective wasn't what upper management wanted this group to produce. I would just have been an irritant—I put my hand up and people *know* what they might hear. I put a first-line supervisor on the team because he *can* see outside the box."

Real-time logics mobilize evidence, knowledge, and methods that are largely experiential and substantive, and not all are quantifiable: most are pointers to states and conditions that have to be understood both on their own terms and in context before inferences can be drawn about their possible consequences.[13] Many unmeasurable conditions were present in the Bhopal catastrophe in India in 1984, where, during a maintenance outage at a Union Carbide chemical processing plant, poisonous gases killed as many as 3,000 people and jeopardized the long-term health of 200,000. The accident inquiry found these unmeasurable conditions: refrigeration was disconnected, workers disbelieved a gauge, investigation of the smell was delayed, vent scrubbers were turned off, observes Nancy G. Leveson, professor of aeronautics and astronautics at the Massachusetts Institute of Technology.[14] Such unmeasurables account for "unrealistic risk assessment."

> Numerical assessments measure only what they *can* measure and not necessarily what *needs* to be measured. The unmeasurable factors (such as design flaws and management errors) are ignored—even though they may have a greater influence on safety than those that are measurable. . . . [A] case can be made that the most important causal factors in terms of accident prevention . . . are often the unmeasurable ones. In addition, the underlying assumptions of the assessment—for example, that the plant or system is built according to the design or that certain failures are independent—are often ignored. The belief grows that the numbers actually have some relation to the real risk of accidents, rather than being a way to evaluate specific aspects of the design.[15]

In an attempt to bring PRA theory closer to operational reality, one NRC study opened its own window onto vital unmeasurables for estimating the "human reliability" metrics of control room operators' activities, to parallel those for equipment reliability. In error-forcing contexts, the study found, twenty factors were defined as safety significant, but these are "not normally considered in PRAs."[16] For example: "instrumentation fails (or is caused to be failed) and fails in many ways"; "the instrumentation used by operators is not necessarily all that is available to them or what designers expect them to use"; "operators can misunderstand how instrumentation and control systems work, resulting in erroneous explanations for their operation and indications"; "one plausible explanation can create a group mindset for an operating crew"; "the recovery of slips may be complicated"; "systems and components are not truly binary state"; "pre-existing plant-specific operational quirks can be important in specific accident sequences"; "dependencies can occur across systems (as well as within systems)"; "the specific, detailed causes of initiating events (especially those caused by humans) can be important to accident response."[17] A culture of control nevertheless has to account for if not anticipate these substantive issues and, in order to locate palliatives, understand how they became issues.[18]

Surprises reveal the subliminal power of risk models: no matter how tentative and fraught with cautions about their limitations they may be, PRAs and other models can set up authoritative *expectations* of what can and should be seen—as when, in the case of Davis-Besse, the NRC had never regarded erosion as a "credible type of concern," according to Brian W. Sheron, its associate director for project licensing and technology assessment. NRC experts "were surprised by the discovery. They said they had never seen so much corrosion in a reactor vessel." Designers' deductions depended on their assumption that "if cooling water leaked from the piping above the vessel and accumulated on the vessel lid, the water would boil away in the heat of over 500 degrees, leaving the boric acid it contains in harmless boron powder form."[19] Even though model-makers themselves may be aware of the limits of their simplifications, models may find themselves doing more heavy lifting than intended when the world goes its own way. What model language calls "ill-structured" problems or "system upsets" are more likely to be real-world situations made more intractable by overstructured expectations that a technology will and should perform as modeled. That nuclear power plant technology should not operate as initially designed is amply attested by the volume of unavoidable design modifications.

Perhaps because real-time logics confront technological and contextual ambiguities and disappointments in much the same way as everyone confronts the ambiguities and disappointments of living—through observation, discussion, experience, judgment, insight, and interpretation—real-time logics are believed to be less rational if not nonrational in science- and technology-driven enterprises. Yet, surely they are as rational when they figure out how to maintain control over a risky technology showing signs of instability: then real-time logics complete the cybernetic loop. That depends on experts' abilities to read, hear, and interpret system signals and devise effective and actionable correctives.

An Infrastructure of Conundrums

Paradoxes, dilemmas, and contradictions appear often enough in technology-driven enterprises to warrant being re-understood as *expectable* outcroppings of complexity: to "manage" a complex system is to keep untying the knots it can get itself into.[20] The premier paradox is that as much as designers and station experts know about the technology's internal workings and its operating environment, they also know it must remain capable of responding to what the culture of control has not imagined. Defending against that paradox's power are margins of error, redundancies, resources for quick response, slack for recovery. Dilemmas are not confined to the tradeoff quandary: when and how to centralize or delegate depends on the situation; procedures cannot be written for unimagined circumstances; upgraded components will highlight flaws in others; career and financial incentives can cloud judgment.

Contradictions can be so numerous that it is difficult to choose, but perhaps three that confront control room operators could head the list, according to Jussi Vuario, Finnish nuclear engineer and probabilistic risk analysis specialist. They stem "in the worst case" from "design-phase errors . . . not always easy to capture" even in a rigorous risk assessment:

1. Contradictory or misleading symptoms.
2. Contradictory goals or supervisor expectations of production and safety.
3. Contradictory or misleading procedures in unanticipated circumstances.[21]

Recognizing the very existence of paradoxes, dilemmas, and contradictions is the obvious first step. But it may be taken only after they have had unwanted consequences. Left unaddressed, the infrastructure of conundrums remains free to stir up conflicts and ambiguities that foment issue upon issue ready for bopping. Those consequences and issues are, as Barry Turner, British engineer and sociologist, tagged them, "decoys" keeping us from considering what precipitates them.[22]

One Overton Station control room crew had not told the next shift about an error it made, discovered, and corrected. That next crew saw what had happened and filed a condition report on the matter. The earlier crew members explained to the event review team that they feared that reporting their near-miss would jeopardize their chances for promotion. Although some members were eligible for open positions, no promotions had been made for an unusually long time: managers had given no explanation for the delay. At a European nuclear power plant, a manager described his job to me as "marketing safety to senior managers. . . . They say that they support 'safety' but they continue to stress 'efficiency.' I find it hard to get my job done with these double meanings." At a U.S. station, despite what seems to be a clear-sighted recognition of policy logics, a review team stops short of asking *why* four "cultural premises" it identified had been "driving the maintenance program" in the first place: "keep the plant operating," "cut operating and maintenance costs," "assume that equipment is operable," "do not admit a lack of knowledge."

"When cultural premises drive a program, individuals at all levels make decisions based on those premises." The team recommended a new premise: "Safely balance plant operation with O&M cost controls." The "significance and consequences" algorithm Doug and Miles proposed at Charles Station is another instance of professional orders being in the position of having to "sell safety" to corporate and market orders. At Electricité de France, as mentioned earlier, finding out how that does or doesn't happen is the job of its "Safety/Availability Monitoring Units": how control room operators and managers negotiate policy rationales to recognize "conflicts" among "a wide-ranging set of requirements" for "nuclear safety," for "personnel safety, health physics and competitiveness" and for "environmental protection." The issue is not the presence of such dilemmas, paradoxes, and contradictions but whether and how utility executives, line managers, engineers, chief financial officers, unions, regulators, and boards of directors recognize them and develop rationales to work them out.

That an infrastructure of conundrums goes with the territory brings onstage a third logics: a *policy logics* in corporate, station, and regulatory orders. In a feedback discussion at Bowie Station with fourteen women and men, I had suggested that paradoxes are expectable consequences of complexity.

> FIRST VOICE: We have the perfect example of a paradox, you know, between middle management saying "safety first" and senior managers saying "schedule first." Every week, we get a goal to meet on the number of tasks to be accomplished that week—95 percent. And our value system tells us that nuclear safety is number one followed closely by personal safety. However, we have to complete 95 percent of our tasks at a minimum every week. What's wrong with this picture?

Where could you take that conversation? Let's say you wanted to have a real discussion about that with the goal of figuring out what could be ameliorated.

> FIRST VOICE: First you'd have to find someone who thinks that's a problem who has a decision-making job.
>
> SECOND VOICE: I think we all recognize we have a problem. I think the real issue is how do we economically—I had to throw that qualifier in—address that problem. We cannot go out and blanket say "We're going to not have a goal for task completion for a week. We're going to drive it entirely on personal safety." Well, then it comes to the point that we don't get anything done, and material condition goes down, then plant reliability goes down, and pretty soon we don't have to worry about anything because we aren't producing power.

That's the problem, that's the balancing act. You can't just focus on the one thing. Of course. So why isn't it a range? Why isn't it between 80 and 95 percent? Why is it an absolute number? That would be a reasonable question.

FIRST VOICE: It's 95 to 100 percent—that's the range.

THIRD VOICE: Talking about that 95 percent completion. They might have that expectation, but at the same time the backlog of unworked items is rising, the number of deferred or cancelled work orders is rising, and so we're getting 95 percent of the work done, but meanwhile we're not getting all of the work there is to do—the backlog of work is going up. At the same time, we just had cuts in the maintenance department.

FOURTH VOICE: One of the central arguments in statistical process control literature is that when you base your decision-making and consequences on specifications like that 95 percent number, instead of looking at the processes and the boundaries and range in which they actually fluctuate around these, and you just put that target there, then there are three ways to respond to that. The people who have to meet that specification can improve the process so it meets that specification all the time. Lacking that, they can distort the process or distort the data. And that backlog rising while we're still meeting the process is an example of one of those other two responses.

FIFTH VOICE: And remember what happened last time when we started lumping different types of this backlog into different categories, saying, "Well, we're only going to look at this category then." And voided a number of items to make the backlog go away. Lots of creative games to make the beans the right color and right number.

SIXTH VOICE: On scheduling to the value [number]—I see the effect of that during outages, where you get to the point where a schedule is not going to be met and the value is in jeopardy. Then there is an enormous amount of almost frenzied energy to find ways to adapt to protect that value. Where a plan that took months to build and is carefully structured and risk-assessed throughout, then suddenly logic ties are broken and things that were a series are jammed into parallel, and people are told, "Make this work."

SEVENTH VOICE: This year, the outage goal in our incentive plan is that you get two days off. We'll get one day if we meet all our goals. We'll get the second day if we have zero lost time accidents, zero recordables [injuries], and zero restricted duties [from injuries]. Zero. Zero's the number. Well, there is no slack there. We're going to lose a day no matter what. As soon as everybody heard that in the presentation, I just know everybody was thinking, "Well, that's one day we're not getting." As soon as the first one [injury] happens, there's no slack, and it will happen within the first few days of the outage.

EIGHTH VOICE: Somebody said it will happen within the first five days. What is our incentive to change our behavior when we know the second day won't be there?

One example of driving toward a target and of the aggrandizing power of policy logics is a dire case in which a board of directors did not question either their "cultural premises" or their "significance and consequences." In their book, *Corporate Profit and Nuclear Safety: Strategy at Northeast Utilities in the 1990s,* Paul W. MacAvoy and Jean W. Rosenthal of the Yale School of Management outline that company's decade-long strategy, which systematically risked license violations at three plants at Millstone Station in Waterford, Connecticut.[23] Developed in 1986 as deregulation came on the horizon, the strategy's priority was to cut costs in Northeast Utility's nuclear subsidiary in order to maintain "low cost dominance" in anticipation of competition. Ultimately, the Connecticut Department of Public Utility Control found the strategy "an overreaction to possible but not certain adverse changes in electricity markets."[24]

By 1991, the program had begun to backfire. Before the company could buy another nuclear power plant, the NRC required improved performance at Millstone Station. Even so, its executives and board kept on with their cost reduction strategy—and forced shutdowns. Some also squelched station experts trying to speak out about operating risks. By 1997 the three plants were on the NRC's "watch list." The Nuclear Regulatory Commission in 1999 imposed a $10 million fine, half of which was for Northeast Utilities' violations in its nuclear operations—said to be the largest fine in the history of the commercial nuclear power industry; Northeast Utilities also pled guilty to criminal charges. Stock prices had been declining for years; by 2000 a company specializing in nuclear power plant operations owned all of Northeast Utilities' nuclear assets.

It is not that the rationale for aggressive cost-cutting, prevalent in this industry throughout the 1980s, is untenable, say MacAvoy and Rosenthal, but that with this particular strategy, the utility "necessarily had its nuclear plants at risk of violating safety requirements." Running so close to the edge, plants were in prolonged shut downs either because of malfunctions or because the NRC shut them down, forcing them to buy replacement power for customers. With all that, the company ultimately incurred "an increase in operating and maintenance costs that eliminated present and prospective future earnings."[25] One reason for that, the authors speculate, could be that the company's executives and its board were "incompetent, or narrowly competent on financial concerns but not on complex nuclear power plant operations," but that is not the most likely explanation. They find instead that "executive management treated cost containment and safety related outlays in nuclear plant operations as if they were tradeoffs and deliberately chose a low-cost/low-safety option. In this view, management was far from incompetent . . . in choosing an option that contained increasing risk of NRC shutdown. With top-down budgeting, it implemented a strategy with significant increases in earnings and with significant and sustained risk of nuclear operational problems." Moreover, "the higher the position in the decision-making hierarchy, and the more identified with the strategy, the higher the survival rate and indeed the better the financial results for that executive. . . . These payments were free of penalties against senior management for destruction of the company."[26] Corporate and market orders swamped all others: "The destruction of Northeast was strategic," the authors conclude.[27]

> The focus with which the management of Northeast Utilities undertook cost containment in nuclear was striking; it set targets for deep cuts in operation and maintenance and in investment in replacement equipment, without questioning whether this would redound on costs, the maintenance of quality, and the reliability of plant performance. The program never established systems for feedback to ensure compliance with operational standards.[28]

The strategy succeeded only in producing bottom-line numbers entitling executives to promised bonuses. Throughout these years, although NRC's senior managers had identified Millstone's maintenance backlogs, they did not tie them to "economic stress and management's response," the policy that the NRC's own consultant had recommended to it for staying current with the safety consequences of downsizing; the NRC did not accept that recommendation.[29]

Whether and how executives and managers engage with the infrastructure of conundrums to consider the "significance and consequences" of their policies is as essential to risk reduction as are calculated and real-time logics. For consequences that become implicated in an event, review teams are in the best position to make those connections and explain how the event is but a decoy. Deference can inhibit that, as at Arrow Station: "[W]e do not mean to limit this term to shortcomings of individual human beings—although those do exist. We mean more generally that our investigation has revealed problems with the 'system' with regards to the operation, maintenance, planning, and scheduling." Without specifics, those "system" problems will persist, leaving corrective actions vulnerable to being ineffective or, not backed up by an explicit rationale, not implemented. An industry workshop in 1999 devoted sessions to problems faced by corrective action programs and their event reviewers, as well as the problem of root cause analyses and "recurrent events." Talking about

"Managing Resistance in Corrective Actions," one station expert "discussed what happens when station management rejects the recommended corrective actions. The prevailing management attitude was that the actions were too extensive and difficult to implement. Instead, corrective actions were focused on localized issues, ignoring the opportunity to address the global issues." Senior managers' resistance comes in four forms: "compliance" with minimum standards; "benign neglect" ("'I don't buy it, but it's OK if you do. I won't fight it, but I won't support it, either.'"); "resistance" ("specious arguments about how the observation . . . is the problem. 'You just don't understand what you're looking at.')"; and "sabotage" ('Go ahead and investigate, but don't look too hard, [**or else!**]')."[30] Another expert addressed the "failure to implement corrective actions." The first of his "ten commandments for improving corrective actions" is, "Make sure [they] address the underlying cause(s) for the event, not the symptoms"—but that may require looking "too hard."

The most well-worn "policy" corrective is, of course, to replace or reshuffle senior managers, but when not also examining the policy logics new managers plan to design and execute, that cycle is likely to recur.[31] The more often reorganizations occur, the more cynical station experts become about what they call "the flavor of the month" new managers sprinkle over the same infrastructure of conundrums.

Control in Real Time

Standing behind a yellow line in the relative quiet of a control room, we watch operators moving between display panels full of meters, gauges, recorders, and control devices, keeping track of trends in thousands of machine components and systems (turbine, valves, reactor cooling water) and varieties of physical processes (electrical supplies, water chemistry, feedwater intake systems). They are noting the conditions of particular components, watching computer screens for condition messages, tracking maintenance evolutions as they occur out in the plant, and adjusting control rods and water chemistry to modulate the nuclear reaction, all in the service of maintaining configuration control. Supporting their vigilance and acuity has had the highest priority in designing control rooms. Operators' most important task, human factors specialists have believed, is monitoring that array of signals, alarms, and messages.

Doing that work twenty-four hours a day are operators, reactor and field, licensed and not yet licensed, together with their shift supervisor in his corner office. Although all keep detailed logs of what they do, they do not record much about how they are doing it. We know most about their ways of working from studies in control room simulators, as they rehearse

Control room

emergency situations and complicated scenarios, as well as from accounts after accidents and events. Studies that observe operators' activities under normal conditions—which is to say, most of the time—are few.[32] Mundane monitoring, industry wags say, is "Ninety-nine per cent boredom, one per cent sheer terror."

To find out just what mundane monitoring consists of in real time, in the early 1990s, under the auspices of the Atomic Energy Control Board of Canada, a group of cognitive and industrial engineers specializing in human-machine interface issues began a "discovery process [that might] draw attention to significant phenomena and suggest new ideas" about "the cognitive complexities that operators confront during normal operations and the active, problem-solving activities that play a fundamental role in monitoring a complex dynamic system."[33] The group's observations began from three propositions based on earlier simulator studies: that "the primary challenge to monitoring is operator vigilance," or, alternatively, that "the primary demands in monitoring relate to selective attention" given the "hundreds of indicators," and, third, that because "the major difficulty in monitoring is one of visual perception," priority belongs to developing "the visual acuity and discrimination skills that are required to detect changes and read indicators accurately." What they found in a "progression" of "field studies" of "cognitive and collaborative processes" confounds and complicates those propositions: none "does justice to the richness of the phenomena we observed." Although all are "relevant issues, we found that there is much more to monitoring than meets the eye."[34]

Their findings come under three main headings: the breadth and variety of information sources operators actively seek out, the contexts in which they are monitoring and how those can work against carrying out their tasks effectively, and the ad hoc strategies they invent to compensate for ill-fitting hardware and software—all to assure that their observations and interpretations are as reliable as possible. Even under routine conditions, these studies demonstrate, the partnership of calculated and real-time logics is essential.

Operators examine gauges, meters, and computer screens and interpret the quality and character of their signals in order to judge, the authors say, "what is relevant to monitor and what deviation or change is meaningful. The same parameter value can be normal in one context and safety threatening in another." Their task is to maintain "an up-to-the-minute, comprehensive, and accurate understanding" of the status of operations. Because "this context is incredibly complex and constantly changing, maintaining it is not a trivial matter."[35] Nor is the control panel, meant to represent the entire plant system, their main source of that contextual information: the information they seek out is "much broader and more diverse."[36] At shift turnovers, incoming operators review current records, evaluate field operators' activities, interpret the results of routine tests, and, walking out into the plant, make field tours of major components for a "process feel" of temperature and of vibration of plant components associated with important assemblies such as the turbine.[37]

The authors keep being surprised. They find that the "challenge" of mundane monitoring "is not how to pick up subtle, abnormal indications against a quiescent background but, rather, how to identify and pursue relevant findings against a noisy background." That, they say, makes mundane monitoring "similar" to the demands of upsets or emergencies.[38] Operators' other duties (signing off on work packages, answering phone inquiries) are part of the "noise." Computer alarm screens, on which operators rely for detecting problems, turn out also to be pressed into service for another function they were "*not* designed to support." Operators use them "to some extent . . . to get an overview of plant status." The group observes "various informal strategies and competencies," which "are not part of the formal training programs or the official operating procedures." Nevertheless, these "are extremely important because they facilitate the complex demands of monitoring and compensate for poor interface design decisions. Thus one could effectively argue that the [control] system works well, not despite, but *because* operators deviate from formal practices."[39]

> Good operators rely extensively on knowledge-driven monitoring instead of rote procedural compliance. This practice allows operators to detect problems before they become significant, to compensate for poor design of procedures, to distinguish instrumentation failures from component failures, and to become better aware (in a deep sense) of the unit's current state.[40]

What makes monitoring difficult? The dynamics of reactor mode changes, questionable equipment reliability, the design of alarm systems, displays, and controls, as well as that of system automation. At these plants, thousands of components, instruments, and equipment "are missing, broken, working imperfectly, or being worked on." Yet "an accurate and comprehensive understanding of the current status" is essential for interpreting which signals are "normal/abnormal." With "so many interactions among components, subsystems, and instrumentation, it is difficult to derive the full implications of the current failures to determine what state any particular parameter should be in."[41]

Credible information is hard to come by. The alarm system's design can get in the way: because alarm "set points are not [generally] context sensitive . . . nuisance (i.e. nonmeaningful alarms) of various types abound." More than 50 percent of alarms "often were not meaningful." Magnifying signal ambiguity are alarms that stay on "because the plant is not currently operated the way it was originally intended to be (e.g., because of equipment upgrades)." Similarly, displays and controls present design "weaknesses," such as indicators "so consistently unreliable that operators do not trust them." Or "when LED's burn out, replacing bulbs is so difficult that information is lost." Or "analog meters may fail but, in those that are motor driven, the needle remains in the same spot," and on some failed instruments, that value is the "same as the low value on the scale. . . . Consequently, these displays require experience, knowledge, and memory to interpret."[42]

Operators develop several strategies to "reduce noise" that prevents them from recognizing "meaningful changes." At shift turnover, they clear the alarm printer of previous data, unclutter the alarm screen, and put out of commission the software controlling "continuous streams of nuisance alarms." They strengthen weak signals ("by expanding the y axis on a trend plot"); they document baselines to facilitate trend analysis; they read logs and keep written records for comparison with changing parameters. They stay aware of plant mode changes that they know from experience are "more likely to cause problems." Making it a priority to understand "the intent" of an equipment test, instead of depending on "rote procedural compliance," they rely on a "knowledge-driven monitoring strategy" that helps them "detect errors as soon as they occur" and may help to "compensate for the limitations of the procedures." They find ways to get information not otherwise provided, sometimes by creating new indicators or alarms, sometimes by testing whether an indicator is valid by manipulating related equipment. And they do what they can via machines or other people to reduce demands on their memory and attention by, for example, using sticky notes or other cues or assigning another operator to track particular indicators or screens.[43]

A singular conclusion is that control room operators "develop many strategies and acquire a great deal of knowledge on the job that goes well beyond the formal training they receive. . . . However, current training and licensing programs are based more on procedural compliance than on knowledge-based understanding."[44] In all, these studies demonstrate how real-time logics augment risk recognition and risk reduction to make good on designers' calculated intentions—so much so, the authors conclude, that training should recognize them. The stress that these unavoidable activities impose also needs attention—as the study's authors observe, the demands of mundane monitoring can resemble those of emergencies. "Problem solving under pressure means coping both with interruptions and with excessive arousal," says Karl Weick, professor of organizational behavior and psychology in the School of Business Administration, University of Michigan. "To cope with mental workload is an arousing, emotional experience, which means that mental processes will be modified by affect," and depending on circumstances, by negative as well as positive emotions and performance.[45]

With a naturalistic approach to the kind of problem "monitoring" is, these findings sketch a general model of how real-time logics systematically and improvisationally reduce risk. Even if these several plants are not typical (I have no basis for comparison), they perhaps for that reason expose more than we might otherwise know of the kinds of knowledge and ways of thinking that configuration control can demand anywhere. In their ways of thinking and in their practices, station experts within and outside control rooms show themselves to be naturalists and archaeologists of a hazardous environment.

Doubt, Discovery, and Interpretation

In their initiatives to uncover the moment-by-moment truth of system conditions, control room operators transform the meanings of "problems," "flaws," "delays," and "errors." These become invaluable sources

of new knowledge. They are identifying both anticipated and unanticipated interactions, not by luck but by intent. Configuration control
through *doubt* shadowed by *discovery*: that is the animating concept of
the second game. The principle of command and control to assure safe
shutdown depends on the principle of doubt and discovery to identify the
impediments.

Automated control systems "do not set machines free but rather reign
them in," says David A. Mindell, electrical engineer and historian of manufacturing and technology at the Massachusetts Institute of Technology.
Like "beasts," he argues, "machinery threatens to run out of control:
airplanes spin, ships veer, guns misfire, and systems oscillate. These wild
behaviors all enact versions of 'instability,' the precise engineering term
for technical chaos. Control systems, like stirrups on a horse, do not create autonomy in the machine but rather harness it, bringing its independence and wildness under the will of human intention."[46] To keep from
slipping into instability, the first game relies on a semantics of "monitoring," "surveillance," "inspection," "vigilance," and "testing," component by component, subsystem by subsystem. Those terms, in obedience
to calculated logics, assume that control can be assured, as in "assume
that equipment is operable"—until it isn't. Incipient instabilities have to
be sought out, which asks far more than "monitoring" and "inspecting"
imply: doubt and discovery have to clear up the opacities the redundancy
principle installs. "Inspections" at Davis-Besse had not sought out the
consequences of a nozzle leak despite warnings to station managers, and
entirely by chance, experts came upon the hole its residues had dug. "Luck
is not a robust barrier," as Doug put it. Doubt and discovery can be.

Doubt and discovery require observation and documentation not only
within the control room but also beyond, as far away as the switchyard
and an executive conference room. But only after having *interpreted* what
is found can experts define next steps.[47] For example, to initiate a condition report and assign its level of significance is a first interpretation. So
is arriving at recommendations for corrective actions: revisiting the context in which the condition arose, searching out performance and maintenance history, considering its links to other equipment and processes, and
so on. These often lead to other tasks: documentation may be hard to
find, when, for example, a plant's original design basis may not exist;
the rationales behind particular operating procedures may be unrecorded;
trend data on a component's performance may remain unanalyzed.

Altogether, doubt, discovery, and interpretation fulfill technologists' intentions. Until a system is operating, calculated logics express only those
intentions, based on what was already known or anticipated via testing
and simulations.[48] They alone cannot make good on them. Real-time logics put intentions into context to find out what they mean, situation by

situation. That depends on experts' exchanges of ideas, information, judgment. In that, there is also more science than meets the eye. As they crystallize interpretations into rationales for next steps, station experts engage in a process little different from that of scientists when interpreting experimental results to evaluate a hypothesis. "In any inquiry, experimenters possess a background set of skills, practices, and other commitments without which there would be no inquiry." A "problematic situation . . . involves a question [requiring] background knowledge, as well as an intimation of how to use it," says Robert Crease, philosopher of science at the State University of New York at Stony Brook. Drawing on that knowledge, experimenters reveal their "skill in judging," a central element of Aristotle's concept of *phronesis*: "being wise in the world through activity," or practical reason. That involves "not deduction or production but deliberation. . . . The deliberation involved in experimentation occurs not only on the level of reading dials, but of planning, construction, and interpretation," skills that display "artistry or prudence."[49]

Once arriving at a coherent image out of the collage of evidence, station experts, like scientists, have to interpret its significance before taking next steps. Then they call on "abduction," a logical process of "forming an explanatory hypothesis. It is the only logical operation which introduces any new idea: for induction does nothing but determine a value, and deduction merely evolves the necessary consequences of a pure hypothesis," proposes the philosopher Charles S. Peirce.

> Deduction proves that something *must* be; Induction shows that something *actually* is operative; Abduction merely suggests that something may be. . . . If we are ever to learn anything or to understand phenomena at all, it must be by abduction that this is to be brought about . . . The abductive suggestion comes to us like a flash. It is an act of *insight*, although of extremely fallible insight. It is true that the different elements of the hypothesis were in our minds before; but it is the idea of putting together what we had never before dreamed of putting together which flashes the new suggestion before our contemplation.[50]

Abduction, ever present in real-time logics, is a mode of reasoning markedly different from that on which calculated logics' additive, linear, and top-down approach depends. The call for a "significance and consequence analysis" for problems on the nonnuclear side at Charles Station acknowledges the need for abductive reasoning. But having only the one game to play, the review team had to call it an "algorithm."[51]

Deductive reasoning alone is insufficient even while designing a technology—that is one moral of the history of a French guided-transportation system intended to combine attributes of automobiles and rail transit. After eighteen years of engineering, planning, and prototyping, in 1987 sponsors halted the project, named Aramis. Speaking through Bruno

Latour, anthropologist of science and technology at the Ecole des Mines who studied the project's history and observed the design process in its final two years, Aramis laments its designers' limited aims and knowledge of the world in which it would be operating:

> [T]hey didn't want to complicate their lives. Everything in its time. Later for the crowd problems; later for the social problems, later for the operating problems. There'll be plenty of time to find a place to use this stuff. As if I were rootless! As if I were a thing! . . . Let's not lose time on complicated problems, you said! But didn't you really lose time, in the long run? . . . "Technologically perfected," you say. But how do you dare treat me that way, when I don't exist? How can you say of something that it is perfected, achieved, finished, technologically impeccable, when it does not have being! . . . They wanted simple, clear, technological solutions. But we technological objects have nothing technological about us. . . . A local elected official knows more about research, about uncertainty, about negotiation, than all of you so-called technicians do. . . . They say they love me and don't want to search for me! They say they love technology and don't want to be researchers![52]

Seeing the process of design also as a "search" outside its designers' box would have let Aramis be "found," as it were.

Finding out is only the beginning; it can end there, too soon for comfort, as Charles Station experts found out after the fact. The principle of doubt and discovery is the reason for its condition-based maintenance program in the first place, but forgotten or discounted in contentions over, or denial of, Paul's interpretation of the thermograms' meanings. Managers also discounted his familiarity with this equipment's thermographic history and with transformer explosions elsewhere and ignored the presence on-site of two other experts. None of that experience-near knowledge was invited across the threshold of that conference room.

By the costs its omission rings up, the value of the doubt and discovery principle is clear. At Davis-Besse, there were "shortcomings in inspections"—perhaps because that was all they were. Inspections saw what calculated logics expected would be seen, as in not regarding erosion as a "credible type of concern."[53] But there had been earlier signs. For example, NRC staff found that even in 1999, air filters in containment "were becoming so filthy with rust and boric acid that FirstEnergy was replacing them every other day for more than two years—far more frequently than the industry norm of once a month." Yet station experts had not reported that to the NRC. That high frequency "should have tipped off FirstEnergy that it had a severe rust problem settling in somewhere on the reactor [according to a senior metallurgical engineer on the NRC staff]."[54] The focus was not on "frequency," which would have sparked curiosity about reasons for this trend, but on *parts*, the dirty filters in and of themselves. The parts template fixated them on "fixing" rather than on discovering why parts were failing so often.

Doubt and discovery are all the more necessary for confronting design-basis legacies that make access to equipment difficult and dangerous. Although Davis-Besse relied on visual inspections every two years, "about 15 percent of [inspectors'] view was "partially obstructed" by the "tight manner in which nozzles are packed together, plus insulation over the reactor head and residue from minor flange leaks," according to a utility spokesman.[55] An NRC letter sent to all plant managers in 1998 "suggested" that they improve ways of gaining access to reactor heads for inspections and maintenance; Davis-Besse was one of seven plants whose designs were "especially vulnerable." It and a station in Arkansas had not "followed through."[56] Only doubt and discovery during operations can call the bluff of command and control assumptions worked into algorithms and risk assessments.

Words, Meanings, and Deeds

One ongoing dilemma that pits command and control against doubt and discovery turns on the question of procedural adherence: whether station experts should exercise "strict compliance," or whether, in some circumstances, they should use their judgment to fit the procedure to the situation. Written as they are with reference to the calculated logics of design, procedures can overlook much of what actually goes on and has to go on while performing a task. The industry term "professionalization" straddles the dilemma: it allows that sometimes station experts' real-time logics can be as informed and as rigorous as the logics of technology designers.[57] Studies show in any case that people will not follow procedures every time, under all conditions.[58] Nor should they under particular conditions, because, observes Yves Dien, senior engineer in the Research and Development Center at Electricité de France, a task procedure controls the person, not the process, yet a task may have to be done when conditions change the process it is part of.[59]

Strict compliance became the watchword at EDF in the years after the accident at Three Mile Island, according to Armand Colas when he was head of the Human Factors Group in the department of Nuclear Power Operations at Electricité de France' headquarters. "Automation was implemented whenever possible; procedures were widely developed, always ensuring their strict application." By the second half of the 1980s, the consequences of this forced march became apparent.

Without realizing it, we gradually transformed the actions and operations to be carried out into a complicated path to follow, strewn with obstacles, one-way roads, never-ending traffic signals, pauses in order to install or remove an item, and so on. It was so complicated, in fact, that the attention of the people assigned to carry out these actions was progressively diverted to the specific details of the path to be followed, thus losing sight of the purpose and reasons of the operation. Unintentionally, we succeeded in transforming people, who, initially, were supposed to be competent and intelligent, into "programmed machines," asking them to relentlessly keep to a pre-defined course. At the same time, prerogatives and responsibilities were separated: engineers (or planners) were given a definition of the course to be followed and "executors" were assigned to carry out actions without any initiative encouraged on their part.

In 1989, incidents occurred at the Gravelines and Dampierre sites which revealed that both plants were affected by operating failures which had gone undetected for several months and which would have had serious consequences in the event of an accident triggered elsewhere in the unit. New weaknesses came to light, namely: the segmentation of activities linked not only to the complex nature of installations, but also to the use of overly specialized procedures, the multiplicity of people involved, and shortcomings in inspections. This time, it was felt that previous solutions based on ergonomics, automation, and the formalization of procedures would have only a limited impact.[60]

How "strict compliance" and "professionalization" work out in practice is a question Mathilde Bourrier, sociologist at the University of Technology at Compiègne, takes up in field studies at two plants in the United States and two in France. In the United States, because stations have procedures for procedure changes, they occur "openly and legally." Not so in French plants, where no such procedures exist, so station experts revise them "secretly and illegally." When finding themselves in "unplanned situations," French experts would "take the responsibility to correct procedures informally" because they "could not find either the support or the resources to modify rules openly and legally."[61] With these "tacit-microadjustments," station experts "accumulate (and sometimes transmit to their peers) a 'private knowledge' of actual operation, . . . confessing that they keep track of the 'real figures' in a personal notebook. This expertise is the basis of their power and their autonomy inside the plant," and they become "key players in a system that needs their knowledge."[62]

"Legally" changing procedures has dollar costs, however: at one U.S. station where every procedure change has to be approved, Bourrier observes, it took a complement of fifty station experts to keep procedure changes "legal" within the time constraints of an outage.[63] Several years later, after reengineering eliminated half those positions and after she had ended her field studies, Bourrier writes, "The intriguing question now, is whether and how the organisation manages to achieve the same level of organisational reliability . . . [which now] must have new social and political foundations."[64] Yes: the foundations need to add a plank that makes it routine to ask, first, What conditions led those experts to discover that procedure changes are needed in the first place? That can signal a "near miss" and disclose new knowledge about system conditions. And to ask next, What technical and contextual paradoxes, dilemmas, and contradictions are relevant to those changes? Why did practice meet untenable theory or unexamined policies?

There are several reasons to change procedures midstream: incomprehensible or misleading language or a procedure that does not take account of related procedures coming before or after a task, for example. Vague verbs (impact, affect, determine), vague adjectives (slow, sufficient, periodical), and vague phrases (as soon as, if required, when directed) as well as procedures having undefined terms and inconsistent terminologies or requiring burdensome memorization, information search, or multiple actions are persistent issues, according to Robert C. Fisher, a root cause specialist.[65] About 35 percent of licensee event reports cite "human performance" issues involving problems with written and verbal communication, an NRC study finds.[66]

Procedures' semantics can also confuse. The implications of "higher risk" in a "minor maintenance work order" on one of the three primary barriers only caught the attention of Mark, the work scheduler at Arrow Station, for which, Rusty said, he should be "commended." With 4,000 valves to look after, a "minor" task also becomes "routine," no matter its location. In a year filled with, say, 10,000 work orders, "minor" and "major" are welcome categories announcing priorities and demarcating responsibilities. But in such "language habits of the group," there is likely to be little difference between naming categories and living up to them, Benjamin Lee Whorf, engineer and distinguished linguist, observed in 1939 in "The Relation of Habitual Thought and Behavior to Language." During his twenty years as a fire prevention engineer at the Hartford Fire Insurance Company, Whorf analyzed "many hundreds of reports of circumstances surrounding the start of fires, and in some cases, of explosions. My analysis was directed toward purely physical conditions, such as defective wiring, presence or lack of air spaces between metal flues and woodwork, etc., and the results were presented in these terms. Indeed it was undertaken with no thought that any other significances would or could be revealed."

> But in due course it became evident that not only a physical situation qua physics, but the meaning of that situation to people was sometimes a factor, through the behavior of the people, in the start of the fire. And this factor of meaning was

clearest when it was a linguistic meaning, residing in the name or the linguistic description commonly applied to the situation. Thus, around a storage of what are called "gasoline drums," behavior will tend to a certain type, that is, great care will be exercised; while around a storage of what are called "empty gasoline drums" it will tend to be different—careless, with little repression of smoking or of tossing cigarette stubs about. Yet the "empty" drums are perhaps the more dangerous, since they contain explosive vapor. Physically the situation is hazardous, but the linguistic analysis according to regular analogy must employ the word "empty," which inevitably suggests lack of hazard. The word "empty" is used in two linguistic patterns: (1) as a virtual synonym for 'null and void, negative, inert,' (2) applied in analysis of physical situations without regard to, e.g., vapor, liquid vestiges, or stray rubbish, in the container. The situation is named in one pattern (2) and the name is then "acted out" or "lived up to" in another (1), this being a general formula for the linguistic conditioning of behavior into hazardous forms.[67]

In the environmental reclamation work at one nuclear weapons installation in the United States, all "minor" work is batched for Fridays; one Friday, a near-miss on one such task could have resulted in an electrocution. At a European station, technicians working on a Friday night who had spent the previous days on a "major" task switched to a "minor" task. Their attention flagged, resulting in a safety system failure. "When you pick up a word, you drag along with it a whole scene," claims Charles J. Fillmore, linguistic theorist at the University of California, Berkeley. In this case, experts "lived up to" its expectation of a low level of safety significance and priority.[68] "Friday" conjures the weekend and its leisure, as in "Thank-God-It's-Friday." Attention is scripted to flag (as Ned's perhaps did in anticipation of his "vacation"). We have already named our consensus about "Monday": a lemon of a car or computer must have been "Made on Monday," the day when assembly line employees are, the idiom imagines, inattentive, recovering from the weekend's proverbial excesses. An internal audit team at a U.S. station was ticking off what was going "wrong" in one of its programs, but when switching to ticking off what was "right," it noted more of what was not happening that should have been. In engineering language, a "fault" in a component turns into a "fault tree" in event analysis, the one usage technically neutral, the other socially blaming; living up to the engineering term "root cause" automatically narrows the scope of event reviews.

A remnant of "empty drums" materialized in the May 1996 crash of ValuJet Flight 592 in Florida, a DC9 in which all 110 aboard died, a tragedy in which the semantics of control played a leading role. The aircraft's cargo hold contained oxygen generators stored in five cartons alongside three tires; the generators initiate the oxygen flow to the masks above each seat. William Langewiesche, correspondent for *The Atlantic Monthly*, describes what happens during the generators' normal operation and what is likely to have happened inside those cartons.

> [T]he passenger pulls a lanyard which slides a retaining pin from a spring-loaded hammer, which falls on a minute explosive charge, which in turn sparks a chemical reaction that liberates the oxygen within the sodium chlorate core [of the generator]. This reaction produces heat, which may cause the surface temperature of the [generator] canister to rise to 500 degrees Fahrenheit when it is mounted correctly in a ventilated bracket and much higher if the canister is sealed into a box with other canisters, which may themselves be heating up. If the materials surrounding the canister catch fire, the presence of pure oxygen will cause them to burn furiously. If those materials are rubber tires, they will provide a particularly rich source of fuel. Was there an explosion? Perhaps. In any event, Flight 592 was blow-torched into the ground.[69]

In his close reading of the report of the National Transportation Safety Board (NTSB), Langewiesche makes as clear as they may ever be the mazes of meanings that ultimately brought on the on-board fire, the direct cause of the accident.[70] A tangle of terms applies to the conditions of generators: "empty," "expired," "fired," "expended," "repairable," "serviceable," "unserviceable," "out of date." Having come "to the end of their licensed lifetimes" but also never having been activated, the "expired" generators had been removed from three secondhand MD80s, which ValuJet was refurbishing. When mechanics removed the oxygen canisters, they wired green tags to most of them; that designated them "repairable," which they were not. Investigators later found two tagged canisters left in a hangar; on one, under "reason for removal" was written "out of date," and on the other, "Generators have been ~~expired~~ fired."[71] Then, when a ValuJet ramp agent accepted delivery for the flight, he violated federal regulations because even if "empty," the airline "was not licensed to carry such officially designated hazardous materials."[72] Not having been fired, and without their firing pins capped as procedures required (and with no caps having been supplied to the mechanics in any case), the generators then went into boxes labeled " 'aircraft parts' " on a shipping ticket marked " '*Oxygen Canisters Empty.*' "

> This required a gang of hard-pressed mechanics to draw a distinction between canisters that were "expired," meaning the ones they were removing, and canisters that were not "expended," meaning the same ones, loaded and ready to fire, on which they were now expected to put nonexistent caps. Also involved were canisters which were expired and expended, and others which were not expired but were expended.[73]

The NTSB report observes that most mechanics were Spanish speakers, but Langewiesche refuses the inference: "quite obviously the language problem lay on the other side with ValuJet and the narrowly educated English speaking engineers who wrote work orders and technical manuals as if they were writing to themselves."[74]

Recall Grant's categories of the "rusty" and "shiny sides of a plant," each loaded with priorities. Recall Brian's concerns with the meanings of safety-related and nonsafety-related.

> The biggest emphasis we have is on safety systems related to safe shutdown in case of an accident. But there's many systems out there that are equally as important. In fact, we just talked about this this morning. . . . [A fuse blew] and operators couldn't find one to fix it. Well, it isn't considered a category-one system [nuclear safety-related], it's not, I guess, really related to safe shutdown of the plant. So you look at it differently. But {voice rising} it can trip a plant, if you don't have the instrument working, it can cause all kinds of problems. . . . "Not related to safe shutdowns," but it's a high cost—it's something that you can't start the plant up without if they're not working right. . . . There's a lot of implications that you should look at these systems a lot differently than the way we used to.

"Looking differently" is the mandate of the NRC's significance determination process, whose outcome often effectively determines the cost of repair or replacement, including time off line. At any plant, the number and categories of safety-significant issues culminate in NRC's ratings of each plant's performance, which also interests market order: Wall Street and insurers take their cues from it. Insofar as risk-based criteria allow, lawyers for both owners and regulator will dominate this definitional process, parsing each term to retain negotiating rights.[75] But conventional industrial language escapes that kind of attention. After a spate of personnel errors at one U.S. station, the corrective actions staff asked forty-two people in various jobs and at several levels of management to suggest why. For one person it came down to Whorf's phrase—"the language habits of the group": "Our terminology puts 'hurry' in the minds of everyone: 'critical path,' 'hours behind,' 'hot maintenance work order.' "

Such semantics of control are among many unmeasurables exerting worldly influences against which there are no physical barriers. Aside from replacing the concepts the semantics express, the only defenses are wider margins for errors, more slack, delays among component interactions, expanded prejob briefs, and meaningful corrective actions. In the same vein, calling real-time logics "informal" or "unofficial" "adaptations" and "adjustments" semantically legitimates the supremacy of calculated logics, when in practice they are partners in fulfilling the technology's intentions. The backstage influence of French station experts is as much testimony to real-time logics' integrity as to the unwarranted and unquestioned dominance of calculated logics.

The industry's advice vocabulary gestures toward doubt and discovery in admonishments to "be alert, anticipatory, generative, learning, proactive, questioning, self-aware, transparent, vigilant."[76] Social scientists, human factors specialists, and regulators also intimate their value, for example, "searching for safety,"[77] "failures of foresight," "accident incubation,"[78] "resident pathogens,"[79] "heedful,"[80] "mindful."[81] "Precursors," "vigilance," "care," "attention" appear throughout industry and regulatory literature. That advice vocabulary is, however, not full-bodied: not itself questioning the one game going, its semantics leave intact the authoritative assumptions of calculated and policy logics and position real-time logics as a collection of untheorized practices. These are likely to be documented and analyzed more in terms of their failures than their successes, in terms of "cognitive bias" and "cognitive error," viewed as inherent human limitations, as in, for example, studies by Kenichi Takano, of the Human Factors Research Center at Japan's Central Research Institute of the Electric Power Industry, and James Reason, emeritus psychologist at the University of Manchester. From analyses of coded event reports in nuclear power plants, they find such "mechanisms" as the frequency bias (habitual action), similarity bias (matching to what is already known), confirmation bias (not seeking contrary evidence), salience bias (picking up on prominent indicators and ignoring others), recency or availability bias (equating a new occurrence with a previous one).[82] Alternatively, with the concept of "social rationality," Jens Rasmussen, a Danish industrial engineer, considers how experts with different perspectives and in different situations take a different "direction of inference" to understanding events: the "individual involved" as a situation unfolds who must take compensatory action; the "repair man" concerned with correcting the situation; and "the attorney" concerned with blame and penalties.[83] Over the last half-century, studies of real-time logics in ongoing situations outside of simulators, such as the Canadian control room studies, are rare.[84]

In any case, a sturdy platform of research from which to launch a systematic science of the real-time logics of control has yet to be built in this industry. For real-time logics to realize the full exercise of their saving graces as well as to prevent them from doing harm, we need to know much more than these three event chapters can tell about what it is people actually do and need to do, alone and with others, to reduce uncertainties and risks. Real-time logics represent intellectual capital whose benefits and costs, in dollars and in trust, have yet to be treated commensurably with their contribution.

Putting doubt and discovery on equal footing with command and control is ever more important in this industry's present and future. Widely believed to have moved through a long "shakedown" period to have arrived at a stage of stable operations, the industry's past and that future are otherwise: decades of essential design modifications without pause now overlap years to come of reactors whose licenses have been extended for another twenty years. Current fleets are uprating power output, upgrading aging equipment, and in some, decommissioning. Configuration control, the industry well knows, has to remain at the top of its agenda. To maintain that control requires the full partnership of calculated, real-time, and policy logics.

Standing in the Way: A System of Claims

Recall how Vince responded to my comment that outages are for finding glitches.

> No, no, no, no. Don't think that. 'Cause they'll run you right out of here. Outages, well, there's no time built into it for that. It always happens. You're talking about theory and reality here, that's the other thing. You're always going to find something unanticipated.

> *I thought that was the point.*

> No. The point is to change the fuel, fix what you know that needs to be fixed, and start it back up. That's the point. And there are certain things you're doing—disassemble, inspect, repair—but you're not supposed to find anything new, which you doubtless do.

Operations and outage managers at an industry workshop also see that theory and reality don't match up for their managers. They recommended that "two types of daily outage meetings should be held: one meeting just for plant management and one for departments. Attendance by the plant manager and/or site vice president has a tendency to restrict an honest discussion of the status of work during the outage." Another: "Most stations do not plan for worst-case scenarios in the outage, and it winds up impacting them. It would be nice if management would buy into the concept."

That bias against doubt and curiosity surfaces at Arrow Station (not radiographing the valve at the outset), and at Charles Station, in its hesitations to track down the source of an anomaly. And evident as well at Davis-Besse in not acting on industry and regulator warnings about nozzles and the reactor head. An industry study of its own black sheep in 1990 saw a "lack of introspection and ability to take a critical look at the operation," a situation that "can lead to a death-spiral effect: violations and regulatory noncompliances leading to ineffective and incomplete corrective actions leading to escalated enforcement actions and plant problems."[85] Those recent and "severe incidents" discussed at the WANO meeting in 2003 appear to be manifestations of that same pattern.

A "production mentality" with little patience for doubt and discovery is certainly a practical hurdle to rethinking the kind of problem it is to operate a nuclear power plant at least risk. But it is the conceptual hurdles that may account for that persistent pattern and for this industry's "collective way of thinking": the claims underpinning the current culture of control rest on assumptions about what converts ambiguity into certainty, how people and machines should relate, and how judgment and reason differ.

In this industry as elsewhere, numbers are the preferred route to actionable knowledge, but here, at the expense of substantive and systematic analyses of utility strategies and station tactics that could help to account for both events and nonevents, and, likely, suggest principled ways to reduce one and increase the other. Quantified evidence is, by definition, more reliably certain than qualitative evidence, the claim runs. Not for all technologists, of course: railing against "the tyranny of the quantitative and the illusion of the precise," Kenneth J. Bell, engineer and editor-in-chief of *Heat Transfer Engineering*, says that unlike scientists, engineers "are paid to make things work . . . and [while] we should—we must—make use of the best tools and information that the scientists can offer us . . . we use these with much other information (mostly qualitative, and never precise) for our own goals, which in the end are given value by society."[86]

In this industry, however, attempts to study industry strategies and tactics for fuller understandings of those contextual influences on risk reduction have all but come to naught. During a three-year research program during the 1980s, the NRC commissioned fourteen studies from academics, national laboratory experts, and industry consultants to develop criteria for indicators relating safe shutdown capabilities to utility and station policies and practices. Only one group was able to gain access to senior managers and utility executives. Coincidentally or not, NRC's funding for these studies was spotty over those years. Asked to characterize the "lessons learned" from doing NRC sponsored research, one study group commented that the "primary lesson . . . is that 'success is failure.' The better the research on the impact of organizational factors (success), the more likely the industry will put pressure on the NRC to cut the funding for future research (failure)." For another group, at "the upper management levels at NRC, there is a general distrust of the social sciences and behavioral science data. . . . Social scientists in an engineering world will always have a tough time."[87]

One obstacle is, of course, legal order: even if executives and managers were willing to discuss their strategies and tactics, they fear that their policies and practices could be vulnerable to charges of "management or operational imprudence." Or lost income may not be allowed as a production expense when it results from schedule delays defined as being within management control. Regulatory order and its penalties can also invite silence, not to mention how they discourage reporting and analyzing near-misses.[88] Legal order may also be narrowing this and other high hazard industries' concepts of risk handling. An industrial engineer at a regulatory agency abroad, versed in human factors studies of nuclear power plant operations, finds that the industry is about fifty years behind the intellectual times and, given issues of liability, "uptight" about the help nontechnical studies can offer.

> Naturally, I believe that we can go a long way generalizing what we already know from social psychology etc. to industrial safety management. This is going to be difficult, as much of industry is even now only just beginning to learn about postwar industrial psychology. Unfortunately, it appears to be somewhat fixated on "touchy-feely" stuff at the moment. . . . My experience so far with proposing knowledge tools to operations for defining relevant situational clues to possible dangers is that people are very uncomfortable with the generality of what can be summarized by way of simple quantifiable principles showing the relationship between these clues and error-making. They would much prefer to rely on their own judgment and experience and are pretty uptight about the possible implications for high hazard safety management. This is still a pretty taboo area for many in industry. Procedures are supposed to be followed in all instances and the fact that sometimes they might not be (and the fact that this is fairly predictable in terms of outcome and extent) is quite a difficult concept for both operators and regulators to grapple with at the moment. I think industry is coming round to the idea, but there will, of course, be far-reaching implications in terms of overall liability, which will need to be investigated both inside and outside any existing legal framework.

Claims about the relation between people and machines remain under the influence of the parts template. When the Institute of Nuclear Power Operators (INPO) began to promote its "human performance" program in the 1980s after the Three Mile Island accident, the focus was on reducing station experts' errors through work observation and task analysis, and people, some say, were seen as "programmed machines." Corrective actions had called mainly for "more training." By the early 1990s, the aims widened to include "error-forcing conditions"—the work-specific circumstances in which errors appear. These conditions, some of which the four event team reports cite as "causes," represent the customary concerns of industrial engineers with formalization, efficiency, optimization of task design, scheduling; of psychologists and cognitive and computer scientists with error types and the human-machine interface; of human factors specialists with eye-hand, cognitive, and ergonomic issues; of occupational safety experts with fatigue, hazards, stress; of training specialists with risk perception and work habits; of psychologists and social psychologists with team work and states of mind. Exhaustive as these condition lists are, naming them is not the same as analyzing the reasons why, in any situation, they appear in the first place. These conditions remain what I call a checklist theory of risk reduction, which, as now used, is unlikely to account systematically for their presence.

But those in this and other high hazard technologies are prone to dismissing those studies that can do so. After thirteen years of studying human error in aviation and space research, a group of cognitive and social psychologists at Ohio State University concludes that credible explanations of accidents and close calls must move from individuals' direct actions into the social and cultural conditions enveloping their work. Nevertheless, the group finds, its studies of all that lies "behind human error" have had remarkably little impact on industries, engineering groups that operate or develop systems, and regulatory bodies. Nor have they affected "decisions about how to manage technology change" or been part of "public debates over accidents and hazardous technologies." Instead, they say, "folk theories" about human error remain "quite prevalent in design and engineering and practitioner communities."[89]

Going "behind human error" is as daunting to others as it was to Keith. After managers restyled a corrective actions program at one U.S. nuclear station, at first, said Josh, assistant human resources director, "managers were nodding their heads, 'good idea,' and behind the scenes, they were trying to sabotage it." Two years later, even though the program began to find its footing, the station continued to base its root cause analyses and corrective actions mainly on equipment fixes.

> It's normal human nature not to want to have to do anything more than they had done in the past. They were all managers with engineering backgrounds. "It's going to take more of my people's time," they claimed, and they wanted to know "What's the value added?" They needed a measure they could understand, with equations and graphics. One day my boss asked me to look through recurring corrective actions—five years of data. We saw weaknesses in communication, supervision, procedures, and training but we hadn't been identifying other

issues. Then a new manager of human resources came into the corporate office, and with that high-level buy-in and senior executives getting more comfortable, that's challenged managers and workers who never had to think this way. Now, the corrective program resources are adequate, but we have not been effective in evaluating the program's consequences—we don't go far enough. A random sample of root cause analyses of level-one [safety significant] condition reports showed that the root cause process is designed for equipment, not for people issues. The program may give lip service to other issues, but the root cause reports don't say specifically what else is going on to provoke an error.

"Lip service" may be left over from an earlier time when some station managers saw as "witchhunting" any efforts to look beyond "what can be done to fix that person's head." "It's hard to get them to understand that the root cause and the person are two different things," says an event review team member at a U.S. station. The manager of a corrective action program at another, formerly a senior reactor operator, comments in an e-mail.

> We struggle with this area. Even yesterday, I was asked during an internal training session of managers and supervisors what a "defense-in-depth philosophy" for human performance means (asked in a derogatory manner). Several people haven't grasped or wouldn't recognize the organizational or cultural underpinnings of performance. If they have to explain human error, it's too hard, and they don't want to be bothered with it. (I'm venting.)

At one feedback session with members of Arrow Station's corrective action program, we discussed other event reports I'd asked them to select as representing what they saw as a blend of soft and hard issues. As we delved into several "philosophic issues" (their phrase), the program manager said, "This discussion is giving us the filling in the sandwich. We've got the two ends—we know what we're supposed to do and what it's supposed to result in. This is talking about what goes into that." Another person commented, "This is at an intellectual level higher than what we're used to around here," wistfully I choose to think, having had a few experiences with a "derogatory manner" and hearing those of others, even with feet in both technical and cultural camps. Over coffee at an international conference devoted to "safety culture," an experienced industry engineer (not from the U.S.) who is also a psychologist commented, "I've been shocked at the bitterness and hostility that many engineers who are here are showing toward the behavioral science presentations. I had thought that anyone coming to the IAEA for a meeting on this topic would be committed to improving the industry's approach to it." At another industry workshop, the manager of a corrective actions program who keeps in touch with his peers around the country commented:

> General managers think they know what the human performance program is based on, but they haven't grasped the idea of error-forcing conditions. Yet they think they're always right. They're looking at people the way they look at machines. The industry is doing better at not shooting the messenger [of bad news] immediately. They might wait a day now.

"Always right" and "folk theories" mean that for some, only calculated logics are allowed to matter. But there is also that profound intellectual animus toward "soft" unmeasurables. For "technical people," grappling with a station's "cultural problems" may be outside their competence yet unmistakably on their agenda; understandably, that frustration can result in some experts' hostility. The sources of this animus are, of course, deeply institutional, in hierarchies of knowledge perpetuated far outside a station's boundaries, which control, for example, the education and credentials of engineers and managers, and, which, by the same token, can keep those in the humanities and the human sciences from engaging intellectually with the peopled worlds of technologies.[90] The animus and the mismatch between the demands of risk reduction and competencies are also elements in the cultures of control in risky technologies to be reckoned with.

So is the persisting demand for cost/benefit analyses of any changes, as at Josh's station. "It's going to take more of my people's time," the managers at Josh's station said. Although policies dictate that changes must pass the value-added test, the bar for "people issues" is likely to be higher on the assumption that the benefits are less certain, compared to the presumed certainty of those of technical changes. Proposed corrective actions that do not also suggest the cost of *not* implementing them are, on the same grounds, susceptible to being ignored. At one U.S. station, several years after a master equipment list with tens of thousands of components had been computerized, the trending group and nuclear oversight found, that because so many fields were unfilled or filled with bad information, control room operators had to search out and cross-check information. Managers decided that the costs of amending the database were too high. After the trending group went ahead on its own and documented the time operators spent tracking down reliable information, managers agreed to support the clean-up effort.

When the rationale for any change is "to improve safety," it meets the plaintive conversation-stopper, "How much safety is enough?" On the one hand, and all to the good for joining theory to reality, the question acknowledges that risk estimation is imperfect and that control can be problematic. On the other, it assumes that "safety" can be measured or that enough is already known about what it takes to reduce risk and recover successfully from mishaps. And it assumes that the tradeoff quandary need be negotiated only once and for all. Chemical process safety experts at a workshop with a varied group of academics made another kind of plea. When recommending process improvements to their managers for reducing risks they had observed, they could articulate the issues, technical principles, and possible outcomes but, unable to quantify their benefits, they could not get managers' approvals. "Can you tell us how to help managers become more comfortable with ambiguity?" None of this is to say, however, that such unmeasurables as professional standards and ethics do not often prevail on the basis of principle and best practice alone, but only that the cost/benefit hurdle usually has first to be overcome.

Crystallizing the Difference: Numbers and Values

At a meeting of the NRC's Advisory Committee on Reactor Safeguards (ACRS), Mark Cunningham, an NRC staff member, was discussing the kinds of criteria that would guide the new risk-based safety significance determination process, which is the centerpiece of the reactor oversight process. The NRC's goal, he said, is the same as that of the NRC's previously "deterministic" approach based on specified thresholds and standards, namely, the "reasonable assurance of adequate protection of the public health and safety." "Will the public health and safety be better or worse as a result?" asked committee member Graham Wallis. Cunningham replied, "We expect . . . as the words say . . . that we will have reasonable assurance that it is protected." "Dr. Wallis: That's not good enough. Unless you have a metric . . . you have no idea if the new . . . is any better than the old . . . and reasonable assurance doesn't mean anything to me. . . . Unless you have answers which are quantitative, you are just invoking words." Gary Holahan of the Division of Regulatory Improvements in the NRC's research group took up that point.

> We've talked for a long time with this committee and a lot of other people in coming to a consensus on how to use not only quantitative risk assessment, but to bring other valuable safety concepts, like defense-in-depth and safety margins, which are sometimes quantitative, but frequently qualitative, into the decision-making process . . . I don't think that we want to be or that we are on the course to converting all of our safety decisions into numerical criteria. . . . There are valued safety concepts which are not necessarily numerical risk calculations.[91]

In quarterly assessments of overall plant performance, the reactor over-sight process juxtaposes on-site inspections with quantitative perfor-mance indicators that each station furnishes unit by unit. That rating de-termines the REGULATORY RESPONSE: whether the NRC will maintain or intensify its basic level of oversight. The ratings range from "very low safety significance" to "high safety significance," each "band" color-coded: green, "no additional regulatory response"; white, "increased reg-ulatory response"; yellow, "required regulatory response"; and red, "un-acceptable performance."[92] A distinction between measurables and un-measurables is basic to the way the NRC arrives at that assessment, which influences local cultures of control.

Four intersecting constructs determine the data used in NRC's plant ratings: CORNERSTONES, PERFORMANCE INDICATORS AND INSPECTION FINDINGS, RISK-INFORMED REGULATION, and CROSS-CUTTING AREAS.[93]

1. SEVEN CORNERSTONES OF PUBLIC HEALTH AND SAFETY The corner-stones contain the physical, chemical, and material resources and pro-cesses that enable a plant's experts to assure safe shutdown and maintain dose control. *Initiating events* (limit the number of unplanned scrams); *mitigating systems* (assure the availability of backup systems); *barrier in-tegrity* (maintain the three primary physical barriers); *emergency pre-paredness* (ensure public safety in a radiological emergency); *occupational radiation safety* (control dose exposure); *public radiation safety* (protect from radiological exposure and routine and inadvertent releases and maintain safe offsite transport of radioactive materials and wastes); and *physical protection* (safeguards against radiological sabotage, internal/external).

2. PERFORMANCE INDICATORS Quarterly, stations report numerical self-assessments of the condition and performance of the specific elements composing each cornerstone in each plant. The NRC measures these against threshold numbers established partly through benchmarking studies the Nuclear Energy Institute conducted at a sample of operating stations.[94] For example, any plant not exceeding the benchmarked thresh-old of 3 unplanned scrams will be coded green; more than 3, white; more than 6, yellow; more than 25, red. Combined with NRC's baseline inspec-tion findings, these make up NRC's quarterly evaluation cornerstone by cornerstone, published on its website. Plants with more than one corner-stone rated below green are subject to additional levels of oversight and/or requirements.[95]

3. RISK-INFORMED The NRC's rationale for introducing performance indicators and the concept of "risk-informed" to replace the "determinis-tic" regulation of the past is that indicators are "objective." "Performance indicators have objective, risk-informed thresholds that identify outliers from nominal industry performance so that deficiencies can be identified

and corrected before they pose an undue risk to public health and safety."
But objectivity has its limits and those keep the door open to "subjectiv-
ity." "The thresholds for some . . . are based on changes in risk from
[PRA] sensitivity analyses. Other thresholds that cannot be assessed using
PRA models are tied to regulatory requirements . . . or are based on the
expert judgment of NRC internal and external stakeholders."[96]

The risk-based approach effectively identifies only those conditions that
indicators and inspections show to need increased attention. Inpections
now check off a shorter list of equipment and processes, a change that
meets one of the NRC's own goals: to reduce its own and station owners'
operating costs.[97]

4. CROSS-CUTTING AREAS Three programs affecting all cornerstones
are zoned into these cross-cutting areas: *human performance* (error prevention and recovery); *management attention to safety and to workers'
ability to raise safety issues* (employee concerns program); *finding and
fixing problems* (corrective action programs). Together with the NRC's
expectation of "management's commitment to safety," these programs accumulate into the regulatory framework for "safety culture."

On the grounds that the conduct and outcomes of these programs are
necessarily "implicit" in the cornerstone indicators, the NRC does not
require stations to meet thresholds or report numerical performance
indicators.

> Licensee deficiencies in these cross-cutting areas manifest themselves as perfor-
> mance issues in the cornerstones and are often the root causes of the issues. The
> NRC reviews ["Problem Identification and Resolution" programs, or corrective
> actions programs] as part of baseline inspections and during a biennial team
> inspection. The establishment of a safety-conscious work environment [em-
> ployee concerns] is monitored throughout the year by the NRC resident staff,
> through review of [employee] allegations, and as part of the PI&R biennial team
> inspection. While there is no specific NRC inspection for human performance, it
> is reviewed as part of a number of baseline inspections and is implicit in the
> data reported for many of the performance indicators.[98]

That definition appeared in a June 2002 revision of this Reactor Oversight Process Handbook. The Davis-Besse event of March 2002 revealed,
however, that the plant's green rating had not recognized the "implicit"
and longstanding "deficiencies" in regulation and self-regulation, which
the vessel head event revealed. Every cornerstone's performance indicator
had passed muster, when, among other nonactions, corrective actions
written in 1999 and 2000 to clean up boric acid on the head had not
been made.

Whether NRC inspectors would have been allowed to pick up on the
performance of these programs in its inspectors' "qualitative" observa-

tions is, in any case, doubtful. The NRC's inspectors' manual, as of January 29, 2004, allows that there can be a "Substantive Cross-Cutting Issue," "as evidenced by a significant number of current inspection findings in programs for human performance, problem identification and resolution, or safety-conscious working environment."[99] The NRC's "presumption [is] that plants which had significant performance issues with cross-cutting areas" would reveal them through cornerstones' "safety-significant" performance indicators and inspection findings. Absent that, "there must be a significant level of concern in the licensee's ability or progress in addressing the cross-cutting area performance deficiency if the agency [NRC] believes that there is a substantive cross-cutting issue at a plant."[100] To make that case, the manual first requires that inspectors tie evidence of deficiencies to specific elements of a cornerstone, and then only after meeting several rigorous criteria are inspectors allowed to describe a "substantive" condition in an official letter report to the NRC.

Given that their plant inspections customarily include their "qualitative" observations, soon after the new oversight process began in 2000, NRC's resident and special inspectors expressed concern about this issue. Although NRC's assessments "allow a qualitative discussion of distinct adverse trends, as indicated by substantial cross-cutting issues," that discussion may not also result in "increased NRC [enforcement] action" in a cornerstone "unless [its quantitative] performance indicators have crossed a threshold or [there are] significant inspection findings." Even so, this internal report concluded a year later, NRC inspectors do "not have sufficient criteria, thresholds, and definitions of cross-cutting issues to ensure consistency in handling" them.

> [Nor is there a] predefined NRC action if the inspection program identifies a substantive crosscutting issue such as a deficient corrective action program. The [reactor oversight process] does not provide for additional NRC engagement on cross-cutting issues unless they are contributing causes to performance indicators or inspection findings that have been characterized as White or greater. Some inspectors are also concerned about the lack of a process to handle low-level human performance trends when it appears that NRC actions could prevent the occurrence of a significant performance issue. The industry believes the [reactor oversight process] should focus on [cornerstone] performance outcomes, of which cross-cutting issues are but one possible cause.[101]

To translate: NRC inspectors want to be able to issue warnings when cornerstone conditions or performance in cross-cutting areas send early signals of "substantive" troubles. The industry wants to limit NRC's qualitative observations: when combined with a cornerstone's numerical threshold rating, as they are intended to be, these could affect a plant's overall quarterly rating. That rating interests not only the public, but Wall

Street and insurers as well. "Low-level" trends may fester until self-regulation voluntarily picks up on their presence or until they become sources of "high-level" conditions impossible to ignore, as in "severe incidents."

The NRC and the industry nevertheless already know that unmeasurables can be problematic for performance. From 1986 to 2000, whenever the NRC's previous oversight regime concluded that program trend data pointed to "management problems," its senior staff followed up with "diagnostic inspections" of station documents and on-site discussions. Nine NRC inspection reports on "executive management" practices at several stations, written between 1987 and 1991, illustrate unmeasurable issues, which the NRC identified as "root causes": decision-making authority for staying on line at too high a level; equipment problem priorities not established; weak self-assessment; strategic plans emphasized new plant construction over improvements in existing plant; initiatives were developed in reaction to NRC or INPO findings, not via self-assessments; poor departmental and corporate communications; production mindset; business diversification; inaction due to management turnover; repetitive problems not addressed; unintegrated management information system; focus on material conditions problems; maximum delegation at low levels; conflicting management estimates of manpower levels and slow hiring. Among the "failure modes" the NRC reports also cite are strategic planning misjudgments, unclear expectations, buying the wrong technology, departmental conflicts, and business plan execution.[102] INPO speaks of "leadership" and "organizational" "weaknesses" in its re-analyses of selected significant events circulated once or twice a year to members and to the NRC, but the few I have seen stay clear of substantive specifics.

Indicators of cornerstone performance are necessarily after-the-fact or "lagging indicators." Inferences about lapses in any of the three cross-cutting programs drawn from those indicators alone may not be timely enough to minimize the duration of their unwanted consequences. "Leading indicators," such as those observed "root causes" and "failure modes," instead warn of the possibility of less than optimum outcomes. The NRC had not inferred from Davis-Besse's cornerstone indicators that anything was amiss: no metric had led it to be concerned with, for example, its managers' repeated neglect of NRC's and INPO's bulletins about nozzle leaks. Nor are inferences likely to pinpoint specific issues, leaving the NRC unsure of "making the right changes" in the scope and substance of its oversight program. Those are likely to involve the "cultural issues and organizational issues" which the NRC has "forbidden" the Advisory Committee on Reactor Safeguards to include in PRA studies, its then chairman, George Apostolakis, reminded the commissioners.[103] The committee further pointed out in a letter to the NRC operations staff that the NRC "has developed its Reactor Oversight Program with the untested hypothesis that degradation of human performance will be detected in a timely way by degradation in plant performance indicators. We remain concerned that this hypothesis may be in error. . . . The NRC may want to follow a program undertaken by the Electric Power Research Institute to find leading indicators of human performance degradation."[104] That untested hypothesis follows from the NRC's and the industry's conviction that activities and outcomes of the three cross-cutting programs are not unequivocally "technical" because, being unquantifiable, they cannot be evaluated "objectively."

The very concerns of each cross-cutting program—reducing operational risk, open listening, and finding and correcting problems—nevertheless validate or call into question the solidity of technical cornerstones for the public and the industry alike. For the public the fact remains that its only deputized witnesses and sources of information about local conditions are NRC on-site inspectors, special inspectors, biennial baseline inspections of these and other programs, and quarterly plant ratings, those being developed partly from performance indicators that stations themselves supply.[105] The Institute of Nuclear Power Operations' peer assessments occur every two years and in any case are not made public, and even then, insiders say, peers make "really sensitive criticisms" orally.

As things stand, the designated responsibility for raising cautions ahead of time falls to each station's self-assessments and the "quality assurance" and "oversight" groups established under the same statutory requirement as mandates the corrective actions program. NRC's oversight process makes these groups' levels of authority, credibility, influence, and resources even more pivotal to self-regulation.

In concept and execution, this regime continues to make issue-by-issue fixes inevitable: tieing the conditions of the three cross-cutting programs to the condition of a specific cornerstone turns them into another kind of "part." In this technically correct discourse, the weight of "cornerstones" contrasts with the airiness of "cross-cutting areas," and while that appears to acknowledge that they are integral to maintaining control, it denies that the qualitative conditions of these programs per se are as amenable to systematic analysis as are cornerstones. This oversight process perpetuates issue-bopping, reinforces the parts template, and strengthens silos. Unless self-regulation consciously overcomes those handicaps, any or all are likely to be implicated in events and in ineffective or unimplemented corrective actions.

Objective and Subjective, Technical and Substantive

After the NRC's own report on the Davis-Besse event documented a history of missteps by both NRC staff and FirstEnergy's executives, including inadequate condition analyses, Ashok Thadani, director of NRC's

Office of Nuclear Regulatory Research, urged that as a technical matter, the NRC consider engaging with, in my terms, policy logics, with respect to criteria for conducting corrective action programs: "Though management and supervision have been shown to be contributors to events . . . the commission directed the staff not to pursue new work in this area until sufficient evidence is developed to serve as a technical basis for modifying this policy. We should discuss whether there is sufficient basis now to develop a position for commission consideration." Finding the hole in the Davis-Besse reactor head, Thadani says, is an "example of how recurrent failures for which thorough root cause analyses are not performed or completely understood and addressed can lead to significant problems."[106] That suggests that, measurable or not, analyses of managerial omissions and commissions belong in event reviews, to try to prevent their recurrence and to provide the basis for effective corrective actions. Whether NRC will rethink its oversight regime's strict limitations on what qualifies as "technical" knowledge remains to be seen, now that it has abandoned the idea of regulating "safety culture."

More fundamentally, distinctions between technical and substantive, objective and subjective, do not conceptually account for nuclear power production as a human and machined system. It cannot be understood otherwise in a production technology that depends on its experts' experience and knowledge to achieve near-constant foresight and control over their own activities and over interactions among assemblies, structures, and components, safety-related and nonsafety-related. How do we think about such complex systems and the information they use and produce to remain viable? Between the Second World War and the 1970s, "systems and systems thinking" depended on "energetic" and "informational" interactions among system constituents. According to Michael D. Gordin and Sam Schweber, historians of science, respectively at Harvard University and at Brandeis University, energetic interactions "are amenable to description in terms of physico-chemical processes," and while the "concept of informational interaction is intuitively clear . . . [it is] much more difficult to formulate and formalize mathematically."[107] Until "various notions of information content and information transfer" were developed after 1970, systems analysts were unable, for example, to "extract and characterize mathematically the information structure" underlying exogenous variables clearly affecting those interactions.[108] Any technology system, by definition working as a "symbiotic whole," Gordin and Schweber suggest, necessarily incorporates "external conditions into internal states of the system."

It is precisely when policy makers perceive the system to be essentially independent of the external environment (not, of course, from the environment it interacts with in the sense of input-output relations, but from the environment, human and social, in which it is embedded) that some of the weaknesses of systems thinking are displayed.[109]

Those weaknesses are particularly apparent, the authors say, when applying the systems approach to contexts whose "information structure" has not mattered analytically in the ways that it matters practically in those contexts. That seems to characterize the NRC's understandings of this production system, framed by its "energetic" cornerstones' internal inputs and outputs excerpted for the purposes of risk estimation and regulation from "human and social" contexts that demonstrably can affect safety margins and risk levels.

For thinking about systematic properties, a concept of "part-whole dialectics" not only acknowledges the continual "interpenetration" of interactive energetics and informational structures. It also helps to account for a system's unpredictability. The population ecologists Richard Levins and Richard Lewontin introduce that concept to explain the development of plant and animal life in context and over time. First, "a whole is a relation of heterogeneous parts that have no prior independent existence *as parts*." Second, "the properties of parts . . . are acquired by being parts of a particular whole." Third, this "interpenetration of parts and wholes is a consequence of the interchangeability of subject and object, of cause and effect." Their mutual influence transmutes the one into the other as "opposing processes [that] are part of the self-regulation and development of the object." In highly complex biological systems, these processes are "dynamically unstable," and systems will "show spontaneous activity" even when they may have been "generated by deterministic processes." Thus it is that parts acquire properties from the whole.[110] The fact that complex, high hazard technologies "show spontaneous activity" that surprises the determinations of calculated logics is just what has to be explained after events and accidents. Then "objects" become "subjects," and "effects" may become "causes," to reveal the myriad ways in which those interpenetrations are inevitably greater than the sums of these systems' parts.

Certainty and Ambiguity, Doubt and Discovery

Technologists' longstanding ambivalence toward collaboration with specialists in human factors and ergonomics is also a consequence of their claims about the relationship between certainty and ambiguity. Or, not at all ambivalent: often enough to be noticeable, technologists dismiss those specialists' contributions entirely.[111] In his intellectual history of human factors and ergonomics, David Meister, cognitive psychologist and member of the first generation after World War II to enter these specialties, chides his fields' "inability to translate behavioral principles into hardware requirements."[112] The "inability" is on the other side: technologists' inability to acknowledge that unspoken claims about the relationship of humans and machines, ambiguity and certainty, and models and reality are already embedded within their calculated logics and hardware designs, as well as the inability to recognize that "behavioral principles" or real-time logics make it possible for hardware to make good its designers' intentions.[113] As things stand, though, the best bet for getting "behavioral principles" recognized *is* to put a hardware label on them. When chemical process safety engineers could not get senior managers to fund a program to study "human factors" in operational issues, they renamed it a "human factors technology program." Then managers signed on.

When PRA experts confront field-based evidence—what control room operators actually do, for example—they are likely to call it "information" rather than "data," the latter having the strict meaning of *numbers*, which, they well understand, are required for talking to design engineers.[114] Even as PRA experts may welcome substantive information for insights about specific conditions or dynamics, their modeling methods will ultimately torture "information" into metrics. Those become a "technology of distance," as Theodore Porter, historian of science and technology at the University of California at Los Angeles puts it. That is, trends and rates are by definition experience-distant (based on past data), anomalies are by definition experience-near (current observations and contextual information).[115] Reduced to shadows of themselves, the meanings—the significance—of the knowledge and practices at issue disappear. When trying to define pointed actions, those meanings have to be found anew.

The claim that "data" consist only of "the numbers" became central to the loss of the *Columbia* shuttle in 2003, when engineers' warnings of possible structural damage from foam strike incidents on a shuttle wing went unheeded. At a public hearing of the Columbia Accident Investigation Board, Sheila Widnall, a board member, astrophysicist, and Institute Professor at MIT, raised the question of numbers and data in terms of the "issue of how an organization that states that safety is its No. 1 mission can apparently transition from a situation where it's necessary to prove that it's safe to fly, to one in which apparently you have to prove that it's not safe to fly."

> I think what's happening is, in fact, that engineers are following the rules but this underlying rule is that you have to have the numbers. . . . So that basically means that [the details of] every flight becomes data and that concern about an anomaly is not [trend] data. . . . So the accumulation of that data, of those

successful flights, puts the thumb on the scale that says it's safe to fly, and people who have concerns . . . in one of these uncertain situations . . . don't have the data. So I think it may be getting at, in some sense, changing the rule to one that [says] it is not okay to continue to operate with anomalies, that the underlying rule of just having data is not sufficient to run an organization that deals with risky technologies. Because otherwise you're just going to end up with a pile of data that says it's okay to fly, and you're not likely to get much data on the other side.[116]

Similarly, at Charles Station, when managers and station experts confronted the thermographic evidence, they did not treat it as its own kind of "information" but gave priority to the accumulated "numbers" of incidents involving circulating current.

These pronounced distinctions between hard and soft and quantitative and qualitative knowledge and evidence are as material to—as influential upon—the ways this industry understands and defines its culture of control as are any other constraints it and we live with. When technologists set aside the demand for metrics and drop their guard to talk about what they call their "soft-edged" issues, executives, managers, and station experts are obviously cogent observers and interpreters of their milieu and its issues. Whether they consider the time required to "step back," and to "punt and think and stop," as Jay recommends, for reconsidering substantive issues to be unproductive overhead or on a par with directly producing electricity is, as at Bowie Station, an open question.

Acknowledging, even if not accepting, that state of affairs seems necessary to make way for conversations about alternative "collective ways of thinking." There are some openings. When events spoil engineering's romance with perfection and precision, those in high hazard industries who are aware of their idealist bent are dismayed but not surprised. They know there is much waiting to be known about reducing operating risk and handling it effectively. And to do that, they will say, "We need to get out of our box," but not so far out as to lose their footing—for our sake as well. Perhaps the principle of *doubt and discovery* and all that precedes and follows from it, already animating a below-stairs second game, stays enough within that box to allow for stepping farther into the world.

Chapter Six

Intellectual Capital for Regulation and Self-Regulation

THE ROUTE *Shouldering Risks* has been taking circles around and into a "reverse salient," a condition in an energized system when components "have fallen behind or are out of phase" and are "in need of attention, such as drag, limits to potential, emergent friction." Reverse salients often inspire engineers toward innovations and inventions, according to Thomas P. Hughes, historian of technology and emeritus professor at the University of Pennsylvania.[1] The "reverse salient" here, by industry experts' own accounts, consists of improvements that don't improve, improvements that aren't realized, and disconnects between theory and practice in design and in operations.[2] And to that add less public trust than the industry hopes for and that we expect it to merit.

By revisiting what has seemed to be a settled question—what it takes to operate and maintain a nuclear power plant at least risk—this book has been exploring the ways of thinking and kinds of knowledge on which that depends: industry experts' ways of understanding a complicated and hazardous technology, the concepts on which they rely, their ways of comprehending their own mistakes and the technology's malfunctions, the kinds of evidence they credit—all those and more in the context of physical, social, political, and financial dynamics bringing the world into their work. As an anthropology of knowledge and meanings, this necessarily is also an anthropology of one risky technology in operation. The metaphysical question of how any of us know what we know is, in this and other risky technologies, practical and portentous. For engineers, generating more knowledge "is not the primary concern" as it is for scientists, claims Walter Vincenti, professor emeritus of aeronautics and astronautics at Stanford University.[3] But generating knowledge and interpreting its significance are by default the paramount concerns of all who anticipate and handle the risks of operating high hazard technologies.

At Charles Station, its experts questioned whether an event was in the making, and after viewing the thermograms, they decided on a proven troubleshooting strategy that dissipated transformer hot spots. Had they recognized that the hot spot was behind two boxes, as Phil did in hindsight (or had a thermography expert pointed that out to them), they all might have been, as he said, "running out of the room screaming." Stable practice, however reliable, says Philip Scranton, historian of industry and technology at Rutgers University, has an ambiguous relation to both failure and novelty.

> Unless practitioners have transdisciplinary competencies (within and beyond engineering), stable practice encourages thinking inside the box about failures and then, perhaps, when the box is unresponsive, a washing of hands and blaming of others (persons, institutions, knowledges). This of course is a profoundly social practice, and a political one as well when power and capital are at stake.

Getting outside the box is equally important in seeking innovations. Then, stable practices undergo "the punishing and stimulating give and take of the conference room, confrontations with component fabricators, or negotiations with corporate vice presidents or federal agencies. Workers, contractors, and funders also have reliable knowledge of matters germane to technical practice [and then] engineering creativity emerges, fully as much as when engineers reflect on foundational knowledge [axioms, algorithms]."[4] After about two hours of give and take, with none that was "punishing," and without reflecting on a "significance and consequence algorithm" or hearing from those experienced in reading thermograms, experts let two risky steps pop out of Charles Station's box of stable practice: verifying the thermograms' images with hand-held pyrometers and taking an infrared reading at a bolt hole. Their wait-and-see tactic put at least several people face-to-face with very high risk and shook station experts' trust in themselves.

A 1995 MIT report based on field studies of nuclear power plant operations, of which I was co-author, stepped outside the box with its suggestion that, to acknowledge overlaps and interdependencies in station activities, an ecological model might replace a machine bureaucracy model and its "silos."[5] Thinking functionally can lead to compartmentalized knowledge, when circumstances require otherwise, as the event at Arrow Station illustrates. "INPO and the NRC have, to a large degree, adopted the military model of the Nuclear Navy," comments Martin, scientist and lawyer who represents nuclear power utilities in a letter responding to the report. "The result is that licensees are reinforced in their use of a machine bureaucracy model even if they would prefer an alternative better suited to attaining the cooperation and communication that are necessary for continued safe operation."[6] The NRC's then-oversight regime fosters "departmentally compartmentalized self-assessment methodologies. . . . Will the new regulatory regime being developed increase licensee ability to adopt ecological, open system organizations?" And to what extent, Martin continues, might NRC and INPO have been "creating expectations" of "organizational structures and managerial strategies and policies that in their effect promote operational difficulties and unsafe behaviors?" The new regime perpetuates these aspects of the old, obviously.

A highly complicated and tightly coupled system of artifacts and people makes unusual knowledge demands: the knowledge of many specialists has to coalesce around any number of issues during the various operational phases. Keeping Martin's question of "structures and strategies" open for the moment, this chapter begins by considering the relations among kinds of knowledge on which this culture of control depends for configuration control and in event reviews. It ends with a thought experiment to re-imagine one with the specific aim of reducing the frequency of good intentions that have disappointing if not threatening outcomes, and along the way, also affect the "cooperation and communication" configuration control requires.

Controlling and Coordinating Knowledge

Cooperation and communication are largely the province of CONTROL-LING DOCUMENTS. Standing out in the forests of station documents, those are a prime element of the culture of control. Manuals, handbooks, and procedures lay out thousands of regulatory, operational, and administrative requirements in a hierarchy of obligation, from "required" to "expected," all in the service of maintaining configuration control and electricity production. Over all of those is each station's unique CONDUCT OF OPERATIONS that translates the requirements of technical specifications, license provisions, NRC requirements, and the defense-in-depth principle into a chain of command. In about fifty pages and written to be compatible with a company's business plan, a Conduct of Operations defines policies, positions, responsibilities, authorities, and tasks of executives and senior managers, and specifies the duties and interdepartmental relations of the operations department. Less official are "Nuts and Bolts" maintenance handbooks for "desktop guidance," which memorialize station-specific rubrics and handy hints of trades, crafts, and professions. Like the "detailed handbooks, trouble-shooting trees and rules of thumb" accumulated during the development of the F-4 Phantom jet, these represent specific real-time logics found trustworthy.[7] Documents control every activity of the dozens of programs for operating, testing, trending, inspections, and repair, which execute what this industry understands to be its "core processes" and its "enabling processes." Each department takes the lead in coordinating those under its wing with others; when managers "reorganize," it is usually to redistribute or rearrange program content and responsibilities among specialists.

OPERATE
PLANT

CORE PROCESSES

CONFIGURATION CONTROL
 DESIGN CHANGES
 FUEL MANAGEMENT
 DECOMMISSIONING

WORK MANAGEMENT
 PLANNING
 SCHEDULING
 PREVENTIVE/CORRECTIVE MAINTENANCE
 RADIATION/CONTAMINATION CONTROL

EQUIPMENT RELIABILITY
 LONG-TERM MAINTENANCE
 SURVEILLANCE AND TESTING
 PREDICTIVE MAINTENANCE

MATERIALS AND SERVICES
 INVENTORY
 CONTRACTING
 PROCUREMENT
 FUEL TRANSPORT AND DISPOSAL

ENABLING PROCESSES

SUPPORT SERVICES
 INFORMATION TECHNOLOGY
 HUMAN RESOURCES
 COMMUNITY/GOVERNMENT RELATIONS
 FACILITIES

LOSS PREVENTION
 SECURITY
 SELF-ASSESSMENT
 CORRECTIVE ACTIONS
 EMERGENCY PLANNING
 FIRE PROTECTION

TRAINING
 DEVELOP
 CONDUCT
 ATTEND

NUCLEAR POWER PLANT STANDARD PROCESS MODEL
AFTER NUCLEAR ENERGY INSTITUTE 2000

Long stowed inside the boxes of this industry's stable practices, the details of program requirements and the knowledge about system conditions they use and produce (test results, inspection and repair history, scheduled maintenance, work orders, backlogs, as-built drawings, mode changes) are now more accessible and more capable of being up to date, coordinated among programs, and circulated efficiently, thanks to computerization. But despite directives, programs can also be, as at Davis-Besse, not only uncoordinated but ineffective: those responsible for about five programs spread among different functions responsible for various activities on or around the reactor head had not called attention to its condition.

Event cause codes would chalk that up to "poor communication." But analytically this industry recognizes "communication" less as a matter of knowledge distribution than as one of clarity and precision in verbal and written communications, such as volume of speech, commonly misheard words, message receipt, verification, and word choices in memos, for example.[8] That sender-receiver model is too limited for the work of control, however, as these comments of several Overton Station experts attest.

> You may know an item of information, but what it means to operations, what the ramifications are, aren't discussed. We need to consult and negotiate.
>
> The twists and turns of running a nuclear power plant, you have to let each hand know, there are so many hands involved. We hold meetings to be sure that interdependencies are explained—people complain about meetings.
>
> People need to find the time and develop the skills to talk about their assumptions and lay out the risks they see. We need to help people to discuss their assumptions.
>
> At the backshift turnover, ops pulled out without talking to anyone about what had been going on. We need to get people talking. They're not there just to fix a valve.

Face-to-face prejob briefs, like hand-offs and shift turnovers, are crucial to maintaining control. Designated a barrier in the defense-in-depth system, only the Conduct of Operations defines this task. At Bowie Station, Greg, formerly a shift supervisor, talks about the overly brief prejob brief Alex held with Ned.

GREG: Everyone's required to know what's in the Conduct of Operations.

They are?

Even Ops technical support knows it.

If you can know all this.

We say, "You should have known this because the Conduct of Operations says it right there." It's almost an administrative procedure, it's pretty big, pretty thick, but you're required to know that.

Does it come with an index?

In the first chapter.

Documents in the hierarchy may themselves be uncoordinated. Cal, a member of Charles Station's corrective action program staff, discusses the relation between the Conduct of Operations and procedures.

What is the status of the Conduct of Operations as a controlling document? How do you think of it?

Ummm. It's supposed to be the philosophies that we use to operate with, providing guidance and instructions if there isn't anything specifically written in a procedure or for things that aren't necessarily covered in the procedure.

Do you think there's ever a time when you would have liked a Conduct of Operations guidance item or philosophy to be in a procedure to make its rationale clearer?

Well, in the event that I'm investigating now, there's a Conduct of Operations statement that says, "During an unplanned plant transient, do not initiate outward rod withdrawal." They pulled control rods to stabilize the plant, and so they were kind of using the procedure that governs it. But then you've got the Conduct of Operations that says, "Don't do this." So they were trying, number one, to rationalize, "Well, were they still in the unplanned plant transient, or was the transient over and now they're trying to stabilize?" Does the procedure really follow that guideline, you know, "Don't pull control rods" or not? So if that guideline had been shared and communicated and that philosophy had been put into the procedure, I wouldn't be doing an event review. . . . And then too, the Conduct of Operations is a kind of a global thing that you can't really pin down or nail down in a procedure necessarily. Such as the peer checking or the prejob brief type of stuff, and we've got reactivity management philosophy in there. . . .

In effect, are you saying that you couldn't carry out the procedure correctly unless you augmented it with the guidance from the Conduct of Operations?

That is one of our actions—it's going to be one of our corrective actions, to review the Conduct of Operations and look for things that would provide guidance that might or should go into a procedure.

The multiplicity of controlling documents and of their sources of authority itself poses a problem of controlling their relationships within the functional division of labor mapped by the Conduct of Operations and its chain of command. These elements of the culture of control can get in the way of the development, circulation, and interpretation of the reliable knowledge on which configuration control depends.

Layered within those elements is the legacy of the project mode of thinking that has guided every plant's years of construction ("South Texas Project," for example, remains the name of one operating plant). Building a nuclear power plant is among the largest of heroic projects in size, cost, and duration. Overton, a two-unit station producing 2,500 megawatts at full power, took ten years to build; the cost for technology, land, and construction was $3.6 billion. From excavating through to assembling, aggregating, and federating its many parts, project management techniques piloted experts through years of construction constraints and contingencies. Likely to have begun their careers during a plant's construction, those now in influential positions exchanged those uncertainties for uncertainties in maintaining configuration control. These are, however, not phase-limited but ongoing. A lingering project template meshed with a machine bureaucracy can impede the continual exchange and synthesis of specialists' knowledge that reducing the uncertainties of configuration control requires.

"What kinds of organizational structures and managerial strategies and policies could reduce operational difficulties and unsafe behaviors?" asks Martin. Any scaffolding would have to support that continual coordination and synthesis of specialists' knowledge essential to reducing the uncertainties of configuration control. That relationship between uncertainty, knowledge for reducing it, and organizational arrangements and strategies has preoccupied Arthur L. Stinchcombe, emeritus professor of sociology at Northwestern University. From his studies of industrial history, Stinchcombe finds that the structures "of organizations, and of parts of organizations, vary according to the sorts of uncertainties they confront." They vary therefore in terms of the "sources of information they depend on" and by "how that information is best got to the decision-making units." Structures and strategies, history reveals, "grow toward sources of news, news about the uncertainties that most affect their outcomes."[9] In the high hazard industry Stinchcombe studied, the Norwegian State Oil Company or Statoil, which designs, builds, and operates rigs in the North Sea for drilling wells and extracting and processing oil and gas, coordination during operations changed little from that in place during construction. For example, in "the last stage of building, what the construction or fabrication people need to know about a change is only what activities they need to do to change it; what the operators and especially maintenance people need to know is how it looks at the end—the 'as-built' drawings and technical data-sheets and spare parts list." This project management template makes operational orphans of as-builts: although that documentation is "crucial for operations," for the project template "it is merely one last bit of paperwork." No longer having "strong motives" and "a strong sense of responsibility to provide quality information," the project template lets as-builts fall between the cracks and accumulate into backlogs. Then when operators and maintenance experts need to know quickly and unambiguously how a component or assembly is configured in place, they are out of luck.[10] The same backlogs often appear in the nuclear power industry.[11]

Managerial strategies that emphasize "people-driving" are irrelevant to assuring the kinds and flow of information needed to reduce uncertainties, Stinchcombe says. "The first idea we have to get *out* of our minds is the 'people-driving' view of what modern management is about." That is because "organization theorists have very little idea of what there is [for managers] to talk about (or write or calculate about), where such information has to flow and why." We know "very little" about how "the hierarchy that appears on the organization chart [relates] to the total flow of communication, because we cannot easily imagine what the communications are other than supervision."[12] Management concerns and commitments need to be reframed to support getting, giving, evaluating, and analyzing information to reduce particular uncertainties, rather than to focus on issuing orders and monitoring work, Stinchcombe is saying. To manage is to manage that *process* of linking information to relevant uncertainties. Out of those linkages and the resources to support them, enterprises develop their internal arrangements, Stinchcombe finds.[13]

Here, the capillary effects of information flow culminate in configuration control. Ideally, those responsible for each kind of uncertainty associated with equipment and programs involved in each operating mode ask for, get, give, and interpret information in a timely way. That system of programs is, then, as essential in the culture of control as the system of signals on a control room board. As both source and user of knowledge on which safe shutdown depends, that program system controls the exchange and interpretation of information. Against that, the people-driving or function-driving extrapolated from the command and control principle, derived as much from being an old-line industry as from continuing naval influences, is misapplied if not obsolete, Stinchcombe's analysis suggests. Simply put, working relationships and arrangements of resources, responsibilities, and accountabilities would be based on the principle of needing to know and needing to tell. I say more about this soon.

"Reorganize based on how we do work"—that's what Jerry, manager of engineering technical support at Arrow Station, hopes for in a looming reorganization in which he is unsure of his say.

> My personal take on it right now, and what I'm trying to get my organization [work group] to understand, is we're going to be an organization that's going to come together and we're going to do what we need to do to get our jobs done. We're going to do our jobs the very best we can, and if we set a shining example, maybe the reorganization will catch on to that and reorganize based on how we do work. I mean that's the only option we have right now. I could spend hours a day worrying about what the organization is going to look like, but we have an outage coming that we're not prepared for, we have a lot of work on our plate.

Managers should be catching on, that is, to the benefits of matching a theory of control to the practices of control.

The Scope of Event Reviews

In Martin's letter commenting on the MIT report, he also asks, "Why have licensees actively opposed the NRC's broad approach to considering the possible 'what if' variations on an event as a means of fully understanding an event's significance?" He poses this question in the context of "the repeatedly observed inability of new senior management to make lasting performance improvements at troubled power plant sites." The short answer is that policy and production logics favor "fixing" over understanding; stations' corrective action programs come under the business heading of "loss prevention."[14] Not "fully understanding an event's significance" accounts in large measure, of course, for corrective actions that miss their mark or are ignored. That full understanding would weight contextual matters on a par with technical matters and recognize their interaction. But writing corrective actions for departmental "interface issues," for example, is so "difficult," staff members at Arrow Station say, that few are. At Bowie Station, the new oversight regime's emphasis on self-regulation led them to see that their corrective actions program was "primarily focused on the worker in the plant rather than on planning, procedure preparation, and administrative activities." Thank the parts template and its "sovereignty of components" for that: a "worker" becomes a fixable part, when looking at people in the same way as "they look at machines." Then "understanding" is limited to corrective actions not going beyond retraining, revising procedures, or disciplining.

Alone among hundreds of built-in controls and feedback mechanisms, event reviews keep experts' fingers on the pulses of technical *and* contextual issues. Once they enter that clearing carved out of routines and schedules for figuring out what happened, station experts are in a position to discover more than anyone already knew about system conditions under specific circumstances. Once in event space, team members are licensed to look up, around, and through the details of mishaps that are not expected to happen. That their lenses tend to magnify technical issues and blur for others does not vitiate the fact that in itself, event space makes room for doubt and discovery and for identifying heretofore unknown instabilities and uncertainties.

Nevertheless, to "fully understand an event's significance" and develop effective correctives, impediments remain. After retiring from the nuclear navy with the rank of admiral, Roger has been the vice-president/nuclear at a generating station, member of a nuclear utility's board of directors, and held a number of committee posts in industry organizations. We were talking about event reviews' effectiveness.

> In the early days of INPO's human performance program, I could see that some managers had to be bludgeoned into it. These are separate kinds of thinking, technical and human performance. I'm all in favor of your side. Most corrective actions fail on the human factors side, in the interpretation of the analysis and what it takes to close it out [correct a condition]. Some see something in an event as trivial, and others take it seriously and see that there would have been three broken brains here. I particularly castigate the training organization for not recognizing issues. That's typically where the breakdown is. Training sets standards. The nub goes back to cultural attitudes, consideration of the human side.
>
> Quick solutions are favored by executives. Hard-core technical people don't want to hear about the soft-side issues. That is one of my difficulties in event reviews. They want to engineer a fix, rather than look to training or discipline. Some is driven by the NRC—they want the pushbutton that makes sure the same thing can never happen again. The most heated debates [between utilities and the NRC] are around this. . . . Before INPO changed the methods for root cause analysis, ten years ago three guys would go and write one up. Now there's special training at INPO, just like on human performance. Not all the people who do this are great. Some review groups can find that an earlier root cause analysis was not good. But it's a quantum step above what it's been.

Lingering in Roger's remarks, nevertheless, are echoes of the parts template and of people-driving: "Human factors," "training," and "discipline" also imply fixes and "pushbuttons." Yet, as Martin says, "the repeatedly observed inability of new senior management to make lasting performance improvements" points to unaccosted conundrums.

To take a "quantum step" in its corrective actions program, Bowie Station managers asked eighteen of its experts who had conducted and written many event reviews to advise them. The team did not stint in identifying policy questions: how to determine the program's effectiveness; what resources are needed "to do the right job"; what the barriers to performing "good" event investigations have been; what staffing options there are; and, not least, what level of authority the program will have. Its lengthy report reveals the conundrums a corrective actions program itself is likely to face: minimal resources allocated, yet expectations of high quality reports; mismatches between available competencies and tasks, mainly trending and root cause analysis; announced versus actual autonomy of event reviewers; and unclear disciplinary consequences, which becomes a disincentive to full disclosure of event details. At Bowie Station as at others, there is also the "boomerang" or "rubber ball" policy: the manager of the group originating any condition report becomes its "owner," a disincentive on its face to file condition reports at all and an incentive to minimize the number made. Further, the same manager also writes an "effectiveness report" within six months of implementing the corrective actions.[15]

In this and other risky technologies, the effectiveness of event review systems is problematic. For example, what the access authorization team's report at Bowie Station did not say was said in discussions with me, yet those oral analyses could have been points of departure for substantive corrective actions and, certainly, for policy reconsiderations. But according to a series of exploratory studies at three nuclear power plants and at one chemical processing plant the analytic scope of event reviews is, on the whole, minimal. Reports leave out details and, short on clarity, insight, and depth, tend to emphasize technical fixes and procedural compliance without also analyzing an event's underlying sources, according to John S. Carroll of the Sloan School of Management at MIT and his collaborators. Team composition can affect quality: better reports on some dimensions (relating corrective actions to causes, for one) come from larger teams whose members are of diverse ages, had teamwork training and more industry experience, spent less time in the military, were more open to questions, and included a range of specialties and managers or supervisors. Teams include one or two members from the corrective action program and depend on others reassigned temporarily from various departments. But middle managers, these studies find, reluctantly release people and when they do, require them to keep up with their regular assignments. Better reports also displayed less conventional thinking and included issues across departments. At a station reputed to have a sophisticated program, its reports had no more analytic depth but were more readable textually and visually. One of its reports, however, included a description of negotiations that reduced a team's twenty-plus recommendations to six, after managers put them through a cost/benefit analysis; four of those were implemented. Whether senior managers act on teams' recommendations depends on the degree to which they take an interest in the issues and find corrective actions on key issues. Whether middle managers take reports at face value depends on their level of trust in the team. At the chemical company, managers had minimal expectations of reports in any case, for fear of opening the plant to regulatory inquiry: written reports were to include only what was legally required (what happened and the proximate causes) without specifying corrective actions or further details. After hearing teams' oral reports, managers would decide whether to request written analyses and whether to develop and implement changes.[16]

Similar weaknesses in the scope and substance of reviews appear in other risky enterprises. The coal industry's reports of accidents in the United States and South Africa provide scant details about working practices, leading to new procedures unrelated to the specifics of the risks, according to Beverly Sauer, professor of management at Johns Hopkins University. Information about the "pit sense" that can keep miners aware of signals of imminent dangers does not appear; mine safety experts, in companies and regulatory agencies far from mines, "theorize the ways that this world works," yet their "disembodied" analyses "construct instructions, policies, and procedures [intended] to prevent disasters in the future."[17] In Holland's steel industry and its health services, the closer to the work, the more willing experts are to discuss the "how and why" of reported incidents, rather than only the "who, what, where and when."[18] Interviews with those knowledgeable about reported incidents, finds Wim van Vuuren of the Safety Management Group of the Technology Management Department at Eindhoven University of Technology, reveal that in health services, incidents were often reported "for liability reasons only, not because doctors believed in the value of incident reporting." Steel industry managers originated improvements; improvements in the medical domain came mainly from localized, hands-on groups, despite managers' not having provided resources. That leads to "suboptimal results and missed opportunities for improvement," and in both domains, although experts saw incidents that reflected managerial failures (of policy, of attention), those were rarely reported—" 'nothing would change anyway,' " those groups felt.[19]

As those cases suggest, the blaming systems of regulatory and legal orders fuel paradoxes within the culture of control. In the management chain, fear of regulatory retribution can eliminate self-analysis; keeping a clean career record may lead station experts not to report near-misses, and in Germany, that prevented nuclear power plant managers from voluntarily telling researchers about near-misses and other incidents, even though the study's aim was to develop a database for improving corrective actions' effectiveness, according to Gerhard Becker, member of a research group at Berlin Technical University and specialist in nuclear plant event and accident analysis. Afraid of being shut down entirely, managers at nuclear power utilities would not disclose information that could give regulators "reasonable doubt about the ability and reliability of the plant management. Given the stringent control by the authorities, the utilities doubt that information regarding non-reportable events and voluntary messages" would be treated confidentially. Even as station experts accepted "that factors from the organisational level are relevant," they did not want the study's analysis to "link" an event "to a specified unit of the organisation."[20] The blaming system and its impediments, Becker concludes, "illustrate again some of the reasons why traditional accident analyses focus on technical matters" and formally limit their curiosity about "human contributions" to events.[21] (Although the German government and the industry agreed in 2001 to a phase-out of all nineteen plants, to begin in 2005, utilities have recently begun to challenge that.[22])

The U.S. National Transportation Safety Board's accident investigations are duty-bound to avoid liability issues yet provide a comprehensive narrative and analysis of antecedents and consequences. The board's reports on aviation accidents reveal nevertheless "*unresolvable tensions*" between "*localizing*" and "*diffusing*" accounts, moving between "causal chains that end at particular sites with a critical action and those that spread out to human interactions and organizational cultures" and to the larger technopolitical regime of commercial aviation, including manufacturing and testing processes, according to Peter L. Galison, physicist, pilot, and historian of science at Harvard University. "Those competing norms of explanation" in these "high-stakes histories" demonstrate "a recurrent strain between a drive to ascribe final causation to human factors and an equally powerful, countervailing drive to assign agency to technological factors."[23] Legal order will, however, interpret those histories in terms of accountability and liability, while corporate order is likely to calculate the difference between the dollar costs of potential liability and the benefits of improving risk reduction; that can lead to not making recommended corrective actions. The deterrent effect of liability law, says Michael Baram, civil engineer and professor of law at Boston University, "depends in part on whether [a company's] liability potential exceeds the gains to be made from increasing productivity without sufficient attention to and investment in safety improvements. [And] its deterrent effect may also be blunted by the availability of insurance at a price less than the investment required to prevent accidents."[24] As a matter of course, these choices are at the center of tradeoff quandaries, especially for corporate order.

Event reviews that are quick sketches rather than careful portraits, warts and all, are products of the hierarchy of knowledge: that hierarchy defines those "competing norms of explanation" in terms of the quantitative and qualitative evidence allowed to matter. One consequence is that although event reviews may name or imply managerial and policy issues, these are not likely to be analyzed because analysis would have to include "nontechnical" evidence. So concludes "Organizational Factors: Their Definition and Influence on Nuclear Safety," a report that nuclear power industry representatives, regulators, and researchers from Finland, France, Germany, Spain, Sweden, and Switzerland prepared for the European Commission in 2000.[25] That leads to "thin" not "thick" accident reviews, as Charles Perrow characterizes their differences. "A thin one is quantitative, precise, logically consistent, economical, and value-free. It embraces many of the virtues of engineering and the physical sciences. . . . A thick description recognizes subjective dimensions and cultural values and . . . shows a skepticism about human-made systems and institutions, and emphasizes social bonding and the tentative, ambiguous nature of experience. A thick description reflects the nature of system accidents, where unanticipated, unrecognizable interactions of failures occur, and the system does not allow for recovery.[26] "Thin" appears to be precise and objective, "thick" records the ambiguities and takes the pulses.

An international workshop on medical errors pondered why that is the case. Titled "A Tale of Two Stories: Contrasting Views of Patient Safety," experts in event and accident analysis (transportation, aerospace, medicine and public health, cognitive psychology, organizational studies) examined the widespread practice of telling stories of accidents and events twice. Following the "first story," which is "relatively straightforward, simple, and easily understood," a "second story" details how "resources, constraints, incentives, and demands produced by [executives, senior managers] shape the environment and influence the behavior of the people [doing the work]." Substantive analyses, predictably, can lead to pointed correctives. After a medical event without serious consequences, a follow-up study asked twenty surgeons and surgical residents to watch videotapes of this risky procedure (which itself relies on live video images) and comment on issues they saw. Their comments shifted the focus from the issue of visualization per se "to define *what* needs to be enhanced, *where* the critical visual cues reside, and *how* the cooperative work of the surgical team is organized."[27] At one U.S. station, such substantive goals motivate meetings with those who report a near-miss: discussions of the details with her/his immediate supervisor and with middle managers, who promise no disciplinary action, allow them all to find out what they might do differently with the resources they control. Fault tree analyses that include the rationales behind *regulators'* policies would round out event reviews, proposes Chris Johnson, computer scientist at the University of Glasgow and head of its Accident Investigation Group: after a railroad accident an inquiry found that regulatory policies allowed changes in signal systems without also requiring analysis of the changes' failure modes and consequences.[28] To replace root cause fault trees, which visualize a linear top-down sequence of occurrences and write two-dimensional stories, Beverly Sauer proposes a three-dimensional analysis in which "human agency, time, and the relative significance of each detail" would appear. That visual and narrative juxtaposition could replace the competing accounts of coal mining companies, unions, and regulators, allowing for a "negotiated view" of culpability and preventive measures.[29] That is in line with a proposal to develop "profound changes to our ways of thinking [that would account] for work-related social and cultural processes by searching out new data [in self-reports] previously ignored or considered to be of secondary importance. These can lead to modes of interpretation that are quite different from the incidents and accidents themselves, and hence to corrective or curative measures that are to a certain extent also different," suggests Michel Llory, director of the Institut du Travail Humain and formerly a member of Electricité de France's human factors research group.[30]

At a nuclear reactor research project in Norway, the first story told about several events, says Erik Hollnagel, cognitive psychologist, "did not lead to significant learning about vulnerabilities or to constructive changes" because, having classified the events into root cause categories, the "interesting, informative aspects" of "the narratives [were] lost."[31] The codes for behavioral "variables" include, for example, "tunnel vision," "nonconservative decision making"). Root cause analysis protocols do not elicit information about "work process(es) and organisational factors [that] played significant roles" in nuclear power operations, says George Apostolakis, PRA specialist and member of the Nuclear Engineering Department faculty at the Massachusetts Institute of Technology.[32] Not only do such categories obliterate the events' dynamics, but their "error-forcing" contexts are not analyzed in parallel.[33] INPO's proprietary reanalyses of highly significant events may be "thicker," discussing, for example, the assumptions a control room crew made.

That bleached evidence contrasts with the stories in the confidential Aviation Safety Reporting System, operated by NASA and funded mainly by the Federal Aviation Administration. Its aim is entirely educational, divorced from regulatory practices and from accident analysis, and free from legal concerns and from "giving guidance about how to solve problems or about which problems are economically or socially worth attention."[34] It depends solely on self-reports of near-misses voluntarily submitted annually by 30,000 pilots, air traffic controllers, mechanics, and flight attendants, whose identities are known only to report analysts, who are "domain experts (e.g., pilots) rather than technicians or clerks." They collate "sets of narratives" around particular themes or questions through an "indexing scheme" to "put together related or contrasting sets of cases for analysis." The narratives circulate back to "the operational community, the people who voluntarily provide the information." The objective is "not to reduce the incident to a category but rather to make sure that the narrative is descriptive, complete, and precise" in a system where "the substance of the narratives is the critical information." These portray real-time conditions, how people understood the conditions they were in, and the reasons for the actions they took in varying situations.

None of that is to say that industry experts do not trade second and thicker stories within their professional networks or follow the daily event reports and technical analyses posted on the NRC's website, or that executives, engineers, and managers do not hash over policy implications of the details of disturbing incidents or events. It is only to say that unless experts write them up as "best practices" and share them across stations, evidence is limited to that coded into industry databases. That leaves little to go on for developing theories and models of risk reduction and risk escalation, when events cannot be analyzed in terms of the characteristics of decisions, constraints, and resources involved; nor are reasons for ineffective or neglected correctives similarly analyzed (yet they are another kind of "event"). Without a framework for understanding the particulars, station experts and managers see each instance as its own story, at their own and at others' stations. When the details don't "roll up" into compelling reasons to revisit policy logics, the "lessons" are "lost," says an Overton Station radiation protection manager about his experiences and those of his peers.

> Although we record details and issues experienced at low levels, these don't get rolled up into final reviews, and lessons are lost. The details of each function's individual improvements get more attention than the details emerging from cross-functional issues. These lessons learned don't roll up into the management systems that go across functions. Those are general and abstract—what happens below that level isn't analyzed for success and failures.

Examining companies' and stations' policy logics is obviously not within the scope of event reviews. Yet the likelihood of improvements that improve depends on the reviews' levels of credibility and authority, which are key to whether managers take them seriously. Then again, teams' resources and authority for producing wider-scope reports depend on policy logics: that catch-22 goes far to account for the felt disparities between teams' "announced and actual" autonomy and influence. Narrow-scope reviews leave it to a station's senior management group to infer which dilemmas, paradoxes, and contradictions these point to and to refer those not within their grasp up a responsive corporate chain of command: that process defines ideal self-regulation. The record shows, however, that such contemplation often needs a kick-start from INPO's peer evaluations, NRC's quarterly ratings, or a serious event at their own or another station.

That may explain why corrective actions the teams at Arrow, Bowie, and Charles Stations recommend appear in two rhetorical styles, one for directly technical, or "hard" issues, the other for administrative, communicative, and resource issues, as they are understood. An action and fixing style addresses improvements in equipment, training, and procedures, a jawboning, pleading, and urging style permeates recommendations for changes in administrative policies and managerial conduct. For line managers, who are responsible for implementing the preponderance of corrective actions, fixing is all of a piece with their jobs: fixes for hard issues are relatively easy to accomplish and likely to be obvious when they aren't made. The soft issues—administrative and policy issues—as the Arrow Station root cause analysis team pleads, would acknowledge "the human element" as itself "an important safety system" thus treating "equipment and human beings" equally. Addressing policy issues directly is likely to be beyond the ken and competence of line managers, and in any case, farther from their influence and control. Perhaps more compelling is that soft fixes are relatively harder to accomplish and whether they are or are not made or are or are not effective is less immediately obvious. The interface and programmatic correctives experts find "difficult to write" are the very issues that fervently preoccupy the team: Arrow Station's peopled "system" has "structural problems," "deficiencies in various processes," and a "lack of precise communication" where needed.

Another source of the problematics of corrective actions in this industry, and perhaps in other risky technologies, is that although event reviews are well within the box of stable practices, not to mention being mandated, the value of the space they open up for self-regulation is underappreciated in the utilitarian scheme of things: that is negative, "indirect" space.[35] Reviews require prime time for "punting and thinking" but, not recognized as being the "real work" of production, they are vulnerable to being shortchanged on resources. Event space does more than go against the grain of production: it is guaranteed only to produce more work immediately, but also perhaps, more trust. In that cultural scheme of things, space and time for "sitting back" become sacred.

"Maintenance Is Going to Save You"

Vince, member of the condition-based maintenance group and among the foursome that discovered the hot spot on Charles Station's generator step-up transformer, explained that he doesn't "have much experience with thermography, the intellectual side." By that, he meant calculating heat transfer rates through different materials or interpreting thermographic images. Early on in Electricité de France's *Nuclear Power Plant Maintenance* published in 1988, its author, Jean-Pierre Mercier, characterizes the "image problem" of maintenance: "dirty coveralls and greasy hands."

> Whether the industry be steel, chemicals, energy . . . production facilities tend to be complex . . . [and] operating company activities fall into only two categories: operation and maintenance. . . . Operation is the most prestigious of the two activities, the one that often gives the industry its image (and its name). . . . The responsibilities of [those] who operate the system are gigantic since the consequences of mistakes can be immediate and very costly. This means that extensive and often very complex training is required. . . . Although maintenance is generally acknowledged to be important, it has an image problem. For most people it means dirty coveralls and greasy hands. Technically, maintenance activities are just as complex and important as operating activities, but they seldom obtain the same recognition as, for instance, design or engineering at least until some failure occurs and the plant is shut down. At this time, maintenance is remembered and often hastily blamed for the failure.[36]

Engineering separates itself from the hands-on work of operations, which separates itself from maintenance in a downward spiral from "mind" to "hand" to "dirty overalls and greasy hands." That manifests industrial culture's claims of a hierarchical relationship of reason to experience. In 1988, managers at the utility that owned the Davis-Besse plant hired a former NRC inspector to tell them what was wrong with maintenance there. What Howard C. Whitcomb found, according to a report in the *New York Times*, was "that management so disdained its craft workers that it had lost touch with the condition of the plant." "Top executives responded swiftly and decisively, he said: They ordered him to change his report. He quit instead." In that report, given to the *Times* in 2002 by an Ohio nonprofit citizens action group, Whitcomb had said, " 'Maintenance has traditionally been regarded in a subservient role.' . . . '[M]anagement needs to recognize the contribution that craft personnel may provide in the development of plant specific maintenance actions.' "

At an MIT workshop in the early 1990s, senior station managers talked about issues they face.

FIRST VOICE: Is there really such an influence of management on plant performance? Doesn't it all boil down to the technical quality of the plant? It may be useful to look at differences in design and at what problems arise afterward. Utilities spend such a lot on redesign.

SECOND VOICE: It's better to have a lousy plant with good operators. I prefer that to a good plant with lousy operators.

FIRST VOICE: It's difficult to say what a bad design is. A good design allows for easy maintenance. But the design for maintainability can't be expressed in a PRA.

Maintainability becomes known only after the fact. For an operations manager at another U.S. station, the image of maintenance has never matched its role. "Maintenance is going to save you. It's the last line of defense. Ingenious operators can get around broken equipment. We need more analytical people. We need to put resources into predictive maintenance and become proactive."

Maintenance is going to save calculated logics, that is: it assures that their intentions will—can be—realized. This industry has long recognized that it requires higher levels of skills; pay scales are about 20 percent higher than in nonnuclear generating stations. Now, in meeting competition, maintenance activities have been intensifying.[37] With the industry's goal of fewer and shorter outages, "only an unusual level of cooperation among operations, maintenance and engineering" can meet it, engineers Walter H. and Thomas C. Esselman warn.

> As performance improves, the factors that detract from performance will become much more subtle. A dramatic improvement in the way that plant data are used should be sought. That includes data recorded by computers, and from system engineer walkdowns, operator rounds, predictive monitoring, surveillance tests, inspections, and many other sources of information.[38]

A "dramatic improvement" depends on the subtleties of the doubt and discovery principle and on a free flow of information and its reliable interpretation. At Charles Station, Jack, a shift manager, talked about his experience at another station where four transformers "were failing one at a time." Although tests showed that "the equipment's OK, all we can say is, 'It didn't fail its test.' That doesn't mean that it's OK. Well, people don't like to hear that, right? They want you to tell them it's OK. And all I can tell you is that it's not bad, because it passed its test, because a test is limited on the things that it can test for." Whether managers see that nuance as a welcome cause for curiosity and a reassuring sign of a shift manager's credibility or as "bad news" is another kind of intellectual challenge.

That image of maintenance at the bottom of an inherited hierarchy is preserved in an industrial division of labor whose occupational categories are "petrified" into outmoded "ideal types" unable to account for the multiple demands of newer jobs (for example, emergency medical technicians and information technology contractors, among others), according to Stephen R. Barley, of the Department of Industrial Engineering and Engineering Management at Stanford University and Gideon Kunda of the Department of Labor Studies at Tel Aviv University.[39] The demands of these nontraditional kinds of work unbutton white- and blue-collar categories, opening up stereotypic differences assigned to "mental" and "manual" work.[40] To define the "core task" of maintenance as its practitioners see it in the two units of a Finnish nuclear power station, Pia Oedewald and Teemu Reiman of VTT Industrial Systems, a Finnish research institute, interviewed 23 experts in various functions and with different job titles, including managers, to learn how they understood their tasks in relation to others and to other activities; a survey of 135 maintenance staff followed. In responding to the constraints and requirements of their working environments, maintenance experts balance among three tasks: anticipating, reacting, and monitoring and reflecting. Flexibility together with a methodical approach and, in my terms, doubting and discovering are key. Constantly, they question the impacts of their activities yet maintain an overview and exercise judgment even as they apply generic rules. In all, this study finds, "maintenance core task demands" are very like "the demands of knowledge-intensive work, where knowledge acquisition, interpretation and sharing are central for maintaining situation awareness" of others' work and ongoing activities.[41]

At Bowie Station, the work of Ned and Meg is understood as being "manual," having been routinized into processes and tasks which others have devised through "mental" or "knowledge" work requiring foresight and planning. For Ned, locating electrical supply cabinets and opening and closing designated breakers are customary tasks; for Meg, reviewing the information assembled in any one contractor's file repeats a process done for hundreds of others. But that understanding of the mind-hand division of labor doesn't hold up, the events suggest. Ned and Meg are expected to augment the skill of their craft with the capacity for the judgment and abductive "insight" associated with "mental" work. Both are counted on to make "interpretations of the information at hand [to] reveal what they believe to be significant," like the machine operators using computers whom Shoshana Zuboff, a social psychologist, observed. Like them, Neds and Megs exercise authority "located in the process of creating and articulating meaning, rather than in a particular position or function."[42] Little doubt that Meg and Ned exercised authority through their knowledge and the meanings they acted on, when in these instances out of hundreds, their observations and interpretations went awry and affected the station's bottom line and its reputation with the NRC.

Splitting "design" from "operations" and then again from "maintenance" by claiming the superiority of reason to experience fundamentally
distorts the culture of control. In many industrial domains, technology
designers do not understand basic interactions sufficiently to model them.
In the cement industry, for example, designers have not understood "fundamental physical and chemical reactions that occur [in kilns]." Com-
puter-based controls not being feasible, operators maintain control over
the cement's quality through "a growing feel for the operation of the
kiln" by continually integrating information about its temperature and
the material's "feed rate, fuel rate, and rotation speed."[43] That is one of
several examples in Larry Hirschhorn's prescient book, *Beyond Mechanization: Work and Technology in a Postindustrial Age*, in which he sees
the nuclear power industry and chemical operations as models "of the
post-industrial integration of labor and technology" also visible in con-
sumer manufacturing. "We do not have to posit a series of extreme break-
downs or accidents to forecast the development of second-order work
at the center of worker responsibility."[44] Ongoing control work can be
"second-order," however, only in a culture of control claiming that design
has the last word.

The kinds of knowledge and ways of thinking technicians' jobs generally demand transcend stereotypes in several industries (automobile, medicine, science, information technologies). The line between them and professionals is finer than corporate order expects, Stephen R. Barley and his
research team find.[45] Technicians speak professionals' language more
from a "contextual perspective," yet technicians "appropriated the professionals' theories, plans, diagnoses, or designs to guide their own work
at the empirical interface." Reciprocally, "some scientists incorporated
. . . without further analysis, into arguments, papers, grants, and theories" data that technicians supplied.[46] Technicians gain access to auxiliary
and substantive knowledge professionals may lack: "semiotic" ("the ability to make sense of subtle differences in the appearance of materials and
the behavior of machines" by distinguishing "colors, shapes, and
smells"); "sensory-motor" ("having a feel" for instruments, materials,
and techniques); "heuristics" ("rules of thumb derived from experience
and reading"); "style of practice" ("knowing how to minimize uncertainty and guard against mistakes . . . behaviors and demeanors with the
moral force of a code of conduct"); "local idiosyncrasies" (knowledge of
the particularities of components, test results, repair history); and "access
to others' knowledge" (knowing the special skills of colleagues, Internet
sources).[47] It is just those kinds of reasoning from experience that attrition, downsizing, and retirements have been depleting in the nuclear
power industry.

When technicians' unique knowledge turns out to be indispensable to that of professionals, that can upset the conventional authority/knowledge hierarchy. No longer unambiguously "workers," their "theoretical sophistication" is at odds with their lower status, Barley finds.[48] Some professionals try to enforce that status, however, by treating technicians as "servants."[49] Or as "parts." Disrupting an intellectual order of things, technicians' work "creates pressures for a more horizontal form": being "vessels of expertise," they become collaborators on a knowledge-based footing.[50] Technicians have "careers of achievement" in conventional industrial environments where "careers of advancement" are more highly valued.[51] That pattern fully characterizes the nuclear power industry: industry experts, whether degreed or declared professionals, gain skill and knowledge as they rotate through different arenas, yet those achievements do not always advance their rank and pay. Richard, now operations manager and at Arrow Station for about eighteen years, talks about the latest wave of reorganizations. "I'm not sure how we built the management structure here we have now. I think some of us are here because we were the only one available to take the job at the time."

Between downsizing and the slow task of recruiting and seasoning specialists, the inverse becomes the problem: newly hired experts fill positions with influence and authority but may not yet have gained the subtle knowledge risk reduction requires. Chuck, senior engineer at Arrow in the operations department, comments about management changes.

> They're bringing in more people who are strictly management type people, rather than people familiar with the technical aspects of it. They say that it's good—they want to have people who look at it from a management and not a technical perspective. But when you do that, if you end up with people who don't have a technical ability or they may have a technical ability but they don't know the specifics, they come in and they have to rely on the people from the departments, engineering and such, who have that technical expertise and explain to them why "It's OK to do this." And then those management people have to make the decision.

Despite the prevalence of joint work and mutual respect in this industry, acknowledging the interdependence, reciprocity, and equality of each professional order struggles against an inherited caste system of credibility. The result is a hierarchy of knowledge that is allowed to matter: engineers over operators, operators over maintenance, and within maintenance, salaried employees over those earning hourly wages ("workers" and, often, union members and contractors). In rueful hindsight, Cliff, operations manager at Charles Station, would have invited "workers" into the conference room.

Looking back on this meeting, we had a lot of supervisors there and very few workers. If I had to do the meeting over again, I would have had only people who were knowledgeable about the issue all the way down to the worker level, and had a vertical slice, if you will, of the organization. So it would have been less intimidating, and you would have had the people that had the right data.

The "right data" and the right stuff: more expertise than designated "knowledge workers" have for interpreting the nuances and subtleties of thermographic images.

As ubiquitous now as they ever have been, the reason/experience distinctions and the disdain they can foster announce an intolerable anachronism. Given the significance of maintenance activities to risk reduction in all high hazard industries, in this twenty-first century a "dirty hands" image marks a cultural lag of "gigantic" proportions. That lag looms larger at a time when maintenance is what aging reactors require more of, more often, and with more sophisticated analyses to guide it.[52]

"Levels of Maturity"

With the industry's third shock—the criticality accident in September 1999 at a uranium processing plant in Tokai village in Ibarki Prefecture, Japan—the question of intellectual capital became one of its maturity. "Methodological Immaturedness—Antimony" is an "inherent and structural" policy problem that the Criticality Accident Investigation Committee "encountered" when considering how to "eliminate the causes of the accident," said Professor Hiroyuki Yoshikawa, chairman of Japan's Nuclear Safety Commission in its Science and Technology Agency.[53] The antimonies are familiar by now:

  A. if safety increases, efficiency decreases [the tradeoff quandary];

  B. if regulations are reinforced, creativity is lost [calculated logics vs. real-time logics];

  C. if surveillance is reinforced, spirit declines [monitoring vs. discovery];

  D. if manuals are introduced, self-management is lost [strict compliance vs. real-time logics];

  E. if fool-proof measures are implemented, the level of skills decreases [rote vs. knowledge-based performance];

  F. if responsibilities are centered on a key person, the group loses concentricity ["owner"-centered vs. process-centered];

  G. if responsibilities are too strict, cover-ups result [sanctions vs. candor];

  H. if information disclosure is promoted, [the] situation becomes too conservative [the blaming system].

The chairman declares, "Specifically, there is no future for nuclear energy unless the safety vs. efficiency antimony . . . is resolved. The same is true for the other antimonies."[54] As welcome as these concerns with the nuclear industry's intellectual maturity are, they themselves illustrate that the industry's maturity is still evolving. A once-and-for-all resolution of the tradeoff quandary is not possible, given variations in the kinds of uncertainties and contingencies that make it necessary. No heroic technology is perfectible once and for all: *doubt and discovery* keep us safe. Calling for these issues to be "resolved" implies a promise that cannot be kept. Unkept promises are themselves sources of distrust not only from publics but from industry experts as well.

What can be "resolved" is an inclusive negotiating process that demands explicit rationales and robust analyses. There will always be situations where choices must be made between top-down and lateral control, between rewarding individuals and rewarding a group, between system training and component training, between depending on contractors and relying on employees, between generalist managers and technically trained managers, between incentives and sanctions. Everywhere, public and private policymakers can resolve to keep that infrastructure of conundrums explicit and discussable, situation by situation, tradeoff quandary by quandary. One industry insider, once on NRC's staff and familiar with the industry abroad, wants "more transparency" of that kind.

> I only wish the nuclear industry and actual plant operations were more transparent than they are, so that more effective critiques could occur. It's nearly impossible for a professor or Washington law-maker to accurately assess nuclear operations and the plant safety culture. It's too complex and too hidden. Even NRC resident inspectors see less than two per cent of all that takes place and they virtually live at a site. What is needed is more transparency. Peer inspections, such as those carried out by INPO and relied upon by the NRC, should be available to the public and to outside nuclear experts—not just the plant management.

But he does not mention true outsiders, like those versed in other risky technologies and experts in nontechnical domains knowledgeable about their political and social complexities and ethical and philosophical implications. For example, Don Ihde, who specializes in the philosophy of science and technology at the State University of New York at Stony Brook, meets with R&D staff members at European companies and research institutes in various fields, at their invitation, to think through with them what Ihde calls their "prognostic predicaments," to consider scenarios of the intended and unintended consequences of cutting-edge inventions and discoveries. These discussions, among other things, help to keep everyone aware of longer time horizons and proliferating effects; they give equal time to wanted and unwanted outcomes, not always easy for technology enthusiasts.[55] Such outsiders can also be a bracing antidote to the "complacency" so often cropping up as a cause of surprising mishaps. As nourishing to morale and as welcome to the bottom line as long runs of exemplary performance are, they can also act as masks and earplugs. At an industry workshop, a utility executive recounted that one of its "star performers" had lost its pedestal, and a few years later regained it. Now, another few years later, its performance continues to be untroubled. "We're on a plateau, which makes me wonder, What are we missing? What aren't we seeing that will unpleasantly surprise us?" So, the search for "significance" is also for the significance of the dog that isn't barking. In "Nothing Recedes Like Success? Risk Analysis and the Organizational Amplification of Risks," William R. Freudenberg, Dehlsen Professor of Environmental Studies at the University of California Santa Barbara, analyzes among other risks that elude risk assessment metrics, "complacency and boredom" and "the atrophy of vigilance" when things keep going right.[56] That can, however, be a dangerous time for other reasons: managers may be tempted to reduce or divert the very resources that make it possible. The presence of outsiders with different interests, questions, and expertise can take many forms and be relatively informal; not all require show-and-tell productions, such as those NRC inspections and INPO assessments inspire. But the tendency to insularity that dogs this industry despite improvements in the last several years requires conscious effort, and resources, to overcome.

An official "peer inspectorate" for any regulated sector is the aim of a comprehensive proposal looking toward a "new form of government" that would decentralize regulatory administration to states and localities and their citizens to strengthen federalism, decrease judiciary burdens, and create a new kind of relationship between firms.[57] Federal regulators would combine their oversight and standard-setting with firms' self-improvement "experiments" and best practices. So proposes "A Constitution of Democratic Experimentalism" by Michael C. Dorf and Charles F. Sabel of the Columbia University Law School. Congress would authorize state and local agencies to participate in benchmarking with regulated firms, whose self-improvements would be reflected in regulatory standards, through an ongoing system of mutual "learning by monitoring" that also respects local and regional contexts.[58] The nuclear power industry is one of four examples through which Dorf and Sabel illustrate their proposal; as mentioned, the Nuclear Energy Institute already provides benchmarking data the NRC uses to set thresholds for performance indicators. Drawing largely on Joseph Rees' 1994 study of INPO, Dorf and Sabel see an existing framework in its relationships with the NRC and with stations. That would require reconsidering INPO's proprietary status, which circumvents the public. Another model for a next stage of industry and of public maturity is the NRC's "Public Roundtable" meetings convened during the months its reactor oversight process was in its pilot phase. From communities surrounding each of eight participating stations, between fifteen and thirty people, including "local officials, interest groups, and members of the public," met to consider the new regime's aims and limitations.[59]

But the industry's maturity has a way to go. After participating in a U.S. peer review of that criticality accident, a seasoned industry manager said at a meeting of the American Nuclear Society that he came to realize that one of reasons "top managers get paid so much money is that they work in two worlds—the public and the regulator. To the public they have to say, 'An accident won't happen here.' To people in plants, they have to encourage them to believe that an accident can happen here and urge them to take all precautions. Rationalizing these two polar assumptions is management's job." In the Tokaimura accident, he said, "the two unfortunately merged and could not be compartmentalized." Now that "regulator" and "self-regulator" are officially more interdependent than ever before, we have to hope that those "polar assumptions" also will have melted away.

To enter into the working life of a nuclear power generating station populated by those who shoulder its risks on behalf of us all is to enter a world where electricity is a by-product. A station's primary product is a cultural commodity: civic and market trust in its managers' and experts' competencies.[60] The primary trust fund on which this industry will continue to draw remains regulation and self-regulation that produces as much evidence of contextual wisdom as of technical wisdom. The breadth and reach of this culture of control in practice calls into question the quarantine of knowledge—objective from subjective, quantitative from qualitative, technical from administrative, material from cultural. Control is a unity that produces outcomes, good to bad, approximate to exact. Technical claims grounded mainly in risk estimation appear, as I have said, in concepts and techniques such as command and control, defense in depth, feedback, margins of safety, procedures, rules, system reliability, training. In operation, other specific and active elements of control temper those claims: the tradeoff quandary, first and foremost, where negotiations among the orders' concerns and commitments occur; the parts template, where analyses leading to corrective actions may disregard context, operating history, and interactions; the status of maintenance, where "disdain" can affect "human performance," "open listening," and corrective actions; and a misplaced project template, a technospeak semantics insensitive to its worldly associations, among others.

These other ways of thinking about the kind of problem it is to operate a nuclear power plant at least risk are far afield from a "definition of a nuclear power plant safety construct" offered by NRC's chairman, Nils J. Diaz, in August 2003: "a hierarchical, techno-legal assembly of regulatory and operational safety systems ensuring the safe design, operation, and maintenance of nuclear power reactors for the benefit of the United States. This definition 'is not complete,' he said, 'but is a good start for a much needed dialogue.' " The goal is for the industry "'to implement a safety construct that leaves little doubt about requirements and responsibilities, for regulators and regulated alike.' "[61] That dialogue is indeed "much needed" as much outside as inside the industry to find out soon if and how "regulators and regulated" can rethink a "techno-legal assembly" as also being a honeycombed culture of control and reconsider their "requirements and responsibilities" in that new light.

By fixing on "elements" of the culture of control, I am trying to make as specific as possible unmeasurable (or thus far unmeasured) "requirements and responsibilities" that palpably influence the technology's design and its operations. Stepping outside that box of stable practices might thus become more practicable. When, where, and how much influence these elements have, we know little about systematically, yet we know much about them on a case-by-case basis after every major accident and serious event. The lack of systematic knowledge or curiosity itself handicaps trust, when, as Martin points out, plant managers do not work out "what-if" scenarios. One of society's values to which those "requirements and responsibilities" look, and which "regulators and regulated," no less than publics, feel on their pulses, is trust or its absence.

Re-Imagining the Culture of Control in the Nuclear Power Industry

This last excursion into the world in which this industry and we live further rearranges today's ways of thinking about the culture of control. Its aim is to respond to this industry's reverse salient with a point of departure for considering innovations that might ameliorate its self-defeating patterns. This thought experiment frees us to ask, What would be the implications for regulation and self-regulation of changes intended to increase substantially the frequency of effective corrective actions? That would also reduce the frequency of events in the first place and decrease the frequency of those that reveal previously ineffective or unmade corrective actions. That could mean more time on line and fewer operating risks all around.

That question and its implications come, however, under circumstances that the designers and owners of this technology had not planned for: they assumed stability—economically, socially, and politically. Over the last fifteen years or so, deregulation and restructuring followed by a still-evolving reactor oversight process have collided with the necessity for intensified security safeguards for both nuclear power plants and the fuel cycle. Station experts have had to initiate and adapt to many kinds of changes yet keep on with familiar routines, while coping with the distraction of flux and new preoccupations.[62] Here, Roger, the former admiral, talks about distractions and events.

> I see events and incidents as an attitude problem, but the attitude may be due to disruption or distraction. In the navy, I insisted that any watch stander be diligent about his duties. I didn't tolerate distractions—telephone calls, people wandering up to ask about the weather. In industry, the watch supervisor in the control room is filling out paperwork, having discussions with others, people calling to find out where someone is. I want to correlate distractions to questionable actions. Was there a distraction? People don't deliberately make mistakes. There must have been a distraction.
>
> The problem is how to get managers to see this as a co-equal part. The big companies are doing better. But if they don't constantly harass about safety, in the early morning meeting they need to list "the distractions today." Senior managers and executives have to provide broad shoulders for what people below want to do, but they don't always know that, or do it. . . . The key is, How does station management recognize those distractions [reengineering, price competition, visits from peer review teams and NRC inspectors] as causing degradation? They need to hold meetings on what's really going to happen—direct, face-to-face communication. We've got too many in the industry who don't know how to do that.

And many people who do know how to do that and a great many other things besides have left the industry or will soon be leaving. Overcoming difficulties in recruiting and retention is a worldwide priority.[63] The most visible distraction brought on by the interaction of demography and deregulation continues to be the loss of knowledgeable people from a knowledge-dependent industry. In the United States, staffing levels in 2003 were 17 percent lower than they were in 1997, a "loss of approximately 1 in every 6" station experts.[64] At Bowie Station, the position of manager for the access authorization program had long been vacant; at Overton Station it was months before managers could replace the one person with training in root cause analysis. It is no secret that downsizing strategies may not be calibrated to the long-term benefits of preventive maintenance. Fewer people can bring about larger backlogs, which lead to urgent issues and "fire drills," according to an MIT model based on staffing and operating data at a U.S. plant.[65] Those "drills" are themselves distractions and introduce instabilities internally. So are reorganizations: responsibility for the condition-based maintenance program and thermography at Charles Station had shifted around so often that it became an analytic outsider.

The industry's gains in time on line (average outages are shorter than ever before, downpowering events fewer) come at a human cost, according to John Jenco, senior manager at the Electric Power Research Institute who has specialized in nuclear power maintenance issues for about fourteen years. "When is enough enough?" he asks, when "in our quest to squeeze every last drop of performance from the tank, we have in many cases driven some very good people away from our industry and created a very high-stress work environment for those that remain." Not that more improvements aren't possible, Jenco says, "But I still believe that we need to at least begin posing the question of diminishing returns for effort expended."[66]

Concern with the safety-related consequences of demographic shifts, shortages of specialists, and deregulation has not yet been a high priority of the NRC, despite the recommendations of a study it commissioned of post-deregulation conditions in the U.S. aviation and railroad industries and in the British nuclear power industry. Led by Vicki M. Bier, member of the faculty of the Department of Industrial Engineering at the University of Wisconsin–Madison and specialist in operations research and risk analysis, a team of economists and a nuclear engineer find that competition spawned several general conditions: experienced staff are not replaced; safety-related investments decrease; managers' time horizons shrink as they navigate conflicts in corporate style and keep up workforce morale; workloads and overtime increase (in the U.K. nuclear industry, contracting increased).[67] Although improved safety and/or safety oversight could result from deregulation, this study finds, it nevertheless "posed substantial challenges to the management of safety" in each industry. In particular, major organizational changes ask managers to accomplish more with fewer resources in uncertain and often confusing work environments as lines of communication and corporate priorities change.[68]

The British Nuclear Safety Directorate, for such reasons, requires evidence that owners have themselves analyzed the safety-related consequences of their strategies (mergers, acquisitions, downsizing). No similar move seems likely to occur in the United States, however, given striking differences in each regulator's analyses of the general situation. The NRC's most recent Strategic Plan for 2000–2006, updated as of June 23, 2003, finds that because the effect of "economic deregulation on maintaining nuclear safety is unclear. . . . We will continue to rely upon our inspection, assessment, and enforcement programs as the primary tool for evaluating and ensuring safe operations at our licensed facilities." Also unclear, the NRC says, is the "potential impact of deregulation on our other performance goals of increasing public confidence, increasing effectiveness, efficiency, and realism, and reducing unnecessary regulatory burden."

> The general public may have increased concerns about the safety of nuclear power plants in a more cost-competitive environment, thereby affecting our efforts to increase public confidence. On the other hand, to remain cost-competitive, licensees put pressure on the NRC to accelerate reform efforts to increase efficiency and effectiveness and reduce unnecessary regulatory burden. Large conglomerates may emerge from consolidation of the nuclear power industry and may necessitate changes in our management and organizational structure to effectively and efficiently regulate the industry.[69]

The U.K. Nuclear Safety Directorate in its Strategic Plan 2003–2006 states that after privatization, the intensifying "commercialisation," "mergers," and new "trading arrangements" bring "pressures on companies to drive down costs and satisfy shareholder expectations. Downsizing, contractorisation, partnering, multiskilling, and shift pattern changes are just some of the ways in which companies have responded to these pressures. . . . While good safety and good commercial performance are both facets of good management, there is potential for tension between them."[70] For those reasons, on the basis of an operator's previous record and the extent of the changes, the Nuclear Installations Inspectorate is assessing "all proposed modifications to licensees' plant, equipment, procedures, safety cases, organisational structure and resources."[71]

The U.K. regulator acknowledges the tensions between costs and safety and is unhesitating in its response; the NRC, seeing itself buffeted by both the public and the industry, equivocates. Perhaps "unclear" consequences of deregulation means that it has underway a program of studies to clarify them, but as of June 2003, that was not the case.[72] Instead, the NRC appears to be waiting to see whether their enforcement practices are capable of anticipating serious problems or of interpreting the significance of company strategies, practices that did not, however, anticipate the significance of Northeast Utilities' strategy to target the company's nuclear assets for cost-reductions. The NRC's task force analyzing the Davis-Besse failures recognized that the new regime did not prevent delays in inspection and repair or take note of unimplemented corrective actions. Since March 2002, the NRC has had the published results of a study it commissioned in 1999 from a national laboratory to evaluate the likelihood that the new oversight regime would "detect human performance

influences" leading to errors that had in fact occurred in safety-critical
operating events and been analyzed in event reviews. On a scale of "highly
likely, "moderately likely," and "less likely" to detect "human performance influences," detection of these is "highly likely":

> improper maintenance of safety grade systems and inadequate operator recov-
> ery for acknowledged sequences.

Detection of these is "moderately likely":

> failure to follow safe work practices involving safety systems, design deficien-
> cies, problems in various maintenance and test activities. . . . the impact of ad-
> verse weather upon staffing levels or ergonomics, any history of false or spuri-
> ous actuations, and licensee failures to follow industry or NRC notices.

These "human performance influences" are "less likely" to be detected:

> crew knowledge regarding ex-control room activities, presence of latent, depen-
> dent failures, improper maintenance of non-safety grade equipment, support
> system failures contributing to atypical plant response, mismatch between plant
> procedures and plant conditions, use of informal procedures, influence of dis-
> tracting conditions on personnel performance, maintainer knowledge deficien-
> cies, and command and control and resource allocation problems.[73]

This study makes two further findings. The reactor oversight process as
of 2001 did not have "a standardized approach to detecting and characterizing" the previous or "latent" errors discovered only after a new event,
and second, that while various kinds of "human errors influenced the
occurrence or severity of operating events," how these "combine to produce failures are neither readily apparent nor easily modeled." The screening methods the oversight process uses "would potentially discard these
smaller latent errors."[74] That leaves the interpretation of the significance
of such likely interactions to self-regulation.

The British requirements represent "a significant change in regulatory
philosophy," say the authors of the deregulation study: the requirements
"formally place the human and organizational contributions to safety on
a par with the hardware contribution."[75] Whether that equalizing philosophy will travel to the United States and to China, Europe, India, Indone-
sia, Japan, the states of the former Soviet Union, remains to be seen.

From Functions to Meanings: A Second Axis for Risk Reduction

Given the NRC's and the industry's stance, self-regulation will be the main
defense against future distractions, flux, and instabilities and the operational uncertainties they introduce. In these times and circumstances, fi-

nancial and political, it matters more than ever who knows what, when they know it, and how credible that knowledge is and is allowed to be. The reverse salient at issue—the presence of weak root cause analyses and policies that can result in ineffective and unimplemented corrective actions—is itself a source of increased uncertainties and risks. The starting point for this thought experiment to re-imagine this industry's culture of control elaborates on Arthur Stinchcombe's findings: To reduce uncertainties inherent in maintaining the capacity for safe shutdown depends on maximizing the free flow of reliable information and on maximizing experts' interpretive competencies. More informative event reviews and more actionable and effective corrective actions depend on both.

With that as a goal, the industry's "collective ways of thinking" would acknowledge that what keeps its experts on a straight path to safe shutdown not only depends on developing and following rules and requirements for reactor control. It also depends on how their experts define, acquire, produce, interpret, and use "information" and "data" to reduce inevitable operating uncertainties. Those knowledge-driven activities are mainly the province of the station programs mapping that path to safe shutdown. When that information is available, reliable, and exchanged in a timely way, experts are more likely to stay on that path, the record shows. But the uncertainties introduced by program activities themselves and by cycles, transitions, and phases built into production processes can throw them off it. During outages, for example, observes a manager at Overton Station: "Most lost time is between the chunks of work, when it's difficult to predict the contingencies. When hand-offs between tasks and shifts aren't smooth—when information isn't exchanged that should be—the schedule lengthens." In the early 1990s, Overton's outage manager recalled:

> The organization had never looked at the flow path of a work package. We visualized it on paper and saw two or three patterns. The interfaces worked or we wouldn't have survived. But we didn't understand how they worked. Through constant critique, we found some places where the organization dropped the ball.

At another U.S. plant, a maintenance manager put a 22-member team together to "look at field relations and communications links to find out why work gets delayed. There are lots of relationships everyone has, and most people don't have a good understanding of what they are." Even though experts know that evaluating uncertainties is vital, that may not be a conscious and central mission. Ken, maintenance manager at Charles Station, was talking about the decision to treat the GSU hot spot as circulating current: "We had experts in there telling us what they thought the issues were. We liked that answer. It appeared to us it was technically correct, it kept the unit on line, which is our mission . . ." That may be the central mission for producing electricity, but it is not always also one that produces trust.

For both, this thought experiment adds an interpretive axis to the functional axis defined by the material and physical requirements for reactor control: an axis of meanings that gives priority to knowledge, policies, resources, and strategies for optimizing information flow and maximizing interpretive competencies. How this axis of meanings rearranges responsibilities and accountabilities depends on how industry experts knowledgeable about each program's concerns and commitments define the kinds of uncertainties it deals with and, in turn, the kinds of information and interpretations each program needs and produces for every other. The contours of those exchanges between and among programs would provide the basis for the social architecture of station relationships, responsibilities, and accountabilities. An axis of meanings acknowledges the living, worldly system that irrevocably parallels the machined system.

At Overton Station, a manager drew an image of overlapping circles to represent their work systems, and when I showed it to a senior engineer from another station whose organizational chart typically showed boxes of functions and positions connected by reporting lines, he fumed, "If boxes became circles, functional boundaries would disappear and there would be chaos. The person inside a box has the job of talking across boxes. But he shouldn't get out of his box and join another. Each function has to specialize and should not overlap." What might be alternative ways of making order to meet the demands of this new slant on the culture of control? Specialists and cornerstones are of course material necessities and givens. Along this axis of meanings, conceptual priority belongs to the ways experts develop and use information, how they interpret the significance of uncertainties, and how they decide what to do. The practical effects of those meanings and actions for reducing uncertainties transcend functions: any scaffolding of responsibilities and accountabilities to support this axis would aim to maximize those effects. That is, instead of being defined in terms of inputs (functions, programs), operational activities would be understood in terms of their outputs (specific kinds of reliable, credible, actionable information and interpretation). The experiment leads to thinking as much about safety-significant relationships among various kinds of *knowledge* for reducing uncertainties as thinking about safety-significant components, processes, and their relationships. Rearraying functional and utilitarian concerns against an axis of meanings inserts other criteria for meeting those concerns, not least criteria that define the competencies and repertoires for enabling unimpeded information flow and reliable interpretation.

An axis of meanings heightens the importance of a singular element of a culture of control in risky technologies: the stress of maintaining control. Reducing uncertainties in itself can reduce stress. Stress in this industry is a fact of this lifeworld for all immersed in it—the physical, emotional, social, financial stress of the "significance and consequence" of most of what has to go on—and the stress of distractions from it. "Occupational health and safety" in the ongoing uncertainties of mergers and downsizing and the push for short outages carries additional and precise meanings for station experts, their families, and friends. "Fitness-for-duty" programs such as drug and alcohol screening and peer observations of fatigue and morale, necessary as they are, do not prevent stress: a culture of control includes controlling the stress inherent in reorganizations, schedules, backlogs, and cost-saving on top of that inherent in the work itself.

The functional division of labor and its hierarchy intensifies stresses when communication is blocked, interpretations are faulty, and mutual respect is lacking. To address Arrow Station's "silos," "pieces," and "owner" issues, a consulting group conducted workshops for managers on "team building" up and down the ladder and across departments. In a coming reorganization, all managers were to be "relieved of their positions" and would have to apply anew for a job. Handing over responsibilities would require unusually high levels of cooperation and coordination. Richard, an operations manager, talks about the workshops.

At the managerial level we have started meeting directly as a group with the consultants and had a two day away-from-site meeting Monday and Tuesday of this week. We have another one coming up in another week, where we get locked into a room. The last one was a barrier-breaking session, taking off the gloves and slugging each other bloody just to clear the air. Having the consultants there was worlds more effective than it would have been had they not been there. You can do a certain amount of building and bonding as the group is getting together, but we are all technocrats when you get right down to it. Some of us are technocrats with better soft skills than others, but none of us are at the level that the consultants are in terms of building organizational cohesiveness.

What kind of soft skills do they seem to be encouraging?

At this point the primary focus is on building channels of communication. There are some of us on that team that have worked together for a long time, but our relationship is built around butting heads until we finally agree. And there are some people who are very new to it.

So, it's becoming more negotiation and mediation?

Yes. And just communication, so issues don't reach the point where you have to butt heads.

Are you saying that these sort of standoffs are habitual here?

It's not the standoffs that are habitual. What's habitual is a lack of regular communication at the department head level. We started having meetings more frequently, which helps. We went through a long period where we were all so busy that we just never got together. But it's also got to get much more to, "We know this problem exists. Let's take a walk out and look at it together and then talk about it," dropping into each other's offices. We do some of that, but we all tend to play favorites and the contacts are not universal with everybody. And our offices are so scattered. I've talked with the director several times about putting the managers together to enhance communication. I'm probably in the worst shape. My office is so far away from everybody else's that it's a real effort for any of them just to be in my neighborhood—my office in a passageway in a service building that has nothing but my office in it. But it's situated to let me get to the control room quickly, not to get to another department head quickly.

Maybe you need two offices?

Another operations manager used to have two offices. When he was told he had to move, he kept his space but took a closet, basically, big enough for a desk, a lamp, and a telephone and established that as his field office.

"Control room" functions, in other words, often have little to do with an operations manager's contributions to and need for the exchange and interpretation of information.

An axis of meanings shifts the kind of problem it is to operate and manage a nuclear power plant. Getting the meanings of feedback signals right enough to prevent a next event is the crux of the matter for writing effective corrective actions no less than for handling any immediate issue. Reliable interpretation that allows for recovering quickly enough to prevent an event's worst consequences is essential: grasping the meanings of the signals of the initiating event at Three Mile Island took experts so long that they were unable to prevent a loss of cooling water large enough to uncover the core. Programs' self-assessments and operational trending analyses also provide signals. When those are uninterpreted or incorrectly interpreted, that can distort the basis of negotiations in the tradeoff quandary and lead to misguided decisions revealed later. Too little interpretation and too few actionable recommendations preceded the *Challenger* disaster: although an engineer's memo had earlier presented crucial o-ring data, he left them uninterpreted; uninflected, the memo carried no meaning for managers responsible for taking actions the data implied.[76] Following the attacks of 9/11/01, chunks of underinterpreted and unsythesized information about heightened terrorist activities turned out to have been long in the possession of the Federal Bureau of Investigation. Any one responsible for national security in its many forms is perforce working in another high-consequence enterprise, and, no differently, we rely on their discovery and interpretive capacities. They also live in a significance culture.

An axis of meanings acknowledges the centrality of ambiguities in the significance determination process: classifying events and adverse conditions begs for fulsome information and well-considered interpretation. An overactive parts template and a residual project template can block off doubt, discovery, and systemic understandings of events and near-misses. Checklists can readily "bucket" condition reports as "level 1's," which usually mandate reviews. "The level 2's are where the rub is," said an Arrow manager: their less obvious or immediate systemwide consequences are more uncertain and more difficult or time-consuming to assess.[77] Yet it is those "benign little transients" that can accumulate into events. To acknowledge these uncertainties would increase the frequency of imagining "unimagined" scenarios and specific significance and consequence analyses.[78]

An axis of meanings intensifies the importance of opening up the infrastructure of conundrums. Contradictions, dilemmas, and paradoxes left unexamined can be prime inhibitors to getting and exchanging information in a timely enough fashion. Chief among the contradictions is the blaming system, whether internal fingerpointing or external threats, when it inhibits information exchange and interpretation, especially about near-misses. Deniability to escape liability seems to account for some managerial silence about rationales for policy logics, and when those are also inaccessible to event reviewers, that can impede information flow and twist interpretation. Competition among nuclear utilities also keeps policy rationales secret. An axis of meanings makes apparent unexamined paradoxes within the institutional infrastructure of regulatory and civil law, insurance law, and competition.

An axis of meanings focuses attention on whatever inhibits information flow and interpretation, from the reluctant acknowledgment of newcomers' observations to unseemly preemptions of rank and specialty. For many years to come, streams of qualified newcomers will populate stations, as much to be educated as to be trained. Mentoring even now belongs in oldtimers' job descriptions and agendas of action items. Category systems ("nonnuclear") and turf "ownership" ("my system") can prescreen information and douse curiosity. Such impediments leaven the frustrations visible in rhetorical strategies needed or used: Ray should have, some said, "forced" or "sold" his concern with stem/disc separation; Paul couldn't convince Jack to put up the danger tape; to get help with a dicey decision, Vince's strategy is to "Try to get buy in. . . . Try to get people in on it." Again, standing behind "try" is "convince"—usually to "convince management," as in the Arrow Station team's repeated pleas: "Management needs to strongly reinforce . . . should hold face-to-face meetings . . . must demonstrate by word and deed." Information lies inert until interpreted. Turning it into reliable meanings depends on open speaking as well as on open listening.

An axis of meanings makes clear the ongoing role of reactor design and modifications in exacerbating uncertainties and the difficulty of getting equipment-based information about them. The design lays the bricks of each cornerstone, leaving to cross-cutting programs and to operations and maintenance the tasks of mortaring them into safe shutdown. But when design and modifications also brick up ready access to safety-critical components (a reactor vessel head) or leave identical components unmarked, that puts information about safety-critical conditions out of reach.

This thought experiment only appears to take a "giant leap" out of the box of functions onto a field of meanings. The pulse of this industry is where it has always been: in operational uncertainties, in the risks they hold, and in the kinds and quality of its experts' significance determination processes.

Into the Next Half-Century

This thought experiment or any other could serve a second purpose: to colonize what is now the wholly imaginary space to be occupied, some technologists tell us, by two heroic possibilities for reducing global warming. Worldwide, as of 2055, 1,000 to 1,500 nuclear reactors would have replaced current fleets and tripled their number.[79] Their design would reduce waste in a once-through fuel cycle to reduce the threat of plutonium proliferation. At about the same time, other experts say, fusion power reactors would have proven their mettle at capturing energy from burning plasma, now that basic science and development initiatives have been restarted.[80] Both technologies from their beginnings could be as grounded in foresight about their embeddedness in the world as in the dynamics of nuclear and plasma physics.

"The Future of Nuclear Power: An Interdisciplinary MIT Study" writes one of the scenarios for mid-century. Developed by eight faculty members at MIT and one at Harvard, led by MIT professors John Deutch and

Ernest Moniz, and published in 2003, the study estimates that new-generation reactors would provide 29 percent of electricity for the "developed world" (17 percent in 2000); 23 percent for the former Soviet Union (16 percent in 2000); and 11 percent in the "developing world" (2 percent in 2000).[81] Nuclear power is one of several options for meeting "future energy needs without emitting carbon dioxide (CO_2) and other atmospheric pollutants," all of which the authors believe should "be preserved," such as "renewables" and "increased efficiency." For the nuclear power option to take hold depends not only on "better economics, improved safety, successful waste management, and low proliferation risk," but also on whether "public policies place a significant value on electricity production that does not produce CO_2." For nuclear power to be competitive with fossil fuels, it would be necessary to increase taxes on their production and use or find "other ways of restricting carbon dioxide emissions."[82] Further, tripling the current number of reactors globally is necessary if nuclear power is to make "a significant contribution to dealing with the greenhouse gas problem."[83]

Four issues, the authors say, are responsible for the prospect of the nuclear industry's "stagnation and decline": costs; safety ("perceived adverse safety, environmental, and health effects" of both reactor safety and that of the fuel cycle); waste disposal ("unresolved challenges in long-term management of radioactive wastes"); and proliferation ("entails potential security risks" and the "current international safeguards regime is inadequate").[84] Moreover, public support is weak and "unlikely," the group's own survey finds, "without substantial improvements in costs and technology" and without greater public awareness of the "link between global warming, fossil fuel usage, and the need for low-carbon energy sources." The "carbon-free character of nuclear power, the major motivation for our study, does not appear to motivate the U.S. general public to prefer expansion of the nuclear option."[85]

To keep the nuclear option open, the study recommends government support for improving its "economic viability" with programs for subsidies, incentives, and R&D. In the near term these would culminate in "a small set of 'first mover' commercial nuclear plants to demonstrate cost and regulatory feasibility."[86] For all this and much more, the study recommends a major series of government R&D programs, including international collaboration, at an estimated cost of $450 million per year for the first five years and $520 million per year for the next five.[87]

On the safety of plant operations, the authors declare, "We do not believe there is a nuclear plant design that is totally risk free. In part this is due to technical possibilities; in part due to workforce issues. Safe operation requires effective regulation, a management committed to safety, and a skilled work force."[88] Pointing to the Davis-Besse event as "a failure on the part of the plant owners" and an NRC misstep, the authors observe that it "is still an open question whether the average performers in the industry have yet incorporated an effective safety culture into their conduct of business." "A major nuclear power initiative will not gain public confidence, if such failures [as Davis-Besse] occur."[89] They cite the need to improve "independent peer review" and "safety culture," on "the principle that the primary responsibility for safe operations . . . rests with the plant owners and operators." To realize the scenario in developed countries, "the rejuvenation of the entire workforce" is essential; in other countries the existing base, now "small or negligible," would have to grow.[90] The NRC "should adapt its inspection activities, reporting requirements, and enforcement actions to reflect the new incentives created by competitive generation markets." Aside from such mentions, the authors acknowledge, safety has not been addressed "as thoroughly as deserved," nor have they addressed the question of "the regulatory regime that provides the best incentive for safe operation."[91] Their R&D strategy includes a "near-term R&D program," government-funded, to "develop more fully the capabilities to improve methods for analyzing life-cycle health and safety impacts of fuel cycle facilities" and to "focus reactor development on options that can achieve enhanced safety standards and are deployable within a couple of decades." Those standards refer to reactor structures, systems, and components for safe shutdown. The authors propose that $50 million annually be devoted to this.[92]

New designs depend on public acceptance, agrees Michael W. Golay, professor of nuclear engineering at the Massachusetts Institute of Technology, writing in another forum. But, he asks, will that result from the better technology designers promise or from greater trust in those responsible for its operation? Any new designs, Golay says, will need to decrease the number of "alarming events" and reduce "mistrust" of those responsible for operations. While "passively safe" reactor designs reduce the risk of core damage, they do not also reduce the risk of "initiating events, occupational accidents and economic failures." "The need for trouble-free nuclear power plant operations has become widely recognized, but has not yet been translated into a requirement for technological innovation. Rather, improved operational performance has come to be viewed as a problem for the team operating the reactor," not as a problem amenable to "better hardware and support systems (including models for improved operational performance)."[93]

From the perspectives of an expanded concept of this industry's culture of control, "enhanced safety standards" and "an effective safety culture" would assume that technology design *includes* its operation with all that implies, within and beyond automation, for acknowledging the partnership of technical and contextual knowledge and of calculated, real-time, and policy logics. Research on reactor development, fission or fusion, would go hand in hand with studies to develop understandings of these logics' structure and dynamics and their part in events and nonevents, to inform *design*. In the nuclear power industry, the record shows that it and its regulator and the U.S. Department of Energy are unlikely to undertake or fund such original research. Yet "first-mover" plants will have already made expensive design commitments; trajectories of innovation once moving are unlikely to change course.[94]

No new generation of reactors can ignore the consequences of the anachronistic status of maintenance. Giving maintenance its due alone redefines the kind of problem designing and operating a nuclear power plant is, as well as the kind of problem operating fusion reactors is likely to be. New designs cannot be considered credible until also analyzed for the accessibility of equipment for inspection, testing, and repair at least risk to plant experts. Recall the comment of a senior manager: "It's difficult to say what a bad design is. A good design allows for easy maintenance. But the design for maintainability can't be expressed in a PRA." It seems to be time for PRAs to account for those risks (of hidden system information, of unisolable valves). That would go far to recognize the depth and breadth—and yes, the costs—of any culture of control in risky technologies and enterprises.

As determined as designers usually are to finesse most relationships between people and machines—to "get them out of the loop" in "passively safe" designs—designers' biases and fallibilities remain. Recall Bart's comments about a "new generation" of plants; before becoming a system engineer at Overton Station, he had been a design engineer at the company's corporate headquarters.

> Most definitely for the new generation of power plants, there needs to be a trial basis—hands-on work in the field to get appreciation for the maintenance work, the operations work, the performance testing that's done—the limitations that the *physical* plant has versus what it has in a designer's mind. That's been a major realization for me.

To develop new designs without also having analyzed the implications of and for their peopled operation perpetuates another anachronism, that of "throwing technology over the wall" to be caught by "the team operating the reactor," and by us. The history of nuclear power operations over the last half-century documents the economic and operational consequences of passing along responsibility for a hazardous technology's limitations even to "a management committed to safety" and "a skilled workforce." Although its calculated logics try to keep this technology true within itself, policy and real-time logics bind it to the world. To value equally the intellectual capital invested in technical and nontechnical ways of thinking and to analyze their systematic relationship throughout design and operation would be marks of this society's maturity on the way to mid-century. That becomes a model for thinking through fusion technology in all its phases, unless, of course, its experts get to this point first. In the meantime, it bears remembering that in the near future about five hundred commercial nuclear reactors, all "actively safe," will have remaining lifetimes ranging from several to forty years and that decommissioning, itself a new technology, brings its own kinds of uncertainties and risks.

To understand what it takes to operate and maintain a nuclear power plant means also to understand that a technology's imperfections and the uncertainties its operation introduces *are* "the technology," just as disconfirming findings in physics are "physical science." So is what experts do to reduce real-time risk as much "the technology" as are the design concepts originating it. This wider conception of "technology" as being far more than the sum of its parts calls into question claims that create the hierarchy of knowledge fabricating that wall between "design" and "operations."[95] In the case of high hazard technologies especially, risk assessments, part by part, assembly by assembly, become the premises of design. But these calculated logics, even with wide safety margins, obviously do not anticipate real-time risks. The record is sufficient to consider them among the many constraints that design by definition confronts. Design concepts uninformed by operational contexts cannot be called design; hubris comes to mind.

That and other claims in the culture of control have made more than walls: they have created the situation where most of the intellectual capital invested in hazardous technologies focuses on estimating the unreliability of parts and assemblies in hopes of maximizing reliability during operations. Least intellectual capital has been invested in understanding what it means for people to handle real-time risks with minimal consequences, some of which the design itself introduces. Once these technologies are out in the world—their reason for being, after all—the statistical arts and politics of risk estimation have no choice but to yield to other concepts and methods for preventing worst-case consequences and, no less important for modifications than for new designs, for understanding the etiology of those that occur or nearly occur and those that do not.

That imbalance raises questions for national and global institutions we rely on as stewards of our own and the planet's well-being. Not only the institutions through which risky technologies are designed, financed, insured, managed, and regulated, but no less, the institutions educating those who make and operate them. In testimony in June 2003 before the U.S. House of Representatives' Committee on Science, Daniel M. Kammen, professor of nuclear engineering and director of the Renewable and Appropriate Energy Laboratory at the University of California, Berkeley, voiced concern with "the overly insular nature of many departments and programs" in nuclear science and technology training. "Engineering programs generally are infamous for packing the schedules of their students so that they have little opportunity to diversify their education," pointing to the need for students to "broaden" their training with other kinds of engineering and with nonengineering courses. "This is absolutely critical to prevent 'in-breeding' and to challenge students and faculty to think in new, innovative ways."[96] A first benefit could be that they learn to recognize "folk theories" about "human error" and "root causes" when they see them.

A second is that they could participate in the "rejuvenation" of the system of claims that govern today's cultures of control. Those claims about the relationships between humans and machines, between models and reality, between ambiguity and certainty cannot, too often for comfort, anticipate or reduce risks unimagined or even already known, measurable and unmeasurable. Which of those claims to keep and to replace are questions for us all. For this century and its ever-increasing technological dependencies and for these times and their uncertainties, these are questions more urgently in need of attention than we have wanted.

• • • • •

Out in deep seas on a three-month mission aboard the Trident nuclear submarine *USS Wyoming*, 173 officers and crew are vulnerable to losing their capacity for depth perception for the duration. The length of one-and-a-half football fields, the submarine is so packed forward and aft with computers, equipment, and other people that for the men to see beyond their immediate surroundings they have to be standing in one narrow aisle 560 feet bow to stern between tubes holding the missiles and torpedoes all are hoping never to use.[97]

Maintaining the capacity for seeing in the round is a struggle of all specialists—technical, cultural, scientific. Refusing "tunnel vision" and keeping their sights on a multidimensional world is especially difficult for those in these complicated enterprises doing their professional best in environments focused on costs and obsessed with time. For those of us not there, if we are to understand what it takes for them and the technology to do their jobs of reducing risks, our jobs are to keep the world in sight.

Senior Management Group
at Overton Station

IN THIS STATION's public documents, managers' biographies cite "industry experience" ahead of formal educaton. Most managers are in the same age range; those who attended college finished their undergraduate degrees between 1969 and 1979; during the 1980s and the late 1990s, others earned external degrees, certificates from executive management courses, or community college associate degrees while working or on company-sponsored leave. Senior managers coming into the industry from the nuclear navy began their military service in the mid-to-late 1960s and left it between the early and late 1970s. Generally, most management positions are filled by white men, except for managers of human resources and industrial safety, some of whom are likely to be persons of color and/or women.

Vice/president nuclear: Responsible for utility's nuclear program. Some stations and just about all utilities have a man in this position, who is usually also a vice-president who serves on the board of directors as well (also sometimes called "chief nuclear officer").

> Industry experience: management positions at an operating plant, contractor during construction of Overton and/or other plants, employee of nuclear engineering firm in design engineering, professional engineer license.
> Education: B.S. in mechanical engineering, business school "advanced management program," INPO senior executive program.

Station manager: Responsible for all aspects of operation, maintenance, chemistry, health physics, including budgets and personnel matters for entire station staff.

> Industry experience: assistant station manager, assistant "station superintendent" at a fossil plant, assistant engineer, lieutenant in U.S. Navy.
> Education: B.S. engineering (U.S. Naval Academy), MBA, INPO senior management program, senior reactor operator license (held for two years)

Assistant station manager: Takes on station manager's duties in his absence. Assists in planning, scheduling, coordination, and direction of station employees activities.

Industry experience: U.S. Navy, engine room supervisor, nuclear power station auxiliary operator, control room operator, shift superintendent, assistant operations manager, operations manager, nuclear safety and oversight manager, technical support manager.

Education: B.S. liberal studies, associate degree, industrial engineering.

Operations manager: Responsible for all licensed activities, senior licensed person for the station, member of operating review committee, resource review committee, management review team.

Work experience: U.S. Navy; nuclear power station: nuclear systems operator, control room operator, unit shift supervisor, shift superintendent, assistant operations manager.

Education: U.S. Navy: electricians mate school, nuclear power school, nuclear power prototype school; B.S. external degree, M.S. in management, external degree.

Maintenance manager: Responsible for maintenance functions and associated staff (160 people): corrective and preventive maintenance, equipment reliability, plant housekeeping, corrective action support, staff development, procedure maintenance, continuous improvements, cost-effectiveness.

Industry experience: Engineering consulting firm startup test engineer; nuclear power plant: startup engineer/supervisor, test group manager, planning, scheduling, and outage manager.

Education: B.S. marine engineering, senior reactor operator license (one year).

Technical support manager: Responsible for managing system and component engineering (45 people).

Industry experience: Naval service; nuclear power plant: system engineer, supervisor maintenance engineering, manager condition-based maintenance, manager component engineering.

Education: B.S. marine engineering.

Chemistry and health physics manager: Responsible for direction of chemistry, radiation protection, and radioactive waste programs.

Work experience: Naval reactors program: radiological controls technician; national laboratory: senior health physics technician; nuclear power plants: chemistry and health physics technician, chemist, chemistry department supervisor.

Education: B.S. chemistry, INPO senior nuclear plant management course.

Nuclear engineering manager: Directs, plans, and manages activities of electrical and mechanical engineering, technical support engineering, engineering performance departments activities: engineering, design, configuration management.

> Work experience: engineering firm: mechanical engineer; state agency: lead mechanical/nuclear engineer; consulting firm: supervising engineer; nuclear power plant: engineering manager.
> Education: B.S. nuclear engineering; M.S. mechanical/nuclear engineering.

Support services manager: Responsible for capital construction, labor relations, backfit-outage support, facilities maintenance, purchasing, inventory, records management, security, telecommunications and information management.

> Work experience: nuclear power station: director of construction, director of corporate services, director of emergency preparedness and community relations.
> Education: B.S. aerospace technology; MBA; MIT/INPO reactor technology program.

Environmental, government, community relations manager: Coordinates activities relating to environmental compliance, interface with state and federal regulatory agencies (not NRC), emergency preparedness, community relations, decommissioning.

> Work experience: engineering consulting firms; nuclear power station: emergency preparedness manager, licensing manager.
> Education: B.S. engineering, M.S. mechanical engineering.

Nuclear oversight manager: compliance with NRC regulations, oversight activities on plant capacity and availability and resource allocations (35 people).

> Work experience: U.S. Navy; engineering consulting firm: quality assurance manager, manager engineering assurance, project quality assurance; nuclear power plant: corporate quality assurance manager/speakout manager, quality assurance manager.
> Education: B.S. mathematics, U.S. Naval Academy, navy nuclear power school and prototype training.

Human resources manager: Responsible for implementing utility's human resources programs, including staffing, compensation administration, EEO/Affirmative Action, and HR-related policies, oversees coordination of on-site employee assistance program and medical program.

> Work experience: utility: personnel assistant; nuclear power station: employment coordinator.
> Education: B.S. business administration.

Appendix Two

Nuclear Power Plant Modes of Operation or Shutdown

The physical position of the reactor mode switch defines six nuclear power plant operating modes. A plant's operating license, including its technical specifications, is based on these six operating states:

Mode 6–Refueling

The reactor coolant is at atmospheric pressure with a temperature of less than 140°F. At least one bolt holding the reactor vessel head to the reactor is loosened.

Mode 5–Cold Shutdown

The reactor core is sub-critical, or not sustaining a nuclear chain reaction. The reactor coolant temperature is less than or equal to 200°F.

Mode 4–Hot Shutdown

The reactor core is sub-critical, or not sustaining a nuclear chain reaction. The reactor coolant temperature is between 200°F and 350°F.

Mode 3–Hot Standby

The reactor core is sub-critical, or not sustaining a nuclear chain reaction. The reactor coolant temperature is over 350°F.

Mode 2–Startup

The reactor core is either sub-critical (i.e., not sustaining a nuclear chain reaction) or is critical (i.e., sustaining a nuclear chain reaction) with its output less than or equal to 5 percent of the licensed power level.

Mode 1–Power Operation

The reactor core is sustaining a nuclear chain reaction with its output ranging between 5 and 100 percent of the licensed power level. The turbine/generator will typically be placed in service when the reactor power level reaches 15 to 20 percent of the licensed power level.

Several other plant conditions supplement the operating states specifically linked to the reactor mode switch position. For example:

Core off-load (or defueled)

All of the reactor core's fuel assemblies have been taken out of the reactor vessel and moved to the spent fuel pool. Depending on the reactor, the number of fuel assemblies off-loaded range from 121 to 800.

Planned transients

A planned transient is the manual change in power level of the reactor core, such as increases during startup and decreases for testing and maintenance.

Unplanned transients

An unplanned transient is the automatic or manual change in power level of the reactor core due to human error or equipment malfunction. The reactor power level can increase, such as in response to a loss of a feedwater heater. The reactor power level may also decrease, such as in response to a loss of offsite power.

Stretch out (also known as "coast down")

Nuclear power plants are refueled once every 18 to 24 months. Toward the end of an operating cycle, the burnable fuel left in the reactor core may be insufficient to permit the plant to reach 100 percent of its licensed output. Plant owners may "stretch out" the operating cycle and allow the reactor core to "coast down" into a refueling outage. The power output of the reactor core drops daily as the nuclear fuel is consumed until being shut down for refueling.

Appendix Three

Study Description

Constance Perin, Ph.D.
National Science Foundation Award #9730605
"Hard" and "Soft" Knowledge in High-Hazard Industries

As a cultural anthropologist, my particular interest is in work systems and the cultural dimensions of efficiency and productivity. My main goal in this study is to develop criteria for a vocabulary or language system that would help to bridge these different ways of viewing organizational and individual behaviors—"hard" being a perspective that seeks "measures" and quantitative data, "soft," a perspective that looks to experience, best practices, policy. I hope to learn what prevents hard and soft knowledge from coming together analytically and practically, as well as what makes their combination possible. Ultimately, I hope to learn more about the reasons why some kinds of operating issues appear to be chronic and why it may be difficult to sustain improvements, especially those recommended by corrective action programs.

There are several questions I want to explore by reading documents of various kinds and interviewing plant staff members.

- What are the conditions under which the understandings and knowledge gained from operating experience, from incident analysis, and from organizational studies blend with the knowledge base of engineering and management specialties?
- What kinds of evidence are credited when decisions are being made about next steps?
- What kinds of corrective actions incorporate both "hard" and "soft" knowledge?

In accordance with National Science Foundation requirements, I will ask each person I interview to read and sign a statement, which I also sign, in which I promise not to reveal their identity and to provide them with feedback about my work.

Notes

Preface
The Culture of Control

1. MacLachlan 2003a, 1. As another expression of the meeting's theme, WANO's staff described a program to broadcast periodically to its members the details of "sentinel events" illustrating "common pitfalls," or what the industry understands as "cultural problems": "acceptance of degraded conditions; 'perceived' undue production pressures; senior management focused on compliance with license conditions and/or distracted by other duties; failure to be self-critical; organizational oversight weaknesses, notably insufficient independence of the oversight function; and 'the most deadly of all, a belief that plant performance was good' . . . [leading to] complacency and 'self-induced isolation' " (MacLachlan 2003b, 8).

2. MacLachlan 2003a, 1.

3. Nor are such failings new to those who operate this and other high hazard technologies or to those studying them. Here is one compilation from accident inquiries in aerospace, civil aviation, chemical processing, nuclear power, radiology:

> disbelief that the accident could ever occur, belief in component independence, over-reliance on component redundancies, inadequate rehearsal of recovery scenarios, neglect of clear warnings from other accidents, budget pressures, morale problems, schedule pressures, irregularities in documentation and certification procedures, flaws in materials or design, lack of data trend analysis, no independent verification of safety practices, clogged communication lines, gradual degradation of hazard analysis and follow-up programs, technical changes not reviewed or communicated, lack of disaster plans, assumptions that risk decreases over time, low priority to safety resources, inadequate supervision of shift turnovers and surveillance procedures, no forum for employees' safety concerns, corporate boards that shortchange engineers' budgets for preventive devices. (After Leveson 1995, 515–648; see also Ontario Hydro 1997)

4. See my acknowledgments for further details.

5. A "loosely-knit group of performance improvement professionals" in the United States and Canada began in 1994 to conduct annual workshops "to facilitate sharing of information and best practices" on "human performance, root cause, and trending" activities. Between 1997 and 2002, plants voluntarily responded to occasional questionnaires about their station's systems for identifying problematic conditions, analyzing events, and developing recommendations for changes. In 1999, for example, 14 plants reported 30–40 root cause event analyses in 1997, 40–50 in 1998, 21–30 in 1999 (HPRCT Business League 1999; see also Nuclear Energy Institute 2001). In 2000, responses from 62 plants range from a

low of 3 root cause analyses to a high of 200, and for 2001, a low of 3 and a high of 75 (some data are at HPRCT Business League 2001; personal communication 2002.) LICENSEE EVENT REPORTS (LERs) are a class of reports of problematic conditions that must be reported to the NRC; not all LERs are license violations.

6. U.S. Nuclear Regulatory Commission 2001c, iii. See the further analysis in U.S. Nuclear Regulatory Commission 2002f, xii.

7. U.S. Nuclear Regulatory Commission 2002f, xii, 8–12.

8. Columbia Accident Investigation Board 2003.

9. The Royal Society 1992, 161–62, 181.

10. This work represents a continuation of my larger project, namely to provide sustained demonstrations of the active role of assumptions, beliefs, and values in contemporary social and economic institutions, largely by examining relationships, or lack of them, among specialists' concepts and knowledge. See entries in the bibliography. See Sahlins 1976.

11. Nuclear Energy Institute 2003, 8, 9, 10, 16. Details appear in chapter 6.

12. The unit "under construction" in the United States refers to the licensed but inoperable unit at the Browns Ferry nuclear station in North Alabama owned by the Tennessee Valley Authority. Unit 1 has been on "administrative hold" since 1985, but not defueled. As of May 2002, work began to return it to service in 2007, at a cost of between $1.7 and $1.8 billion (Tennessee Valley Authority 2002).

13. World Nuclear Association 2004a and 2004b. The total of U.S. "licensed nuclear reactors" is 104; until Browns Ferry comes back on line, 103 reactors are operating. In 56 countries, there are 284 research reactors (World Nuclear Association 2004c).

14. "Capacity factor is the ratio of electricity generated to the amount of energy that could have been generated" (U.S. Nuclear Regulatory Commission 2004, 27).

15. Toulmin 1990, 179–80; italics in original.

Chapter One
Complexities in Control

1. Rees 1994, 14.

2. In Rees 1994, 190; see also Pool 1997, 272. The French utility, Electricité de France (EDF), whose fleet of plants is second in size to that of the United States, also did not begin to shift its understandings until after the accident at Three Mile Island (TMI) in 1979. From 1977 to 1982, according to Christophe Roux-Dufort and Emmanuel Metais at the EDHEC Graduate School of Management in Lille, its "technocratic culture" continued to focus on "technical considerations" alone, only later widening, through about 1988, to include the "human factors" that TMI analyses highlighted. Executives brought into corporate offices a group consisting "almost exclusively" of outside "sociologists, ergonomists, psychologists, and specialists in communications," who analyzed plant incidents as "consultants" from headquarters. After the Chernobyl accident in 1986, from 1988 to 1995 the construct "safety culture" began to take hold, but not directly

because of that accident: Russian plant designs, EDF experts believed, were not comparable. Only after other analyses of that accident began to emphasize "certain values, behavior, and objectives" and the "devotion and responsibility of operators" did EDF extend the human factors initiative to emphasize wider self-analyses of incidents by plant experts themselves (Roux-Dufort and Metais 1999, 118–26).

3. Two books published in 1997 examine the institutional and economic contexts of those years. In *Beyond Engineering: How Society Shapes Technology* Robert Pool, science writer, reconsiders what he had seen as a "line between technical and nontechnical, which had at first seemed so clear but slowly dissolved [as I] came to see the development of nuclear power as a collaboration—albeit an unwitting and often uncomfortable one between engineers and the larger society" (1997, 5–6). In his book, *Too Cheap to Meter: An Economic and Philosophical Analysis of the Nuclear Dream*, Steven Mark Cohn, economics professor at Knox College, recounts the interplay of government and industry between 1950 and 1970 during their collaborations in developing strategies and policies for financing, technical analysis, and risk assessment, and follows the story of public costs and private returns on investment into the U.S. industry's contraction between 1975 and 1995. Cohn's book ends with an economic analysis of the relationship between global warming issues and nuclear power's competitive position (Cohn 1997). Documenting the industry's earlier history are works by Balogh 1991; Jasper 1990; Rees 1994. Two histories of the beginnings of the Nuclear Regulatory Commission are Walker 1992; Mazuzan and Walker 1984. Among book-length studies of citizen protest and the history of particular plants are Nelkin 1971, 1982, and Aron 1997. A comprehensive text on the design and operation of commercial nuclear power plants is Ramsey and Modarres 1998.

4. The phrase belongs to Zev Lanir, a social psychologist specializing in decision making processes (Lanir 1986). Three Mile Island was a surprise, however, only because information about two earlier near-misses under similar circumstances had not been widely circulated (in 1974 in Switzerland and in 1977 in Ohio). See Snook 2000, 214–18 for a discussion of an unacknowledged near-miss with many of the same conditions present as those in the friendly-fire shootdown of U.S. Black Hawk helicopters in 1991. The Chernobyl accident in 1986 seems to have been more significant to Europe and Asia than to the United States, not only because of their regions' proximity to airborne radioactivity, but also because protective designs on Russian-made reactors are different from the containments required for all American commercial reactors. In his study of "nuclear politics" in the United States, France, and Sweden, James M. Jasper observes: "American nuclear experts reacted [to Chernobyl] in the same unhelpful way that French nucleocrats had reacted to TMI: 'It couldn't happen here.' Perhaps an identical accident could not, but many other, equally devastating accidents are possible and likely, since any reactor is a fragile and dangerous system" (1990, 213–14).

5. On September 16, 1954, Admiral Lewis L. Strauss, then chairman of the U.S. Atomic Energy Commission, whose mandate was to promote as well as oversee the industry, had made the industry's most famous promise: "It is not too much to expect that our children will enjoy electrical energy in their homes too cheap

to meter." Speaking at a meeting of the National Association of Science Writers, Strauss was talking, however, not about energy from nuclear fission but about the long-range prospects of nuclear fusion (Ford 1982, 50). Even so, the phrase took on a life of its own when the Atomic Energy Commission forecast in 1967 that 1,000 nuclear plants would be on line in the United States by 2000. In an article first appearing in a 1955 *Fortune* magazine series looking ahead to 1980, John von Neumann, professor at the Institute of Advanced Sciences, participant in the Manhattan Project, and, in that same year, appointed to the Atomic Energy Commission, wrote of "free energy":

> fission is not nature's normal way of releasing nuclear energy. In the long run, systematic industrial exploitation . . . may shift reliance onto other and still more abundant modes. Again, reactors have been bound thus far to the traditional heat-steam-generator-electricity cycle, just as automobiles were at first constructed to look like buggies. It is likely that we shall gradually develop procedures more naturally and effectively adjusted to the new source of energy, abandoning the conventional kinks and detours inherited from chemical-fuel processes. Consequently, a few decades hence energy may be free—just like the unmetered air—with coal and oil used mainly as raw materials for organic chemical synthesis. . . . [The] 'natural' sites for [nuclear reactions] are entire stars (von Neumann 1956, 37).

6. Balogh 1991; Cohn 1997, 47–48; Gilinsky 1991, 1992; Pool 1997, 228–31.

7. U.S. Department of Energy 2002.

8. The American Nuclear Society is a not-for-profit, international, scientific and educational organization with a membership of about 11,000 engineers, scientists, administrators, and educators in public and private institutions.

9. Verna 1994, 32–33.

10. Run-to-failure was the rule of thumb among paper mill owners in early modern France into the eighteenth century. Owners systematically ignored warning signs of wear and tear for as long as possible; brief shutdowns and patches would suffice until production levels could no longer be sustained. Reynard 1999.

11. Petryna 1995, 2002; see also Liberatore 1999.

12. Pool 1997, 303.

13. Nuclear Energy Institute 1994, III-12.

14. Nuclear Energy Institute 1994, II-5.

15. Fertel 2001. NEI represents nearly 275 companies, including every U.S. utility licensed to operate a commercial nuclear reactor, their suppliers, fuel fabrication facilities, architectural and engineering firms, law firms, radiopharmaceutical companies, research laboratories, universities, and international nuclear organizations. The groups consolidating into NEI were the Atomic Industrial Forum, U.S. Council on Energy Awareness, the Nuclear Power Oversight Committee, and the Nuclear Management and Resources Council. The NEI also conducts benchmarking studies and related programs for maximizing operating efficiencies. NEI activities and position papers are available at http://www.nei.org.

16. Bier et al, 2003, 214.

17. The 1992 Energy Act also included provisions changing various aspects of nuclear plant regulation and nuclear waste management, as well as provisions

supporting advanced reactor research. U.S. electric utilities' monopolistic practices were limited in the late 1970s by the Public Utilities Regulatory Policies Act, but the extended absence of an "oil crisis" and passage of the Energy Policy Act of 1992 largely account for the precarious financial situations of some nuclear utilities and the spate of mergers and acquisitions throughout the 1990s. While the costs of fuel are lower in nuclear power production compared to other methods of producing electricity, labor costs are considerably higher. In 1990, coal plant production costs were 76 percent for fuel, 17 percent for direct labor, and 7 percent other; for nuclear units, production costs were 31 percent fuel, 55 percent direct labor, and 14 percent other. *Nuclear News* 1993, 26.

18. Nuclear Energy Institute 2002; U.S. Nuclear Regulatory Commission 2004b.

19. In 1993, the American Nuclear Society (ANS) conducted a three-day international workshop on the coming competition for nuclear executives, plant managers and other specialists, and industry consultants, including talks by the then-chair of the NRC, a Wall Street analyst, utility executives, among others. According to one of its organizers, one impetus for the workshop was the difficulty of getting utilities to share strategies and data with peers. As members of the Organization and Management Study Group in the MIT International Program on Enhanced Nuclear Power Plant Safety, John S. Carroll, Alfred A. Marcus, and I were invited to present early findings from our studies as well as to structure the discussions to maximize exchanges among the 60 participants. Carroll and Perin 1995; Tomkiewicz 1993. Under ANS auspices, dozens of such self-organized workshops and conferences on scientific, technical, and industry issues occur annually.

20. At Overton Nuclear Power Station, about 360 employees hold managerial jobs, 100–150 are in supervisory positions, and 540 are technicians, nonsupervisory employees, and clerks, mostly nonsalaried employees and, by federal law, eligible for overtime pay. Some belong to the International Brotherhood of Electrical Workers (IBEW), a unit of the AFL-CIO, which claims 15,000 members at 66 percent of U.S. nuclear generating stations; about 2,200 at 7 operating stations belong to the Utility Workers of America (UWA). The Nuclear Energy Institute (NEI) backs up the industry's policy of "union avoidance" with a program of information and training for station and utility managers. As of 2002, the average complement at single-unit stations is about 850 employees. *Nuclear News* 2002, 16.

21. Science and Technology Agency 1999. In 1964, the only previous criticality accident occurred at a commercial fuel plant in the United States, resulting in one death. Other criticality incidents in U.S. and Russian military plants and laboratories have been reported. Uranium Research Centre 2002b.

22. Hibbs 2002; MacLachlan 2003a.

23. U.S. Nuclear Regulatory Commission 2002b, v.

24. Nucleonics Week 2002; Uranium Information Centre 2003. The International Nuclear Event Scale (INES) uses these categories: major accident 7; serious accident 6; accident with off-site risk 5; accident without significant off-site risk 4; serious incident 3; incident 2; anomaly 1. This fact sheet gives these "examples of classified nuclear events:

The 1986 accident at the Chernobyl nuclear power plant in the Soviet Union (now in the Ukraine) had widespread environmental and human health effects. It is thus classified as Level 7.

The 1957 accident at the Kyshtym reprocessing plant in the Soviet Union (now in Russia) led to a large off-site release. Emergency measures including evacuation of the population were taken to limit serious health effects. Based on the off-site impact of this event it is classified as Level 6.

The 1957 accident at the air-cooled graphite reactor pile at Windscale (now Sellafield) facility in the United Kingdom involved an external release of radioactive fission products. Based on the off-site impact, it is classified as Level 5.

The 1979 accident at Three Mile Island in the United States resulted in a severely damaged reactor core. The off-site release of radioactivity was very limited. The event is classified as Level 5, based on the on-site impact.

The 1973 accident at the Windscale reprocessing plant in the United Kingdom (now Sellafield) involved a release of radioactive material into a plant operating area as a result of an exothermic reaction in a process vessel. It is classified as Level 4, based on the on-site impact.

The 1980 accident at the Saint-Laurent nuclear power plant in France resulted in partial damage to the reactor core, but there was no external release of radioactivity. It is classified as Level 4, based on the on-site impact.

The 1983 accident at the RA-2 critical assembly in Buenos Aires, Argentina, an accidental power excursion due to nonobservance of safety rules during a core modification sequence, resulted in the death of the operator, who was probably 3 or 4 metres away. Assessments of the doses absorbed by the victim indicate 21 Gy for the gamma dose together with 22 Gy for the neutron dose. The event is classified as Level 4, based on the on-site impact.

The 1989 incident at the Vandellos nuclear power plant in Spain did not result in an external release of radioactivity, nor was there damage to the reactor core or contamination on site. However, the damage to the plant's safety systems due to fire degraded the defence-in-depth significantly. The event is classified as Level 3, based on the defence-in-depth criterion.

The vast majority of reported events are found to be below Level 3. Although no examples of these events are given here, countries using the Scale may individually wish to provide examples of events at these lower levels." IAEA 2003.

25. Union of Concerned Scientists 2002, 1.

26. *Nuclear News* 1999, 23. Team inspections also occur periodically, such as a biennial engineering and design inspection (400 hours) and a fire protection inspection every three years (200 hours). The NRC has two resident inspectors for each unit at each station; other inspectors with particular specialties are available from regional offices. Utilities pay for oversight inspections (about $150 per hour for one NRC inspector's time); that is in addition to about $3 million annually per reactor for license fees, which are the statutory sources of the NRC's total budget. Authorized by and reporting only to the U.S. Congress, the commission's budget in 2002 was about $560 million; reactor fees account for 73 percent of the 100 percent budget that federal recovery law requires. Of its "personnel ceiling" of 2,842 for 2002, about 52 percent work in nuclear reactor safety as

inspectors, researchers, and administrators (U.S. Nuclear Regulatory Commission 2002e, 14, 17).

27. Other license conditions define standards for, among others, the location of the reactor on the site, fuel handling, nuclear waste storage, emergency evacuation. To shut down a reactor, licensed operators insert control rods to halt the chain reaction. A quick or immediate shutdown, manual or automatic, is usually called a TRIP in pressurized water reactors and a SCRAM in boiling water reactors. Whether automatic or manual, gradual or immediate, trips and scrams are UNPLANNED OR FORCED SHUTDOWNS, usually required when an unexpected interaction or equipment glitch threatens to impair safety-significant systems or their availability. PLANNED OUTAGES for major equipment repairs and REFUELING OUTAGES are scheduled months, sometimes years, in advance. In between outages, to make certain tests or repairs possible, operators moderate the chain reaction to lower the level of power output. Appendix 2 lists typical plant modes.

28. Center for Strategic and International Studies 1999, 16. An interdisciplinary working group and steering committee in CSIS' Energy and National Security group produced this report, which previews the central issues the new oversight regime addresses. John F. Ahearne, former chairman of the Nuclear Regulatory Commission and director of Sigma Xi's Program in Research Ethics, chaired the group, which included House and Senate members and their staffs, utility executives, two Nuclear Regulatory Commissioners, the Natural Resources Defense Council, Resources for the Future, the Union of Concerned Scientists, the Nuclear Energy Institute, the American Nuclear Society, reactor vendors, the U.S. Department of Energy, the Electric Power Research Institute, The Atlantic Council, and officials of the state of Connecticut.

29. INPO maintains strict control over information about all of its activities. Only a few of INPO's experts have been accessible throughout the years of my research, and that rarely and under limitations. When writing the only book to examine INPO's activities, *Hostages of Each Other: The Transformation of Nuclear Safety Since Three Mile Island* (1994), Joseph V. Rees, political scientist at Virginia Polytechnic Institute and State University, had to seek other sources for establishing his conclusion that INPO is a "unifying institution" and source of a unique self-regulating industrial "community" (Rees 1994, 176). After publication, INPO offered cooperation on his further studies. Personal communication.

30. Riccio and Freedman 1993. In 1984, Public Citizen sued under the Freedom of Information Act for the NRC to release its INPO documents. After eight years in the courts, the U.S. Court of Appeals upheld INPO's right to confidentiality.

31. Because Congress created the NRC, it alone has oversight over its activities; U.S. Code of Federal Regulations 1974. In 1997 the NRC's effectiveness in staying ahead of problems became the concern of Senators Joseph L. Lieberman and Joseph R. Biden, Jr., who requested the U.S. General Accounting Office (GAO), Congress's oversight arm, to study how the NRC "defines nuclear safety, measures and monitors the safety condition of nuclear plants, and uses its knowledge of safety conditions to ensure [their] safety." The 1997 GAO report examines NRC's activities in three plants with a history of poor performance. The study concludes, among other things:

Identifying and correcting safety deficiencies are among the licensees' most important safety responsibilities and a major focus of NRC's inspection program. Yet NRC allows licensees repeated opportunities to correct their safety problems, often waiting for a significant problem or series of events to occur at a plant before taking tough enforcement action. General Accounting Office 1997, 10

32. Appendix B to Part 50, 10CFR, section I Organization. U.S. Code of Federal Regulations 1970.

The persons and organizations performing quality assurance functions shall have sufficient authority and organizational freedom to identify quality problems; to initiate, recommend, or provide solutions; and to verify implementation of solutions. Such persons and organizations performing quality assurance functions shall report to a management level such that this required authority and organizational freedom, including sufficient independence from cost and schedule when opposed to safety considerations, are provided. Because of the many variables involved, such as the number of personnel, the type of activity being performed, and the location or locations where activities are performed, the organizational structure for executing the quality assurance program may take various forms provided that the persons and organizations assigned the quality assurance functions have this required authority and organizational freedom. Irrespective of the organizational structure, the individual(s) assigned the responsibility for assuring effective execution of any portion of the quality assurance program at any location where activities subject to this appendix are being performed shall have direct access to such levels of management as may be necessary to perform this function.

33. A literature in the social and behavioral sciences on the organizational characteristics associated with accidents and with risky system in operation debates two approaches. One finds that because they are so complex socially and technically, they ultimately harbor the seeds of their own failures—the thesis of Charles Perrow's 1984 book, *Normal Accidents*; the other says that while that is true, risky technologies fail so infrequently that that is what needs to be explained—known as "high reliability theory." From field studies (nuclear power plants, aircraft carriers, air traffic control, the marine industry), this group concludes, among other things, that these enterprises both centralize and localize authority, engage in incessant training, follow procedures, offer incentives for reporting errors and learning from mistakes, maintain high levels of technical competency, value safety on a par with production, and are continuously improving (e.g., LaPorte 1994a, 1994b, 2001; LaPorte, Roberts, and Rochlin 1989; Schulman 1989, 1993a, 1993b). Scott Sagan's book *The Limits of Safety* (1993) was the first of several empirical studies to compare "normal accident" and "high reliability" theories. In his study of near-misses in the U.S. weapons complex, Sagan finds that conflicts among military units over influence, careers, and recognition inserts layers into an already layered technical system, which relies on the redundancy principle. Despite the fact that military values and structures align with many of those of high reliability theory, Sagan finds that the social and cul-

tural opacity and the resulting difficulties in information exchange and open communication point to the validity of normal accident theory for explaining more about the sources of near-misses than does the absence of discipline and rule-following, for example. In 1996, Diane Vaughan's study, *The Challenger Launch Decision: Risky Technology, Culture, and Deviance at NASA*, examined the interplay of engineering and bureaucratic norms with reference to both approaches. In his study of the 1991 accidental shootdown of U.S. Black Hawk helicopters over Northern Iraq published in 2000, Scott Snook examines the specific circumstances in light of those other approaches to arrive at his analyses of the individual, group, and organizational "levels" contributing to the tragedy (Snook 2000, especially pp. 218–26).

In his second edition of *Normal Accidents* (1999), Perrow's new Afterword surveys a "vast outpouring of books and articles dealing with the issue of accidents and high-risk systems," concluding that "while we do not seem to have made any progress in preventing accidents, we have made great progress in interpreting them." Perrow comments on those studies and elaborates his theory with a call for more research to distinguish the characteristics of systems prone to be "error-avoiding," "error-inducing," and "error-neutral" (Perrow 1999, 371–72). Nuclear power remains on his list of those that are "error-inducing." For the principals' debate of the finer points of their positions, see the journal symposium, "Systems, Organizations and the Limits of Safety" (LaPorte and Rochlin 1994; LaPorte 1994a; Perrow 1994a; Sagan 1994).

Risk Assessment: The Human Dimension by Nick W. Hurst, who was, before his early death, a research chemist on the Laboratory staff of the U.K. regulator, the Health and Safety Executive, is an industry-originated study that engages with that literature; to my knowledge, no parallel study appears in the professional and research literature on the nuclear power industry. Hurst's observations, from on-site assessments at operating chemical process facilities, lead him to find both relevant. Instead of framing them as "pessimistic" and "optimistic," which some commentators on this literature do, Hurst sees high reliability theory as "ideal" and normal accident theory as "real." "Ideal world organisations" depend on several "theories of idealness": high reliability theory, strong safety culture, the system paradigm, successful health and safety management. "Real world organisations" depend on "theories of the 'real' world: normal accidents, system failures, latent failures. . . . The discrepancies between [them] are what drive the faults and problems within real organisations." Differences between the two approaches, I suggest, also qualify as being "constitutive" and "regulative": both assume given "conditions" on the one hand, and malleable "states" on the other. My work speaks to both approaches in that those responsible for understanding their own systems are providing most of the data: because the characteristics producing their usual "high reliability" have somehow failed them, they try to understand systemic preconditions that set up the failures.

34. The thresholds and standards calculated into each reactor's DESIGN BASIS reappear as TECHNICAL SPECIFICATIONS that define the operational conditions required to support safe shutdown. These include LIMITING CONDITIONS OF OPERATIONS that define allowable durations of repair or testing when backup systems can remain inoperable. These also control employees' exposures to radiation,

depending on the work tasks, under the evolving principle of "As Low As Reasonably Achievable" (ALARA). Almost no activity occurs without a work order written in accordance with the technical specifications, nor does any task, administrative or technical, occur without a written procedure to guide it. There are about 4,000 written procedures at Overton Station, for example; not following a safety-related procedure can be a license violation. Procedures are often revised, or need to be revised; yes, there are procedures for doing that.

35. Perrow 1986, 1999; Sagan 1993, 1994.

36. In addition, OFF-NORMAL conditions can put a unit beyond its licensed design basis. Over a three-year period, at a time when 111 reactors were licensed in the United States, operators at 102 plants reported a total of over 500 instances of operating outside the conditions specified in their license (Wald 1999, A14, which cites an analysis of NRC documents by James Riccio of Critical Mass, a citizen oversight group). These frequencies are low (an average of five incidents per plant), but the demands they make on the skill and judgment that configuration control requires are high. Averages are misleading, however, in this industry: the 1997 GAO report cited earlier found that each of the three problem plants had been allowed for periods of years to operate outside their design basis, after reporting their condition to the NRC (U.S. General Accounting Office 1997, 37, 48, 59).

37. Hannaman and Singh 1993.

38. Vaurio 1998, 336.

39. Fourest 2000, 1, 2, 6. In his 1990 book, *Nuclear Politics*, Jasper says: "Because nuclear energy is still controversial in the United States, the nuclear industry pretends for strategic reasons that nuclear energy is a perfectly safe energy source, continually underestimating the potential for serious accidents. The French nuclear industry has full government support, which allows it to admit there are serious risks" (Jasper 1990, 260).

40. After that symptom had become known worldwide, the NRC's task force said, "NRC agreed to review the safety assessments conducted by the PWR [pressurized water reactors] owners groups"—primarily utility engineers who confer about such issues, often also involving the vendors. The U.S. owners group concluded that nozzle cracking "was improbable and boric acid attack of the [reactor head], if it were to occur, would be discovered through boric acid walkdown inspections well before safety margins would be compromised. In a safety evaluation dated November 19, 1993, the NRC agreed with this assessment, but reserved judgment regarding . . . cracking on a case-by-case basis" (U.S. Nuclear Regulatory Commission 2002b, 2).

41. Horner and Twachtman 2003, 6. Even as other vessel heads await replacement, "EDF has never seen a leak in service on a [reactor vessel head] much less major corrosion of the vessel head steel as happened at Davis-Besse" (MacLachlan 2002, 1).

42. The NRC's Davis-Besse task force continues:

While much was known within the NRC about nozzle cracking and boric acid corrosion, other important details associated with these two issues, such as the number of nozzle cracking events, as well as insights from foreign operating experience and domestic research activities, were not widely recognized or were viewed as not being applicable. The NRC accepted industry positions regarding the nature and significance of [vessel head] nozzle cracking without having independently verified a number of key assumptions. . . . None of the NRC's previously identified generic issues pertained directly to either . . . nozzle cracking or boric acid corrosion; although, there was one generic issue that pertained, in part, to boric acid corrosion of fasteners. This generic issue was classified as resolved in 1991. . . . For a number of years, the NRC was aware of the symptoms and indications of active . . . leakage [at Davis-Besse]. The NRC even reviewed some of these individual symptoms during routine inspections; however, the NRC failed to integrate this information into its assessments. . . . As a result, the NRC failed to perform focused inspections of these symptoms. (2002b, viii, ix).

43. Although INPO had sent its members 18 documents between 1981 and 2002, specifically addressing the corrosive effects of boric acid and giving examples of some stations' repair outages, it did not speak to Davis-Besse's situation. But in "July 2001 [INPO sent a] report to members [in which it] emphasized the importance of inspecting for corrosion after a less severe problem was found at a similar plant in South Carolina. . . . The institute [now] said [Davis-Besse] managers suffered from 'isolationism' " (Wald 2002a, A20).

44. Union of Concerned Scientists, 2002, 5–6.

45. Policy Statement on the Conduct of Nuclear Power Plant Operations, 54 Federal Register 3424 (1989).

46. International Atomic Energy Agency 1992, 1. See also International Atomic Energy Agency 1991, 8; Sorenson 2002.

47. The Atomic Energy Act of 1954 established the Advisory Committee on Reactor Safeguards to advise the NRC. Its responsibilities are to comment annually on the NRC's Safety Research Program, and as it decides, to review specific safety-related issues as they arise. The Commission refers to it licensing questions in terms, for example, of the adequacy of proposed reactor safety standards, including the technical and NRC policy issues of new plant designs. The Committee may also respond to requests from the U.S. Department of Energy with respect to its nuclear activities and facilities, and provides technical advice to the DOE Nuclear Facilities Safety Board. The NRC's web site posts the meeting agendas and transcripts of the Committee and its subcommittees (www.nrc.gov).

48. U.S. Nuclear Regulatory Commission 2000c.

49. Marcus, Alfred A. et al. 1990; U.S. Nuclear Regulatory Commission 2000c.

50. U.S. Nuclear Regulatory Commission 2002c, 108.

51. Sorenson 2002, 201.

52. Meserve 2002, 2–6. See also Bier et al. 2001 for a discussion of the British practice, discussed further in chapter 6.

53. Horner and Weil 2003, 11.

54. A fire spread throughout the Browns Ferry reactor building and burned for seven hours, and "finally, every means of core cooling to the reactor was lost." A candle's flame started the fire. To test the leak rate of polyurethane foam seal, which maintains the required air pressure in the Browns Ferry reactor building,

the practice was for an electrician to carry a lighted candle; if the wall seal pulls the flame toward it, that marks locations where air is entering the building. After finding one hole in the seal and stuffing it, an electrician brought the candle closer to verify the seal; the foam caught fire. Although no radioactivity was released, the event changed regulatory requirements and stations' practices (Ramsey and Modarres 1998, 105–6). See also Weil 1984.

55. Rasmussen 1992, 13; see also Rasmussen 1994, 31; Gilinsky 1992, 1991; A. Marcus 1995; Vaughan 1996, 422.

56. Meserve 2002, 2–6; Sorensen 2002.

57. This strategy is in the anthropological tradition of studying the "trouble case," in which the whole of a local world can be revealed economically—how things were, how they were unsettled, why it matters to those experiencing it. See Ihde 1991, 54–55 on philosophic interest (Heidegger, Kuhn) in such disclosing or revealing ruptures in technological and scientific practice.

58. For discussions of what I call that "new work at work" (Perin 1998b, 85), see other papers in the same volume, (G. E. Marcus 1998), especially the individual articles on American corporations by Cefkin, Davis-Floyd, and Newfield.

59. Perin 1995a.

60. MacLachlan 2003a, 1.

61. MacLachlan 2003a, 1.

62. A large literature speaks to occupational cultures, discourse communities, and to "communities of practice." A discussion of the different views of "new automation technology" held by "operators" and "engineers" in electric utility companies generally is Von Meier 1999. See Davis 1998 for a philosopher's field-based discussion of engineers' and managers' ethical stances.

63. Like academic disciplines, as Michel Foucault proposed in *The Order of Things*, these industrial orders are "regional ontologies which attempt to define what life, labor, and language are in their own beings" (Foucault 1973, 347).

64. The U.S. Department of Energy, which oversees military reactors and other nuclear-related activities, contracts for INPO products and services.

65. For variations in station structures and practices in six nuclear power stations with a total of 16 units in the Czech Republic, France, Hungary, Korea, Spain, and the United States, see International Atomic Energy Agency 1999.

66. Thus being in its early phase an "official technology," defined as one that "enjoys strong state support, the sponsorship of a significant representative of private capital, the promoted aura of 'the coming technology,' and the capture of path dependent advantages." So Steven Mark Cohn proposes in his "economic and philosophic" analysis of the history and prospects of nuclear power (Cohn 1997, 4–5; Jasper 1990). The earlier development and use of light water nuclear reactors for seagoing vessels has been a continuing influence that distinguishes the American nuclear power industry from that of other countries, which initially developed "indigenous reactor designs" not then based on light water technology, as well as having different traditions of labor-management relations (Jasper 1990, 64; see also Balogh 1991; Hewlett and Duncan 1974). Reinforcing that military-civilian connection from another direction is the industry's reliance on cybernetic and risk modeling concepts and techniques grounded in wartime use of operations

analysis and research, still proliferating in systems analysis in science, government, industries, and disciplines (Rau 2001). Even earlier is the influence of the Army Corps of Engineers, whose systematic development of cost/benefit analysis dates from the 1920s, when the politics of the time first required it to justify its projects in civilian arenas (Porter 1995, 153–55), now of course a staple of private and public talking points. See also Mindell 2002.

67. Waller 2001, 20.

68. Waller 2001, 180.

69. For a positive view of hierarchy, see Hirschhorn 1993.

70. Rees 1994, 61.

71. Rockwell 1992, 348–49. John M. Deutch, now Institute Professor at the Massachusetts Institute of Technology and then director of energy research and acting assistant secretary at the U.S. Department of Energy, urged the Commission to hear from Rickover.

72. Carter transferred from Georgia Tech to the U.S. Naval Academy; after graduating and studying nuclear physics at Union College, he was invited to join Rickover's staff; Carter served as an officer on the nuclear submarine *Sea Wolf*. Carter asked for Rickover's comments on May 31, 1979. The occasion was a dinner at Rickover's apartment, with Mrs. Carter and daughter Amy, which Mrs. Rickover had "secretly arranged [because] she had never been able to surprise the Admiral," cooking and serving it herself to circumvent the Secret Service. Carter later wrote, "Admiral Rickover had a profound effect on my life—perhaps more than anyone except my own parents" (quoted in Rockwell 1992, 350–51).

73. Rockwell 1992, 350–53. GPU Corporation, then owner of Three Mile Island, later commissioned Rickover's assessment of its organization and senior management in terms of its capacity to operate the other Three Mile Island unit and other plants, which was published in 1983 (Rees 1994, 191).

74. Perrow 1999, 337–38; see also 61, 305, 330–39.

75. Rees 1994, 94–95.

76. Rees 1994, 95–96.

77. Rees 1994, 96.

78. 2002, personal communication.

79. The authority for licensees' corrective actions programs is 10 CFR (Code of Federal Regulations) Part 50, Appendix B, "Quality Assurance Criteria for Nuclear Power Plants and Fuel Reprocessing Plants." Under the heading, "Corrective Action," it further specifies:

> Measures shall be established to assure that conditions adverse to quality, such as failures, malfunctions, deficiencies, deviations, defective material and equipment, and nonconformances are promptly identified and corrected. In the case of significant conditions adverse to quality, the measures shall assure that the cause of the condition is determined and corrective action taken to preclude repetition. The identification of the significant condition adverse to quality, the cause of the condition, and the corrective action taken shall be documented and reported to appropriate levels of management. . . . These criteria will also be used for guidance in evaluating the adequacy of quality assurance programs in use by holders of construction permits and operating licenses.

80. Some data are at HPRCT Business League 1999, 2001; others are personal communication 2002. LICENSEE EVENT REPORTS (LERs) are a class of reports of problematic conditions that must be reported to the NRC; not all LERs are license violations.

81. Nuclear Energy Institute 2001.

82. NEI/INPO/EPRI Industrywide Human Performance Process Benchmarking Report. NEI 2000a, Z-4. EPRI is the Electric Power Research Institute, a member research and consulting group funded by electric utilities using all fuel sources; its reports are either proprietary or carry industrial strength prices.

83. U.S. Nuclear Regulatory Commission 2000e.

84. These range from a session of CONSTRUCTIVE COUNSELING between an employee directly involved in a mishap and an immediate boss, to some number of days off without pay, to probation, to deprivation of bonuses, to demotions and pay cuts, to job termination; other than the last two, those actions usually remain confidential. At Overton Station, for example, there is a first level of counseling with the supervisor to see what can be done to prevent a mistake in the future; at a second level, a "reminder" that the mistake involved failure to adhere to a clear EXPECTATION is placed in the person's record; a third level requires one to three days of time off with pay, to come to terms with the possibility of discharge and then returning to comply with an action plan (for training, for counseling), which a manager develops for both the employee and his/her supervisor; a fourth level is "termination."

85. My acknowledgments provide details; Carroll and Perin 1995.

86. Any anthropology of thought and knowledge owes much to Clifford Geertz, professor at the Institute of Advanced Study. Thought is to be found in the "outdoor activities" of practice, no less than it can be found in the interiors of mind and psyche. That stand and his concern with the relationship between the "radical variousness" of modern thought and "the larger framework of our moral existence" have reinforced my longstanding concerns with specialists' ways of thinking (Geertz 1983c, 161). "The problem of the integration of cultural life becomes one of making it possible for people inhabiting different worlds to have a genuine, and reciprocal, impact upon one another. If it is true that insofar as there is a general consciousness it consists of the interplay of a disorderly crowd of not wholly commensurable visions, then the vitality of that consciousness depends upon creating the conditions under which such interplay will occur" (1983c, 161). My "profusion of orders" and their amalgam represents that "disorderly crowd." My concern with semantics and knowledge is a "practical epistemology" of this risky technology, whose sources lie well beyond it (1983c, 151).

To stay close to those visible practices for what they can reveal of the culture of control, I do not rehearse the largely psychological perspectives most associated with this and other high hazard industries, such as those on error, leadership, learning, team dynamics, risk perception, social climate, and stress. Those are already well distributed in understandings of control and loss of control. Searching instead for "outdoor" thoughts and practices, I take station experts' "subjectivity" as pointers to specific conditions of their world to which they respond and adapt. Because they do not overlook them, we must not. Yet overlooked they often are, when translations and generalizations into "objectivity" via formal or bureaucratic languages dry them out, or when managers do not consider experience-based recommendations seriously. In a feedback session with senior managers at Bowie Station where I quoted anonymously from some of my interviews, there was a chorus of "We never hear that! We didn't know that's how they see things," in a welcoming, if not deprived, tone. But the managers did not also exclaim that they had not asked station experts to express themselves on these subjects. That response confirms what these self-ethnographies reveal: the circumscribed influence of station experts, or in sociological jargon, their "agency" vis-à-vis the given "structure" of constraints within which any of us must live and work. Their and others' event reports express what I have come to think of as "tantalizing agency": their event reviews are a chance to influence the wider system, but at the same time, their perspectives are effective only to the extent managers allow them to be. See Llory 1991, 1997.

Chapter Two
Arrow Station: A Leaking Valve in Containment

1. Mercier 1988, 86–87.
2. The event review team interviews 24 people, the root cause analysis team interviews 39, five of whom are at other nuclear power stations or are employed by equipment suppliers, and the independent review team interviews 44. The 14 members of the three teams interview the same 10 people; the ERT and the RCAT interview the same 11 people, the RCAT and the IRT interview the same four people, and the ERT and the IRT interview the same three people.
3. Rasmussen 1990.
4. Perin 1988, 1994a.
5. Bier et al., 2003, 186.
6. Carroll 1995, 4.
7. Pool 1997, 116.
8. Scientech 2001, 18.
9. That was the finding of a federal inquiry into the World Trade Center Towers' fires and collapse by the Federal Emergency Management Agency and the American Society of Civil Engineers. Testing for fire resistance proceeds one part at a time in a furnace (a procedure known as ASTM E-119), which "does not mimic how a real fire sweeps through rooms in a building, creating structural stresses in one place that can lead to failures elsewhere in the building's interconnected skeleton. Within the cramped furnace, the test involves individual beams or columns and does not even check whether, once mounted in a building, the bolted, welded or riveted connections between them are equally resistant to failure in a fire" (Lipton and Glanz 2002, A1, A12).
10. See also Vincenti 1990, 201, 216.
11. Bugos 1996, 3, 4.
12. Bugos 1996, 285.
13. Bugos 1993, 279, 280.

14. Bugos 1993, 286.

15. Vincenti 1991, 762–63.

16. Leveson 1995, 76.

17. In Japan, plants are built according to designs followed stringently during construction. In France, regional differences are significant, despite having a standardized reactor technology. French units become differentiated by their date of construction; those built later may incorporate design changes resulting from the experience of predecessors, and one by one, units may come to differ further as particular equipment problems require design changes. The Chinese nuclear power plant construction program gives provinces leeway in choosing their reactor designs.

18. The Kemeny Commission found that information about valve failures similar to the one at Three Mile Island (TMI) in 1979 had not been circulated or acknowledged. These had nearly happened twice before (in 1974 in Switzerland and in 1977 at the Davis-Besse plant in Ohio); the particular relief valve that had not closed on the TMI reactor had failed nine times previously in similarly designed reactors (Rees 1994, 22).

Chapter Three
Bowie Station: A Reactor Trip and a Security Lapse

1. Hursh 2001.

2. Shinohara, Kotani, Tsukada 1996, 310–15.

3. Tokuine 1996, 343–44.

4. Tokuine 1996, 343–45.

5. Tokuine 1996, 345.

6. Tokuine 1996 346–47.

7. Corcoran 2000, 2–3.

8. "The most frequent contributing causes included design errors dating back to the time of original plant licensing (70 percent), procedure deficiencies (28 percent), human error (23 percent), poor work control practices (15 percent), and plant modifications (14 percent)." Of 26 safety-related plant system categories, 6 accounted for about 64 percent of all reported design-based issues in 1997: emergency core cooling (16 percent), emergency AC/DC power (14 percent), containment and containment isolation (12 percent), primary reactor (9 percent), essential service water (6 percent), and auxiliary/emergency feedwater (7 percent) (Lloyd, Boardman, and Pullani 2000, xi).

9. Lloyd, Boardman, and Pullani 2000, xi, xiii.

10. Nuclear Energy Institute 2003a.

11. Hanes, Gross, and Ayres 2001, 1; italics in original.

12. Ten in Illinois, which Commonwealth Edison had owned, and two in Pennsylvania, formerly owned by PECO; with AmerGen Energy, Exelon operates one plant in Illinois, one in New Jersey, and one in Pennsylvania.

13. *Nuclear News* 2001, 24.

14. Institute of Nuclear Power Operations 1985.

Chapter Four
Charles Station: Transformer Trouble

1. Rockwell 1992, 352.

2. The film *The China Syndrome*, released a few months before the Three Mile Island accident, dramatized the fictional threat of an accident when turbine vibrations at a nuclear power plant signaled a potential disaster; the film centers on managers' resistance to a control room shift supervisor's observations.

3. The "kinds of argument [that] count, for whom, [and] under what circumstances" constitutes "the 'sociology of proof,'" Donald MacKenzie concludes, in his study of the "unsuccessful quest for a mathematical proof of a fail-safe software system." MacKenzie 1996, 164; see also Pinch 1993.

Chapter Five
Logics of Control

1. U.S. Nuclear Regulatory Commission 2002d, 16.

2. Schulman 1989 discusses limitations to the concept of "bounded rationality," which neglects the presence of self-defeating "organizational irrationality."

3. One of the studies that the NRC shut down "abruptly and rudely" was trying to amplify the reliability of risk assessments with policy logics, by developing empirically a typology of "management and organizational style" as "organizational paradigms [that] might employ different means to explore options and seek solutions" (Blackman et al. 1998a, 2293).

4. Krohn and Weingart 1987, 53.

5. Wynne 1988, 150.

6. Snook 2000, 197.

7. Geertz 1983a, 57–59. For "error management tools" developed from and for workplace analyses of ongoing tasks, contextual influences, and failures, see Reason 1997, 131–54.

8. Ambiguities about their place in a station's hierarchy of control documents often leave plant experts questioning their "formality," hence authority—a paradox the next chapter discusses.

9. For example, Lave 1988.

10. In their introduction to *Ambiguity and Command: Organizational Perspectives on Military Decision Making* (1986), James G. March and Roger Weissinger-Baylon say:

> This book is about military decision making under conditions of ambiguity. . . .
> It is clear that the idea of ambiguity is alien to ancient military traditions. Although observers of warfare have often noted the confusions of battle, the ideology of military decision making emphasizes the imposition of order through organization and command and the importance of clarity, coherence and comprehensiveness. As a result, examining ambiguity in military decision making is a little like examining the sexual habits of Victorian England. It requires a willingness to accept the possibility that things are not exactly what they appear

to be, or are supposed to be. At the same time, it also requires a recognition that the fact that things are not exactly what they appear to be does not imply that they are necessarily exactly the opposite. (1986, 1)

11. Bucciarelli 1994, 2003; Forsyth 1993; Porter 1995; Vincenti 1990; Winsor 1996, 99–100; Wise 1995.

12. Weick 1988 offers a perceptual and cognitive analysis of "enacted sense-making."

13. See Forsythe 2001 for a cultural anthropologist's study of conceptions of knowledge held by "knowledge engineers," who elicit the practical knowledge of domain experts for encoding in artificial intelligence software. See Searle 2001 for a philosopher's theory of practical reason, which, in recognizing varieties of rational action, amends understandings of rationality. But without providing algorithms for decision-making: "[T]he search for a formal deductive logical structure of practical reason is misguided. Such models either have little or no application, or, if they are fixed up to apply to real life, it can only be by trivializing the essential feature of practical deliberation: the reconciliation of conflicting desires and conflicting reasons for action generally and the formation of rational desires on the basis of the reconciliation" (255–66).

14. Leveson 1995. See also Shrivastava 1992; Fortun 2001.

15. Leveson 1995, 58; italics in original. See also Carlisle 1997 for an early history of probabilistic risk assessment.

16. U.S. Nuclear Regulatory Commission 2000b, xv–xvi.

17. U.S. Nuclear Regulatory Commission 2000b, 5–19–21.

18. Unrealistic risk analysis may also result from simplifying or oversimplifying heuristics, which are, aware or not, part and parcel of model-making, in science as well. Scientists' "problem-solving strategies" when making mathematical models of evolutionary processes in biology display "systematic biases," finds William C. Wimsatt, philosopher of science at the University of Chicago. Some Wimsatt identifies are: assuming the system's environment is constant or context-free, thereby omitting possible variability; seeing the internal properties of processes as being more fundamental than their systemic relationships; taking internal or structural properties as being more significant than functional or adaptive properties; believing that internal mechanisms are more significant than evidence of adaptations evoked by contexts; not appreciating intersystemic phenomena; in improving a model, changes may elaborate only the problem's internal structure and ignore new knowledge of its context; excluding environmental variables and omitting data to reveal interactions or patterns, temporally or locationally; keeping contextual variables constant, thus reducing the possibility of finding causal variables. After Wimsatt 1986, 301–3; Perin 1995a.

19. Wald 2002a, A1, A20.

20. By "expectable" I don't mean "normal" in the same sense as Charles Perrow's concept of "normal accidents" brought about by unknowns or unknowables in complex, highly interdependent systems (Perrow 1999). See also Clarke and Perrow 1996. The conundrums can readily be "known," if only they would be. Nor are paradoxes or contradictions "deviant" in the sense of the "normalization of deviance," when small technical compromises harden into standards, which

Diane Vaughan, sociologist at Boston College, sees as being central to the *Challenger* accident (Vaughan 1996). Conundrums in and of themselves are cause for neither surprise nor alarm—insiders can readily recognize them for what they are.

21. Vaurio 1998, 37–38. See also Östberg 1992.

22. Turner and Pidgeon 1997, 48–49. In 1978, Barry Turner published *Man-Made Disasters*, which, to the best of my knowledge, was the first study to identify a pattern of background conditions in events he reanalyzed, as documented in 84 official accident reports occurring in the U.K. between 1965 and 1975 in many kinds of industries. After Turner's death in 1994, Nicholas Pidgeon published as this second edition its ten chapters; Pidgeon added another chapter with recent cases he analyzes in Turner's framework.

23. MacAvoy and Rosenthal, in press.

24. MacAvoy and Rosenthal, in press.

25. MacAvoy and Rosenthal, in press. See also Marcus and Nichols 1999.

26. MacAvoy and Rosenthal, in press.

27. MacAvoy and Rosenthal, in press. The authors' evidence comes from company documents available in the files of the Securities and Exchange Commission and from files of the Nuclear Regulatory Commission and the Connecticut Department of Public Utility Control; many details are from interrogatories resulting from the Connecticut Department's investigations into costs that the utility incurred in the shutdown, as well as from civil and criminal actions brought by the U.S. Attorney for Connecticut. Public inquiries into several major accidents—Kemeny Commission report on Three Mile Island (Kemeny et al. 1979) and the extensive literature on the Chernobyl accident (Liberatore 1999; Meshkati 1991; Petryna 1995, 2002; U.K. Atomic Energy Authority 1987) and the disaster at Bhopal (Shrivastava 1992)—are other exemplary sources of systematic accounts of the operations of policy logics in high consequence industries. For aviation, the National Transportation Safety Board's investigations are indispensable (www.ntsb.gov); a Rand Corporation study of the Board's structure and operations and its investigative approaches, made at its request, is Lebow et al. 1999. In marine and rail accidents, several public inquiries also include witness and participant accounts at all corporate levels—for example, the Clapham Junction Railway accident (Hidden 1989); the roll on/roll off ferry capsize, *Estonia* (Joint Accident Investigation Commission of Estonia, Finland, Sweden 1997); roll on/roll off ferry capsize, *Herald of Free Enterprise* (U.K. Department of Transport 1987).

28. MacAvoy and Rosenthal, in press.

29. The NRC commissioned the firm of Arthur Andersen in 1996 to study its senior management process for designating what were then "watch list" plants. Based on two of three case studies that found statistically significant links between financial and safety issues, the consultants recommended, as mentioned in chapter 2, that the NRC " 'should evaluate economic, management and operational factors in order to prevent future events. . . . Given the economic factors behind production and safety, assessing indicators of economic stress and management's response should allow the NRC to achieve . . . earlier identification of problems' " (in Bier et al. 2003, 186). By some accounts, because no single quantifiable indicator could be defined, that recommendation went no further.

30. HPRCT Business League 1999. Emphasis in original.

31. As things stand, policy logics act largely as an "unobtrusive control," in Charles Perrow's term, compared to the "obtrusive controls" of orders, rules, and procedures. Policymakers first establish the "premises of decision making," as James March and Herbert Simon suggested, which allow them to limit the scope of an issue and the information a decision requires. The premises thereby also limit the subsequent range of possible action. Such limiting or "control premises" in themselves are rarely studied, Perrow suggests (Perrow 1986, 128–31). My concern here is with their being made as explicit as any "obtrusive" controls are in high consequence enterprises, where employees are the first to experience their effects and to extrapolate their implications for risk reduction. In this industry, the catchall "safety culture" refers to both obtrusive and unobtrusive controls, but it does not include as part of that "culture" the risk escalating or risk reducing implications of "premise control," such as "assume that equipment is operable."

32. Rochlin and von Meier 1994.

33. Mumaw et al. 2000, 37. The article "There Is More to Monitoring a Nuclear Power Plant than Meets the Eye," one of several coming out of this fieldwork, appears in a "special section" of six articles devoted to "contextual" studies in the *Journal of the Human Factors and Ergonomics Society*. The authors, with one another or with others, have been publishing on various aspects of this work since 1994, e.g., Vicente, Roth, and Mumaw 2001. In four cumulative studies, the group made about 180 hours of observations and interviews with 52 reactor and plant operators during day and night shifts in two four-unit stations. At each station, all operators worked in the same control room where each unit's control panel was visible to everyone; the panel configurations and levels of computer support were different at each station. To evaluate the generality of its first case study, the group solicited comments from still other operators on its written reports. Each of the next three studies also "bootstrapped," leading them to conclude that their findings "held across individuals, across time, and across plants that differed in sophistication of automation and user interface technology" (Mumaw et al. 2000, 38–42).

34. Mumaw et al. 2000, 38.
35. Mumaw et al. 2000, 52.
36. Mumaw et al. 2000, 41, 43–44.
37. Mumaw et al. 2000, 41, 43–44.
38. Mumaw et al. 2000, 50.
39. Mumaw et al. 2000, 52; italics in original.
40. Mumaw et al. 2000, 51–53.
41. Mumaw et al. 2000, 44–45.
42. Mumaw et al. 2000, 45.
43. Mumaw et al. 2000, 47–50.
44. Mumaw et al. 2000, 53.
45. Weick 1990, 23, 29.
46. Mindell 2000, 206.

47. In engineering, "technological hermeneutics" occurs on three levels, according to Hans Poser, philosopher of science and technology at Berlin Technical University: when a particular situation requires understanding or "real action," when engineers connect various situations to appropriate available rules, and

when "local conditions" require specific if not unique rules to mesh with their characteristics (Poser 1998, 89–90).

48. A field study of "disturbance handling" in an automated manufacturing system offers a related perspective. Although machine operators figured out design changes that could overcome production bottlenecks, which "clearly challenged the framework of the given system," management denied resources for revisions. So finds Leena Norros, cognitive psychologist at a Finnish research institute. Norros sees operators' feedback as "design-oriented operation," which produces new knowledge for enhancing designers' application of the command-control principle that motivates their "operations-oriented design" (Norros 1996, 171–72. See also Vicente 1999).

49. Crease 1993, 114–15, italics in original. Anecdotal evidence suggests that scientists dislike stepping out of their box; they "frequently hold themselves and their colleagues to an exacting, uncompromising, unsentimental, and ultimately even unrealistic standard" of quality that refuses to acknowledge the inherent risk and uncertainty of their experimental activities as well as their own "artistry and prudence" (118). See also Gooding 1990 for an extended discussion of the "interdependence" of scientific thought and experimental actions (143) and the "craft skills and technologies [that] have always been important to scientific activity" (214).

50. Abduction is the name Charles S. Peirce, the American philosopher who originated pragmatism, gave to this thinking process. In Shapiro 1983, 68–69; italics in original. Abduction has been experiencing a controversial renaissance, especially in the philosophy of science and studies of scientific reasoning, as well as in artificial intelligence/robotics research and cognitive science generally. Magnani 2001 discusses variations in abductive reasoning; most directly related to these interests is medical reasoning, scientific and clinical (71–94).

51. William R. Corcoran, an engineer consulting to this and other high consequence industries on root cause analysis, publishes a monthly newsletter of "Event Investigation Organizational Learning Developments" in which he frames his advice on most topics—for example, conducting prejob briefs and postjob debriefs—as "algorithms." Back issues are available from http://groups.yahoo.com/group/Root Cause State of the Practice/.

52. Latour 1996 [1993], 295–296. See also Perin 1970.

53. Wald 2002b, A1, A20.

54. Henry 2002a, 2.

55. Henry 2002b, 2.

56. Henry 2002b, 3.

57. Industry advocates of professionalization moderate the expectation of "strict compliance" with procedures through "levels of adherence" and "levels of use," which take into account both experts' experience and the frequency of task performance. For example, procedure adherence is graded by the type of work: step-by-step, general intent, continuous use, reference use. In all cases, the text of the procedure is at the job site, except when being read for information alone, as in planning a work package.

58. Reason 1990.

59. Dien 1998, 181. Under simulated accident conditions, operators use the "know-how" gained in routine operations and a "habit of being disinvolved, of 'standing back' " from the procedure, the better to judge its appropriateness for the situation at hand. Dien calls this "controlled initiative" especially valuable under emergency operating conditions (185).

60. Colas 1995, 218–19.

61. At stations where procedure revision is supported and "legal" they are, Bourrier concludes, "self-designing" or "self-correcting" organizations (Bourrier 1998, 137).

62. Bourrier 1998, 141. See also Hecht 1999, especially 163–99.

63. Bourrier 1998, 140.

64. Bourrier 1998, 144.

65. After Fisher 2001.

66. U.S. Nuclear Regulatory Commission 1997, 1–1.

67. Whorf 1971, 135.

68. Fillmore 1977, 114; Lakoff and Johnson 1980.

69. Langewiesche 1998, 208–09.

70. Langewiesche 1998; National Transportation Safety Board 1997.

71. Langewiesche 1998, 230.

72. Langewiesche 1998, 212.

73. Langewiesche 1998, 228; italics in original.

74. Langewiesche 1998, 228–29.

75. Trubatch 2001, for example, provides a detailed legal discussion of rules for companies' undertaking risk-based maintenance, by parsing words and phrases such as "reasonable assurance" that require NRC interpretation and judgment. He examines these "subjective" terms to help utilities evaluate "regulatory risk," that is, the risk that the NRC will find their policy logics violate the rules.

76. Advisory Committee on the Safety of Nuclear Installations 1993; International Atomic Energy Agency 1991.

77. Wildavsky 1988; the phrase refers to a macro-level process of social "learning from error over time" (30) not only within risky enterprises, but also by regulators (224–25). Wildavsky's concerns are framed, however, not for their relevance to operational issues, with which the phrase is often associated, but to risk forecasting for policymakers. For him the macro-policy question is whether an "alleged risk is real" at all, and if so, "compared to what?" to be followed by the question of whether "the remedy might itself be more dangerous" (221–22). See also Schulman 1993b, 368; Westrum 1993.

78. Turner 1978.

79. Reason 1990.

80. Reason 1990.

81. Weick and Sutcliffe 2001.

82. Takano and Reason 1999, 1042–43. For a systematic analysis of the possibility of anticipating errors, see Williams 1997.

83. Rasmussen 1993, 985–87.

84. See Hutchins 1995 and Klein 1998 for field-based studies of naturalistic decision-making, the one aboard ship, the other mainly in aircraft. In the early 1990s, Electricité de France's research group announced a program that combined

simulator and field-based studies of control room activities to "understand the operators' understanding" in order to pursue observations of "gaps between . . . theoretical concepts and the operators' logic" (Llory 1990); no published studies are available. For a discussion of absolute rationality, bounded rationality, and social and cultural rationality in analyzing risky technologies and in forming perceptions of risk, see Perrow 1999, 315–28. For a discussion of dynamic decision-making, see Brehmer 1992b.

One research group is trying to systematize real-time logics to understand "when and why [a] heuristic works well." That requires, as Herbert Simon's constructs of "bounded rationality" and "satisficing" suggest, looking "at the structure of the information in the environment." Situation by situation, people have to act on approximations and tradeoffs. To acknowledge the role of context, which mainstream cognitive sciences tend to neglect, a group at the Max Planck Institute for Human Development in Berlin, in a Center for Adaptive Behavior and Cognition led by Gerd Gigerenzer, considers two other kinds of rationality, ecological and social. Real world decisions are made in ongoing life situations, include other people, and cannot be informed by a computationally exhaustive search for information, they claim. Instead, they propose "fast and frugal heuristics, which perform limited search [and can] exploit [information in the environment] to yield adaptive decisions. Partly complementary to constructs such as cognitive bias seen as an inherent cognitive deficit and partly a departure, the group seeks to develop "tools for adaptive and accurate decision making in real environments" (Gigerenzer, Todd, and the ABC Group 1999, 14–16).

85. This industry-commissioned "white paper" reanalyzed NRC's assessments of plants it had then rated as "problem plants" or "marginal performers." The NRC identified as "root causes," among other conditions, "deficiencies in or characteristics of management processes" (Tenera, L.P. 1990, 9).

86. Bell 1994, 3.

87. U.S. Nuclear Regulatory Commission 1991, A-40; A-43–44. A proposal for an "observatory" to keep managers at Electricité de France (EDF) informed of events and incidents in their own and other risky technologies declares that "a number of major obstacles litter the path" to systematic studies of the relationship between "critical events" and, in effect, policy logics. For managers and experts, organizationwide research takes second place, if that, to psychological and behavioral approaches to event analysis focused on "the bottom rung." Another obstacle is not wanting to disclose company information. Systematic studies are impossible from "most incident and accident databases which most frequently give only information about technical failures and human errors by operators or agents" (Labadié, Montmayeul, and Llory 1998, 9). Similar observations appear in Baumont et al. 2000; Becker 1997, 1999; Carroll, Rudolph, and Hatakenaka 2002. The NRC halted studies along these lines again in the 1990s; some analyses appear in research proceedings (Blackman et al. 1998a, 1998b) and in Levy 1997.

88. Baram 1997; Becker 1997, 1999; Pidgeon and O'Leary 2000. Such regulatory contradictions appear in aviation as well. Comparing four aircraft maintenance companies, a study for the European Commission finds that "there was no difficulty in getting examples of technical defects or discrepancies eliciting appropriate design changes [but] it was very difficult to elicit examples of systematic or

routine procedures for changing the situation in a way that would prevent repetition in response to identified human and organisational defects or failures." Even in the one company making an effort to collect that information, it "appeared to have considerable difficulty in translating this into effective remedial action." To the contrary, "there was a strongly expressed belief that the existence of this information exposed the company to criticism from the regulatory authorities" (McDonald et al. 2000, 172–73).

89. Woods et al. 1994, xvii. Or, as a Dutch accident research group comments, "mythology."

> The beliefs and attitudes of people, both in industry and in the general population, are riddled with misconceptions about how and why accidents occur and what can be done to prevent them. This amounts to a mythology which is as rich as the Greek or Celtic. A few of the beliefs which can strongly influence people's decisions and actions and prevent the effective use of their knowledge and skills are the following:
> —beliefs in the inevitability of accidents: "this work is just plain dangerous," "people are incorrigibly fallible," Murphy's law, etc.
> —beliefs in the superiority of technical fixes: "automation will solve our problems," "people cannot be changed, so let's concentrate on the hardware."
> —beliefs in unicausality: "there is always one root cause of an accident which will make everything OK if we remove it," often coupled with a search for someone to blame for the accident.
> —a static view of safety, a belief in "one right answer" which can be formulated in rules which will cover all eventualities. (Hale, Goossens, and Gerlings 1991, 14–15).

90. See Latour 1996, viii.

91. U.S. Nuclear Regulatory Commission 1999, 3, 5.

92. U.S. Nuclear Regulatory Commission 2003g, Part II, 13. The ratings determine the level and kind of NRC "response" based on PLANT ISSUES MATRICES, from which regulators write an ACTION MATRIX ("NRC Response Plan") of reparative steps required. For example, with a finding of one repeatedly "degraded" performance band, or multiple degraded bands, or multiple yellow ratings, or a single red rating, the NRC's "response" is that its executive director for operations will hold a public meeting with senior utility management. In those cases NRC will ask the utility to develop a PERFORMANCE IMPROVEMENT PLAN, which it will monitor.

93. U.S. Nuclear Regulatory Commission 2003c.

94. Nuclear Energy Institute 2000, 2001.

95. U.S. Nuclear Regulatory Commission 2003d.

96. U.S. Nuclear Regulatory Commission 2003g, Part II, 8. The concept of risk-informed regulation is in the process of becoming a working practice for both stations and NRC inspections: few stations have up-to-date PRAs of their plants as currently configured and not all failure sequences may be identified. A full-scope PRA costs between $1 and $2 million, depending on data already available. Without that scope, decisions remain "risk-based"—experts' judgments available based on previous INDIVIDUAL PLANT EVALUATIONS, on standards and operating

experiences at other plants, and on expert opinion. Until the risk-informed principle propagates throughout the NRC's staff and throughout all nuclear utilities, inspections and self-assessments continue to rely largely on deterministic criteria such as those in technical specifications. To acknowledge the distinction I continue to use the term risk-based, as do discussions at the NRC.

Ultracomplex mathematically, PRAs are likely to be incomprehensible to all but their makers; even statistically knowledgeable station experts call PRA's "blue sky." Their best use, all seem to agree, is to provide well-worked criteria for making specific, often expensive decisions about investments for equipment involved in safe shutdown and dose control; in that, they act as "boundary objects" organizing negotiations among the orders, e.g., Henderson 1991. See Apostolakis 2000 for a comprehensive discussion of PRA methods and issues.

97. One analysis suggests that utilities spend more for capital improvements than to meet NRC license requirements (Verma and Marcus 1995).

98. U.S. Nuclear Regulatory Commission 2002g, Part I, 4.

99. U.S. Nuclear Regulatory Commission 2004a, 3.

100. U.S. Nuclear Regulatory Commission 2004a, 25.

101. U.S. Nuclear Regulatory Commission 2001a, 10

102. Gouldy and Grazio 1993. One station's licensing staff made a summary of the NRC reports, which I paraphrase.

103. Weil 2002.

104. U.S. Nuclear Regulatory Commission 2002i, 2. See also Knapik 2002a.

105. Other public inspectors include federal regulators who make periodic visits or analyze station documents for the Environmental Protection Agency and the Occupational Health and Safety Administration as well as state and local agencies concerned with building and fire codes, for example.

106. Knapik 2002b, 5. This news report quotes from an August 2002 memo from Thadani to the director of the NRC's Office of Nuclear Reactor Regulation.

107. Gordin and Schweber 2002, 391.

108. Gordin and Schweber 2002, 392.

109. Gordin and Schweber 2002, 392.

110. Levins and Lewontin 1985, 273-74, 281, 119-20; italics in original.

111. Perrow 1983.

112. Meister 1999, 197.

113. Turner and Pidgeon 1997, 137-40 describe how "decision premises" enter into operational decisions at all levels.

114. U.S. Nuclear Regulatory Commission 2000c, 9, 18.

115. "Rigid insistence on statistical tests, now common in a wide range of scientific, social-scientific, and medical fields, is a . . . way of standardizing people, organizing a discourse, and imposing values that promote scientific unity, even if they may occasionally stand in the way of understanding the phenomena." So Porter argues in his history of "quantification [as] a technology of distance . . . [that] minimizes the need for intimate knowledge and personal trust" (Porter 1995, ix). See also Miller 1995, 1999a, 1999b; Potter, Wetherell, and Chitty 1991; Sauer 2003; Winsor 1996. For an historical account of "the moralization of objectivity" in science at the turn of the nineteenth century to "reveal both the diversity

and contingency of the components that make up the current concept" with respect to subjectivity, see Daston and Galison 1992, 80–81.

116. Columbia Accident Investigation Board 2003, 49.

Chapter Six
Intellectual Capital for Regulation and Self-Regulation

1. Hughes 1983; 1987, 73.

2. Full credit is not possible even for "risk reductions due to plant design or operation changes before [their] effectiveness . . . has been empirically demonstrated," concludes Vicki Bier, professor of industrial engineering at the University of Wisconsin in a discussion of "illusions of safety." Inappropriate or badly designed technical improvements can bring new troubles, but in situations where routine testing will not discover the new faults and they do not come to light immediately, their duration itself leaves the system at more than usual risk. Of five equipment improvements that could have caused serious trouble, two were not found for 15 days, one remained in place for 8.5 months, another for 2 years, and the duration of one, which made relief valves inoperable, had lasted an unknown length of time. In another case, a misunderstanding of the rationale of the system design led to an improvement that tripped the reactor every time a particular system was tested. Another improvement introduced the potential of spurious pump trips when service water flows were high, thereby shutting off the flow entirely; that condition lasted about two years (Bier 1997). Whatever shortcomings may be reflected in these new flaws—inadequate analyses of consequences, for example—their duration becomes the most pressing operating issue, against which only a systematic doubt and discovery orientation skeptical toward ultimate effectiveness is likely to be a barrier. See also Dowell and Hendershot 1996.

3. Vincenti 1990.

4. Scranton 2000, 762–63. This article responds to one by Constant 1999; see also Constant's rejoinder to Scranton 2000, 776–82.

5. Management and Organization Study Group of the MIT International Program for Enhanced Nuclear Power Plant Safety, Final Report. Carroll and Perin 1995.

6. In his study of organizational reliability at the Diablo Canyon nuclear power station, Paul Schulman, political scientist at Mills College, found in the early 1990s that the NRC and the California Public Utilities Commission put pressure on the station to "tighten up its chain of command and clarify lines of responsibility and accountability. Unambiguous lines of responsibility would clarify accountability for the regulators. . . . But yielding to this pressure might well deny Diablo Canyon some very important organizational protections from an overly rigid approach to reliability. . . . It would be painfully ironic if, while trying to improve regulatory responsiveness, regulating agencies themselves were to decrease the organizational slack used to promote reliability" (Schulman 1993b, 370).

7. Codified work instructions much like those "in a military organization," which have different "handbooks" for different ranks, have long been in the culture of control in manufacturing. In his history of statistical quality control, Denis

Bayart, historian of technology, finds that after the Second World War, "in the firm, we find a scientific treatise for the engineers, a popularized text for the directors, a technical manual for the supervisors . . . and a list of instructions for the machine attendant. Each of these texts gives some rules of conduct, but with less and less freedom to maneuver as we descend the hierarchy, and with less and less information in them. The engineer can choose among different types of control charts, the supervisor among different ways to make a measurement, but the worker only has one rule to apply: to call the machine setter if the points recorded on the chart exceed the control limits" (Bayart 2000, 170).

8. In *Fatal Words: Communication Clashes and Aircraft Crashes*, Steven Cushing, linguist and designer of aviation interface systems, examines black box recordings retrieved from crashes and after near-misses. In cockpit conversations and exchanges with air traffic controllers, he finds various semantic and linguistic sources of miscommunication—for example, misunderstandings of the intention of various speech acts (statements, questions, requests, promises), unclear pronoun references, inferences made on false assumptions, mistaken repetitions in readbacks. Outright misinformation occurs, such as incorrect numerical designations and number reversals, overlaps in numerical ranges assigned to different flight parameters (vectors, heading, airspeed, level). Material conditions of communication are a factor as well: a radio goes out of commission or is not used, and social conditions: not cooperating with air traffic controllers (Cushing 1994).

Words can lose face value, Charlotte Linde, a sociolinguist, finds, when overlaid with rank and its meanings. A co-pilot politely warns his captain about worrisome takeoff conditions, and instead of listening to the language, the captain hears the politeness. Taking that as his due, he does not acknowledge the warning; nor does the co-pilot, in his dedication to deference, insist on it; there is a crash (Linde 1988a, 1988b). Language practices are of course crucial in professional life generally (Boden 1994; Zabusky 1995); they remain pivotal for risk reduction (Herndl, Fennell, and Miller 1990; Manning 1992a, 1992b; Myers 1999; Moore 1992; Sauer 2003; Winsor 1990). See also Weick 1993, 185–87.

9. Stinchcombe 1990, 3, 6. See also Stinchcombe and Heimer 1985; Chandler 1991.

10. Stinchcombe 1990, 88.

11. Mismatches between types of problems and types of projects also occur, the most well known being NASA's original approach to conceptualizing the space shuttle as an aircraft. For the still poorly understood problem of how to clean up contaminating waste produced for decades at nuclear weapons manufacturing sites, a study for the U.S. Department of Energy of the superfund programs at their outset concluded that its "centralized control structure, which relies on contractor firms employing thousands, and a management plan that gives great weight to cost effectiveness, tight scheduling, and technical means for reaching the primary policy goal . . . emphasizes perfectability and the minimization of error . . . [giving] little indication of being responsive to uncertainty and error or capable of learning and adaptation" (Cook, Emel, and Kasperson 1990, 343, 349, 353, 359). For typologies matching kinds of uncertainty and appropriate project management approaches, see Shenhar 1991, 1992, 1998; Shenhar and Bonen 1997.

12. Stinchcombe 1990, 74–75; italics in original.

13. Stinchcombe 1990, xi.

14. Preventing mistakes like Ned's is of course an industry preoccupation in terms of preventing injury as well as loss of assets. In the best case, calculated safety margins make room for mistakes and work packages give due attention to the possibility; prejob briefs tailor them to the job and supervisors follow up with postjob debriefs; morning meetings and work group discussions make error avoidance a priority. At one U.S. station, as reported at an industry workshop, industrial safety managers designate "error-likely days" based on trend data on days of the week and the month; on the kind of work planned for the day and its known risks; on upcoming holidays; on company-related distractions and on other recognized error precursors. On a day when the schedule shows possible convergence between the work load and day of the week, a "highly visible traffic light," yellow glowing, stands at the plant entrance, and meetings and prejob briefings add reminders, higher risk work has extra barriers, and managers and supervisors make a special effort to observe ongoing tasks.

15. For a resource-oriented view of risk reduction see Marcus, Nichols, and McAvoy 1993.

16. Carroll, Rudolph, and Hatakenaka 2002. Sachi Hatakenaka is also at the Sloan School; Jenny W. Rudolph is at the Boston College Carroll School of Management. The study used multiple methods: a few case studies; questionnaires to line managers and members of 20 teams; and a self-administered diagnostic of cognitive style. This work develops a "four-stage model of organizational learning that illustrates different approaches to control and learning," "control" referring to the emphasis reports place on physical barriers, supervision, and procedures, and "learning" referring to systemic analyses of sources of problems; see also Carroll 1998.

17. Sauer 1998, 159.

18. van Vuuren 1999, 27.

19. van Vuuren 2000, 27, 42, 43.

20. Becker 1998, 153.

21. Becker 1998, 155.

22. Hibbs 2003.

23. Galison 2000, 3, 4; italics in original.

24. Baram 1993, 233.

25. Baumont et al. 2000. For working papers and reports of this group, see http://www.vtt.fi/virtual/learnsafe/workingpapers/index.htm.

26. Perrow 1999, 328.

27. Cook, Woods, and Miller 1998, 17; italics in original.

28. Johnson 1999. See the Group's website for its research papers and links to others: http://www.dcs.gla.ac.uk/research/gaag. See Ludwig Benner's website, Investigation Research Roundtable and Library, a clearinghouse for research on accident investigation methodologies, at www.iprr.org.

29. Sauer 1994a.

30. Llory 1997, 1153.

31. Cook, Woods, and Miller 1998, 42. Lists of precoded causes can also foster surface perspectives. "Shortened search strategies" in event reviews in German

nuclear power plants, say Babette Fahlbruch and Bernhard Wilpert, psychologists at the Research Centre for Systems Safety at the Berlin University of Technology, can produce incomplete or distorted results when event reviewers use predetermined data collection procedures or follow checklists. Items "at the beginning of a checklist tend to be chosen more frequently as causes than items at the end," and if a cause is not itemized, "it will probably not be found because, as investigations with error trees show, even experts tend to overlook missing branches" (Fahlbruch and Wilpert 1997, 119).

A voluminous record published in 1992 of the Wilberg coal mine fire in Utah in 1984 in which 27 miners died includes one survivor's handwritten testimony and the sometimes conflicting testimony of 13 miners who had observed the fires. Out of those materials and accounts, a consultant produced a "consistent and coherent" report for the Mine Safety and Health Administration using "a series of commonplaces familiar to all involved with mine fires and explosions." The report fails "to identify the specific practices, materials, repairs, or [lack of] preventive measures that might have caused the Wilberg fire," nor does it "connect [the commonplaces] to Wilberg." Again, the report does not attempt to "answer questions about why miners focused on production missed the signs of imminent danger" (Sauer 2003, 129, 150–51, 152).

32. Apostolakis 1999, 158.

33. Including context-based "human reliability" estimates in PRAs is a worthy goal. In a methodological experiment to translate qualitative data derived from direct observation into model metrics, a Finnish team of system reliability engineers and psychologists made observations of operators rehearsing an accident scenario at a control room simulator. From the operators' explanations of what they did and why, the team analyzes their activities and explanations "as realistically as possible" in context and from the operator's "point of view." The qualitative data include operators' "decision rationales" and the observations of team members, each from their specialist's perspective. They arrive at an agreement to restate these qualitative data as probability estimates for risk analysis models. That "makes it possible to formalize human activity in a comprehensive way. The contextual psychological models help in the validation of decision analytic and reliability models because the operators' bases of inference can be made more visible [leading] to the possibility of using new types of evidence in determining human error probabilities" (Holmberg et al. 1999, 239, 242, 245, 249). By combining experience-near and experience-distant evidence, this becomes a true "trading zone," an exchange in which specialists stipulate how they will listen intelligibly to one another (Galison 1997, 803). The study demonstrates, in my terms, the possibility of juxtaposing the data of calculated and real-time logics, and were operators' decision "inferences" to be analyzed further, they might reveal needed or possible ways to ameliorate policy logics, as the EDF "safety and reliability" studies are likely to do.

34. Cook, Woods, and Miller 1998, 38–39. See Tamuz 2000, 2001 for "learning disabilities" arising from aviation and medical reporting systems prompted by enforcement-based reporting vs. self-reports for understanding what, why, and how. Scott Sagan, political scientist at Stanford University, finds in his study of

near-misses in the U.S. weapons system during the Cold War years that so many sociological and political layers impede military communication and learning (information control, secrecy, short time horizons, interservice rivalries, career interests, competition for funding) that a more actionable palliative, he says, would be for weapon systems designers to reconsider the fail-safe redundancy principle to reduce the opacities of "interactive complexity." Sagan 1993, 275–77; 1994.

35. Corrective action programs are a kind of internal "counter-institution," like "research and development laboratories" in many industries, whose task is "to renew crucial aspects of current routines." In "hierarchically specialized" enterprises, however, there is a "danger of stultification" and resistance to their laboratories' recommendations (Helper, MacDuffie, and Sabel 2000, 464). So too for the nontechnical recommendations coming from corrective action programs. Similarly, the "conceptual slack" that experts cut themselves to reconsider their processes, as Paul Schulman, professor of political science at Mills College, names it, is also an element of the culture of control (Schulman 1993b, 364). That slack sometimes appears in temporary task forces and committees on particular topics, but at Arrow Station, such "stepping back," as Jerry discussed, is for "people appointed to do that" and for specific meetings.

36. Mercier 1988, 14. From a machine bureaucracy perspective, maintenance is likely to be regarded as "articulation work" carried on "behind the scenes" and often "deleted" from research attention (Star 1992, 276). Historians of technology also ignore maintenance, says Pierre Claude Reynard, who studied French paper mill owners of the eighteenth century. Maintenance "has traditionally been regarded [by scholars] as secondary to the initial choice, design, and evolution of a technology, and the interpretation of maintenance costs requires chronological series that are difficult to assemble." An "outstanding exception" to this indifference is Fernand Braudel, a French historian of everyday social practices, who saw the "constant deterioration of equipment during the early modern period as a pernicious economic disease. . . . a debilitating condition [that] limited the accumulation of capital" (Reynard 1999, 238). Furthermore, Reynard observes, only original archival research "will take researchers past the heavily mediated comments of professional writers and illustrators, engineers, and entrepreneurs subject to the influence of Diderot's *Encyclopédie* images of papermaking [which] made little room for artisans and workers and their knowledge. In particular, these representations ignored the challenges they faced every day from less-than-perfect and relentlessly deteriorating machinery. . . . By their very nature maintenance practices are likely to remain a secondary parameter of production, hidden behind the technological, financial, and human resources at the disposal of entrepreneurs" (Reynard 1999, 259, 262).

37. Makansi 1999.

38. Esselman and Esselman 2000, 51. At an American Nuclear Society conference in 2002 after the discovery at Davis-Besse, Dave Morey, vice president at the Farley Nuclear Station, owned by the Southern Nuclear Operating Company, observed that some new-found material problems had not been thought about 25 years ago. "So, what is going to raise its head five years from now, ten years from now? . . . People need to be looking at what research needs to be done in order to handle the problems that are going to be coming up." Advocating long-term

thinking, Morey calculates roughly that the industry spends on research less than 1 percent of what is spent to operate plants.

> And I had to include a lot of different things from a research standpoint to get up to that less than 1 percent. I think we need to quit focusing on the costs and we need to focus on our revenue that we generate. . . . If that revenue is going to stay for the next 40 years, we are going to have to spend a little more than 1 percent on research. We're going to have to get especially into the area of research for materials and material issues. (Michal 2002, 65)

See Morgan and Tierney 1998 for an analysis of historically low levels of research funding across the entire electrical industry.

39. Barley and Kunda 2001, 82–84.

40. Two related categories are similarly implicated. "Knowledge workers" (in bioscience, information technology, financial services) have had the lion's share of research interest over the last 20 years or so; their opposites are, the language assumes, nonknowledge workers. Under the heading of "the anthropology and sociology of knowledge," studies examine the intellectual engagement of those in academic or industrial institutions, while labor studies examine "work" largely among those with "jobs" and less formal education, lower pay, and prestige. What scientists and engineers do, for example, is called "knowledge construction and production," which positions their work philosophically; studies of occupations such as computer programmers and radiology technicians position them politically, emphasizing their problematic rights to influence and power, while those of knowledge workers, studies assume, are undoubted (Brint 1994). Robert M. Solow, Nobel laureate and economist at MIT, observes that it is "anthropologically interesting that in our culture the phrase 'manpower policy' or 'manpower specialist' tells you immediately that we are talking about the low end of the labor market, low skills, low wages, low status. . . . Subsidization of medical education is not described as 'manpower policy' " (Solow 1987, 2). In the philosophy of technology, observes Carl Mitcham, philosopher at Pennsylvania State University, despite technology's "modern significance . . . there is surprisingly little by way of explicitly philosophical analyses of work, and what exists emphasizes work as labor" (Mitcham 1994, 241). For the parallel and relatively recent realization that "artisanal knowledge," skills, and practices are central to science and practiced by scientists themselves as well as by those making and maintaining equipment for their experiments, see Jackson 1999 for a review of works in the cultural history of science. See Joyce 1987 for a collection of historical studies "concerned with work as a cultural activity, rather than simply an economic one, and with the discourses with which this activity has been invested in the past" (1).

41. Oedewald and Reiman 2003.

42. Zuboff 1988, 308.

43. Hirschhorn 1988, 53–54.

44. Hirschhorn 1988, 99–101.

45. Barley 1996, 77.

46. Barley 1996, 421, 422.

47. Barley 1996, 425–29.

48. Barley 1996, 412.

49. Barley 1996, 439, 434.
50. Barley 1996, 435.
51. Barley 1996, 438.
52. Stations have been increasing power output using much the same equipment (uprating), and, with or without renewed licenses, they continuously upgrade equipment. Of 103 operating commercial reactors in the United States, the NRC has renewed fourteen plant licenses to operate for another twenty years; another sixteen are in the approval pipeline, and twenty are planning to apply in the next several years. (U.S. Department of Energy 2003, 3–12) That assures production revenues, which foot the bill for otherwise unaffordable repairs and replacements usually of the biggest and costliest safety significant structures, systems, and components designed for that original lifetime. License renewal also pays for having demonstrated to the NRC's satisfaction that systems can withstand further aging. Electrical cable systems, piping corrosion, steam generator tube cracks, reactor vessel embrittlement, and nozzle cracks in the control rod drive mechanism (as at Davis-Besse) the industry deems to be the most vulnerable and the most likely to be added to maintenance's work schedule (Amber 2001, 14). A Nuclear Utility Obsolescence Group of almost all companies in the United States and Canada is developing equipment inventory databases, sharing information on spare parts and likely equivalents, and developing specifications with and for vendors (Michal 2001, 37–41). See also Lochbaum 2004.
53. Prof. Yoshikawa is president of the International Council for Science, specialist in artificial intelligence, and recipient of the Japan Prize for General Design Theory in 1997 (Science and Technology Agency 1999, 17). This report summary appears on the website of the Ministry of Education, Culture, Sports, Science and Technology in a "provisional" English translation. I have been unable to locate a final translation.
54. Science and Technology Agency 1999, 19. Another "inherent and structural" policy problem Yoshikawa names is "the lack of clear allocation" of high-level authority, in this case among four main Japanese agencies in their relations with one another and their relations with the public: their responses were initially slow and not candid, leading to a crisis in public trust.
55. Ihde 2002, 103–12. Such discussions exercise the "requisite imagination" high consequence systems deserve, as Ron Westrum, sociologist of large technical systems at Eastern Michigan University, puts it, in a "culture of conscious inquiry" (Westrum 1993, 402).
56. Freudenberg 1992, 7–9.
57. Dorf and Sabel 1998, 267.
58. Dorf and Sabel 1998, 374.
59. U.S. Nuclear Regulatory Commission 2000a, 5; Attachment 2, 17.
60. Freudenberg 1993; Garrick 1998; LaPorte 2001.
61. Kovan, Michal, and Sinco 2003. For that dialogue and many others concerning the NRC's reactor oversight process, see the NRC's website and newsletters and magazines dedicated to this industry (*Inside N.R.C.*, *Nuclear News*, *Nucleonics Weekly*).
62. Marcus and Nichols 1999 offer a field-based catalog of distractions and flux in two nuclear power plants through the mid-1990s.

63. International Atomic Energy Agency 2002; Organisation for Economic Co-Operation and Development, Nuclear Energy Agency, 2000. In the United States, the Nuclear Energy Institute estimates that the nuclear industry as a whole will need "90,000 new workers [in all specialties] . . . . from 2002 to 2011." In nuclear power, a "first wave" of retirements will occur within five years, with "a far more significant number" seven to ten years hence. And for nuclear engineers, "demand will be about 150 percent of supply" over the next ten years. For "skilled craft," now less than 4 percent of the total workforce, staffing will need to double, and for "operators and technicians," now about 1 percent, that will need to increase to about 7 percent of all "available new workers" to supply the current number of power plants in the United States (Nuclear Energy Institute 2003b, 8, 9, 10, 16).

64. Industry estimates of attrition specify affected work categories. Estimates by 29 U.S. nuclear generating stations with 44 operating plants expect retirements and departures in all work categories between 2003 and 2006; most will occur in maintenance and engineering and next most in support services. This survey, published in March 2003, finds that average attrition estimated at two-unit stations between 2003 and 2006 is 100 per plant, and over the next five years, 166. At one-unit stations, 64 will be leaving over the next three years, 100 over the next five. The variance five years out is wide, with estimates ranging from 46 to 349 total at two-unit stations and from 20 to 200 total at one-unit stations. At one-unit stations, for example, total losses from maintenance and engineering combined are expected to be 49.5 percent of all attrition. In the work categories "safety" and "radiation protection," attrition is expected to remain low, at about 1 percent per year. Asked about recruiting to offset these losses (about 6 in 100), most two-unit stations report they will replace about half, the rest to be supplemented by contractors; in one-unit stations, managers estimate replacing about four of ten people with contractors. At two-unit stations, reductions in the scope of work and technology and process improvements are expected to compensate for about 18 percent of losses, compared to 10 percent in one-unit stations (Goodnight Consulting, Inc., 2003b, 1–4).

65. Hansen, Golay, and Kwak 2001. The plant is not one that Northeast Utilities had owned. See also Hansen and Golay 1997. Engineers, operations researchers, and economists use and promote various techniques for determining relationships among maintenance costs, economic return, and equipment reliability. See Sherwin 1999 for a constructive critique of one popular technique, which cogently sketches the general problem and the often unrealistic assumptions behind these techniques. See also Carroll, Sterman, and Marcus 1998.

66. *Nuclear News* 2000, 48.

67. Several other findings: Keeping up good marks from regulators and markets is, allegedly, an incentive to underreport near-misses and personal injuries; before and after deregulation, some actions can mitigate poor outcomes, particularly improved training programs, increase in automation, and more effective preventive maintenance. In the U.S. railroad and aviation industries, there is some but not definitive evidence of links between safety outcomes and companies' financial condition. After deregulation of U.S. railroads, accidents and deaths occurred; that industry's regulator became generally more active and, specifically,

322   NOTES TO PAGES 268–269

developed requirements for pre-merger safety management plans (Bier et al. 2003, 150–70); the NRC published the original report in 1997, the authors' book appeared in 2003. As is customary, both publications carry the NRC disclaimer of responsibility for the authors' findings. See also a short article based on the report, Bier et al. 2001. In 2003, Britain took maintenance of its rail system out of the hands of private contractors and made it the responsibility of the government-supported Network Rail, after "decades of underinvestment" and several fatal crashes (Cowell 2003).

68. Bier et al. 2003, 216.

69. U.S. Nuclear Regulatory Commission 2003c. The full quote is: "The pace of the deregulation of the electric power industry will increase and there is potential for considerable change in the nuclear power industry. Although we do not believe economic deregulation will affect our strategic goals, the effect of deregulation on maintaining nuclear safety is unclear. Deregulation could result in improvements to safety through standardization of best practices, maintenance of the status quo, or degradation of safety through excessive efforts to reduce costs. We will continue to rely upon our inspection, assessment, and enforcement programs as the primary tool for evaluating and ensuring safe operations at our licensed facilities. The potential impact of deregulation on our other performance goals of increasing public confidence, increasing effectiveness, efficiency, and realism, and reducing unnecessary regulatory burden is also unclear. The general public may have increased concerns about the safety of nuclear power plants in a more cost-competitive environment, thereby affecting our efforts to increase public confidence. On the other hand, to remain cost-competitive, licensees put pressure on the NRC to accelerate reform efforts to increase efficiency and effectiveness and reduce unnecessary regulatory burden. Large conglomerates may emerge from consolidation of the nuclear power industry and may necessitate changes in our management and organizational structure to effectively and efficiently regulate the industry."

70. U.K. Health and Safety Executive 2003, 7. The full quote is: "Many of the main influences within the nuclear sector are continuations of structural changes which have been in play for a decade or so. The deregulation of electricity markets and the privatisation of some nuclear power generating capacity has contributed to a much more commercial environment across the whole industry. This brings pressures on companies to drive down costs and satisfy shareholder expectations. Downsizing, contractorisation, partnering, multiskilling, and shift pattern changes are just some of the ways in which companies have responded to these pressures. The commercialisation of the operating environment is likely to increase as the new electricity trading arrangements settle in and with any further nuclear sector privatisations. Even without further privatisation, mergers and changes of ownership will put pressures on licensees and regulators alike. While good safety and good commercial performance are both facets of good management, there is potential for tension between them."

71. A pilot "system for rating the quality and completeness of proposals for, and implementation of, change and modification" is underway. "The outputs will be the basis for future regulatory programmes and to inform future NSD strategic plans" (U.K. Health and Safety Executive 2003, 12).

72. U.S. Nuclear Regulatory Commission 2003e.

73. U.S. Nuclear Regulatory Commission 2002e, 23–24.

74. U.S. Nuclear Regulatory Commission 2002f, xii–xiii.

75. Bier et al. 2003, 217.

76. Herndl, Fennell, and Miller 1990; Winsor 1990.

77. Studies for the NRC of the ways that the risk-informed reactor oversight process takes into account "human performance" issues, conducted by the Idaho National Engineering & Environmental Laboratory, find that in a study of 37 operating events identified as being ACCIDENT SEQUENCE PRECURSORS, "certain latent failures in non-safety grade systems without a clear impact upon safety functions may not be fully characterized due to the risk-informed approach to regulation (i.e., only risk-significant failures are to be reported). Even if a deterministic approach were to be taken, it is not known which small latent errors are more likely to combine to help cause or contribute to events. Results from operating events demonstrated that non-safety grade failures have the potential to affect the context of events and risk" (U.S. Nuclear Regulatory Commission 2002f, 33).

78. Clarke 1999.

79. Massachusetts Institute of Technology 2003.

80. U.S. Department of Energy 2003; National Academy of Sciences 2003. These are portals into activities stimulated by the United States' decision in January 2003 to renew its investments in domestic plasma physics research and to participate in negotiations to build a model for an operating reactor, known as the International Fusion Research Project.

81. Massachusetts Institute of Technology 2003, ix, 2, 3. Support for the study came from the Alfred P. Sloan Foundation and from MIT's Office of the Provost and the Laboratory for Energy and the Environment. Massachusetts Institute of Technology 2003, vii. The study group members represent these disciplines: chemistry, economics, engineering (electric, mechanical, nuclear), environmental science, physics, political science.

82. Massachusetts Institute of Technology 2003, 3–4.

83. Massachusetts Institute of Technology 2003, 28.

84. Massachusetts Institute of Technology 2003, ix.

85. Massachusetts Institute of Technology 2003, 6. A survey of 1,350 adults in the U.S., which the group commissioned, produced three "important and unexpected results." Perceptions of the technology inform attitudes "almost entirely" aside from "politics or . . . demographics such as income, education, and gender." Views of "nuclear waste, safety, and costs" weigh heavily against support for future expansion, yet "[t]echnological improvements that lower costs and improve safety and waste problems can increase public support substantially."

86. Massachusetts Institute of Technology 2003, 8.

87. Basic research is the initial priority, in order be able to "justify" a "development and demonstration program" (Massachusetts Institute of Technology 2003, 92, 94).

88. Massachusetts Institute of Technology 2003, 9.

89. Massachusetts Institute of Technology 2003, 47.

90. Massachusetts Institute of Technology 2003, 49–50.

91. The authors declare, however, that the NRC's "regime is based on prescriptive regulation, accompanied by inspection and enforcement of rules by an independent regulatory commission governed by strict procedural rules." (That is not how the NRC or the industry would characterize the risk-based and performance-based regime adopted in 2000, I suggest.) Those rules do, the authors say, nevertheless "offer a very important opportunity for public involvement. . . . If a different regulatory process is adopted the interveners who seek a voice in the decision will not go away. . . . So changing the rules for safety decisions should not be used as a device for stifling the legitimate expression of different views about the benefits and costs of nuclear power" (Massachusetts Institute of Technology 2003, 85).

92. Massachusetts Institute of Technology 2003, 14, 91.

93. Golay 2001, 1, 2, 7, 8.

94. Cohn 1997, 17–62, 310–14. These pages analyze the sources of nuclear power's momentum and the decisive position of "first movers"; the entire book stands as one of several institutional and economic studies of nuclear power's history that are indispensable for considering fusion power's development and diffusion. See also, e.g., Aron 1997; Balogh 1991; Hecht 1999; Jasper 1990; Liberatore 1999; Morone and Woodhouse 1986; Pool 1997.

95. Even in design per se, the whole is not the sum of its parts, proposes Louis L. Bucciarelli, Jr., professor emeritus of engineering at the Massachusetts Institute of Technology, whose PhD is in aeronautics and astronautics. Although engineers try to bring all uncertainties into "an object world for instrumental assessment," that still eludes the "perfection" of the whole: "Analytical exactness and completeness may hold within [separate] object worlds, but the behavior of the whole, in a sense, is not fully defined by the behavior of its parts. It is this fundamental feature of designing which makes engineering the challenge that it is and denies the possibility of achieving technical perfection" (Bucciarelli 2003, 26, 31).

96. Kammen 2003, 8.

97. C-Span 2000; Waller 2001, 133.

Bibliography

Adams, John
  1995   *Risk*. London: UCL Press.
Adams, R., G. Apostolakis, K. Davoudian, O. Grusky, D. Okrent, J. S. Wu, and
  Y. Xiong
  1992   Inclusion of organizational factors into probabilistic safety assess-
         ments of nuclear power plants. In *Human Factors and Power Plants*,
         381–88. Conference Record for 1992 IEEE Fifth Conference, 7–11
         June 1992.
Adato, Michelle, James MacKenzie, Robert Pollard, and Ellyn Weiss
  1987   *Safety second: The NRC and America's nuclear power plants*.
         Bloomington: Indiana University Press.
Advisory Committee on the Safety of Nuclear Installations
  1993   *Human factors study group third report: Organising for safety*. Health
         and Safety Executive. London: HMSO.
Amber, David P.
  2001   Extending life by half. *IEEE Spectrum Online* 8/8/01: 1–5. http://
         www.spectrum.ieee.org/WEBONLY/publicfeature/nov01/nreco.html.
Apostolakis, George
  1999   Organisational factors and nuclear power plant safety. In *Nuclear
         safety: A human factors perspective*, ed. Jyuji Misumi, Bernhard Wil-
         pert, and Rainer Miller, 145–59. London: Taylor and Francis.
  2000   Apostolakis: On PRA. *Nuclear News*. March, 27–31.
Apostolakis, George E., and J-S. Wu
  1995   A structured approach to the assessment of the quality culture in nu-
         clear installations. In *Safety culture in nuclear installations: Confer-
         ence proceedings*, ed. A. Carnino and G. Weimann, 517–26. Vienna:
         American Nuclear Society, Austria Local Section.
Aron, Joan
  1997   *Licensed to kill? The Nuclear Regulatory Commission and the Shore-
         ham Power plant*. Pittsburgh: University of Pittsburgh Press.
Balogh, Brian
  1991   *Chain reaction: Expert debate and public participation in American
         commercial nuclear power, 1945–1975*. New York: Cambridge Uni-
         versity Press.
Banaghan, Ellen A.
  1991   Developing performance indicators for complex organizations: A case
         study in nuclear power. M.S. thesis. Sloan School of Management,
         Massachusetts Institute of Technology, Cambridge, MA.
Baram, Michael
  1993   Industrial technology, chemical accidents, and social control. In *Relia-
         bility and safety in hazardous work systems: Approaches to analysis*

Baram, Michael (*cont.*)

and design, ed. Bernhard Wilpert and Thoralf Qvale, 223–36. Hillsdale, NJ: Lawrence Erlbaum.

1997   Shame, blame and liability: Why safety management suffers organisational learning disabilities. In *After the event: From accident to organisational learning*, ed. Andrew Hale, Bernhard Wilpert, and Matthias Freitag, 197–214. London: Pergamon.

Barley, Stephen R.

1996   Technicians in the workplace: Ethnographic evidence for bringing work into organization studies. *Administrative Science Quarterly* 41(3): 404–41.

1990   The alignment of technology and structure through roles and networks. *Administrative Science Quarterly* 35: 61–103.

1983   Semiotics and the study of occupational and organizational cultures. *Administrative Science Quarterly* 28: 393–413.

Barley, Stephen R., and Gideon Kunda

2001   Bringing work back in. *Organization Science* 12 (1): 76–95.

Batteau, Allen W.

2001   Negations and ambiguities in the cultures of organization. *American Anthropologist* 102 (4): 726–40.

Bax, Erik H.

1995   Organization and the management of risk in the chemical process industry. *Journal of Contingencies and Crisis Management* 3 (3): 165–80.

Baumont, Geneviève, Björn Wahlström, Rosario Solá, Jeremy Williams, Albert Frischknecht, Bernhard Wilpert, Carl Rollenhagen

2000   Organisational factors: Their definition and influence on nuclear safety. Final report. Contract No. ERB FI4S-CT98_0051. Commission of the European Communities, Fourth Framework Programme on Nuclear Fission Safety. Final report. http://www.vtt.fi/virtual/learnsafe/links/orfa_final_report.pdf.

Bayart, Denis

2000   How to make chance manageable: Statistical thinking and cognitive devices in manufacturing control. In *Cultures of control*, ed. Miriam R. Levin, 153–76. New York: Harwood Academic Publishers.

Beck, Ulrich

1995   [1991] *Ecological enlightenment*. Atlantic Highlands, NJ: Humanities Press International.

Becker, Gerhard

1997   Event analysis and regulation: Are we able to discover organisational factors? In *After the event: From accident to organisational learning*, ed. Andrew Hale, Bernhard Wilpert, and Matthias Freitag, 197–214. London: Pergamon.

1998   Layer system for learning from human contributions to events—A first outline. In *Safety management: The challenge of change*, ed. Andrew Hale and Michael Baram, 149–64. Oxford: Elsevier Science.

1999   From theory to practice: On the difficulties of improving human-factors learning from events in an inhospitable environment. In *Nuclear safety: A human factors perspective*, ed. Jyuji Misumi, Bernhard Wilpert, and Rainer Miller, 113–125. London: Taylor and Francis.

Bell, Kenneth J.
1994   The tyranny of the quantitative and the illusion of the precise. *Heat Transfer Engineering* 15 (2): 3.

Bier, Vicki M.
1997   Illusions of safety. Paper for workshop, "Organizational Analysis in High-hazard Production Systems: an Academy-Industry Dialogue." http//www.engr.wisc.edu/centers/CHPRA/pdfs/IllusionsofSafety.pdf.

Bier, Vicki M., James K. Joosten, David Glyer, Jennifer A. Tracey, and Michael P. Welsh
2001   Deregulation and nuclear power safety: what can we learn from other industries? *The Electricity Journal* May: 49–60.
2003   *Effects of deregulation on safety: Implications drawn from the aviation, rail, and United Kingdom nuclear power industries.* Boston: Kluwer Academic Publishers.

Blackman, Harold S., David I. Gertman, Bruce P. Halbert, Donald L. Schurman, and Catherine Thompson
1998a   Management and organizational factors research: The socio-organizational contribution to risk assessment and the technical evaluation of systems (SOCRATES). In *Probabilistic Safety Assessment and Management*, PSAM 4, 2289–95. Proceedings of the 4th International Conference on Probabilistic Safety Assessment and Management, 13–18 September. New York.
1998b   Integrating safety culture. In *Probabilistic Safety Assessment and Management*, PSAM 4, 2296–302. Proceedings of the 4th International Conference on Probabilistic Safety Assessment and Management, 13–18 September. New York.

Blommaert, Jan, and Chris Bulcaen
2000   Critical discourse analysis. *Annual Review of Anthropology* 29: 447–66.

Boden, Deirdre
1994   *The business of talk: Organizations in action.* Cambridge, UK: Polity Press.

Bourrier, Mathilde
1998   Elements for designing a self-correcting organisation: Examples from nuclear plants. In *Safety management: The challenge of change*, ed. Andrew Hale and Michael Baram, 133–48. Oxford: Elsevier Science.
1999   Constructing organisational reliability: The problem of embeddedness and duality. In *Nuclear safety: A human factors perspective*, ed. Jyuji Misumi, Bernhard Wilpert, and Rainer Miller, 25–48. London: Taylor and Francis.

Brehmer, Berndt
1988   Organization for decision-making in complex systems. In *Tasks, errors and mental models*, ed. L. P. Goodstein, H. B. Andersen, and S. E. Olsen, 116–27. New York: Taylor & Francis.
1992a   The Zeebrugge disaster. Mimeo, Managing technological risk in industrial society. Paper for 11th Network Workshop, Werner-Reimers-Stiftung, Bad Homburg, Germany, May.

Brehmer, Berndt (*cont.*)

    1992b   Dynamic decision making: Human control in complex systems. *Acta Psychologica* 81: 211–41.

Brint, Steven

    1994   *In an age of experts: The changing role of professionals in politics and public life.* Princeton, NJ: Princeton University Press.

Brown, Gillian, and George Yule

    1983   *Discourse analysis.* Cambridge: Cambridge University Press.

Bucciarelli, Louis L., Jr.

    1985   Is idiot proof safe enough? *International Journal of Applied Philosophy* 2 (4): 49–57.

    1994   *Designing engineers.* Cambridge, MA: MIT Press.

    2003   *Engineering philosophy.* Delft: Delft University Press.

Bugos, Glenn E.

    1993   Manufacturing certainty: Testing and program management for the F–4 Phantom II. *Social Studies of Science* 23: 265–300.

    1996   *Engineering the F-4 Phantom II: Parts into systems.* Annapolis: Naval Institute Press.

C-Span

    2000   Aboard a boomer: The *USS Wyoming* Trident Nuclear Submarine. http: //www.c-span.org/submarine.

Carlisle, Rodney P.

    1997   Probabilistic risk assessment in nuclear reactors: Engineering success, public relations failure. *Technology and Culture* 38 (4): 920–41.

Carroll, John S.

    1995   Incident reviews in high-hazard industries: Sensemaking and learning under ambiguity and accountability. *Industrial and Environmental Crisis Quarterly* 9 (2): 175–97. (Special Issue: *Managing with danger*)

    1998   Organizational learning activities in high-hazard industries: The logics underlying self-analysis. *Journal of Management Studies* 35 (6): 699–717.

Carroll, John S., and Constance Perin

    1995   Organizing and managing for safe production: New frameworks, new questions, new actions. Organization and Management Study Group, Final Report. The MIT International Program for Enhanced Nuclear Power Plant Safety. Massachusetts Institute of Technology, Center for Energy and Environmental Policy Research, Report No. NSP 95–005. June.

Carroll, John S., Constance Perin, and Alfred A. Marcus

    1991   Organizational learning at nuclear power plants. Cambridge, MA: MIT, Center for Energy Policy Research, 90–004WP.

    1992   Organization and management in the nuclear power industry. Cambridge, MA: MIT Sloan School of Management Working Paper.

    1993   Management research on outages and maintenance. Report of the Second Nuclear Industry Executives Advisory Panel Meeting. Cambridge, MA: MIT Sloan School of Management Working Paper.

Carroll, John S., Jenny W. Rudolph, and Sachi Hatakenaka

    2002   Learning from experience in high-hazard organizations. In press.

Carroll, John S., Sachi Hatakenaka, and Jenny W. Rudolph
  2001   Problem investigation teams in high-hazard industries: Creating and
          negotiating organizational learning. In press.
Carroll, John S., Sachi Hatakenaka, Jenny W. Rudolph, and Marcello Boldrini
  1999   The difficult handoff from incident investigation to implementation.
          Paper presented at the New Technologies and Work Conference, Bad
          Homburg, Germany, May.
Carroll, John S., John Sterman, and Alfred A. Marcus
  1998   Playing the maintenance game: How mental models drive organiza-
          tional decisions. In *Debating rationality: nonrational elements of orga-
          nizational decision making*, ed. J. J. Halpern and R. N. Stern, 99–121.
          Ithaca, NY: Cornell University ILR Press.
Casson, Ronald W.
  1983   Schemata in cognitive anthropology. *Annual Review of Anthropology*
          12: 429–62.
Cebon, Peter B.
  1995   When the chemistry is right: A study of work organization and change
          in two chemical plants. Ph.D. dissertation. Sloan School of Manage-
          ment, Massachusetts Institute of Technology, Cambridge, MA.
Cefkin, Melissa
  1998   Toward a higher-order merger: A middle manager's story. In *Corpo-
          rate futures*, ed. George E. Marcus, 89–112. Limited Editions Series,
          5, Chicago: University of Chicago Press.
Center for Strategic and International Studies
  1999   The regulatory process for nuclear power reactors: A review. A report
          of the CSIS Nuclear Regulatory Process Review Steering Committee.
          CSIS Panel Report. Washington, DC: The CSIS Press. http://www
          .csis.org/energy/NucReg.htm
Chandler, Alfred D.
  1991   Review, *Information and organizations* by Arthur L. Stinchcombe.
          Contemporary Sociology 20 (May): 337–40.
Cho, Guk-Hyun
  1995   Task characteristics and organizational demography: Their influence
          on organizational outcomes at nuclear power plants. Working Paper.
          Sloan School of Management, Massachusetts Institute of Technology,
          Cambridge, MA.
Citizens' Nuclear Information Center
  2000   STA [Science and Technology Agency] adds 229 to its list of exposed
          people due to JCO accident. http://www.cnic.or.jp/english/topics/JCO/
          reports/repo41.html.
Clarke, Lee B.
  1992   Context dependency and risk decision making. In *Organizations, un-
          certainties, and risk*, ed. J. F. Short, Jr., and L. Clarke, 27–53. Boulder,
          CO: Westview Press.
  1993   Drs. Pangloss and Strangelove meet organizational theory: High relia-
          bility organizations and nuclear weapons accidents. *Sociological
          Forum* 8 (4): 675–89.

Clarke, Lee B. (*cont.*)
  1999   *Mission improbable: Using fantasy documents to tame disaster.* Chicago: University of Chicago Press.
Clarke, Lee B., and Charles Perrow
  1996   Prosaic organizational failure. *American Behavioral Scientist* 39: 1040–56.
Cohn, Steven Mark
  1997   *Too cheap to meter: An economic and philosophical analysis of the nuclear dream.* Albany: State University of New York Press.
Colas, Armand
  1995   Human factors and safety at Electricité de France. *Industrial and Environmental Crisis Quarterly* 9 (2): 213–24. (Special Issue: *Managing with danger*).
Columbia Accident Investigation Board
  2003   Public hearing. Houston. April 23. http://www.nasa.gov/columbia/caib/PDFS/VOL6/H08.PDF.
Constant, Edward W., II
  1999   Reliable knowledge and unreliable stuff: On the practical role of rational beliefs. *Technology and Culture* 40: 324–57.
  2000   Rejoinder to Constant. *Technology and Culture* 41: 776–82.
Cook, Brian J., Jacque L. Emel, and Roger E. Kasperson
  1990   Organizing and managing radioactive waste disposal as an experiment. *Journal of Policy Analysis and Management* 9 (3): 339–66.
Cook, Richard I., David D. Woods, and Charlotte Miller
  1998   A tale of two stories: Contrasting views of patient safety. Report from a Workshop on Assembling the Scientific Basis for Progress on Patient Safety. Chicago, IL: National Health Care Safety Council of the National Patient Safety Foundation of the American Medical Association. http: //www.npsf.org/exec/front.html.
Cooper, J. Arlin, Scott Ferson, and Lev Ginzburg
  1996   Hybrid processing of stochastic and subjectivity uncertainty data. *Risk Analysis* 16 (6): 785–91.
Coquelle, J. J., B. Cura, and B. Fourest
  1995   Safety culture and quality systems. In *Safety culture in nuclear installations*, ed. A. Carnino and G. Weimann, 193–202. Vienna: American Nuclear Society, Austria Local Section.
Corcoran, William R.
  2000   Mix-ups in high hazard industries. *The Firebird Forum* 3 (1). Newsletter of Event Investigation Organizational Learning Developments. firebird.one@alum.mit.edu.
Couture, Barbara
  1992   Categorizing professional discourse: Engineering, administrative, and technical/professional writing. *Journal of Business and Technical Communication* 6 (1): 5–37.
Cowell, Alan
  2003   Concerns of safety push Britain to reassume control of rail maintenance. *New York Times*, October 25: B4.

Crease, Robert P.
    1993   *The play of nature: Experimentation as performance.* Bloomington:
            Indiana University Press.
Crick, Malcolm
    1982   Anthropological field research, meaning creation, and knowledge con-
            struction. In *Semantic anthropology,* ed. David Parkin, 15–37. New
            York: Academic Press.
Cushing, Steven
    1994   *Fatal words: Communication clashes and aircraft crashes.* Chicago:
            University of Chicago Press.
Czarniawska-Joerges, Barbara
    1992   *Exploring complex organizations: A cultural perspective.* Newbury
            Park, CA: Sage Publications.
Daston, Lorraine, and Peter Galison
    1992   The image of objectivity. *Representations* 40: 81–128.
David, Paul A., R. Maude-Griffin, G. Rothwell, and R. Sturm
    1991   European nuclear power plants and their less reliable American cous-
            ins: International differences in the distributions of reactor operating
            spell durations. CEPR Publication no. 273. Center for Economic Pol-
            icy Research, Stanford University.
Davis, Michael
    1998   *Thinking like an engineer: Studies in the ethics of a profession.* New
            York: Oxford University Press.
Davis-Floyd, Robbie E.
    1998   Storying corporate futures: The Shell scenarios. In *Corporate futures,*
            ed. George E. Marcus, 141–76. Limited Editions Series, 5. Chicago:
            University of Chicago Press.
DiBella, Anthony J.
    1991a   Advantages and disadvantages of the French nuclear power system.
            Cambridge, MA: MIT Sloan School of Management, unpublished
            manuscript.
    1991b   Change and variation amidst standardization. Cambridge, MA: MIT
            Sloan School of Management, unpublished manuscript.
    1991c   Staff development at Electricité de France. Cambridge, MA: MIT Sloan
            School of Management, unpublished manuscript.
    1993   EDF's performance feedback system at work: The case of the "pi-
            quage" (WP3532–93). Cambridge, MA: MIT Sloan School of Man-
            agement working paper.
    1995   Organizational change and stability in French nuclear power opera-
            tions. *Industrial and Environmental Crisis Quarterly* 9 (2): 224–41.
            (Special Issue: *Managing with danger*).
Dien, Yves
    1998   Safety and application of procedures, or "How do 'they' have to use
            operating procedures in nuclear power plants?" *Safety Science* (29):
            179–87.

Dorf, Michael C., and Charles F. Sabel
   1998   A constitution of democratic experimentalism. *Columbia Law Review*
            98 (2): 267–488.
Douglas, Mary, and Aaron Wildavsky
   1982   *Risk and culture: An essay on the selection of technical and environ-
            mental dangers.* Berkeley: University of California Press.
Dowell, A. M., and D. C. Hendershot
   1996   No good deed goes unpunished: Case studies of incidents and potential
            incidents caused by protective systems. Paper presented at the Ameri-
            can Institute of Chemical Engineers, 31st Annual Loss Prevention Sym-
            posium, Houston, TX, March 13. Mimeo.
Downey, Gary L.
   1988   Reproducing cultural identity in negotiating nuclear power: The Union
            of Concerned Scientists and emergency core cooling. *Social Studies of
            Science* 18: 231–64.
Downey, Gary L., and Juan C. Lucena
   1995   Engineering studies. In *Handbook of science and technology studies,*
            ed. S. Jasanoff, G. Markle, J. Petersen, and T. Pinch, 167–88. New
            York: Academic Press.
Dwyer, Tom
   2001   *Life and death at work: Industrial accidents as a case of socially pro-
            duced error.* New York: Plenum Press.
Enders, John H.
   1993   The role of feedback in the airline industry. In *Proceedings of the
            American Nuclear Society conference: Risk management—Expanding
            horizons,* ed. Ronald A. Knief, 15–19. La Grange Park, IL: American
            Nuclear Society.
Esselman, Walter H., and Thomas C. Esselman
   2000   Nuclear power: Viable in a competitive market? *Nuclear News.* Janu-
            ary, 48–52.
Fahlbruch, Babette, and Bernhard Wilpert
   1997   Event analysis as problem solving process. In *After the event: From
            accident to organisational learning,* ed. Andrew Hale, Bernhard Wil-
            pert, and Matthias Freitag, 113–29. London: Pergamon.
Farrell, Thomas B., and G. Thomas Goodnight
   1981   Accidental rhetoric: The root metaphors of Three Mile Island. *Com-
            munication Monographs* 48: 271–300.
Fertel, Marvin S.
   2001   Testimony for the record, hearings by the U.S. Senate Energy and Natu-
            ral Resources Committee. July 12, 2.
Fillmore, Charles
   1975   An alternative to checklist theories of meaning. In *Proceedings of the
            first annual meeting of the Berkeley Linguistics Society,* ed. C. Cogen
            et al, 123–31. Berkeley, CA.
   1977   Topics in lexical semantics. In *Current issues in linguistic theory,* ed.
            R. W. Cole, 76–138. Bloomington: Indiana University Press.

Fisher, Robert C., Jr.
  2001   Troubleshooting procedures: A root cause analyst's look at common procedure related problems. Performance Improvement International©. Human Performance and Root Cause Trending Workshop, Baltimore. June.

Foley, Brendan P.
  2003   Fighting engineers: The U.S. Navy and mechanical engineering, 1840–1905. Ph.D. thesis, Program in Science, Technology, and Society, Massachusetts Institute of Technology, Cambridge, MA.

Ford, Daniel
  1982   *Cult of the atom.* New York: Simon and Schuster.

Forsythe, Diana E.
  1993   Engineering knowledge: The construction of knowledge in artificial intelligence. *Social Studies of Science* 23: 445–77.

  2001   *Studying those who study us: An anthropologist in the world of artificial intelligence.* Edited, with an introduction, by David J. Hess. Stanford: Stanford University Press.

Fortun, Kim
  2001   *Advocacy after Bhopal: Environmentalism, disaster, new global orders.* Chicago: University of Chicago Press.

Foucault, Michel
  1973   [1966] *The order of things: An archeology of the human sciences.* New York: Vintage Books.

Foulke, Larry R.
  2002   A perspective: Status and future of nuclear power in the United States. Americas Nuclear Energy Symposium, October 16. http://www.ans.org/pi/documents/1035997602.PDF.

Fourest, Bernard
  2000   Safety/availability monitoring units: A means of developing safety culture. Advisory Committee of Experts for Nuclear Reactors (GPR) France. Paper presented at the Quadrilateral Meeting, Berlin. October 23–25.

French, Howard W.
  2003   Tokyo is told: Go nuclear or go dark. *New York Times*, April 13: A13.

Freudenburg, William R.
  1988   Perceived risk, real risk: Social science and the art of probabilistic risk assessment. *Science* 242: 44–49.

  1992   Nothing recedes like success? Risk analysis and the organizational amplification of risks. *Risk: Issues in Health and Safety* 3 (1): 1–35. http://www.piercelaw.edu/Risk/Vol3/winter/Freudenb.htm.

  1993   Risk and recreancy: Weber, the division of labor, and the rationality of risk perceptions. *Social Forces* 71: 909–32.

Gal, Susan, and Judith T. Irvine
  1995   The boundaries of languages and disciplines: How ideologies construct difference. *Social Research* 62 (4): 967–1001.

Galison, Peter L.
1997   *Image and logic: A material culture of microphysics.* Chicago: University of Chicago Press.
2000   An accident of history. In *Atmospheric flight in the twentieth century,* ed. P. Galison and A. Roland, 3–43. Dordrecht: Kluwer Academic Publishers.

Garrick, B. John
1998   Technological stigmatism, risk, perception, and truth. *Reliability Engineering and System Safety* 59: 41–45.

Geertz, Clifford
1973   Thick description: Toward an interpretive theory of culture. In *The interpretation of cultures: Selected essays,* 4–30. New York: Basic Books.
1983a   "From the native's point of view": On the nature of anthropological understanding. In *Local knowledge: Further essays in interpretive anthropology,* 55–70. New York: Basic Books.
1983b   Common sense as a cultural system. In *Local knowledge: Further essays in interpretive anthropology,* 73–93. New York: Basic Books.
1983c   The way we think now: Toward an ethnography of modern thought. In *Local knowledge: Further essays in interpretive anthropology,* 147–63. New York: Basic Books.

Gephart, Robert P., Jr.
1993   The textual approach: Risk and blame in disaster sensemaking. *Academy of Management Journal* 36 (6): 1465–514.

Gigerenzer, Gerd, Peter M. Todd, and the ABC Research Group
1999   *Simple heuristics that make us smart.* New York: Oxford University Press.

Gilinsky, Victor
1991   Nuclear power: What must be done? *Public Utilities Fortnightly* June 1: 25–26.
1992   Nuclear safety regulation: Lessons from US experience. *Energy Policy* 1992 (August): 704–11.

Goble, Robert L., and Gordon R. Thompson
1995   The use of probabilistic risk assessment in emergency-response planning for nuclear power plant accidents. In *Preparing for nuclear power plant accidents,* ed. D. Golding, J. X. Kasperson, and R. E. Kasperson, 165–80. Boulder, CO: Westview Press.

Goffman, Erving
1974   *Frame analysis: An essay on the organization of experience.* New York: Harper & Row.

Golay, Michael W.
2001   On social acceptance of nuclear power. New Energy Technologies: A Policy Framework for Micro-Nuclear Technology. The James A. Baker III Institute for Public Policy of Rice University. http://www.rice.edu/projects/baker/Pubs/workingpapers/2001_nuclear/.

Gonyeau, Joseph
2002   The virtual nuclear tourist. http: //www.nucleartourist.com/.

Gooding, David
  1990   *Experiment and the making of meaning: Human agency in scientific observation and experiment.* London: Kluwer Academic Publishers.
Goodnight Consulting, Inc.
  2003a Nuclear Newsletter: 2003 U.S. nuclear plant staffing. September.
  2003b Nuclear Newsletter: U.S. nuclear plant personnel attrition. March.
Gordin, Michael D., and Sam Schweber
  2002   Thinking systematically: Thomas and Agatha Hughes, *Systems, Experts, and Computers. Technology and Culture* (43): 390–97.
Gouldy, Russ, and Robert Grazio
  1993   Diagnostic evaluation study. Nuclear Licensing Department. Juno Beach: Florida Power & Light Company. Mimeo.
Grabowski, Martha, et al.
  2000   Risk modeling in distributed, large-scale systems. *IEEE Transactions on Systems, Man, and Cybernetics—Part A: Systems and Humans* 30: 651–60.
Grabowski, Martha, and Karlene Roberts
  1996   Human and organizational error in large scale systems. *IEEE Transactions on Systems, Man, and Cybernetics—Part A: Systems and Humans* 26: 2–16.
Gras, Alain, Caroline Moricot, Sophie L. Poirot-Delpech, and Victor Scardigli
  1994   *Faced with automation: The pilot, the controller and the engineer.* Condensed version of *á Face a l'automate: Le pilote, Le contrôleur et l'ingénieur.* Translated by Jill Ludsten. Série Homme et Société 20. Paris: Publications de la Sorbonne.
Guillén, Mauro
  1994   *Models of management: Work, authority, and organization in a comparative perspective.* Chicago: University of Chicago Press.
Gusterson, Hugh
  1996   *Nuclear rites: A weapons laboratory at the end of the cold war.* Berkeley: University of California Press.
Hale, Andrew, Bernhard Wilpert, and Matthias Freitag, eds.
  1997   *After the event: From accident to organisational learning.* London: Pergamon.
Hale, Andrew R., L.H.J. Goossens, and P. Oortman Gerlings
  1991   Safety management systems: a model and some applications. 9th Net-Work (New Technology and Work) Workshop on Safety Policy. Bad Homburg. May.
Halliday, Michael A. K.
  1978   *Language as social semiotic: The social interpretations of language and meaning.* London: Edward Arnold.
Hanes, Lewis F., Madeleine M. Gross, and Thomas J. Ayres
  2001   Knowledge documentation problems and efforts in electric utilities. Presentation. 7th Annual Human Performance/Root Cause/Trending Workshop, Baltimore, MD. June. Palo Alto, CA: EPRI Strategic Human Performance Program.

Hanks, William F.
  1996   *Language and communicative practices*. Boulder, CO: Westview Press.
Hannaman, G. W., and A. Singh
  1993   Human reliability assessments and applications to enhance availability
          and reduce risk during less-than-full power operations. In *Proceedings
          of the American Nuclear Society conference risk management—Ex-
          panding horizons*, ed. R. A. Knief, 180–83. La Grange Park, IL: Ameri-
          can Nuclear Society.
Hanners, David
  2002   Xcel nuclear lapses recurrent, feds say Monticello, Prairie Island
          plants not unsafe, though. *Saint Paul Pioneer Press*, November 17.
          http://www.twincities.com/mld/pioneerpress/business/4532619.htm.
Hansen, Kent F., and Michael W. Golay
  1997   Systems dynamics: An introduction and applications to the nuclear
          industry. In *Advances in nuclear science and technology*, ed. J. Lewins
          and M. Becker, 191–221. New York: Plenum Press.
Hansen, Kent F., Michael W. Golay, and Sangman Kwak
  2001   Modeling organizational influence on nuclear power plant perfor-
          mance. Department of Nuclear Engineering, Massachusetts Institute
          of Technology. December.
Harvey, Joan, et al.
  2002   An analysis of safety culture attitudes in a highly regulated environ-
          ment. *Work and Stress* 16 (1): 18–36.
Hastings, Kevin B., and John Wilson
  1997   Maintenance rule supports Millstone Station's recovery efforts. *IEEE
          Sixth Annual Human Factors Meeting*. Proceedings Nov. 6–10. Or-
          lando, Florida.
He, Wei Ugo, and Norman C. Rasmussen
  1993   Estimating management impact on core-melt frequency. In *Proceed-
          ings of the American Nuclear Society conference: Risk management—
          Expanding horizons*, ed. Ronald A. Knief, 303–04. La Grange Park,
          IL: American Nuclear Society.
Hecht, Gabrielle
  1994   Political designs: Nuclear reactors and national policy in postwar
          France. *Technology and Culture* October: 657–85.
  1999   *The radiance of France*. Cambridge, MA: MIT Press.
Helmreich, Robert L., Earl L. Wiener, and Barbara G. Kanki
  1993   The future of crew resource management in the cockpit and elsewhere.
          In *Cockpit resource management*, ed. E. L. Wiener, B. G. Kanki, and
          R. L. Helmreich, 479–501. New York: Academic Press.
Helper, Susan, John Paul MacDuffie, and Charles Sabel
  2000   Pragmatic collaborations: Advancing knowledge while controlling op-
          portunism. *Industrial and Corporate Change* 9 (3): 443–88.
Henderson, Kathryn
  1991   Flexible sketches and inflexible data bases: Visual communication,
          conscription devices, and boundary objects in design engineering. *Sci-
          ence, Technology and Human Values* 16 (4): 448–73.

Henry, Tom
  2002a   NRC rips safety flaw at reactor: Corrosion 'worst ever'; no radia-
          tion risk seen. *The Blade.* http://www.toledoblade.com/apps/pbcs.dt
          ...Kategori-NEWS06.
  2002b   Warning signs went unheeded: Corrosion was evident in '99, First
          Energy says. *The Blade.* http://www.toledoblade.com/apps/pbcs.dt
          ...Kategori-NEWS06.
Herbold, Ralf
  1995   Technologies as social experiments: The construction and imple-
          mentation of a high-tech waste disposal site. In *Managing technology
          in society: The approach of constructive technology assessment,* ed.
          A. Rip, T. J. Misa, and J. Schot, 185–98. New York: St. Martin's
          Press.
Herndl, Carl G., Barbara A. Fennell, and Carolyn R. Miller
  1990   Understanding failures in organizational discourse: The accident at
          Three Mile Island and the shuttle *Challenger* disaster. In *Textual dy-
          namics of the professions: Historical and contemporary studies of writ-
          ing in professional communities,* ed. C. Bazerman and J. Paradis, 279–
          305. Madison: University of Wisconsin Press.
Hewlett, Richard G., and Francis Duncan
  1974   *Nuclear navy: 1946–1962.* Chicago: University of Chicago Press.
Hibbs, Mark
  2002   METI rules out legal action in response to Japan cover-up. *Nucleonics
          Week* 43 (40): 1.
  2003   German energy debate spills over into open challenge to phase-out.
          Nucleonics Week 44 (37): 2.
Hidden, Anthony
  1989   *Investigation into the Clapham Junction Railway accident.* Depart-
          ment of Transport. London: HMSO.
Higgins, James C., and John M. O'Hara
  2000   Proposed approach for reviewing changes to risk-important human
          actions. NUREG/CR–6689. Washington, DC: U.S. Nuclear Regula-
          tory Commission.
Hilgartner, Stephen
  1992   The social construction of risk objects: Or, how to pry open networks
          of risk. In *Organizations, uncertainties, and risk,* ed. J. F. Short, Jr.,
          and L. Clarke, 39–53. Boulder, CO: Westview Press.
Hirschhorn, Larry
  1988   [1984] *Beyond mechanization: Work and technology in a postindus-
          trial age.* Cambridge: MIT Press.
  1993   Hierarchy versus bureaucracy: The case of a nuclear reactor. In *New
          challenges to understanding organizations,* ed. Karlene H. Roberts,
          137–49. New York: Macmillan.
Holmberg, J., K. Hukki, L. Norros, U. Pulkkinen, and P. Pyy
  1999   An integrated approach to human reliability analysis—decision ana-
          lytic dynamic reliability model. *Reliability Engineering and System
          Safety* 65 (3): 239–50.

Hopson, Michael E.
   1992   Organizational restructuring of a nuclear power plant. M.S. thesis.
           Sloan School of Management, Massachusetts Institute of Technology,
           Cambridge, MA.
Horlick-Jones, Tom
   1998   Meaning and contextualisation in risk assessment. *Reliability Engi-
           neering and System Safety* 59: 79–89.
Horner, Daniel, and Gregory Twachtman
   2003   Calvert Cliffs joins the crowd of units replacing vessel heads. *Inside
           N.R.C.*, May 5.
Horner, Daniel, and Jenny Weil
   2003   Davis-Besse safety culture draws mixed reviews from NRC. *Inside
           N.R.C.*, October 6.
HPRCT Business League
   1999   5th Annual Human Performance/Root Cause/Trending Conference,
           Kansas City, MO. May. http://hprct.dom.com/1999/index.htm.
   2001   7th Annual Human Performance/Root Cause/Trending Conference,
           Baltimore, MD. June. http://hprct.dom.com/2001/index.htm.
Hughes, Thomas Parke
   1983   *Networks of power: Electrification in Western society, 1880–1930.*
           Baltimore, MD: Johns Hopkins University Press.
   1987   The evolution of large technological systems. In *The social construc-
           tion of technological systems*, ed. Bijker, Wiebe E., Thomas P. Hughes,
           and Trevor Pinch, 51–82. Cambridge, MA: MIT Press.
Hug, Richard W.
   1998   Is there hope for the error prone organization?: The mystery of HROs.
           A response to Todd La Porte and Paula Consolini. *International Jour-
           nal of Public Administration* 21 (6–8): 853–55.
Hursh, Steven R.
   2001   Fatigue and alertness management using FAST™. Presentation, 7th
           Annual Human Performance/Root Cause/Trending Workshop. Balti-
           more, MD. June 4–7, 2001. Hursh@saic.com.
Hurst, Nick W.
   1997   *Risk assessment: The human dimension.* London: Royal Society of
           Chemists.
Hutchins, Edwin
   1995   *Cognition in the wild.* Cambridge, MA: MIT Press.
Ihde, Don
   1991   *Instrumental realism: The interface between philosophy of science and
           philosophy of technology.* Bloomington: Indiana University Press.
   2002   *Bodies in technology.* Minneapolis: University of Minnesota Press.
Institute of Nuclear Power Operations
   1985   Japan's nuclear power operation: A U.S. nuclear utility report. Novem-
           ber. Atlanta: Institute of Nuclear Power Operations.
   1988   Performance indicators for the U.S. nuclear utility industry. Atlanta:
           Institute of Nuclear Power Operations.

1990   Increasing personnel awareness of frequent causes of human performance problems. (INPO 90–001). Atlanta: Institute of Nuclear Power Operations.

1992a   Reducing the occurrence of plant events through improved human performance (SOER 92–01). Atlanta: Institute of Nuclear Power Operations.

1992b   Managing outage risk: Operations/outage managers workshop. Volumes 1 and 2, August. Atlanta: Institute of Nuclear Power Operations.

International Atomic Energy Agency

1988   *Basic safety principles for nuclear power plants: A report by the International Nuclear Safety Advisory Group.* (75-INSAG–3). Vienna: International Atomic Energy Agency.

1991   *Safety culture.* Safety Series. International Nuclear Safety Advisory Group (75-INSAG–4). Vienna: International Atomic Energy Agency.

1992   Information sheet. Technical Committee Meeting on "Impact of Management and Organization on the Safe Operation of Nuclear Power Plants." Ref.: J4-TC–804. Vienna. August–September.

1999   Evaluating and improving nuclear power plant operating performance. Nuclear Power Engineering Section. July. 152 IAEA-TEC-DOC–1098. www.iaea.or.at/programmes/ne/nenp/npes/download/tecdoc1098.PDF.

2002   Managing nuclear knowledge. Scientific Forum, 46th regular session of the IAEA General Conference. Vienna. 17–18 September.

2003   The international nuclear event scale. http://www.iaea.or.at/worldatom/Periodicals/Factsheets/index.

International Energy Agency

2001   Nuclear power in the OECD. Presentation by Peter Fraser at the World Nuclear Association Symposium. London. September. http://www.world-nuclear.org/sym/2001/.

Irvine, Judith

1989   When talk isn't cheap: Language and political economy. *American Ethnologist* 16 (2): 248–78.

Jackall, Robert

1988   *Moral mazes: The world of corporate managers.* New York: Oxford University Press.

Jackson, Myles W.

1999   Labor, skills, and practices in the scientific enterprise: Recent works in the cultural history of science. *Journal of Modern History* 71 (December): 902–13.

Jaliff, Juan O.

1991   Organization and management characteristics of a nuclear power plant. M.S. thesis, Sloan School of Management, Massachusetts Institute of Technology, Cambridge, MA.

Jasanoff, Sheila

1986   *Risk management and political culture.* New York: Russell Sage Foundation.

Jasanoff, Sheila (*cont.*)
   1995   *Science at the bar: Law, science, and technology in America.* Cambridge, MA: Harvard University Press.
Jasper, James
   1990   *Nuclear politics: Energy and the state in the United States, Sweden, and France.* Princeton, NJ: Princeton University Press.
Joerges, Bernward, and Barbara Czarniawska
   1998   The question of technology, or how organizations inscribe the world. *Organization Studies* 19 (3): 363–85.
Johnson, Chris W.
   1999   Visualizing the relationship between human error and organizational failure. In *Proceedings of the 17th International Systems Safety Conference*, ed. J. Dixon, 101–10. Unionville, VA: The Systems Safety Society.
Joint Accident Investigation Commission of Estonia, Finland, Sweden
   1997   *Final report on the capsizing on 28 September 1994 in the Baltic Sea of the RO-RO Passenger Vessel MV Estonia.* December. http://www .edita.fi/aib_finland/estoneng/index.html.
Joyce, Patrick, ed.
   1987   *The historical meanings of work.* Cambridge: Cambridge University Press.
Kammen, Daniel M.
   2003   The future of university nuclear science and engineering programs. U.S. House of Representatives, Committee on Science, Subcommittee on Energy. June 10. www.house.gov/science/hearings/energy03/jun10/ kammen.pdf.
Kemeny, John G., et al.
   1979   *The need for change: The legacy of Three Mile Island: Report of The President's Commission on the accident at TMI.* Washington, DC: U.S. Government Printing Office.
Klein, Gary
   1998   *Sources of power: How people make decisions.* Cambridge, MA: MIT Press.
Knapik, Michael
   2002a   ACRS, concerned about human performance, urges expanded RES effort. *Inside N.R.C.*, October 21.
   2002b   RES [NRC Office of Nuclear Regulatory Research] urges NRR [NRC Office of Nuclear Reactor Regulation] to cooperate on new approach to evaluate utility caps [corrective action programs]. *Inside N.R.C.*, August 26.
   2003   Staff to clarify guidance on PRA quality. *Inside N.R.C.*, August 25.
Kochan, T., J. C. Wells, and M. Smith
   1991   Managing workplace safety and health: The case of contract workers in the U.S. petrochemical industry. Final Report to the Occupational Safety and Health Administration, U.S. Department of Labor.

Kochan, Thomas A., and Saul A. Rubinstein
  2000   Toward a stakeholder theory of the firm: The Saturn partnership. *Organization Science* 11 (4): 367–86.
Kouts, Herbert J. C.
  1995   Safety management and conduct of operations at the Department of Energy's Defense Nuclear Facilities. Washington, DC: Defense Nuclear Facilities Safety Board. http://www.deprep.org/archive/techrpts/bm95o06a.htm.
Kovan, Dick
  2002   NUMEX 2002: Excellence rewarded. Special section, Plant maintenance. *Nuclear News*, October, 50.
Kovan, Dick, Rick Michal, and Patrick Sinco
  2003   Nuclear has a lot going for it. Report of the American Nuclear Society annual meeting. *Nuclear News*, August, 35.
Krohn, Wolfgang, and Peter Weingart
  1987   Commentary: Nuclear power as a social experiment—European political "fall out" from the Chernobyl meltdown. *Science, Technology, and Human Values* 12 (2): 52–58.
Krohn, Wolfgang, and Johannes Weyer
  1994   Society as a laboratory: The social risks of experimental research. *Science and Public Policy* 21 (3): 173–83.
Kunda, Gideon
  1992   *Engineering culture: Control and commitment in a high-tech corporation.* Philadelphia: Temple University Press.
Kunreuther, H., and P. Slovic, eds.
  1996   Challenges in risk assessment and risk management. In *The Annals of the American Academy of Political and Social Science*, 545. Thousand Oaks, CA: Sage Periodicals Press.
Labadié, Gerard, René Montmayeul, and Michel Llory
  1998   What lessons can be learnt from incidents and accidents? Working towards a permanent monitoring system. ESReDA International Seminar on Accident Data Bases as a Management Tool. Anverpen, November 16–17. Mimeo.
Lakoff, George, and Mark Johnson
  1980   *Metaphors we live by.* Chicago: University of Chicago Press.
Lal, Bhavya
  1992   A framework for incorporating best practices at nuclear power plants. M.S. thesis, Technology and Policy Program, Department of Nuclear Engineering, Massachusetts Institute of Technology, Cambridge, MA.
Langewiesche, William
  1998   *Inside the sky: A meditation on flight.* New York: Pantheon Books.
Lanir, Z.
  1986   *Fundamental surprise.* Eugene, OR: Decision Research.
LaPorte, Todd R.
  1994a   A strawman speaks up: Comments on *The Limits of Safety. Journal of Contingencies and Crisis Management* 2 (4 December): 207–11.

LaPorte, Todd R. (*cont.*)
  1994b   Large technical systems, institutional surprises, and challenges to polit-
          ical legitimacy. *Technology in Society* 16 (3): 269–88.
  2001   Highly reliable operations and the rigors of sustained legitimacy: Mat-
          ters of public trust and institutional constancy. (English version of
          Fiabilite et legitimaite soutenable [reliability and sustainable legiti-
          macy]). In *Organiser la Fiabilite*, ed. Mathilde Bourrier, 71–106. Paris:
          L'Harmattan.
LaPorte, Todd R., and Paula Consolini
  1991   Working in practice but not in theory: Theoretical challenges of high
          reliability organizations. *Journal of Public Administration Research
          and Theory* 1 (1) (Winter): 19–47.
  1998   Theoretical and operational challenges of "high-reliability organiza-
          tions": Air-traffic control and aircraft carriers. *International Journal
          of Public Administration* 21 (6–8): 847–52.
LaPorte, Todd R., and Gene Rochlin
  1994   Rejoinder to Perrow. *Journal of Contingencies and Crisis Management*
          2 (4 December): 221–27.
LaPorte, Todd R., and Craig W. Thomas
  1995   Regulatory compliance and the ethos of quality enhancement: Sur-
          prises in nuclear power plant operations. *Journal of Public Administra-
          tion Research and Theory* 5 (1): 109–33.
LaPorte, Todd R., Karlene Roberts, and Gene Rochlin
  1989   High reliability organizations: The research challenge. Institute of
          Governmental Studies, University of California, Berkeley. April.
Latorella, Kara A., and Prasad V. Prabhu
  2000   A review of human error in aviation maintenance and inspection. *In-
          ternational Journal of Industrial Ergonomics* 26 (1): 133–61.
Latour, Bruno
  1987   *Science in action: How to follow scientists and engineers through soci-
          ety.* Cambridge, MA: Harvard University Press.
  1994   [1991] *We have never been modern.* Cambridge, MA: Harvard Univer-
          sity Press.
  1996   *Aramis or the love of technology.* Trans. Catherine Porter. Cambridge,
          MA: Harvard University Press.
Lave, Jean
  1988   *Cognition in practice: Mind, mathematics and culture in everyday life.*
          Cambridge: Cambridge University Press.
Lebow, Cynthia C., Liam P. Sarsfield, William L. Stanley, Emile Ettedgui, and
  Garth Henning
  1999   Safety in the skies: Personnel and parties in NTSB aviation accident
          investigations. Institute for Civil Justice, 56. Washington, DC: RAND
          Corporation.
Lee, Terence, and K. Harrison
  2000   Assessing safety culture in nuclear power stations. *Safety Science* 34
          (1–3): 61–97.

Leveson, Nancy G.
   1995   *Safeware: System safety and computers*. Reading, MA: Addison-Wesley.
   2002   A new accident model for engineering safer systems. 27 pp. http://
          sunnyday.mit.edu/accidents/esd.pdf.
Levins, Richard, and Richard Lewontin
   1985   *The dialectical biologist*. Cambridge, MA: Harvard University Press.
Levinson, Stephen C.
   1983   *Pragmatics*. Cambridge: Cambridge University Press.
Levy, Paul
   1997   Draft letter report for comment: Annotated bibliography for the man-
          agement and organization factors workshop. For the U.S. Nuclear
          Regulatory Commission. November. Idaho Falls: Idaho National Engi-
          neering Laboratory. INEEL/EXT–97–01293.
Liberatore, Angela
   1999   *The management of uncertainty: Learning from Chernobyl*. London:
          Gordon and Breach.
Lienhard, John H.
   2000   *The engines of our ingenuity: An engineer looks at technology and
          culture*. New York: Oxford University Press.
Linde, Charlotte
   1988a The quantitative study of communicative success: Politeness and acci-
          dents in aviation discourse. *Language in Society* 17: 375–99.
   1988b Who's in charge here?: Cooperative work and authority negotiation
          in police helicopter missions. Publications of the ACM: *Computer Sup-
          ported Cooperative Work* 282 (9): 52–64.
Lipton, Eric, and James Glanz
   2002   Towers' collapse raises new doubts about fire tests. *New York Times*,
          April 8, A1, A12.
Llory, Michel A.
   1990   Research on human factors: Generic operator models, on-site and sim-
          ulator studies. 1990 ANS Winter Meeting. Washington, DC.
   1991   Human reliability and human factors in complex organizations: Epis-
          temological and critical analysis—Practical avenues to action. SMIRT
          11th Post-Conference Seminar on Probabilistic Safety Assessment
          Methodology. Kyoto, August 26–27.
   1997   Human- and work-centered safety: Keys to a new conception of man-
          agement. *Ergonomics* 40 (10): 1148–58.
Lloyd, Ronald L., John R. Boardman, and Sada V. Pullani
   2000   Causes and significance of design-basis issues at U.S. Nuclear Power
          Plants. NUREG SR1275, Vol. 14. Regulatory Effectiveness Assessment
          and Human Factors Branch, Division of Systems Analysis and Regula-
          tory Effectiveness, Office of Nuclear Regulatory Research, U.S. Nu-
          clear Regulatory Commission. Washington, D.C. November.
Lochbaum, David
   2004   U.S. nuclear plants in the 21st century: The risk of a lifetime. Washing-
          ton, DC: Union of Concerned Scientists. http://www.ucsusa.org/
          documents/nuclear04fn1.pdf.

Lucy, John A.
  1997   Linguistic relativity. *Annual Review of Anthropology* 26: 291–312.
MacAvoy, Paul W., and Jean W. Rosenthal
  2004   *Corporate profit and nuclear safety: Strategy at Northeast Utilities in the 1990s.* Princeton, NJ: Princeton University Press. In press.
MacKenzie, Donald
  1990   *Inventing accuracy: A historical sociology of nuclear missile guidance.* Cambridge, MA: MIT Press.
  1996   *Knowing machines: Essays on technical change.* Cambridge, MA: MIT Press.
MacLachlan, Ann
  2002   A decade later, regulators, EDF say vessel head change-outs paid off. *Nucleonics Week* 43 (44): 1.
  2003a Complacency, negligence threaten nuclear industry, WANO warns. *Nucleonics Week* 44 (42): 1.
  2003b WANO analyzing 'sentinel' events to steer operators away from pitfalls. *Nucleonics Week* 44 (43): 8.
Magnani, Lorenzo
  2001   *Abduction, reason, and science: Processes of discovery and explanation.* New York: Kluwer Academic/Plenum.
Mailer, Norman
  1970   *Of a fire on the moon.* Boston: Little, Brown.
Makansi, Jason
  1999   Special report: Get the most from the existing asset base. *Power* 143 (3): 30–40.
Maltz, Daniel N., and Ruth A. Borker
  1982   A cultural approach to male-female miscommunication. In *Language and social identity,* ed. John J. Gumperz, 195–216. Cambridge: Cambridge University Press.
Manning, Peter K.
  1992a *Organizational communication.* Hawthorne, NY: Aldine de Gruyter.
  1992b Managing risk: Managing uncertainty in the British Nuclear Installations Inspectorate. In *Organizations, uncertainties, and risk,* ed. J. F. Short, Jr., and Lee Clarke, 255–73. Boulder, CO: Westview Press.
March, James G.
  1991   Exploration and exploitation in organizational learning. *Organization Science* 2 (1): 71–87.
March, James G., Lee S. Sproull, and Michal Tamuz
  1996   [1991] Learning from samples of one or fewer. In *Organizational learning,* ed. Michael D. Cohen and Lee S. Sproull, 1–19. Thousand Oaks, CA: Sage Publishers.
March, James G., and Roger Weissinger-Baylon
  1986   *Ambiguity and command: Organizational perspectives on military decision making.* Marshfield, MA: Pitman Publishing.
Marcinkowski, K., G. Apostolakis, and R. Weil
  2001   A computer-aided technique for identifying latent conditions (CATI-LaC). *Cognition, Technology and Work* 3 (2): 111–26.

Marcus, Alfred A.
   1995   Managing with danger: An introduction. *Industrial Crisis Quarterly* 9
           (2): 139–51.
Marcus, Alfred A., and Mary L. Nichols
   1999   On the edge: Heeding the warnings of unusual events. *Organization
           Science* 10 (4): 482–99.
Marcus, Alfred A., et al.
   1990   Organization and safety in nuclear power plants. U.S. Nuclear Regula-
           tory Commission, Office of Nuclear Regulatory Research, Division of
           Systems Research. (NUREG/CR–5437). Washington, DC: U.S. Nu-
           clear Regulatory Commission.
Marcus, Alfred A., M. L. Nichols, and G. E. McAvoy
   1993   Economic and behavioral perspectives on safety. *Research in Organi-
           zational Behavior* 15: 323–55.
Marcus, George F.
   1991   Past, present and emergent identities: requirements for ethnographies
           of late twentieth-century modernity worldwide. In *Modernity and
           identity*, ed. Scott Lash and Jonathan Friedman, 309–30. London:
           Basil Blackwell.
Marcus, George E., ed.
   1998   *Corporate futures*. Limited Edition Series, 5. Chicago: University of
           Chicago Press.
Massachusetts Institute of Technology
   2003   The future of nuclear power: An interdisciplinary MIT Study. http://
           web.mit.edu/nuclearpower/.
Maurino, Daniel E., James Reason, Neil Johnston, and Rob. B. Lee
   1995   *Beyond aviation human factors*. Brookfield, VT: Ashgate Publishing.
Mayo, Deborah G., and Rachelle D. Hollander, eds.
   1991   *Acceptable evidence: Science and values in risk management*. New
           York: Oxford University Press.
Mazuzan, George T., and J. Samuel Walker
   1984   *Controlling the atom: The beginnings of nuclear regulation 1946–
           1962*. Berkeley: University of California Press.
McDonald, N., S. Corrigan, C. Daly, and S. Cromie
   2000   Safety management systems and safety culture in aircraft maintenance
           organisations. *Safety Science* 34: 151–76.
Meister, David
   1999   *The history of human factors and ergonomics*. Mahwah, NJ: Lawrence
           Erlbaum.
Mercier, Jean-Pierre
   1988   *Nuclear power plant maintenance*. English adaptation of "La Mainte-
           nance des Centralés Nucleaires" published for Electricité de France
           1987. 2nd edition. Paris: Editions Kirk.
Meserve, Richard A.
   2002   Safety culture: An NRC perspective. 2002 INPO CEO Conference, No-
           vember 8. http://www.nrc.gov/reading-rm/doc-collections/commission/
           speeches/2002/s-02–033.html.

Meshkati, Najmin
 1991 Human factors in large-scale technological systems' accidents: Three
 Mile Island, Bhopal, Chernobyl. *Industrial Crisis Quarterly* 5: 133–54.
Michal, Rick
 2001 The *Nuclear News* interview: Caragher on equipment obsolescence at
 Fermi-2. October: 37–41.
 2002 Utility Working Conference: A revival through improved plant operations. *Nuclear News*, October, 65–69.
Miller, Carolyn R.
 1995 The roots of risk analysis: Chauncey Starr's management of rhetorical
 pathos. Conference paper, Society for the Social Study of Science and
 Technology.
 1999a The presumption of expertise: *Ethos* in risk analysis. Conference paper,
 American Association for the Studies of Rhetoric in Science and Technology, National Communication Association. Chicago. November.
 1999b Nuclear power and risk analysis: A rhetorical alliance for managing
 emotion. Annual Conference, National Communication Association,
 Association for the Study of Rhetoric in Science and Technology, Panel:
 "Multiple perspectives on nuclear energy: Classical rhetoric, critical
 theory, and public communication." November 3. Chicago.
Mindell, David A.
 2000 Beasts and systems: Taming and stability in the history of control. In
 Cultures of Control, ed. Miriam R. Levin, 205–24. New York: Harwood Academic Publishers.
 2002 *Between human and machine: Feedback, control, and computing before cybernetics*. Baltimore, MD: Johns Hopkins University Press.
Mitcham, Carl
 1994 *Thinking through technology: The path between engineering and philosophy*. Chicago: University of Chicago Press.
Moore, Patrick
 1992 Intimidation and communication: A case study of the *Challenger* accident. *Journal of Business and Technical Communication* 6 (4 October): 403–37.
Moray, Neville P., and Barbara M. Huey
 1988 *Human factors research and nuclear safety*. Washington, DC: National
 Academy Press.
Morgan, M. Granger, and Susan F. Tierney
 1998 Research support for the power industry. National Research Council
 Issues in Science and Technology Online. Fall. http: //www.nap.edu/
 issues/15.1/morgan.htm.
Morone, Joseph G., and Edward J. Woodhouse
 1986 *Averting catastrophe: Strategies for regulating risky technologies*.
 Berkeley: University of California Press.
Mumaw, R. J., E. M. Roth, K. J. Vicente, and C. M. Burns
 2000 There is more to monitoring a nuclear power plant than meets the eye.
 Human Factors (42): 36–55.

Mumby, Dennis K.
  1988   *Communication and power in organizations: Discourse, ideology, and domination.* Norwood, NJ: Ablex.
Myers, Greg
  1996   Out of the laboratory and down to the bay: Writing in science and technology studies. *Written Communication* 13 (1): 5–43.
Myers, H. R.
  1994   Nuclear oversight by Congress. In *Controlling the atom in the 21st century,* ed. D. P. O'Very, C. E. Paine, and D. W. Reicher, 241–59. Boulder, CO: Westview Press.
National Academy of Science
  2003   A burning plasma program strategy to advance fusion energy. Report of the Fusion Energy Sciences Advisory Committee. http://www.ofes .science.doe.gov/More_HTML/FESAC/FESAC9–02/Prager.pdf.
National Transportation Safety Board
  1997   Aircraft accident report: In-flight fire and impact with terrain, ValuJet Airlines, Flight 592 DC–9–32, N904VJ, Everglades, near Miami, Florida, May 11, 1996. Report PB97–910406. August 19.
Negroni, Christine
  2000   *Deadly departure: Why the experts failed to prevent the TWA Flight 800 disaster and how it could happen again.* New York: Cliff Street Books.
Nelkin, Dorothy
  1971   *Nuclear power and its critics: The Cayuga Lake controversy.* Ithaca, NY: Cornell University Press.
  1982   *The atom besieged: Extraparliamentary dissent in France and Germany.* Cambridge: MIT Press.
Newfield, Christopher
  1998   Corporate culture wars. In *Corporate Futures,* ed. George E. Marcus, 23–62. Limited Editions Series, 5. Chicago: University of Chicago Press.
Norros, Leena
  1996   System disturbances as springboard for development of operators' expertise. In *Cognition and communication at work,* ed. Yrjö Engström and David Middleton, 159–76. Cambridge: Cambridge University Press.
Nuclear Energy Institute
  1994   The U.S. nuclear industry's strategic plan for building new nuclear power plants: Fourth annual update. Washington, DC: Nuclear Energy Institute Executive Committee.
  1999   Nuclear energy: 2000 and beyond—1999 update to "A Strategic Direction for Nuclear Energy in the 21st Century." Washington, DC. May.
  2000a   Corrective action program benchmarking report. NEI Industrywide Benchmarking Report LP002. Washington, DC: Nuclear Energy Institute. November.

Nuclear Energy Institute (*cont.*)

2000b   Regulatory assessment performance indicator guideline. NEI 99–02 revision. 28 March.

2000c   The standard nuclear performance model: a process management approach. Revision 1. December.

2001   Human performance process benchmarking report. NEI/INPO/EPRI Industrywide Benchmarking Project, LP 002. Washington, DC: Nuclear Energy Institute. May.

2003a   State electric industry restructuring: Nuclear plants in states considering retail choice. http://www.nei.org/documents/nuclearplants.pdf.

2003b   Testimony before the Energy Subcommittee, House Science Committee, U.S. House of Representatives. Angelina S. Howard, Executive Vice President. June 10. www.house.gov/science/hearings/energy03/jun10/howard.pdf.

Nuclear Safety Review Concepts Corporation

n.d.   Diagnostic evaluation study: Executive summary. Windsor, CT. Mimeo.

Nuclear News

1993   Nuclear utilities must cut costs: ANS Meeting. July, 26–31.

1999   Trial run nears for new inspection program. May, 23.

2000   Nuclear plant maintenance: An EPRI manager's perspective. October, 41.

2001   Job cuts announced for nuclear plants. August, 24.

2002   Number of employees declines at nuclear plants. October, 16.

2003   Status of license renewal applications in the United States. August, 22.

Nuclear Power Oversight Committee

1992   Strategic plan for building new nuclear power plants. Second annual update. November. Washington, D.C. (Replaced in 1994 by the Nuclear Energy Institute Executive Committee.)

Nucleonics Week

2002   NRC confirms INES level 3 rating for Davis-Besse head corrosion. 43 (25): 2.

Numark, Neil J., and Robert P. Grant

2001   Impact of electricity deregulation on the U.S. Nuclear industry. Global Foundation Annual Conference, "Competition in Electricity Marks: Deregulation, the Environment and Security of Supply." London. December 4. http: //www.numarkassoc.com/Londonspeech.pdf.

Ochs, Elinor, and Sally Jacoby

1997   Down to the wire: The cultural clock of physicists and the discourse of consensus. *Language in Society* 26: 479–505.

Oedewald, Pia, and Teemu Reiman

2003   Core task modelling in cultural assessment: A case study in nuclear power plant maintenance. *Cognition, Technology and Work* 5 (4): 283–93.

Olsen, John, et al.

1988   *Development of programmatic performance indicators.* NUREG/CR–5241. Washington, DC: Nuclear Regulatory Commission.

Ontario Hydro Nuclear
  1997   A report to Ontario Hydro Nuclear Management: The IIPA [Indepen-
          dent Integrated Performance Assessment]/SSFI [Safety System Func-
          tional Inspection] Evaluation, Findings, and Recommendations. Parts
          I and II. July 21. http: //www.ccnr.org/hydro_report.html.
Orasanu, Judith
  1993   Decision-making in the cockpit. In *Cockpit resource management*, ed.
          Earl L. Wiener, Barbara G. Kanki, and Robert L. Helmreich, 137–72.
          New York: Academic Press.
Organisation for Economic Co-Operation and Development
  1991   *Regulatory requirements and experience related to low-power and shut-
          down activities: A report on a survey of national practices.* Committee
          on Nuclear Regulatory Activities. Paris: OECD Publications Service.
  1994   *Nuclear safety research in OECD countries: A report by an NEA
          group of experts.* Nuclear Energy Agency. Paris: OECD Publications
          Service.
  2000   Workshop on assuring nuclear safety competence into the 21st century.
          Budapest, October 1999. Nuclear Energy Agency, Committee on Nu-
          clear Regulatory Activities. NEA/CNRA/R(2000)1.
Östberg, Gustaf
  1992   Inspecting nuclear pressure vessels: The conundrum of minimizing
          risk. Institute of Mechanical Engineering Proceedings 206, Part A:
          Journal of Power and Energy: 53–57.
Pasqualetti, M. J.
  1994   Decommissioning nuclear power plants. In *Controlling the atom in the
          21st century*, ed. D. P. O'Very, C. E. Paine, and D. W. Reicher, 315–
          35. Boulder, CO: Westview Press.
Pate-Cornell, M. Elisabeth
  1990   Organizational aspects of engineering system safety: The case of off-
          shore platforms. *Science 250*: 1210–16.
Perin, Constance
  1970   *With man in mind: an interdisciplinary prospectus for environmental
          design.* Cambridge: MIT Press.
  1977   *Everything in its place: Social order and land use in America.* Prince-
          ton: Princeton University Press.
  1988   *Belonging in America: Reading between the lines.* Madison: University
          of Wisconsin Press.
  1991   The moral fabric of the office: Panopticon discourse and schedule flex-
          ibility. In *Research in the sociology of organizations*, Vol. 8, Organiza-
          tions and Professions, ed. Pamela S. Tolbert and Stephen R. Barley,
          243–70. Greenwich, CT: JAI Press.
  1992   The communicative circle: Museums as communities. In *Museums and
          communities: The politics of public culture*, ed. Ivan Karp, Christine
          Mullen Kreamer, and Steven Lavine, 182–220. Washington, DC:
          Smithsonian Institution Press.
  1993   What kind of problem is an outage? In *Transactions of the American
          Nuclear Society*, "Risk management—Expanding horizons," ed. Ron-
          ald A. Knief, 57–59. LaGrange Park, IL: American Nuclear Society.

Perin, Constance (*cont.*)

1994   The reception of new, unusual, and difficult art. In *The artist outsider: Creativity and the boundaries of culture*, ed. Michael Hall and Eugene Metcalf, 172–97. Washington, DC: Smithsonian Institution Press.

1995a   Organizations as contexts: Implications for safety science and practice. *Environmental and Industrial Crisis Quarterly* 9 (2): 152–74.

1995b   How organizational, technical, and cultural processes work together for safety. Proceedings, *Safety Culture in Nuclear Installations*. American Nuclear Society/Austria Local Section and International Atomic Energy Agency. Vienna, Austria, 303–10.

1998a   Operating as experimenting: Synthesizing engineering and scientific values in nuclear power production. *Science, Technology & Human Values*, Special Issue, *New Anthropological Approaches to Science, Technology, and Society* 23 (1): 98–128.

1998b   Making more matter at the bottom line. In *Corporate futures*, ed. George E. Marcus, 63–88. Limited Editions Series, 5. Chicago: University of Chicago Press.

1998c   Work, space, and time on the threshold of a new century. In *New international perspectives on telework: From telecommuting to the virtual organisation*, ed. P. J. Jackson and J. M. Van der Wielen, 40–55. London: Routledge.

Perin, Constance, and John S. Carroll

1997   Organizational analysis in high-hazard production systems: An academy-industry dialogue. Final Report of a Workshop with members of the Center for Chemical Process Safety and academics funded by the National Science Foundation. October.

Perron, M. J., and R. H. Friedlander

1996   The effects of downsizing on safety in the chemical processing industry and the hydrocarbon process industry. *Process Safety Progress* 15 (1): 18–25.

Perrow, Charles

1983   The organizational context of human factors engineering. *Administrative Science Quarterly* 28: 521–41.

1984   *Normal accidents: Living with high-risk technologies*. New York: Basic Books.

1986   *Complex organizations: A critical essay*. 3rd ed. New York: McGraw Hill.

1994a   The limits of safety: The enhancement of a theory of accidents. *Journal of Contingencies and Crisis Management* 2 (4): 212–20.

1994b   Accidents in high-risk systems. *Technology Studies* 1 (1): 1–19.

1999   *Normal accidents: Living with high-risk technologies*. With a new Afterword and a postscript on the Y2K problem. Princeton, NJ: Princeton University Press.

Petryna, Adriana

1995   Sarcophagus: Chernobyl in historical light. *Cultural Anthropology* 10 (2): 196–220.

2002   *Life exposed: Biological citizens after Chernobyl.* Princeton, NJ: Princeton University Press.

Pidgeon, Nick, and M. O'Leary
2000   Man-made disasters: Why technology and organizations (sometimes) fail. *Safety Science* 34: 15–30.

Pinch, Trevor
1993   "Testing—One, Two, Three . . . Testing!": Toward a sociology of testing. *Science, Technology, and Human Values* 18 (1): 25–41.

Pool, Robert
1997   *Beyond engineering: How society shapes technology.* The Sloan Technology Series. New York: Oxford University Press.

Porter, Theodore M.
1995   *Trust in numbers: The pursuit of objectivity in science and public life.* Princeton, NJ: Princeton University Press.

Poser, Hans
1998   On structural differences between science and engineering. *Techné: Journal of the Society for Philosophy and Technology* 4 (2): 81–92. http://scholar.lib.vt.edu/ejournals/SPT/spt.html

Potter, Jonathan, and Margaret Wetherell
1987   *Discourse and social psychology: Beyond attitudes and behaviour.* London: Sage Publications.

Potter, Jonathan, Margaret Wetherell, and A. Chitty
1991   Quantification rhetoric: Cancer on television. *Discourse and Society* 2 (3): 333–65.

Powell, Walter W.
1990   Neither market nor hierarchy: Network forms of organization. *Research in Organizational Behavior* (12): 295–336.

Putnam, Linda L., and Gail T. Fairhurst
2001   Discourse analysis in organizations: Issues and concerns. In *The new handbook of organizational communication: Advances in theory, research, and methods,* ed. Fredric M. Jablin and Linda L. Putnam, 78–136. Thousand Oaks, CA: Sage Publications.

Rabinow, Paul
1999   *French DNA: Trouble in purgatory.* Chicago: University of Chicago Press.

Raiffa, Howard
1968   *Decision analysis.* Reading, MA: Addison-Wesley.

Ramsey, Charles B., and Mohammad Modarres
1998   *Commercial nuclear power: Assuring safety for the future.* New York: John Wiley & Sons.

Rasmussen, Jens
1990   The role of error in organizing behaviour. *Ergonomics* 33 (10/11): 1185–99.
1992   Small and large-scale accidents. Overhead presentation, New Technologies and Work Study Group, Bad Homburg, Germany.
1993   Diagnostic reasoning in action. *IEEE Transactions on Systems, Man, and Cybernetics* 23 (4): 981–92.

Rasmussen, Jens (*cont.*)
  1994   Open peer commentary on "Accidents in High-Risk Systems," article
          by Charles Perrow. *Technology Studies* 1 (1): 25–34.
  1996   Cognitive control and human error mechanisms. In *New technology
          and human error*, ed. J. Rasmussen, K. Duncan, and J. Leplat, 53–61.
          London: John Wiley & Sons.
Rasmussen, Jens, and Roger Batstone
  1989   Why do complex organizational systems fail? Environment Working
          Paper no. 20, Policy Planning and Research Staff, Environment De-
          partment. Washington, DC: The World Bank. October.
Rau, Erik P.
  2001   Technological systems, expertise, and policy making: The British ori-
          gins of operational research. In *Technologies of power: essays in honor
          of Thomas Parke Hughes and Agatha Chipley Hughes*, ed. Michael
          Thad Allen and Gabrielle Hecht, 215–52. Cambridge, MA: MIT Press.
Reason, James
  1987   Generic error-modelling systems (GEMS): A cognitive framework for
          locating common human error forms. In *New technology and human
          error*, ed J. Rasmussen, K. Duncan, and J. Leplat, 63–83. London: John
          Wiley & Sons.
  1990   *Human error.* Cambridge: Cambridge University Press.
  1997   *Managing the risks of organizational accidents.* Brookfield, VT: Ash-
          gate Publishing.
  1999   Are we casting the net too widely in our search for the factors contrib-
          uting to errors and accidents? In *Nuclear safety: A human factors per-
          spective*, ed. Jyuji Misumi, Bernhard Wilpert, and Rainer Miller, 199–
          208. London: Taylor and Francis.
Rees, Joseph
  1994   *Hostages of each other: The transformation of nuclear safety since
          Three Mile Island.* Chicago: University of Chicago Press.
Reynard, Pierre Claude
  1999   Unreliable mills: Maintenance practices in early modern papermaking.
          Technology and Culture 40 (2): 237–62.
Riccio, Jim, and Matthew Freedman
  1993   Hear no evil, see no evil, speak no evil: What the Nuclear Regulatory
          Commission won't tell you about America's nuclear reactors. Critical
          Mass Energy Project. Washington, DC: Public Citizen.
Rijpma, Jos A.
  1997   Complexity, tight-coupling and reliability: Connecting normal acci-
          dents theory and high reliability theory. *Journal of Contingencies and
          Crisis Management* 5 (1): 15–23.
Rip, Arie, Thomas J. Misa, and Johan Schot, eds.
  1995   *Managing technology in society: The approach of constructive tech-
          nology assessment.* New York: St. Martin's Press.
Roberts, Karlene
  1990   Some characteristics of one type of high reliability organization. *Orga-
          nization Science* 1 (2): 160–76.

1993   *New challenges to understanding organizations*. Editor. New York: Macmillan.

Rochlin, Gene I.
1991   Iran Air Flight 655: Complex, large-scale military systems and the failure of control. In *Responding to large technical systems: Control or anticipation*, ed. Todd LaPorte, 95–121. Dordrecht: Kluwer Academic Publishers.
1994   Social and cultural dimensions of operator performance: Some empirical observations. First International Conference on Human-Factor Research in Nuclear Power Plant Operations: Berlin, November. Mimeo.

Rochlin, Gene I., and Alexandra von Meier
1994   Nuclear power operations: A cross-cultural perspective. *Annual Review of Energy and the Environment* 19: 153–87.

Rockwell, Theodore
1992   *The Rickover effect: how one man made a difference*. Annapolis, MD: Naval Institute Press.

Roth, George L.
1992   Managing structural tensions in maintaining a high-reliability organization: The study of 'River Point' Nuclear Power Plant. Cambridge, MA: MIT Sloan School of Management, unpublished manuscript.

Rothwell, Geoffrey
1996   Organizational structure and expected output at nuclear power plants. *The Review of Economics and Statistics* 78 (3): 482–88.

Roux-Dufort, Christophe, and Emmanuel Metais
1999   Building core competencies in crisis management through organizational learning: The case of the French nuclear power producer. *Technological Forecasting and Social Change* 60 (2): 113–27.

Royal Society
1992   *Risk: Analysis, perception, and management*. London: The Royal Society.

Ryle, Gilbert
1949   *The concept of mind*. London: Hutchinson & Co.

Sagan, Scott D.
1993   *The limits of safety: Organizations, accidents and nuclear weapons*. Princeton, NJ: Princeton University Press.
1994   Toward a political theory of organizational reliability. *Journal of Contingencies and Crisis Management* 2 (4): 228–40.
1996   When redundancy backfires: Why organizations try harder and fail more often. *American Political Science Association Annual Meeting*. San Francisco, CA.

Sahlins, Marshall
1976   *Culture and practical reason*. Chicago, IL: University of Chicago Press.

Sauer, Beverly A.
1992   The engineer as rational man: The problem of imminent danger in a non-rational environment. *IEEE Transactions on Professional Communication* 35 (4): 242–49.

Sauer, Beverly A. (*cont.*)
  1993   Sense and sensibility in technical documentation: How feminist inter-
          pretation strategies can save lives in the nation's mines. *Journal of
          Business and Technical Communication* 7 (1): 63–83.
  1994a   The dynamics of disaster: A three-dimensional view of documentation
          in a tightly regulated industry. *Technical Communication Quarterly* 3
          (4): 393–419.
  1994b   Fatal grammar: The rhetoric of disasters. *Technical Communication,
          First Quarter 1994,* 154–58.
  1998   Embodied knowledge: The textual representation of embodied sensory
          information in a dynamic and uncertain material environment. *Writ-
          ten Communication* 15 (2): 131–69.
  2003   *The rhetoric of risk: Technical documentation in hazardous environ-
          ments.* Mahwah, NJ: Lawrence Erlbaum.
Schatzki, Theodore R.
  1983   The prescription is description: Wittgenstein on the human sciences.
          In *The need for interpretation,* ed. Sollace Mitchell and Michael Rosen,
          118–40. London: Athlone Press.
Schieffelin, Bambi B., K. A. Woolard, and P. V. Kroskrity
  1998   *Language ideologies: Practice and theory.* New York: Oxford Univer-
          sity Press.
Schon, Donald A.
  1983   *The reflective practitioner: How professionals think in action.* New
          York: Basic Books.
Schulman, Paul R.
  1989   The "logic" of organizational irrationality. *Administration and Society*
          21 (1): 31–53.
  1993a   The analysis of high reliability organizations: A comparative frame-
          work. In *New challenges to understanding organizations,* ed. K. H.
          Roberts, 33–54. New York: Macmillan.
  1993b   Negotiated order of organizational reliability. *Administration and So-
          ciety* 25 (3): 353–72.
Schwartzman, Helen B.
  1989   *The meeting: Gatherings in organizations and communities.* New
          York: Plenum Press.
Schwoebel, Richard L.
  1999   *Explosion aboard the Iowa.* Annapolis, MD: Naval Institute Press.
Science and Technology Agency of Japan
  1999   A summary of the report of the criticality accident investigation com-
          mittee. The Nuclear Safety Commission. December 24. Provisional
          translation. Press release. http: //www.mext.go.jp/english/news/1999/
          12/g991209.htm.
Scientech
  2003   Commercial nuclear power plants. Edition no. 22. March. http://www
          .scientech.com/downloads/index.html.

Scranton, Philip
   2000   Missing the target? A comment on Edward Constant's "Reliable Knowledge and Unreliable Stuff." *Technology and Culture* 41: 752–64.
   2000   Rejoinder to Constant. *Technology and Culture* 41: 776–82.
Searle, John R.
   1969   *Speech acts.* London: Cambridge University Press.
   2001   *Rationality in action.* Cambridge, MA: MIT Press.
Shapiro, Michael
   1983   *Sense of grammar: Language as semeiotic.* Bloomington: Indiana University Press.
Shenhar, Aaron J.
   1991   Project management style and technological uncertainty (part 1): From low- to high-tech. *Project Management Journal* 22 (4): 11–14, 47.
   1992   Project management style and the space shuttle program (part 2): A retrospective look. *Project Management Journal* 23 (1): 32–37.
   1998   From theory to practice: Toward a typology of project-management styles. *IEEE Transactions on Engineering Management* 45 (1): 33–44.
Shenhar, Aaron J., and Zeev Bonen
   1997   The new taxonomy of systems: Toward an adaptive systems engineering framework. *IEEE Transactions on Systems, Man, and Cybernetics—Part A: Systems and Humans* 27 (2): 137–45.
Sheridan, Thomas B.
   2002   *Humans and automation.* New York: John Wiley & Sons.
Sherwin, David J.
   1999   A constructive critique of reliability-centered maintenance. *IEEE Proceedings, Annual Reliability and Maintainability Symposium:* 238–44.
Sherzer, Joel
   1987   A discourse-centered approach to language and culture. *American Anthropologist* 89: 295–309.
Shinohara, Hirofumi, Fumio Kotani, and Tetsuya Tsukada
   1996   Human factors as revealed by the use of natural language in near-incidents at nuclear power plants. In *Nuclear safety: A human factors perspective*, ed. Jyuji Misumi, Bernhard Wilpert, and Rainer Miller, 305–30. Philadelphia: Taylor & Francis.
Short, James F., Jr., and Lee Clarke
   1992   Social organization and risk. In *Organizations, uncertainties, and risk*, ed. J. F. Short, Jr., and Lee Clarke, 309–21. Boulder, CO: Westview Press.
Shrivastava, Paul
   1992   *Bhopal: Anatomy of a crisis.* 2nd edition. London: Paul Chapman.
Silva, Franco
   1993   Managing high-risk, technology-intensive companies in heavily regulated environments: Two case studies in the nuclear industry. Master's thesis. Cambridge, MA: MIT Sloan School of Management.

Silverstein, Michael
    1998   The uses and utility of ideology: A commentary. In *Language ideolo-gies: Practice and theory.* ed. B. B. Schieffelin, K. A. Wollard, and P. V. Kroskrity, 123–45. New York: Oxford University Press.
Slaton, Amy
    2001   "As near as practicable": Precision, ambiguity, and the social features of industrial quality control. *Technology and Culture* 42: 51–80.
Slovic, Paul
    1991   Perceived risk, stigma, and potential economic impacts of a high-level nuclear waste repository in Nevada. *Risk Analysis* 11 (4): 683–96.
    1995   Judgment and decision making in emergency situations. In *Preparing for nuclear power plant accidents,* ed. D. Golding, J. X. Kasperson, and R. E. Kasperson, 165–80. Boulder, CO: Westview Press.
Snook, Scott A.
    2000   *Friendly fire: The accidental shootdown of U.S. Black Hawks over Northern Iraq.* Princeton, NJ: Princeton University Press.
Solow, Robert M.
    1987   Government and the labor market. Paper prepared for conference on "New Developments in Labor Markets and Human Resource Policies." Massachusetts Institute of Technology, Endicott House (June).
Sorensen, J. N.
    2002   Safety culture: A survey of the state-of-the-art. *Reliability Engineering and System Safety* 76: 189–204.
Star, Susan Leigh
    1992   Craft vs. commodity, mess vs. transcendence: How the right tool be-came the wrong one in the case of taxidermy and natural history. In *The right tools for the job: At work in twentieth-century life sciences,* ed. Adele E. Clarke and Joan H. Fujimura, 165–80. Princeton, NJ: Princeton University Press.
Stinchcombe, Arthur L.
    1990   *Information and organizations.* Berkeley: University of California Press.
Stinchcombe, Arthur L., and Carol A. Heimer
    1985   *Organization theory and project management: Administering uncer-tainty in Norwegian offshore oil.* Oslo: Norwegian University Press.
Suchard, Alexandra, and Gene Rochlin
    1993   The control of operational risk in nuclear power plant operations: Some cross-cultural perspectives. In *Proceedings of the American Nuclear Society Conference Risk Management-Expanding Horizons,* ed. Ronald A. Knief, 190–92. La Grange Park, IL: American Nuclear Society.
Suchman, Lucy A.
    1987   *Plans and situated actions: The problem of human-machine communi-cation.* Cambridge: Cambridge University Press.

Takano, K., K. Sawayanagi, and T. Kabetani
  1994   System for analyzing and evaluating human-related nuclear power plant
          incidents. *Journal of Nuclear Science and Technology* 31: 894–913.
Takano, Kenichi, and James Reason
  1999   Psychological biases affecting human cognitive performance in dy-
          namic operational environments. *Journal of Nuclear Science and Tech-
          nology* 36 (11): 1041–51.
Tamuz, Michal
  2000   Defining away dangers: A study in the influences of managerial cogni-
          tion on information systems. In *Organizational cognition: Computa-
          tion and interpretation,* ed. Theresa K. Lant and Zur Shapira, 157–83.
          Mahwah, NJ: Lawrence Erlbaum.
  2001   Learning disabilities for regulators: The perils of organizational learn-
          ing in the air transportation industry. *Administration and Society* 33
          (3) 276–302.
Tannen, Deborah
  1984a   *Coherence in spoken and written discourse.* Norwood, NJ: Ablex.
  1984b   *Conversational style: Analyzing talk among friends.* Norwood, NJ:
          Ablex.
Tasca, Leo
  1990   *The social construction of human error.* Ph.D. dissertation, Depart-
          ment of Sociology, State University of New York at Stony Brook.
Tenera, L. P.
  1990   *Excellence in nuclear operations: An assessment of lessons learned
          from problem plant indicators, attributes and symptoms.* An industry
          white paper. April. Mimeo.
Tenner, Edward
  1996   *Why things bite back: Technology and the revenge of unintended con-
          sequences.* New York: Alfred A. Knopf.
Tennessee Valley Authority
  2002   TVA board approves Browns Ferry Unit 1 recovery, extended opera-
          tion. News release, May 16. http://www.tva.gov/news/releases/
          0502bferry.htm.
Thomas, Robert J.
  1994   *What machines can't do: Politics and technology in the industrial en-
          terprise.* Berkeley: University of California Press.
Thompson, Charles C.
  1999   *A glimpse of hell: The explosion on the USS Iowa and its cover-up.*
          New York: W. W. Norton.
Thompson, James D.
  1967   *Organizations in action: Social science bases of administrative theory.*
          New York: McGraw-Hill.
Tokuine, Teruo
  1996   A review of human error prevention activities at Kansai Electric's nu-
          clear power stations. In *Nuclear safety: A human factors perspective,*

Tokuine, Teruo (*cont.*)
>   ed. Jyuji Misumi, Bernhard Wilpert, and Rainer Miller, 343–47. Phila-
>   delphia: Taylor and Francis.

Tomkiewicz, Bob
  1993   Newport: A summary and analysis. American Nuclear Society Execu-
          tive Conference, "The Management Challenge: Better, Safer, Cheaper
          Nuclear Power." May 16–19. Mimeo.

Tompkins, Phillip K.
  1993   *Organizational communication imperatives: Lessons of the Space Pro-
          gram*. Los Angeles: Roxbury.

Toulmin, Stephen E.
  1990   *Cosmopolis*. New York: Free Press.

Trubatch, Sheldon
  2001   A legal perspective on the NRC's Maintenance Rule. *Nuclear News*,
          May, 26.

Tuler, Seth
  1995   Organizational decision-making theory and technological emergen-
          cies. In *Preparing for nuclear power plant accidents*, ed. D. Golding,
          J. X. Kasperson, and R. E. Kasperson, 253–88. Boulder, CO: Westview
          Press.

Turner, Barry
  1978   *Man-made disasters*. London: Wykenham.
  1993   Software and hazard management: The text and vocabulary of system
          failure. Middlesex University Business School, Occasional Paper 6.

Turner, Barry, and Nick Pidgeon
  1997   *Man-made disasters*. 2d edition. London: Butterworth.

Twachtman, Gregory
  2003   Can safety culture evaluations be a regulatory tool? ACRS asks. *Inside
          N.R.C.*, June 16, 4.

U.K. Atomic Energy Authority
  1987   *Chernobyl and its consequences*. London: HMSO.

U.K. Department of Transport
  1987   *Herald of Free Enterprise: Formal report*. London: HMSO.

U.K. Health and Safety Executive
  2003   Nuclear Safety Directorate Strategic Plan 2003–2006. June 2003.
          http://www.hse.gov.uk/nsd/stratplan14.pdf.

U.K. Health and Safety Executive, Advisory Committee on the Safety of Nuclear
  Installations
  1993   *Human factors study group third report: Organising for safety*. Lon-
          don: Health and Safety Executive.
  2000   Behaviour modification to improve safety: Literature review. Prepared
          by The Keil Centre for the Health and Safety Executive. London: Her
          Majesty's Stationery Office.
  2001   Root causes analysis: Literature review. Prepared by WS Atkins Con-
          sultants Ltd for the Health and Safety Executive. London: Her Majes-
          ty's Stationery Office.

2002   Strategies to promote safe behaviour as part of a health and safety management system. Prepared by The Keil Centre for the Health and Safety Executive. London: Her Majesty's Stationery Office.

U.S. Code of Federal Regulations

1974   Title 10-Energy. Chapter 1-Nuclear Regulatory Commission, Parts 1–171. Part 50-Domestic Licensing of Production and Utilization Facilities: Sections 11–120, Appendices A-S. http: //www.access.gpo.gov/nara/CFR/waisidx_02/10cfrv1_02.html.

U.S. General Accounting Office

1997   *Nuclear regulation: Preventing problem plants requires more effective NRC action.* (GAO/RCED–97–145). Washington, DC: General Accounting Office.

2004   *Nuclear regulation: NRC needs to more aggressively and comprehensively resolve issues related to the Davis-Besse nuclear power plant's shutdown.* Washington, DC: General Accounting Office. GAO-040415.

U.S. Department of Energy

2002   U.S. nuclear reactor list-shutdown. July. http.//eia.doe.gov/cneaf/nuclear/page/nuc_reactors/shutdown.html.

2003a   U.S. Fusion Energy Science Program, Office of Fusion Energy Sciences. http://wwwofe.er.doe.gov/.

2003b   Nuclear reactors built, being built, or planned in the United States: 2003. Office of Nuclear Energy, Science and Technology. Washington, DC: DOE/NE-0118. December. http://www.ne.doe.gov/reports/bluebook2003.pdf.

U.S. Department of Labor

2002   Nuclear engineers. *Occupational outlook handbook.* Washington, DC: Bureau of Labor Statistics. http://www.bls.gov/oco/ocos036.

2002   Public utilities. *Career guide to industries.* Washington, DC. http://www.bls.gov/oco/cg/PDF/cgs018.PDF.

U.S. Nuclear Regulatory Commission

1975   *Reactor safety study.* (WASH–1400). NUREG–75/014). Washington, DC: Nuclear Regulatory Commission.

1991   Organizational factors research: Lessons learned and findings. Human Factors Branch, Division of Systems Research, Office of Nuclear Regulatory Research. August. Draft.

1992   Shutdown and low-power operation at commercial nuclear power plants in the United States. Draft report for comment. February. NUREG–1449.

1997   Evaluation criteria for communications-related corrective action plans. Office of Nuclear Reactor Regulation, Office of Nuclear Regulatory Research. Washington, DC, NUREG-1545.

1998   NRC Human performance plan. SECY–98–244. October 22, 1998. http://www.nrc.gov/reading-rm/doc-collections/commission/secys/1998/secy1998-244/1998-244scy.html.

1999   Reliability and probabilistic risk assessment, plant operations, and regulatory policies and practices committee. Advisory Committee on Reac-

U.S. Nuclear Regulatory Commission (*cont.*)

       tor Safeguards. Transcript. July 13. http://www.nrc.gov/reading-rm/
       doc-collections/ACRS/tr/subcommittee/1999/pr990713.html

2000a Results of the revised reactor oversight process pilot program. Part
       I. Secy–00–0049. March 28. http://www.nrc.gov/reading-rm/
       doc-collections/commission/srm/2000/2000–0049srm.html.

2000b Technical basis and implementation guidelines for a technique for
       human event analysis (ATHEANA). Division of Risk Analysis and Ap-
       plications, Office of Nuclear Regulatory Research. Washington, DC,
       NUREG-1624, Rev. 1.

2000c Human factors committee meeting, Advisory Committee on Reactor
       Safeguards. Transcript, 57 3/15/00. http: //www.nrc.gov/reading-rm/
       doc-collections/ACRS/tr/subcommittee/2000/hf000315.html.

2000d Safety Research Program Subcommittee, Advisory Committee on
       Reactor Safeguards, 194–96. November 1. http://www.nrc.gov/
       reading-rm/doc-collections/ACRS/tr/subcommittee/2000/
       sr001101.html

2001a Reactor oversight process: Initial implementation evaluation panel.
       Final report. May 10. http: //www.nrc.gov/NRR/OVERSIGHT/ROP/
       iiep_final_report050801.PDF.

2001b Regulatory assessment performance indicator guideline. November.
       http://www.nrc.gov/NRR/OVERSIGHT/nei_9902rev2.pdf.

2001c Review of findings for human error contribution to risk in operating
       events. Prepared by David I. Gertman, Bruce P. Hallbert, Mark W.
       Parrish, Martin B. Sattision, Doug Brownson, James P. Tortorelli.
       Idaho National Engineering and Environmental Laboratory. August.
       NUREG CR-6753. http://www.nrc.gov/reading-rm/doc-collections/
       nuregs/contract/cr6753/.

2002a Safety culture: A survey of the state-of-the-art. Prepared by J. N. Soren-
       sen for the Advisory Committee on Reactor Safeguards. Advisory
       Committee on Reactor Safeguards. Washington, DC: U.S. Nuclear
       Regulatory Commission. NUREG–1756.

2002b Davis-Besse Reactor Vessel Head Degradation: Lessons-Learned Task
       Force Report. September 30. http://www.nrc.gov/reactors/operating/
       ops-experience/vessel-head-degradation/news.html.

2002c 498th meeting of the Advisory Committee on Reactor Safeguards.
       Transcript. http://www.nrc.gov/reading-rm/doc-collections/ACRS/tr/
       fullcommittee/2002/ac120502.PDF.

2002d Detailed ROP [reactor oversight program] description. http://www
       .nrc.gov/reactors/operating/oversight/ROP-description.html.

2002e Human performance characterization in the reactor oversight pro-
       cess. Prepared by David I. Gertman, Bruce P. Hallbert, David A.
       Prawdzik. Idaho National Engineering and Environmental Labora-
       tory. March. http://www.nrc.gov/reading-rm/doc-collections/nuregs/
       contract/cr6775/.

2002f   Human factors information system: Definitions. http: //www.nrc.gov/
         reactors/operating/ops-experience/human-factors/definition-list.html

2002g   Reactor oversight process. Volume 8, Licensee Oversight Programs.
         Handbook 8.13 Parts I–II. June 19.

2002h   Nuclear reactors (stations) operating in the United States 2000, by
         state. http://www.eia.doe.gov/cneaf/nuclear/page/nuc_reactors/reactsum
         .html

2002i   Human factors and human reliability analysis research plans. Letter
         from the Advisory Committee on Reactor Safeguards to William D.
         Travers, Executive Director for Operations, September 24. Washing-
         ton, DC: U.S. Nuclear Regulatory Commission. http://www.nrc.gov/
         reading-rm/doc-collections/acrs/letters/2002/4952008.html.

2003a   Information digest 2003 edition. NUREG 1350, Vol. 15. August.
         http://www.nrc.gov/reading-rm/doc-collections/nuregs/staff/sr1350/.

2003b   Fact sheet on reactor license renewal. August. http://www.nrc.gov/
         reading-rm/doc-collections/fact-sheets/license-renewal.html.

2003c   Strategic Plan: Fiscal Year 2000–Fiscal Year 2005, Appendix.
         NUREG-1614. Vol. 2, Part 2. Last revised Monday, June 23, 2003.
         http://www.nrc.gov/reading-rm/doc-collections/nuregs/staff/sr1614/
         v2/part1/.

2003d   503rd Meeting of the Advisory Committee on Reactor Safeguards. June
         12. Transcript. http://www.nrc.gov/reading-rm/doc-collections/ACRS/
         tr/fullcommittee/2003/ac061203.PDF.

2003e   Davis-Besse reactor vessel head damage: NRC update. May. http://
         www.nrc.gov/reactors/operating/ops-experience/vessel-head-degrada
         tion/vessel-head-degradation-files/dbnews-05–03.PDF.

2003f   Public meeting between U.S. Nuclear Regulatory Commission and
         FirstEnergy Region III, Lisle, IL. Davis-Besse Nuclear Power Station:
         Safety culture and safety conscious work environment. Open meet-
         ing, January 30, 2003. http://www.nrc.gov/reactors/operating/
         ops-experience/vessel-head-degradation/vessel-head-degradation-files/
         01–30–03-mtg-transcript1.PDF.

2003g   ROP cornerstone and performance indicators. http://www.nrc.gov/
         NRR/OVERSIGHT/ASSESS/cornerstone.html.

2004a   NRC inspection manual. Manual chapter 0305, Operating reactor as-
         sessment program. January 29. http://www.nrc.gov/reading-rm/
         doc-collections/insp-manual/manual-chapter/mc0305.pdf.

2004b   Fact sheet on effects of electric utility deregulation. January 2004. http://
         www.nrc.gov/reading-rm/doc-collections/fact-sheets/effects.html.

U.S. Office of Technology Assessment

1993   *Aging nuclear power plants: Managing plant life and decommis-
         sioning.* OTA-E–575. Washington, DC: U.S. GPO.

Union of Concerned Scientists

2002   Davis-Besse: The reactor with a hole in its head. http: //www.ucsusa
         .org/energy/bf_davisbesse.html.

Union of Concerned Scientists (*cont.*)
2003   Davis-Besse: One year later. http://www.ucsusa.org/publication.cfm
        ?publicationID–589.
Uranium Information Centre
2003   Briefing papers: The International Nuclear Event Scale. http.//www
        .uic.com.au/ines.htm.
Van Dijk, Teun A.
1977   *Text and context: Explorations in the semantics and pragmatics of
        discourse.* New York: Longman.
van Vuuren, Wim
1999   Organisational failure: lessons from industry applied in the medical
        domain. *Safety Science* 33: 13–29.
2000   Cultural influences on risks and risk management: Six case studies.
        Safety Science 34: 31–45.
Vaughan, Diane
1996   *The Challenger launch decision: Risky technology, culture, and devi-
        ance at NASA.* Chicago: University of Chicago Press.
1998   Rational choice, situated action, and the social control of organiza-
        tions. *Law and Society Review* 32 (1): 23–62.
1999   The dark side of organizations: Mistake, misconduct, and disaster.
        American Review of Sociology 25: 271–305.
Vaurio, Jussi K.
1998   Safety-related decision making at a nuclear power plant. *Nuclear Engi-
        neering and Design* 185: 335–45.
Verma, Kirin, and Alfred A. Marcus
1995   Causes and effects of rising production costs in the U.S. nuclear power
        industry. *Industrial and Environmental Crisis Quarterly* 9 (2): 242–
        58. (Special Issue: *Managing with danger*)
Verna, Bernard J.
1994   On line with Verna. *Nuclear News*, September, 32–33.
Vicente, Kim
1999   *Cognitive work analysis: Toward safe, productive, and healthy com-
        puter-based work.* Mahwah, NJ: Lawrence Erlbaum.
Vicente, Kim, Emilie M. Roth, and Randall J. Mumaw
2001   How do operators monitor a complex, dynamic work domain? The
        impact of control room technology. *International Journal of Human-
        Computer Studies* 54: 831–56.
Vincenti, Walter G.
1990   *What engineers know and how they know it: Analytical studies from
        aeronautical history.* Baltimore, MD: Johns Hopkins University Press.
1991   The scope for social impact in engineering outcomes: A diagrammatic
        aid to analysis. *Social Studies of Science* 21: 761–67.
von Meier, Alexandra
1999   Occupational cultures as a challenge to technological innovation.
        IEEE Transactions in Engineering Management 46 (1): 101–14.

von Neumann, John
    1956   Can we survive technology? *The fabulous future: America in 1980.* As seen by David Sarnoff and others, 32–47. With an introduction by the editors of *Fortune.* New York: Dutton.

Wahlstrom, B., and E. Swaton
    1991   The influence of organization and management on the safety of NPPs and other complex industrial systems: Report of a consultants meeting organized by the International Atomic Energy Agency and the International Institute for Applied Systems Analysis. (WP–91–28). Laxenburg, Austria: International Institute for Applied Systems Analysis.

Wald, Matthew L.
    1999   Nuclear safety flaws are found. *New York Times,* August 11, A14.
    2002a   '88 warning was rejected at damaged nuclear plant. *New York Times,* September 30, A14.
    2002b   U.S. alarmed by corrosion, orders checking of reactors. *New York Times,* March 26, A1, A20.

Walker, J. Samuel
    1992   *Containing the atom: Nuclear regulation in a changing environment, 1963–1971.* Berkeley: University of California Press.

Waller, Douglas C.
    2001   *Big red: Three months on board a Trident nuclear submarine.* New York: HarperCollins.

Weart, Spencer R.
    1988   *Nuclear fear: A history of images.* Cambridge, MA: Harvard University Press.

Weick, Karl E.
    1979   Cognitive processes in organizations. *Research in Organizational Behavior* 1: 41–74.
    1987   Organizational culture as a source of high reliability. *California Management Review* 29 (2): 112–27.
    1988   Enacted sensemaking in crisis situations. *Journal of Management Studies* 25 (4): 305–17.
    1990   Technology as equivoque: Sensemaking in new technologies. In *Technology and Organizations,* ed. Paul S. Goodman, Lee S. Sproull and Associates, 1–44. San Francisco: Jossey-Bass.
    1993   [1990] The vulnerable system: An analysis of the Tenerife air disaster. In *New Challenges to Understanding Organizations,* ed. Karlene H. Roberts, 173–97. New York: Macmillan.
    1997   The *Challenger* launch decision. Book review symposium. *Administrative Science Quarterly* 42: 395–401.

Weick, Karl E., and Karlene M. Roberts
    1993   Collective mind in organizations: Heedful interrelating on flight decks. *Administrative Science Quarterly* 38: 357–81.

Weick, Karl E., and Kathleen M. Sutcliffe
    2001   *Managing the unexpected: Assuring high performance in an age of complexity.* San Francisco: Jossey-Bass.

Weil, Jenny
    2002   ACRS chair urges consideration of safety culture at nuclear plants. *Inside N.R.C.* July 15, 1.

Weil, Vivian
    1984   Browns Ferry case. In *Professional responsibility for harmful actions*, ed. Martin Curd and Larry May, 402–11. Dubuque, IA: Kendall Hunt.

Westrum, Ron
    1987   Management strategies and information failure. In *Information systems failure analysis*, ed. J. A. Wise and A. Debons, 109–27. NATO ASI Series F. Computer and Systems Science 3. Berlin: Springer-Verlag.
    1993   Cultures with requisite imagination. In *Verification and validation of complex systems: Human factors issues*, ed. John A. Wise, V. D. Hopkin, and P. Stager, 401–16. New York: Springer-Verlag.
    1997   Social factors in safety-critical systems. In *Human factors in safety-critical systems*, ed. F. Redmill and J. A. Rajan. London: Butterworth/Heineman.

White, Geoffrey M.
    1987   Proverbs and cultural models: An American psychology of problem solving. In *Cultural models in language and thought*, ed. Dorothy Holland and Naomi Quinn, 151–72. Cambridge: Cambridge University Press.

Whorf, Benjamin Lee
    1971   [1956] *Language, thought, and reality.* Cambridge, MA: MIT Press.

Wicker, Allan W.
    1987   Behavior settings reconsidered: Temporal stages, resources, internal dynamics, context. In *Handbook of environmental psychology*, ed. D. Stokols and I. Altman, 613–54. New York: John Wiley & Sons.

Wiegmann, Douglas A., Hui Zhang, Terry von Thaden, Gunjan Sharma, and Alyssa Mitchell
    2002   A synthesis of safety culture and safety climate research. Aviation Research Lab, Institute of Aviation, University of Illinois at Urbana-Champaign. Federal Aviation Administration. Technical Report ARL-02–3/FAA-02–2.

Wiener, Earl L., Barbara G. Kanki, and Robert L. Helmreich
    1993   *Cockpit resource management.* New York: Academic Press.

Wildavsky, Aaron
    1988   *Searching for safety.* New Brunswick, NJ: Transaction Books.

Williams, Jeremy C.
    1991   Safety cultures—Their impact on quality, reliability, competitiveness and profitability. Mimeo. Paper for presentation at conference, "European Reliability." June.
    1997   Assessing and reducing the likelihood of violation behavior. Institution of Nuclear Engineers Conference (U.K.) October. Mimeo.

Wimsatt, William C.
  1986   Heuristics and the study of human behavior. In *Metatheory in social science: Pluralisms and subjectivities*, ed. Donald W. Fiske and Richard A. Shweder, 293–314. Chicago: University of Chicago Press.
Winkler, A. W.
  1993   *Life under a cloud: American anxiety about the atom.* New York: Oxford University Press.
Winner, Langdon
  1986   *The whale and the reactor: A search for limits in an age of high technology.* Chicago: University of Chicago Press.
Winsor, Dorothy A.
  1990   The construction of knowledge in organizations: Asking the right question about the *Challenger. Journal of Business and Technical Communication* 4 (2): 7–20.
  1996   *Writing like an engineer: A rhetorical education.* Mahwah, NJ: Lawrence Erlbaum.
Wise, M. Norton, ed.
  1995   *The values of precision.* Princeton, NJ: Princeton University Press.
Wolf, Frederick, and Bruce Finnie
  2001   Balancing competing demands: Organizational factors and risk in complex technical systems. *Journal of Applied Management and Entrepreneurship* 7 (1): 3–29.
Woods, D. D., L. J. Johannesen, R. I. Cook, and N. B. Sarter
  1994   *Behind human error: Cognitive systems, computers and hindsight.* University of Dayton Research Institute, Department of Defense. Wright-Patterson Air Force Base, Ohio: Crew Systems Ergonomics Information Analysis Center.
Woolgar, Steve
  1991   The turn to technology in social studies of science. *Science, Technology, and Human Values* 16 (1): 20–50.
World Nuclear Association
  2000   Tokaimura criticality accident. http://world-nuclear.org/info/inf37.htm.
  2003   World nuclear power reactors 2002–2003 and uranium requirements. http://world-nuclear.org/info/reactors.htm.
  2004a   Nuclear power reactors 2002–2004 and uranium requirements. March 17. http://www.world-nuclear.org/info/reactors.htm.
  2004b   Plans for new reactors worldwide. March. http://www.world-nuclear .org/info/inf17.htm.
  2004c   Nuclear power in the world today. March. http://www.world-nuclear .org/info/inf01.htm.
Wu, J. S., G. E. Apostolakis, and D. Okrent
  1991   On the inclusion of organizational and managerial influences in probabilistic safety assessments of nuclear power plants. In *The analysis, communication, and perception of risk*, ed. B. J. Garrick and W. C. Gekler, 429–39. New York: Plenum Press.

Wynne, Brian
  1988   Unruly technology: Practical rules, impractical discourses and public understanding. *Social Studies of Science* 18: 147–67.
Yakura, Elaine
  1995   Transferring best management practice across cultural and organizational boundaries: Japanese and U.S. nuclear power. *Industrial and Environmental Crisis Quarterly* 9 (2): 198–212.
Zabusky, S. E.
  1995   *Launching Europe: An ethnography of European cooperation in space science*. Princeton, NJ: Princeton University Press.
Zonabend, Françoise
  1993   [1989] *The nuclear peninsula*. New York: Cambridge University Press.
Zuboff, Shoshana
  1988   *In the age of the smart machine*. New York: Basic Books.

Index

abduction, definition of, 215, 259. *See also* real-time logics

access authorization: and administrative or technical work classifications, 140–42; criteria for, 121

accident sequence precursors, 6; design basis issues in, 114

accidents and events in risky technologies: accounts of, 307n27; contextual sources of, 289n3; Wilberg coal mine fire (Utah 1984), 317n31

Advisory Committee on Reactor Safeguards (ACRS), 230; attempt of to study "safety culture," 14; and NRC cancellation of studies of operational issues and practices, 14, 225–26, 234, 311n87; and public hearing on "safety culture" oversight, 16; and regulating "safety culture, report on, 15; statutory establishment of and responsibilities to NRC, 299n47; and study of "safety culture" metrics, 15

agency-structure relationship, 303n86

Ahearne, John F., 295n28

Alfred P. Sloan Foundation, 323n81

algorithms, as technical advice, 309n51

Amber, David P., 320n52

ambiguity and certainty, assumptions about, xii, 225

Ambiguity and Command (March and Weissinger-Baylon), 305n10

American Nuclear Society: goals of, 292n8, 295n28, 318n38; international workshop on energy competition of, 293n19

anomalies, 238–39

antimonies, 262–63. *See also* infrastructure of conundrums

Apostolakis, George, 14–15, 254, 234–35, 313n96

Aramis, 215

Arthur Andersen, 307n29

as-built drawings: backlogs of, 247; definition of, 11

"As low as reasonably achievable" (ALARA) radiation exposure, 298n34

Atlantic Council, The, 295n28

Atlantic Monthly, The, 221

Atomic Energy Act of 1954, 299n47

Atomic Energy Commission: forecast of plant population in 2000 of, 292n5; mandate of, 23

Atomic Energy Control Board of Canada, 210

Aviation Safety Reporting System, 254

axis of functions, definition of, xvi, 272

axis of meanings: definition of, xvi; implications of, 272–76

backlogs, 206, 268

balance of plant, definition of, 7

Baram, Michael, 252

Barley, Stephen R., 259, 260–61

Bayart, Denis, 314n7

Becker, Gerhard, 252

beliefs, about plant safety, 11

Bell, Kenneth J., 225

benchmarking, 264

Benner, Ludwig, 316n28

Beyond Engineering (Pool), 291n3

Beyond Mechanization (Hirschhorn), 260

Bhopal catastrophe (India, 1984), 202

Biden, Joseph R., Jr., 295n31

Bier, Vicki, M. 268, 307n29, 314n2, 321n67, 322n68

Blackman, Harold S., 305n3

blaming system, 26, 251; and effect on self-reports, 275; and event analysis, 252; and self-regulation, 29

Bonaca, Mario, 16

Bonen, Zeev, 315n11

Bourrier, Mathilde, 218, 310n61

Braudel, Fernand, 319n36

Brehmer, Berndt, 311n84

Brint, Steven, 319n40

Browns Ferry event (Alabama, 1975), 16, 299n54

Browns Ferry Nuclear Station, status of, 290nn12–13

Bucciarelli, Louis L., Jr., 324n95

Bugos, Glenn E., 90–91

calculated logics, 262; assumptions underlying, 238; characteristics of, xv, 197–203; semantics of, 201